# GUIDANCE OF YOUNG CHILDREN

## Ninth Edition

### MARIAN MARION

Boston   Columbus   Indianapolis   New York   San Francisco   Upper Saddle River
Amsterdam   Cape Town   Dubai   London   Madrid   Milan   Munich   Paris   Montreal   Toronto
Delhi   Mexico City   São Paulo   Sydney   Hong Kong   Seoul   Singapore   Taipei   Tokyo

**Vice President and Editorial Director:** Jeffery W. Johnston
**Senior Acquisitions Editor:** Julie Peters
**Editorial Assistant:** Andrea Hall
**Vice President, Director of Marketing:** Margaret Waples
**Senior Marketing Manager:** Krista Clark
**Development Project Management:** Carol Bleistine, Aptara®, Inc.
**Project Manager:** Laura Messerly
**Operations Specialist:** Michelle Klein
**Senior Art Director:** Diane Lorenzo

**Photo Coordinator:** Jorgensen Fernandez
**Cover Art:** KidStock/Blend Images/Corbis
**Cover Designer:** Suzanne Behnke
**Full-Service Project Management:** Karen Jones, Aptara®, Inc.
**Composition:** Aptara®, Inc.
**Printer/Binder:** Courier/Kendallville
**Cover Printer:** Courier/Kendallville
**Text Font:** ITC Berkeley Oldstyle Std

Credits and acknowledgments for materials borrowed from other sources and reproduced, with permission, in this text appear on the appropriate page within the text.

Every effort has been made to provide accurate and current Internet information in this book. However, the Internet and information posted on it are constantly changing, so it is inevitable that some of the Internet addresses listed in this textbook will change.

**Photo Credits:** David Kostelnik/Pearson Education: pp. 3, 10, 37, 46, 61, 87, 100, 103, 121, 146 (bottom), 167, 187, 289, 324 (top and bottom); Mangostock/Fotolia: p.23; Monkey Business/Fotolia: p. 30; Lorraine Swanson/Fotolia: p. 80; Hope Madden/Merrill Education/Pearson Education: p. 97; Petro Feketa/Fotolia: p. 101; Krista Greco/Merrill Education/Pearson Education: p. 127; LenaLeonovich/Fotolia: p. 133; Subbotina Anna/Fotolia: p. 146 (top); Sonya Etchison/Fotolia: p. 158; Ben LaFramboise/Pearson Education: pp. 163, 207; Carla Mestas/Pearson Education: pp. 183, 338; Mariiya/Fotolia: p. 192; Michaeljung/Fotolia: pp. 199, 278; Suzanne Clouzeau/Pearson Education: p. 212; Laura Bolesta/Merril Education/Pearson Education: p. 221; Dron/Fotolia: p. 238; Rob/Fotolia: p. 241; Katelyn Metzger/Merrill Education/Pearson Education: pp. 254, 314; Atm2003/Fotolia: p. 266; Andrea Berger/Fotolia: p. 280; KidStock/Blend Images/Getty Images: p. 296; Christian Schwier/Fotolia: p. 333; Kenishirotie/Fotolia: p. 351

**Library of Congress Cataloging-in-Publication Data**
Marion, Marian
  Guidance of young children / Marian Marion.—Ninth edition.
    pages cm
  ISBN 978-0-13-342722-6—ISBN 0-13-352206-7 (coursesmart)—ISBN 0-13-352146-X (e-pub)—ISBN 0-13-352158-3 (updf)
  1. Child psychology.  2. Child rearing.  I. Title.
  HQ772.M255 2015
  649'.1—dc23

2013045545

10 9 8 7 6 5 4 3 2 1

ISBN 13: 978-0-13-342722-6
ISBN 10:    0-13-342722-6

# Dedication

For Lucy Anne, rottweiler, now 13 years old
and who has sat under the computer table
through the writing of four editions of this book.

Also for Leo Allesandro, Francesca Louisa,
Anna Maria, and Vito Luca, my feline companions.
You all bring joy to my life.

# Preface

Welcome to the ninth edition of *Guidance of Young Children*. My purpose in writing the ninth edition is the same as for earlier editions—to give students a book grounded in solid theory and research, a book that will help them understand the process of child guidance. This book is based on my beliefs about children, and these are stated near the end of this Preface.

## ∷ NEW TO THIS EDITION: PEARSON ETEXT FEATURES AND CONTENT CHANGES

This edition has several digital elements in the Pearson eText that make e-reading and studying engaging and interactive. For example:

- **NAEYC Standards and Key Elements** that pertain to each chapter are embedded in the Pearson eText and pop up when clicked on so that students can connect these standards to their practice.
- **Questions for Reflection** pop up from the Pearson eText to provoke students to think about past experiences, their thoughts about appropriate practice, or feelings about a situation.
- Embedded **videos** in each chapter (roughly three per chapter) illustrate key concepts and strategies
- **Focus on Practice** boxes are video-based learning experiences with questions that help students to deepen their understanding of theory and practice.
- **Glossary**

The ninth edition retains features that have helped students construct a developmentally appropriate approach to guiding children. It also contains updated research throughout and new content and features designed to make the teaching and learning processes for instructors and students even more effective, efficient, and enjoyable. Following are some examples.

- **Expanded Information on Challenging Behavior** (Chapter 11). This chapter has been revised significantly and now includes information on functional behavioral assessment. The functional behavioral assessment process is explained, and then students learn how to use the A-B-C, that is, the antecedent, behavior, consequence method to collect the data that they need before they can handle with challenging behavior. Students will use these processes to learn how to work with six specific challenging behaviors—interruptions, teasing, biting, whining and pestering, tattling, and aggressive behaviors (for example, hitting, kicking, damaging and destroying things, and temper tantrums). The chapter now contains a section on supporting infants and toddlers with challenging behaviors.

- **New Content on Bullying** (Chapter 10). Students will understand the nature of *cyberbullying* as a form of aggression and bullying. Students will understand the different, currently used methods that the cyberbully uses. Students will also read about what they can do to help victims of bullying defend themselves. Special emphasis is placed on helping victims deal with teasing and other forms of face-to-face bullying.

- **Revised Content on Social Emotional Learning (SEL)** (Chapter 8). This chapter now includes a listing and discussion of *essential topics* in SEL. Students will learn how to deliberately plan for teaching these topics, such as at large-group time and throughout the day. Specific information on helping children handle disappointment and anger as well as on building friendship skills are now included.

- **Focus on the Role of Culture in Guiding Children** (Chapters 1, 2, 3, 5, 6, 10). *Focus on Culture* boxed information targets the role that *cultural scripts* play in guiding children. Cultural scripts are acquired by members of a culture and affect them in ways that we might not have thought about. For example, Chapter 5's Feature on Culture explains how the *extra talk cultural script* affects a teacher's limit setting in a classroom.

- **Implications of Theories Added** (Chapter 2). This chapter now contains information on the implications of all theories presented. That is, what are the practical applications of each theory for an early childhood teacher? Students will now have access to brief and clearly explained implications.

- **Expanded Coverage of Child Development Information** (Chapter 3). This chapter now outlines the major facets of social and emotional growth in children during early childhood. This information is presented by age groups: birth to 8 months, 8 to 18 months; 18 months to 3 years, 3 to 4 years, 4 to 5 years, and 6 to 8 years.

- **New Information on Sensory Stimulation in Infancy and Toddlerhood** (Chapter 4). Chapter 4 now looks at room design chronologically—that is, starts with room design for infants and toddlers first and then is followed by that information for preschool through third grade. The role of sensory stimulation in a child's first 3 years is now emphasized. Students will learn about presenting appropriately timed sensory stimulation to infants and toddlers.

- **How to Develop Good Relationships Information Added** (Chapter 1). Expanded coverage of the importance of good teacher–child relationships in guiding children. Specifically, students will now study the practical steps that they can take to develop caring and positive relationships with young children.

- **Expanded Coverage of Schedules** (Chapter 4). This new section focuses on elements of appropriate time schedules. In addition, examples of appropriate schedules for different age groups within the early childhood period are given and the effect of appropriate schedules on children's development and learning are explained.

- **Expanded Information on Observation** (Chapter 6). This chapter now includes a discussion of the role of assessment in schools of today, achieving objectivity in observing, and using portfolios in the assessment process.

## :: FEATURES RETAINED FROM THE PREVIOUS EDITION

My goal has always been to write a *student-friendly* textbook. Within that framework, I want students to see that a research- and theory-based textbook can challenge them to think critically about guiding children. These effective features from the last edition have been retained, but have been refined to make them even more useful:

- **Writing Style.** Conversational *and* informative.
- **Bold Font.** Emphasizes definitions and terms seen for the first time.
- **Use of Three Teachers from the Same School.** Mr. Bensen (infant–toddler), Mrs. Johnson (preschool), and Mr. Santini (kindergarten through Grade 2, multiage, looping classroom) appear throughout the text and deal with guidance problems faced in real classrooms every day.
- **Chapter-Opening Vignettes.** Vignettes open every chapter and focus on children and teachers in early childhood classrooms. Students will read vignettes from the infant–toddler, preschool, and kindergarten–primary classrooms. Occasionally, there is one longer vignette instead of three. The vignettes illustrate major points in each chapter.
- **Analyze Vignettes.** Students apply newly acquired knowledge from the chapter to the chapter-opening case study. Students come full circle in each chapter.
- **Questions for Reflection.** At the ends of major chapter sections, these are designed to encourage higher level thinking and analysis when reflecting on the chapter's main points.
- **Apply Your Knowledge.** An end-of-chapter feature focusing on the application level in the cognitive domain.
- **Examples.** Gleaned from real classrooms, these illustrate guidance in early childhood classrooms at all levels.
- **Appendix.** Summarizes major positive guidance strategies.

## :: THIS TEXTBOOK HAS EVOLVED FROM A SET OF BELIEFS

This edition continues to reflect my core beliefs about children and child guidance; it is these beliefs that I want to pass on to students.

- **I believe that protecting children is our most important role.** Students reading this text should understand that we teach and protect children most effectively by making active, conscious decisions about positive strategies. *We protect children when we refuse to use strategies that are degrading or hurtful or have the potential to harm or humiliate children.* Some strategies denigrate and dishonor children and should never be used, such as biting, shaking, hitting, and other forms of physically hurtful interaction; hostile humor; embarrassment; ridicule; sarcasm; judging; manipulating; playing mind games; exerting hurtful punishment; ignoring; terrorizing; isolating; and violating boundaries. These are personality-numbing horrors. They are abusive and have no place in our lives with children.

The National Association for the Education of Young Children (NAEYC), in its *Code of Ethics*, notes that the most important part of the code is that early childhood professionals never engage in any practice that hurts or degrades a child. Therefore, this textbook takes this approach: first of all, do no harm. Students who use this textbook will learn *only* positive strategies and a respectful approach to guiding children.

- **I believe that we have a choice about how we think about and behave with children.** John Steinbeck, in *East of Eden*, described the beauty inherent in the ability to make choices. Students need to know that what they choose to think about children, how they act with them, and the discipline strategies they use *do* matter. Using a positive, constructivist approach on a daily basis has a long-term impact on children—helping them become self-responsible, competent, independent, and cooperative people who like themselves and who have a strong core of values.

- **I believe that an adult's "style" of guiding children does affect children.** It affects several parts of their personality and their approach to life—for example, their moral compass, emotional intelligence, level of self-esteem, how they manage anger and aggression, how they handle stress, their willingness to cooperate with others, whether they can take another person's perspective, and their social skills.

  Therefore, the organizing force for this text is the concept of styles of caregiving—a concept presented right away in Chapter 1. Students should come away from that chapter with a clear idea of the authoritarian, authoritative, and permissive styles. They will learn about adult beliefs and behavior in each style and about the likely effect of that style on children. They will then encounter the concept of caregiving style woven into almost every chapter.

- **I believe that constructivist, positive, and effective child guidance is based on solid knowledge of child development.** Without this knowledge, adults might well have unrealistic expectations of children. Having this knowledge gives professionals a firm foundation on which to build child guidance skills.

- **I believe that there is no one right way to deal with any issue but that there are many good ways.** I do *not* give students a set of tricks to use with children. However, students will find numerous exercises and questions designed to help them construct basic concepts of child guidance. They might enjoy thinking critically about typical guidance issues and even more challenging behaviors.

- **I believe that we should each develop a personal approach to guiding children, one built on theoretical eclecticism.** In this text, students will study and use the decision-making model of child guidance, a model that evolves from understanding various theoretical approaches to guiding children. Students will apply the major theories forming our beliefs and perspectives on guiding children.

## ⠿ ANCILLARIES FOR THIS EDITION

- **Online Test Bank with Answers,** separate from the Instructor's Manual. The test bank is easy to use and provides different types of questions. All online ancillaries can be downloaded from the Instructor Resource Center at Pearson's Higher Ed website by adopting professors and instructors.
- **Online Instructor's Manual.** This manual has been updated and refined. I have retained the teaching objectives and suggestions for teaching each section. Handouts are included that support teaching and learning.
- **Online PowerPoint® Presentations.** There is one PowerPoint® presentation for each chapter. These are intended to decrease the time that you have to spend preparing materials for the class.
- **TestGen.** TestGen is a powerful assessment generation program available exclusively from Pearson that helps instructors easily create and quizzes and exams. You install TestGen on your personal computer (Windows or Mac) and create your own exams for print or online use. It contains a set of test items organized by chapter, based on this textbook's contents. The items are the same as those in the Online Test Bank. The tests can be downloaded in a variety of learning management system formats.

## ⠿ ACKNOWLEDGMENTS

My early childhood colleagues with whom I work most closely at Governors State University, Jeannine Klomes and Evie Plofsky, are unrelentingly positive in their interactions with students, excellent models of professionalism. I do like working with them.

The professionals at Pearson support authors as they write. I thank my editor, Julie Peters, and Andrea Hall, editorial assistant.

Reviewers have been generous in offering ideas for enriching the content and structure of *Guidance of Young Children*. Several colleagues from around the country reviewed the material for the ninth edition: Kara Hoffmann, Waukesha County Technical College; Alexandra Remson, Housatonic Community College; Lori Schonhorst, Des Moines Area Community College; and Gia Smith, Savannah Technical College. Reviewer feedback was exceptionally helpful and constructively given. My guess is that their students receive the same type of helpful feedback. The reviewers made several specific suggestions that I have heeded. For example, I added information on functional behavioral assessment and the A-B-C method of data collection to the chapter on challenging behavior, and have included information on cyberbullying in the chapter on aggression and bullying. The chapter on social emotional learning now contains information on helping children deal with disappointment and anger as well as on how to develop friendship skills. Their feedback has reshaped the structure of parts of this textbook.

Once again, please feel free to email me with questions, comments, or suggestions about *Guidance of Young Children*, Ninth Edition.

*Marian Marion*
Email: *mariancmarion94@yahoo.com*

# Brief Contents

# Contents

## Chapter 5   Positive Guidance and Discipline Strategies: Direct Guidance   121

## Chapter 6   Using Observation in Guiding Children   158

## PART III   SPECIAL TOPICS IN CHILD GUIDANCE   181

## Chapter 7   Self-Esteem and the Moral Self   181

# Guiding Young Children
## *Three Essential Elements*

**Chapter 1**   A Teacher's Role in Guiding Children

This chapter emphasizes the importance of building a caring relationship with children. It then describes three adult caregiving styles—authoritarian, authoritative, and permissive—explaining the concept of developmentally appropriate practice as part of the authori*tative* style. It focuses on the processes that adults use to influence children. The feature on culture in this chapter focuses on the effect of a person's cultural scripts on how they guide children.

**Chapter 2**   Theoretical Foundations of Child Guidance

Chapter 2 describes theory as a firm foundation on which to base decisions about guiding young children. The goal is *not* to memorize information about different theories but to understand that, without theory, we would not have a foundation for our profession. The chapter explains three categories of theories: theories explaining how children's behavior develops in different systems; theories focusing on how children construct ideas; and theories examining children's psychological, emotional, and social learning needs. Direct and practical implications of each theory are described. The feature on culture for this chapter focuses on understanding the effect that poverty has on a child's life.

**Chapter 3**   Understand Child Development: A Key to Guiding
Children Effectively

This chapter opens by describing what to expect in general about the social and
emotional development of children in the different phases of early childhood. Then,
we shift to perception and memory, two parts of a child's cognitive development that
are important in how children take in, organize, and remember what they see and
hear during interactions. Then, we will examine how children understand the behavior of others, how they view friendship, and how they understand accidental versus
intentional behavior. Finally, we will look at how children build on perception,
memory, and social cognition to develop self-control and to become compassionate
and caring individuals. The feature on culture for this chapter focuses on the impact
of individualistic and interdependent cultures on your guidance of children from
such cultures.

# CHAPTER 1
# A Teacher's Role in Guiding Children

## Learning Outcomes

- State the focus of this text
- Summarize a teacher's vision for working with children
- Explain the two major dimensions of a teacher's style of caregiving
- Describe major caregiving styles in terms of an adult's level of demandingness and responsiveness
- Summarize the effects of different styles of caregiving on children's development and behavior
- Explain the basic processes through which teachers influence children
- Explain the function of cultural scripts in guiding children

### VIGNETTES

#### BLAKE IGNORES HIS MOTHER'S REQUEST

*Blake left his scooter in the middle of the living room. His mother called out to him, "Put the scooter outside, Blake." Blake heard but ignored her as he walked away. "Blake, did you hear me? Put that scooter outside this instant. I mean it. No water park for you this afternoon if you don't put that scooter outside!" Blake shuffled down the hall to his room and Mom continued in an exasperated tone, "Blake, get back here. I want that scooter put away."*

*Finally, Mom just turned back to the kitchen. "That boy never listens to me."*

*Blake pays little attention to his mother's limits. He also knows that she hardly ever follows up on her threats. That afternoon, for example, Mom took Blake to the water park, after saying, "Next time, Blake, you'd better listen to me when I tell you to do something." Blake turned his head away from Mom and rolled his eyes.*

#### DAVID DOES WHATEVER HE WANTS TO DO

*At 18 months, David, when visiting a friend with his mother, banged on the friend's television screen and pushed at the door screen. His mom said nothing until the friend expressed concern for her property. Then she said, "David, do you think you should be doing that?" To the friend she said, "You know, I don't think I should order him around." When he was 4 years old, David stayed up until 11:30 when company was over. To the friend who inquired about his bedtime, Mom replied, "Oh, I let David make decisions on his own." David fell asleep in the book corner at his preschool the next day. At 6 years of age, David pushed ahead of others at a zoo exhibition. Mom ignored what had happened to the other children and said, "Go ahead. Can you see? Move up closer."*

#### PATRICK'S PROBLEMS HAVE DEEP ROOTS

*Patrick's father is irritable around his children. His sister-in-law has watched him for years and now thinks that he really dislikes being a father. He tells his three children, including Patrick, what he wants them to do by cursing at them and barking and snapping orders. He expects his children to obey immediately despite anything else they might be doing. He laughed when he recited his "motto" to one of the other men at work: "My kids know that I mean business! When I say jump, they know that they'd better say, 'how high?'" Patrick has watched as Dad used a belt on an older brother.*

*When Patrick was a toddler and learning how to use the toilet, Dad spanked him when he had an accident. When Patrick was 4 years old Dad grabbed one of his arms and yanked him to make Patrick move along at the store, saying, "#%&\*#$# [curse word] I'm sick of you holding us up all the time." At preschool, Patrick had trouble with other children because he hit them when he was angry and the other children started to leave him out of activities.*

### LEAH BITES ROBERT

*Leah's mother is a home child-care provider for Leah, 18 months old, and her friend's two children, Robert, aged 24 months, and Steven, aged 9 months. Steven's mother asked Leah's mom what to do when Steven bites her during feeding. "Quickly tell him no and pull his mouth off your breast. Don't make a joke of it, either, or he'll think you're playing a game." Leah wanted a toy that Robert had but did not seem to have the words for asking. She grew more agitated and then, even to her own surprise, she bit him! Leah's mother, also surprised, immediately took care of the bite on Robert's arm. Then, to her daughter, she said, "No, Leah. Biting is a no-no. Biting hurts Robert. If you need help, come to Mommy and I will help you get a toy."*

## :: INTRODUCTION

This entire textbook focuses on positive, authori*tative* child guidance, based on principles of developmentally appropriate practice. Many adults, like Leah's mother and many teachers, use developmentally appropriate, authoritative child guidance. They are warm, very responsive, and supportive, while they also have reasonable and high expectations of children. Their beliefs about discipline and guidance are developmentally appropriate. Their practices are also developmentally appropriate, with their beliefs "in sync" with their practices. This first chapter describes developmentally appropriate or authoritative child guidance. Other adults, like Patrick's father, use the developmentally inappropriate practices of the authoritarian. Still others, like David's and Blake's parents, use a developmentally inappropriate style of guidance known as permissiveness.

In this chapter, you will first read about building good relationships with children, the most important part of your professional role. Then you will read about the authoritarian and permissive styles, but the emphasis is on positive authoritative guidance. We will first examine each style of caregiving and its effect on children's development. Then we will focus on the ways in which all adults, whether they are authoritative, authoritarian, or permissive, influence children. Finally, you will learn about the effect of culture on a teacher's role in guiding children.

## ∷ BEGINNING THE CIRCLE: OUR HOPE FOR CHILDREN

As teachers, we have a vision for our work and a hope for children. We hope to help them develop in all domains and to satisfy their inborn curiosity by learning eagerly and joyfully. Our vision is to help children to, first, feel safe and secure, and to develop healthy self-esteem as well as a strong moral compass. We want them to honor and respect themselves and others and to learn how to deal with a variety of stressors. We can help children understand and deal effectively with an array of feelings, such as joy, anger, sadness, love, and jealousy. Most of all, we can help children become compassionate individuals who can walk a mile in another person's shoes—or an animal's tracks. Thus, we help them to develop empathy, what every society needs for survival.

## Developing Good Relationships with Children

Bringing our vision to life takes some thinking and reflection. We as teachers need to acknowledge our role in the process, and the most significant part of this role is the ability to build good relationships with children. This text is about guiding children, but guidance starts with adult reflection, looking at oneself first in the guidance process. We are the ones responsible for constructing the interpersonal environment, the relationships, in which children develop. That is, we have a big part in setting the tone in a classroom and in how we interact with children. We are the adults. We have the life experience. We have the knowledge about children's development. We understand how to teach. Yes, children certainly have a part in interactions with us, but we are the adults and have the responsibility in guiding children.

The very first step in guiding children effectively is to develop a good relationship with them. If teachers do not have a strong and positive bond with children, then they cannot expect to guide them well. Here are some practical strategies that help many teachers establish a friendly, positive relationship with children (Pearson, n.d.). All of the strategies revolve around being respectful, warm, and responsive (Pearson, n.d.).

- Demonstrate respect and show interest. Show appropriate interest in and genuine respect for each and every child's family.
- Acknowledge children. Acknowledge each child every day at school. Welcome each one warmly with a friendly greeting. Make eye contact if the child's culture accepts direct eye contact and smile if that is a part of your personal style.
- Learn about each child. Get to know each child by observing that child working and playing with equipment and with other children. You can discover the types of things that a child likes to do. You can also observe how that child interacts with others.
- Discover what is important to children. Ask children appropriate questions so that you can discover what is important to them and the things that they like to do.
- Show respect by paying attention. When you talk to children, pay attention to what they say. Look at them and avoid doing anything else. This tells that child that you are indeed interested in the child's ideas and what the child thinks about things. If another person, adult or child, interrupts, simply say that you will get

to that person after you are finished your conversation with this child. Paying attention to a person you are talking to and not doing anything else (no phone, no texting, no Internet, for example) is a loud and clear sign of real respect.

- Show appreciation. Communicate to each child, gradually, of course, some of the things that you appreciate about that child. For example, if a child listens well during a lesson, then quietly let him know that you noticed. If a child speaks softly and shows kindness to the class pet, let her know that you noticed this and like this about her. If a child is helpful, then notice and communicate your appreciation to that child. You will be validating that child's positive characteristics, and validation is an essential need of every human being.

- Express enjoyment in your interactions. Teachers have different styles, of course, with some teachers smiling easily and others showing humor effortlessly. Others can show real enjoyment more quietly but in ways that are equally effective in communicating genuine liking for children. Whatever your personal style, develop good relationships by appropriately expressing the pleasure you get from being with young children directly to them.

Teachers hope to help children learn eagerly and joyfully. As you watch this video, notice how the teacher's focus on science through combining two colors to make another has engaged all of the children. Look for the signs telling you that the child she talks to is delighted with his learning and his accomplishment. Look for signs that this teacher has established a positive bond or relationship with this child.

## :: MAJOR DIMENSIONS OF CAREGIVING STYLES

Researchers have long been interested in how one parent or teacher differs from others. Researchers have also been interested in how these differences affect children. For example, almost 60 years ago, Becker (1954) analyzed several studies and classified a parent's style by looking at whether the parent was (a) hostile or warm and (b) restrictive or permissive. Then and now, we know that warmth is probably the single most important factor in an adult's relationship with a child.

Diana Baumrind (1967, 1971, 1977, 1979, 1996; Baumrind & Black, 1967) built on the foundation of the earlier research. She is acknowledged as one of the most influential researchers in this area. She has found that two major factors—responsiveness and demandingness—determine an adult's style of caregiving. Some adults are highly responsive to children, whereas others are not very responsive. Some adults are high in demandingness, whereas others make very few demands. (See Figure 1.1.) Other researchers now use Baumrind's framework, examining the role of responsiveness and demandingness (Ciairano, Kliewer, Bonono, & Bosma, 2008; Mansager, 2004; Shek, 2007; Walker, 2008).

### Responsiveness

**Responsiveness** is one of two major caregiving dimensions. It refers to the degree of adult supportiveness, the degree to which an adult is tuned in to a child's developmental level, and whether the adult meets a child's needs. Figure 1.1 shows that responsiveness is on a continuum. A person can exist anywhere along the

**Responsiveness**
One of the elements of a person's caregiving style; whether an adult meets a child's needs and understands child development

**FIGURE 1.1**    Two major dimensions of caregiving

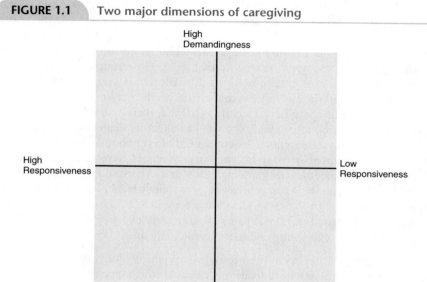

continuum. Some adults are highly responsive to children, whereas others are not. This section and Figure 1.2 describes several important aspects of responsiveness, including warmth, whether an adult knows child development, whether he views children and adults as partners in interaction, communication style, and whether an adult uses good explanations along with guidance strategies (Baumrind, 1996).

**Warmth**
Emotional expression of fondness

**Warmth**    **Warmth** is the emotional expression of liking or love. Observe a group of adults, either parents or teachers, as they interact with young children. You will observe differences in how warm they are toward children. Some teachers and parents are highly responsive: they show a high degree of sincere warmth. But others are low in responsiveness and do not express affection or love at all or do not express it appropriately.

There are many ways to show warmth; no one way is best because we each have our own approach. Whatever our culture or personal manner, however, the common thread in warmth is making it clear to a child through our interactions that we genuinely like or love him. Our warmth shows a genuine concern for that child's welfare, as shown in the next three examples.

**EXAMPLE**    Lev's father is not given to extravagant expressions of emotion. When Lev said before dinner, "Can I feed Sam [the cat] before we sit down to eat? He looks hungry," Dad thought that Lev had done a good thing but said little. He expressed his warmth, however, during the prayer before eating: "I am also thankful for a son who thinks about his cat first." Lev kept his head down but shifted his eyes to look quickly at his dad and then back at his plate. Lev is secure in his father's love and affection.

| FIGURE 1.2 | What is responsiveness? What is demandingness? |
|---|---|

| Responsiveness | Demandingness |
|---|---|
| • **Warmth**<br>Do I show that I like children? Do I show appropriate affection and support? Are my expressions of warmth sincere? | • **Boundaries, limits, and expectations**<br>Do I have age- and individually appropriate expectations for behavior? Do I clearly state appropriate limits? |
| • **Child development knowledge**<br>Do I have a good knowledge base in child development? Do I understand how families affect children? Do I understand how a child's culture affects him or her? | • **Monitoring and supervising**<br>Do I know how to create an orderly, consistent environment? Do I monitor children and supervise them well? |
| • **Children and adults as partners in interaction**<br>Do I really understand that both adults and children have a part in any interaction? Do I also understand that my adult role carries greater responsibility? | • **Discipline strategies**<br>Are my discipline strategies positive, age appropriate, individual appropriate, and culturally sensitive? |
| • **Communication style**<br>Do I communicate in an open and direct way? How do I send messages, especially limits? | • **Style of confrontation**<br>Am I willing to confront children when necessary? Do I confront in a firm yet kind way? |
| • **Giving explanations**<br>Do I use a reason along with a guidance strategy? Do I know how to state reasons well? | |

**EXAMPLE**    Mr. Santini said to his first graders, who were sitting in a circle, "When I was driving to school this morning, I thought about how happy I was that I would see all the children in my class again." He then looked at each child, saying his or her name. "Susan, Tom, Vinnie, Sam, Reese . . . let's hold hands and make a circle of friends. This circle of friends is going to help each other to have a good week at school."

Warmth is an important part of responsiveness (Belsky, Sligo, Jaffee, Woodward, & Silva, 2005). Children are often quite aggressive when their parents are not warm, when they are negative and irritable (Grusec & Lytton, 1988). These children act out in school when their parents are angry, nonaccepting, and disapproving. Baumrind (1996) cautions that warmth should be sincere. She believes that false expressions of affection prevent parents and teachers from appropriately managing discipline encounters when limits are necessary.

**Child Development Knowledge**    Teachers using positive child guidance have usually taken formal course work in child development. Parents, too, can take formal course work, or they can acquire **child development knowledge** by reading and attending parent education classes (Patterson, Mockford, & Stewart-Brown, 2005). This knowledge base allows adults to have realistic expectations of children of different ages in terms of motor, physical, cognitive, social, and emotional development. It also enables adults to understand the role that families play in a young child's development.

**Child development knowledge**
Ability to describe and explain different aspects of children's growth

**EXAMPLE**    Mr. Santini, the primary grade teacher, realizes that his children feel emotions such as anger and that they express their angry feelings. He also knows that children do not understand anger. Nor can they manage their feelings on their

**Highly responsive teachers convey warmth and understand child development.**

own. Therefore, he helps them label feelings and he gives them the words to use for expressing feelings.

**Partners in Interaction**   Researchers started to think about this concept in the late 1960s (Bell, 1968; Bell & Harper, 1977). We know that children are active partners in every interaction with other children or with adults. Adults who use developmentally appropriate child guidance believe that children have an important part in any interaction, but at the same time, they know that adults always have a greater responsibility (Maccoby & Martin, 1983).

> **EXAMPLE**   Mr. Santini has a right to expect his class to put things away after using them. The teacher also realizes that he has a greater responsibility in that he has to make the cleanup limit clear. He also has to teach children how to put things away, and he has to manage the classroom so that cleanup is simple. In addition, he has to pay attention to the children when they do put things away and acknowledge their efforts.

**Communication Style**   Highly responsive adults communicate in an open, congruent, validating, and direct way. They deliver messages simply, kindly, firmly, and consistently. Children tend to accept this type of communication willingly because the adult uses persuasion, not force, to make a point. Children are socialized most effectively by adults who use this type of communication, and who enforce their directives (Baumrind, 1993, 1996). Such a positive **communication style** indicates that they also see children as competent, as having choices, and as worthy of respect.

**Communication style**
Manner in which an adult delivers messages to children; indicative of the adult's view of children

> **EXAMPLE**   Vinnie and Sam scooted off to the computer, leaving their library books on the table even though the classroom limit is that people put things away before they start a new activity. Mr. Santini, responsive in this discipline encounter, used a

direct and validating style of communication: "I know that you've been waiting for your turn at the computer and I'll save your spot for you. First, though, I want you to put your library books in your cubbies."

Highly responsive adults communicate in an open, congruent, validating, and direct way. As you watch this **video**, notice the teacher states directions for the breathing exercise in a kind but firm way. She validates their need for a cool-down but directs the activity well, communicating openly.

**Giving Explanations**   Giving explanations to children is good for both children and adults. We all, and that includes children, tend to be more cooperative when we know why somebody wants us to do something or even to stop doing something. It is a sign of respect to give an explanation, and children deserve to know why we ask them to do something.

Giving explanations benefits adults, too. Already using positive guidance strategies, highly responsive adults are even more effective because they state a reason along with the guidance strategy. Discipline encounters usually deal with one specific act (a child leaving books strewn about the library). A good strategy—simply reminding the child to put the books away—helps a child understand what is appropriate for that incident. However, giving a reason along with the strategy paints a broader picture for the child. It tells him that the appropriate behavior would apply in many other cases, too (Baumrind, 1996).

> **EXAMPLE**   Mr. Santini says to Reese, one of his first graders, "Reese, I noticed that you left the library books on the floor near the beanbag chair. Please put the books back up on the shelf, standing up in their places. Then the other children can see them easily and the books won't get stepped on."

# Demandingness

**Demandingness** is the other major caregiving dimension. This text uses research that has shaped thinking about how we interact with young children and explains things using terms *from* that research. The word *demandingness* is the official term used in the caregiving style research, from Baumrind's earliest work to publications in 2009, as noted in the introduction. Demandingness, an off-putting word to some, merely refers to an adult's overall views on control and deals with the following elements (Baumrind, 1996):

Understanding and setting boundaries, limits, and expectations

How adults monitor and supervise

The type of discipline strategies used

An adult's style of dealing with conflict or confrontation

Adults differ in how demanding they are with children. Figure 1.1 shows that demandingness, like responsiveness, is on a continuum. A person can exist anywhere along the demandingness continuum. Some adults are on the higher end, whereas others tend to be at the lower end of the continuum—some are high, some lower in making expectations known to children. The following subsection and Figure 1.2 explain the elements of demandingness.

**Demandingness**
One of the elements of a person's caregiving style: whether and how the person sets limits and monitors, supervises, and faces issues

**Boundaries, Limits, and Expectations**  Adults differ in their ability and willingness to help children understand that there are boundaries, or limits, on behavior. They differ in how they state expectations (how they request or ask) for cooperative, helpful, appropriately self-controlled behavior from children. Demanding and responsive adults understand the importance of proper boundaries and appropriate limits in guiding young children. They develop and clearly communicate appropriate limits. The key is to combine high demandingness with warmth, understanding of child development, and giving explanations (high responsiveness).

**Monitoring and Supervising**  One part of demandingness is whether adults monitor and supervise children's activities and behavior and whether they provide an orderly and consistent physical environment and time schedule. Authoritative adults steadfastly believe that monitoring and supervising children is essential (Barnard & Solchany, 2002). Their actions or practices are in harmony with their beliefs because they are willing to commit themselves to the time necessary to monitor children in a classroom or at home. They fully understand that continuous but not annoying monitoring, combined with appropriate supervision, prevents or ends some inappropriate behavior in children (Baumrind, 1996). Early childhood students learn quickly that, when in a classroom with young children, they must be aware of the entire room or playground and what is going on. They learn that they must monitor all activities. It also takes time, effort, and skill to develop a responsive physical environment and time schedule (Haupt, Larsen, Robinson, & Hart, 1995).

**Guidance and Discipline Strategies**  Adults believe in and use a variety of guidance or discipline strategies. Some adults use guidance strategies that are age, individually, and culturally appropriate. Other adults use strategies that are not appropriate for the age or individual needs of a child and very often focus on punishing a child. Other adults use unhelpful discipline strategies. The strategies are not hurtful but they do not help children, either. The strategies are simply confusing.

Age-appropriate guidance strategies are suitable for the general age group of the children being taught. For example, it would be age appropriate to teach all the children in a group of 3-year-olds to label feelings.

An individually appropriate strategy is suitable for a specific child, regardless of the child's age. It would be individually appropriate to teach David, one of the case study children who is now 8 years old, how to put labels on his feeling of frustration when his dog does not sit on command. Why? David did not learn how to label feelings when he was a preschooler, and he needs to learn the lesson now.

**Style of Confrontation**  **Style of confrontation** refers to facing something and coping with it. In child guidance, confrontation deals with how an adult faces and copes with behavior that is clearly hurtful or inappropriate, such as name calling or physical aggression. Adults differ in how they face issues. Some adults are firm yet kind and are willing to take a stand even if doing so provokes a conflict.

**Style of confrontation**
Facing something, often irritating or hurtful, and coping with it

> **EXAMPLE**  Mr. Santini heard Jack say to a child in a wheelchair, "We don't want you to play with us. Get that stupid chair out of here." He quietly asked Jack to come with him so that he could talk to (confront) him in private. Mr. Santini did

not accuse him but dealt with this discipline encounter by using a discipline strategy called an I-message: "I heard you say . . . to Pippin. I was surprised to hear you say that because we have talked about kindness in our room, and I know that you are usually very kind."

This teacher statement started a short conversation that gave Jack an opportunity to tell Mr. Santini that he was afraid of the wheelchair. He was also afraid that Pippin would fall out of the wheelchair. Jack did not think that Pippin would be able to work very well with the science equipment while seated in the wheelchair. Mr. Santini then realized that Jack needed to know more about Pippin's wheelchair and that Pippin could do all the class activities, but that she had to do them sitting down.

## :: STYLES OF CAREGIVING

Baumrind's longitudinal study is called the Family Socialization and Developmental Competence Project. The focus of this research, begun in the 1960s, is on the relation between adult authority and developmental outcomes for typically developing children. Over time, Baumrind has studied the effects of demandingness and responsiveness on the same children's development at three stages—preschool, school age, and adolescence. She assessed parents' specific discipline strategies but focused most pointedly on their overall levels of demandingness and responsiveness (Baumrind, 1996).

Baumrind identified and labeled several styles of parenting or caregiving based on the adult's level of demandingness and responsiveness, as shown in Figure 1.3.

| **FIGURE 1.3** | **Authori*tative* caregivers combine high responsiveness with high demandingness** |

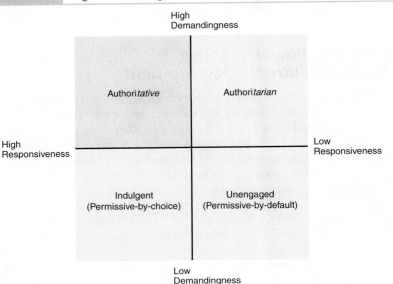

These caregiving styles are the authoritative, authoritarian, and permissive styles. For each, you will read about an adult's level of demandingness and responsiveness and the impact of the style on children. I will emphasize, though, the positive authoritative style.

## The Authoritative Style

**Authoritative style of caregiving**
Combination of high demandingness and high responsiveness; considered a positive approach

Authoritative caregivers possess qualities that help children develop equally positive qualities.

## High Demandingness, High Responsiveness

Figures 1.1 and 1.3 show that authoritative caregivers are high in both demandingness and responsiveness. In terms of demandingness, they expect developmentally appropriate, mature behavior. They set and maintain reasonable, fair limits and closely supervise and monitor children's activities. They are willing to confront a child when necessary, but they confront in a respectful, kind way. In terms of responsiveness, authoritative adults are warm and nurturing. They understand child development and tend to have realistic expectations from children of different ages.

Authoritative adults have a clear communication style. They deliver messages simply, kindly, firmly, and consistently. They use persuasion, not force, to help children understand things. They use positive, developmentally appropriate discipline strategies which focus on teaching and not on punishment. Authoritative adults believe in giving simple and clear reasons and explanations in discipline encounters. Recent research with families of Mexican descent in the United States found that parents in this group reported using authoritative practices more often than authoritarian strategies (Varela, Sanchez-Sosa, & Riveros, 2004).

## Positive and Powerful Effect on Young Children's Development

**The Authoritative Style Helps Children Feel Safe and Secure**    One of a child's most basic needs is for safety and security. Authoritative caregivers help children feel both psychologically and physically safe. They clearly communicate rules that say, "I will never hurt you and I expect you to treat others with respect." Adults who use positive discipline speak to children respectfully and refuse to degrade or demean children. Authoritative adults know that children control their own behavior best when they feel safe and secure (Baumrind, 1993).

**The Authoritative Style Encourages Self-Responsibility**    Children learn to take responsibility for their own actions when they have good models of self-responsible behavior. Authoritative caregivers use positive discipline strategies such as I-messages that model self-responsible behavior. They accept responsibility for their actions and do not blame others for how they themselves feel or act. They are nonjudgmental as they explain the consequences of a child's choice of unsafe behaviors. They model self-responsible behavior.

### The Authoritative Style Fosters Competence and Healthy Self-Control

Authoritative caregiving helps children become competent. Children of authoritative parents tended to be socially responsible and independent when they are first observed in preschool. When these same children were 8 and 9 years old, both boys and girls from authoritative families were still quite competent in the cognitive and social spheres (Baumrind, 1996; Baumrind & Black, 1967).

Our long-range goal in guiding children is to help them achieve healthy self-control. We want children to be able to regulate their own behavior and to want to behave appropriately in school as well as 5, 10, or 20 years from now. Children develop the ability to regulate or control their behavior when they interact with warm and supportive adults who use positive discipline (Hart, DeWolf, Wozniak, & Burts, 1992). Authoritative teachers and parents help children become self-controlled because they:

- Model self-control.
- Clearly communicate their expectation that children will show the level of self-control that they are capable of showing (Healy, 2004, 2005).
- Give specific information on how children can control themselves.
- Recognize and encourage children who act in an age-appropriate, self-controlled way.

The authoritative style helps children develop empathy. Piaget (1970) believed that there are classical factors of development—maturation, social interaction, and physical activity. He noted that social interaction helps children gradually become less egocentric and more empathic because contact with other children and adults exposes children to ideas different from their own. Authoritative adults are themselves more empathic (Brems & Sohl, 1995). They model empathy and encourage children to look at things from someone else's perspective. Adults can guide children's understanding of an alternative viewpoint by taking the time to explain the other person's perspective.

> **EXAMPLE**    Mr. Santini had playground duty and observed that one of the first graders hit a kindergarten child. Mr. Santini, after first helping the kindergarten child, said to the first grader, "I think that you hurt Cody when you hit him. I can tell because he is crying."

Mr. Santini's discipline strategy was developmentally appropriate. It will help the child understand how Cody seems to feel. The teacher has actually told the child how Cody feels and has avoided simply asking, "How do you think Cody feels?"

The authoritative style builds authentic self-esteem and a strong core of personal values. Competence, confidence, and a sense of worthiness are the cornerstones of positive self-esteem. One of our goals as early childhood educators is to help each child develop authentic self-esteem. Along with authentic self-esteem, we want to help children develop a strong core of personal values that guides them to believe in the rights of others to dignified, fair treatment.

Children are motivated by a need to be competent and to have confidence in their ability to do things well, whether it is identifying birds, finger painting, making and keeping friends, doing math problems, or taking care of a horse. The authoritative style helps children feel competent and confident enough to behave appropriately.

It takes time, effort, and creativity to use positive discipline strategies well, and children who experience positive discipline view themselves as worthy of an adult's time and effort. Adults who rely on positive discipline strategies also model, expect, teach, and encourage fair, dignified treatment of other people and animals.

**EXAMPLE**  Mr. Santini quietly and calmly introduced the gerbils to his first graders during morning meeting. With the teacher's guidance, the entire group developed the kindness rules for dealing with the gerbils. They printed the kindness rules and posted them near the gerbil house. Mr. Santini reminded the children about the kindness rules at other group times, and he pointed to the rule about being quiet around the gerbils when Jessie and Lee started talking too loudly near the gerbils' house.

---

## :: Question for Reflection

---

## The Authoritarian Style

**Authoritarian style of caregiving**
Combination of high demandingness and low responsiveness; considered a negative approach

The **authoritarian** style differs significantly from the more positive authoritative style just described. Authoritarian caregivers very often have a negative impact on children's development.

## High Demandingness, Low Responsiveness

Figure 1.3 shows the authoritarian style in the upper right quadrant, where high demandingness meets low responsiveness—not a good combination.

**Demandingness**  Think about the differences between the high demandingness of an authoritative and an authoritarian caregiver. Both set limits, but authoritarians develop arbitrary limits and then state them poorly. Authoritarian caregivers do not monitor or supervise children's activities very well, then they punish when a child does something of which they disapprove. Smith and Farrington (2004) found that males who were poorly supervised by their parents were themselves poor supervisors as adults. When authoritarians confront children, they tend to do so in an inconsiderate, inept, or mean-spirited way. They try to exert a great deal of psychological control.

**EXAMPLE**  Patrick and his family were eating at a buffet-style restaurant. Six-year-old Patrick ran to the serving area by himself, despite the rule requiring an adult to accompany children to the buffet. His father just kept on eating. After about 5 minutes, however, Dad sighed, got up, and went to the buffet to get Patrick. They came back, Dad belittling Patrick and Patrick carrying a dish overflowing with ice cream.

Dad was furious because Patrick had slopped ice cream on the counter, himself, and the floor. (Patrick's father could easily have prevented this whole episode by monitoring his son's activity and by setting some limits.)

Authoritarian adults like Patrick's father rely on negative discipline strategies and equate discipline with punishment. Patrick's father does not use just one negative discipline strategy. He uses a combination of negative discipline strategies such as harsh corporal punishment, threats, lies, shame or ridicule or sarcasm, hostile humor, love withdrawal, and refusal or inability to teach a different way to behave. These negative discipline strategies reflect his need to control and blame, and he gets very frustrated and angry after his negative discipline strategies do not "work."

**Responsiveness**    Patrick's father is like many authoritarian parents—not very responsive to his children. He is often irritable and angry. He does not like being a parent and really does not know how to deal with the role of parent. He is rigid in his interactions with his children and speaks negatively about them, especially Patrick. Parents who are unresponsive and who emotionally neglect their children set up their children for acting out types of problem behavior.

Patrick's father knows very little about child development. Consequently, he has unrealistic expectations of Patrick.

> **EXAMPLE**    Dad expects 6-year-old Patrick to sit quietly in a doctor's office or other public place, no matter how long they are there. Dad makes no attempt to help Patrick find something to read or to do while he waits. He does not know that young children are just developing self-control (Raffaelli, Crockett, & Shen, 2005). He does not attempt to talk to Patrick except to scold him.

Like many authoritarian adults, Patrick's dad rarely even thinks about how Patrick might feel, what Patrick might try to tell him, or what Patrick needs. He uses force (coercion) and places great value on unquestioning obedience. He punishes any attempt from his children at verbal give-and-take and suppresses any attempt at independence or autonomy.

Patrick's father also communicates in an unhelpful, hurtful way. He orders: "I said to get over here. Do it now." He blames: "I hope you're satisfied. You made a real mess at the ice cream machine." He distracts: He avoids issues and occasionally makes completely irrelevant statements. When Patrick complained that his brother had pinched him, Dad only said, "Patrick, pass the mustard." Dad criticizes by focusing on the negative. He criticizes even when Patrick does something Dad asked him to do: "Yeah, I see. You raked the leaves but you missed that whole pile!"

Patrick's father never thinks about the long-term effects of his authoritarian style; he is concerned only about short-term control. He does not know any good child guidance skills. He rarely gives a good reason to help Patrick understand a limit. The few reasons that he does give tend to be related to his adult power.

> **EXAMPLE**    When Patrick asked his father why his brother never had to empty the trash, Dad said, "I don't have to explain myself to you, boy. You hear me?"

Over the years, all of these negative interactions add up, making it difficult for children like Patrick to believe that their parents love them (see Figure 1.4).

| FIGURE 1.4 | Green jelly beans: Authoritarian caregivers make it difficult for children to behave well |
|---|---|

Hurtful discipline strategies are a lot like green jelly beans. Yell at a child; drop a green jelly bean in his memory jar. Make fun of him; green jelly bean. Slap him; several green jelly beans. Some children end up with a memory jar chock-full of green jelly beans.

The children with whom you work, from different backgrounds, will be affected by their culture's views on discipline and their family's caregiving style. Children who come from authoritarian homes will have hundreds or thousands of bad experiences with discipline. They will have experienced some or all of the situations listed below. Knowing this might help you understand that those children, when confronted with a problem, often reach into that jar of jelly beans and come up with a green jelly bean—a hurtful, unhelpful strategy, which they themselves then use.

Authoritarian adults often use:

- **Harsh physical punishment.** They use physical force to try to change a behavior. They do not understand or refuse to take a child's perspective and defend their right to use harsh punishment. They minimize the real harm that they do. Parents who, as children, experienced harsh physical discipline are at high risk for using harsh physical discipline with their children (Tajima & Harachi, 2006).

- **Threats.** Threats create fear and anxiety and are negative and harmful. Some children are terrorized through threats, a form of psychological abuse.

- **Lies.** We are talking here about a nasty pattern of lying to children, a form of manipulation aimed at changing or controlling a child's behavior.

- **Shaming, ridicule, sarcasm, humiliation.** Such strategies foster a negative view of the self and make unpleasant feelings and moods fester.

- **Hostile humor.** Patrick's father often cloaks his aggression as humor, but it is still aggression and is always disrespectful. **Example:** When Patrick had his first ice-skating lesson, he was afraid of falling down. His dad called him a sissy and made him get moving. At home that night, Dad cruelly imitated what he called "sissy-boy Patrick's" fearful approach to the ice and his wobbly start on skates. Patrick burned with embarrassment.

- **Disconnecting (clamming up).** They refuse to talk or listen to, threaten to leave or abandon, or glare at a child. **Example:** Patrick was slow in getting into Mom's car after Little League practice. Mom was angry and Patrick sensed it when she refused to talk to him and stared straight ahead. She looked at him a few times but only shook her head.

## Negative Effect on Young Children's Development

Authoritarian caregiving sets the stage for harm to children (Baumrind, 1996).

**Authoritarian Caregiving Fosters Negative Self-Esteem**   Patrick experiences negative discipline and has developed negative self-esteem. He has not developed the competence, confidence, or sense of worthiness on which self-esteem is built. Instead, he mirrors the lack of trust that his parents communicate. He feels degraded by their authoritarian tactics.

**Authoritarian Caregiving Results in Poor Self-Control**   Patrick's father, like many authoritarian adults, aims to control his children. He believes that he has to control Patrick (external control) and does not help Patrick learn to control himself (self- or internal control). He does not teach Patrick about how his behavior affects others. Therefore, it is difficult for Patrick to act in a self-controlled way in school or anywhere else.

**Authoritarian Caregiving Teaches and Encourages Aggression**   Children who experience negative discipline tend to be more aggressive than children whose parents and teachers use discipline that is more positive. Either they aim their aggression toward the adult who hurt them, or they recycle their anger and use the same degrading behavior with people or animals that had nothing to do with hurting the child.

EXAMPLE  Dad, angry with 6-year-old Patrick for crying, said, "Cut the crying or you'll really get something to cry about." Patrick stopped crying and walked outside. His dog barked a greeting to him but Patrick threw a rock that smashed against his dog's kennel.

## Authoritarian Caregiving Does Not Stop Unacceptable Behavior

Researchers have known for decades that high levels of punishment can restrain behavior only for a short time and, surprisingly, can make the undesired behavior even worse (Church, 1963; Rollins & Thomas, 1979). Undesired behavior seems to occur at a more intense level than it did before the punishment. This is a phenomenon called response recovery. After the punishment is meted out, the behavior appears to cease. However, when the adult stops punishing, the behavior often recurs and is more intense.

## Authoritarian Caregiving Negatively Reinforces Adults for Using Harsh Discipline

Authoritarian adults who rely on negative discipline strategies wrongly believe that this sort of discipline works because they have been reinforced for using it. For example, when Patrick was a toddler and kicked his high chair, his teacher slapped Patrick's legs and Patrick stopped kicking. The teacher was reinforced for using slapping. The sequence went like this:

Patrick kicked his high chair (a behavior that annoyed the teacher).

Teacher slapped Patrick's legs (negative discipline strategy).

Patrick was surprised and stopped kicking—but only for the moment.

Teacher thought, "Hmm, that worked." (Teacher was reinforced because the negative discipline strategy of hitting seemed to work to stop an annoying behavior.)

The next day, Patrick kicked his high chair again. (Response recovery is operating. The negative discipline strategy stopped the behavior only temporarily.)

Teacher slapped Patrick again. (Remember, slapping seemed to work yesterday.)

The real problem here is that hitting Patrick became firmly entrenched in this caregiver's repertoire of disciplinary strategies. She had begun to believe that hitting was effective. It becomes easy for adults to rely on an ineffective discipline strategy, especially when they do not know or do not practice strategies that are more effective or when they rationalize their harsh behavior. Note also that Patrick's teacher used negative, hurtful discipline. She violated the National Association for the Education of Young Children (NAEYC) Code of Ethical Conduct.

In its extreme form, hitting is child abuse. First, we live in a society accepting of violent conflict resolution. Many parents reflect this idea by using violence to solve family problems; they use physical or psychological force as discipline and such discipline can easily injure a child. Second, negative discipline seems to work but really does not. Negative discipline is very ineffective. Third, adults are reinforced for using negative discipline and tend to use the same method again. Finally, an adult who relies on harsh negative discipline strategies soon discovers that she must increase the intensity of the punishment in order for it to be "effective." She must yell more loudly or hit harder, intensifying the strategy.

---

## :: *Question for Reflection*

---

**Permissive style of caregiving**
Low in demandingness

## The Permissive Style
## Low Demandingness

Figure 1.3 shows that *all* **permissive** adults are low in demandingness. They allow children to regulate their own behavior and to make their own decisions. They establish very few guidelines, even about when children eat, watch television, or go to bed. They make few demands for mature behavior, such as showing good manners or carrying out tasks. They avoid imposing any controls or restrictions and have a tolerant, accepting attitude toward the child's impulses, even aggressive ones.

Permissive adults are alike because they are all low in demandingness; they differ, however, in their degree of responsiveness. Some permissive adults are highly responsive to children, but others are quite low in responsiveness (Figure 1.3). Thus, there are two types of permissive adults—but both are low in demandingness.

## Indulgent: Low Demandingness
## Plus High Responsiveness

**Indulgent/permissive style of caregiving**
Combination of low demandingness and high responsiveness; person chooses to be permissive

**Indulgent** caregivers are permissive by choice. They are low in demandingness and high in responsiveness. Members of this group are permissive because they choose to be permissive. Their view is part of their belief system about how to treat children. They firmly believe that children have rights with which adults should not interfere. These parents do not demand much from their children, but they are highly responsive. They are warm and understand child development. They give their child much of what he needs, except for good limits.

## Uninvolved: Low Demandingness
## Plus Low Responsiveness

**Uninvolved/permissive style of caregiving**
Combination of low demandingness and low responsiveness; also known as unengaged; person would rather not be permissive

**Uninvolved** or unengaged caregivers are also low in demandingness, which places them in the permissive category. The similarity ends here, however. Uninvolved, unengaged caregivers are also low in responsiveness. Members of this group have drifted into being permissive. They are permissive *not* because of a strong philosophical belief in a child's rights but because their method of discipline has been so ineffective. They would like to be able to set and maintain limits, but have been so ineffective in getting compliance from children that they have given up trying. They might even begin to see some behaviors, such as aggression, as normal.

Once on the slippery slope of permissiveness, these adults could not get off and have become unresponsive and indifferent toward children—they have become "permissive by default." Think about it this way: If you forget to set the margins on your word processor, the computer sets the margins by default. Similarly, a parent who does not consciously decide on and choose a style of caregiving has his style set by default.

Permissive adults tend to use ineffective discipline. They do not hurt children, but they are not very helpful, either. For example, permissive adults often fail to set appropriate limits, and even when they do set a limit, they frequently fail to maintain it.

> **EXAMPLE**    Liza's mother told Liza to clean up her space at the table. When Liza left the table without cleaning her space, Mom just shrugged her shoulders and walked away.

We guide children effectively by giving them enough of the right type of information so that they will be able to act appropriately under different conditions. Liza's mother did not follow through with her legitimate limit.

Permissive-by-default, uninvolved adults tend to natter and nag. These adults have tried to set limits but have been very ineffective. On occasion, they still try to set limits, but they tend to talk so much that the child ignores their limits.

Some permissive adults use inconsistent discipline, which is related to breaking rules, aggression, and defiance (Stanger, Dumenci, Kamon, & Burstein, 2004). There are two ways to be inconsistent:

> ***Within-a-person inconsistency:*** This person deals differently with the same situation each time it occurs. Take biting as an example. Jared's father was inconsistent when he ignored Jared's biting one day and the next day told him, "No, no, Jared. Biting hurts." The third time he bit another child, Dad ignored him. This is inconsistency within the same individual.

> ***Between-two-or-more-people inconsistency:*** Two adults deal with the same behavior differently. Parents might disagree about how they will deal with any number of issues. Patrick's parents, for example, inconsistently dealt with Patrick's biting when Patrick was a toddler. Dad hit him and Mom ignored the biting. Both techniques are ineffective and negative.

## How Permissiveness Affects Young Children

Both children and adults pay a heavy price when adults refuse to make or give up making demands for maturity or to set clear, firm standards of behavior. Children from permissive systems tend to be low in impulse control. They are not very self-reliant or self-responsible. They tend to be dependent and are not very competent, either socially or cognitively. These results held when the children were 8 and 9 years old (Baumrind, 1967, 1971).

## :: BASIC PROCESSES ADULTS USE TO INFLUENCE CHILDREN

**Basic processes of influencing children**
Direct and indirect methods of persuasion used by any adult in an interaction with a child

All adults—authoritarian, authoritative, indulgent/permissive, or uninvolved/permissive—use these basic processes of influencing children directly and indirectly. In this section, you will read about each of the basic processes that are used by adults, whatever the caregiving style, to influence children. For example, all adults use the basic process of modeling, but an authoritarian adult demonstrates behavior that is very different from that modeled by an authoritative adult. The process is the same, but the content is different. The processes include:

Modeling (M)

Instruction and practice (I)

Feedback (F)

(Management of the) physical environment (P)

Expectations (E)

Change (help the child change understanding and attitude) (C)

Just as we help children learn memory skills, you can use a memory skill to remember this list. Use the mnemonic MIFPEC as an aid to fix the list in your memory.

## Modeling

**Modeling**
Performing an activity and having a child observe it

Much human behavior is learned simply by watching someone else perform the behavior. The other person is the model, and the basic process is modeling. Perhaps the best-known researcher to give us information about this process is Albert Bandura. His classic research (1971) demonstrates that children can effectively learn a behavior just by watching it. Although children can learn from several types of models (cartoon characters, pictures in books, and movie or video characters), Bandura's group showed just how powerful adult models are in demonstrating aggression. Adults can also model other behaviors such as kindness or fear.

Children learn undesirable behaviors—such as aggression or abusiveness—by observing models. An authoritarian parent or teacher who disciplines by hitting or by responding with sarcasm actually models (demonstrates) aggressive behavior. You will also see evidence throughout this book that children just as effectively learn more desirable and positive behaviors—such as generosity, cooperation, kindness, and helpfulness—through the same basic process. An authoritative adult who uses positive discipline teaches a different lesson than does the authoritarian adult.

**Imitation**
Performing an action modeled by someone else

Imitation is different from modeling. A child might learn, for example, how to be kind to animals by observing her teacher model the behavior. The child learns the behavior. There is no guarantee, though, that the child will also perform the behavior that she has learned. When she does perform a behavior learned via modeling, then she has imitated the behavior. Children in this country observe thousands of acts of violence on television and in video games before they enter first grade. Thus, they have several thousand sessions of modeling of aggression and violence. They learn the violence. Whether they imitate what they have observed is another story. Avoid saying, "She modeled after the television violence." Instead, consider saying, "She imitated the violence modeled in the television show."

## Instruction and Practice

Direct instruction involves intentional and explicit teaching. There are many examples of adults influencing children through direct instruction. Teacher education students take curriculum courses so that they can learn developmentally appropriate methods of giving instruction in math, science, social studies, and language arts. Adults also instruct children in physical safety, such as traffic safety, safe use of toys, and how to recognize "good" and "bad" touches. We instruct children about so many things: the correct way to hold a baseball bat, build a campfire, ride a horse, or execute a figure 8 on skates.

Consider the benefits of instructing children in social skills—how to make and keep friends, how to take another person's perspective, how to work cooperatively with friends, and how to resolve conflicts (Lavallee, Bierman, & Nix, 2005).

The next step, after giving instruction, is to encourage a child to practice a new skill. It is very helpful to give on-the-spot guidance or coaching as the child practices.

**EXAMPLE**    Mr. Santini had taught Patrick how to wait for his turn at the computer (he is working on helping Patrick be more observant about approaching activities and other children because Patrick just barges right in). The teacher believes that Patrick will make changes, but Patrick is going to do so gradually. Now, he is at the computer with Patrick. He encourages Patrick to go through the steps that he has modeled and taught: First, check the list of names to see who is next. Second, put his name on the list, if necessary. Third, find something else to do while he waits for his turn and ask for help if he needs it. The teacher coached Patrick through each

**Adults influence children through direct instruction.**

step. "What's the first thing to do, Patrick? Right! Look at the list." He continues this coaching. Mr. Santini believes that this is a much better approach than punishing Patrick for pushing ahead of others on the list to use the computer. It actually teaches something positive.

## Feedback

It is important to give accurate feedback as children are learning and developing. Adults influence children by giving them feedback.

**Feedback**
Information that an adult gives to a child about how the child did something

**Feedback** is advice, pointers, and information from adults about how a child has done something. Feedback is critical to constructing skills and competencies as well as for making changes. Giving good feedback means that teachers give positive feedback and suggestions for change, when appropriate.

**Positive, Unconditional Feedback**   This is positive information independent of anything that the child has done; the child does not have to earn the feedback. Examples include "I love you," or "I like being your teacher" (teacher to class).

**Positive, Conditional Feedback**   These are positive comments expressed after a child has done a specific task—for example, "Thank you, Reese, for showing Sam how to feed the gerbils without disturbing them" or "The fire alarm was very loud but everybody listened so carefully to my instructions." This is positive, meaningful feedback, not empty flattery. It should help children build a healthy view of their competence.

**Feedback That Helps Children Construct More Helpful Skills or Competencies**   Adults, with their expert knowledge and skills, can help children construct positive and satisfying interaction skills. For example, Mrs. Woodward, a preschool teacher, said to Jackie, "You look upset. Is that right?" Jackie told her "yes" and that Ralph would not give him the wagon. Mrs. Woodward had observed Jackie capture the wagon, pushing Ralph in the process. He needed to learn a better way to get what was rightfully his. "I see. Now, everybody is upset. Let's figure out how to use words to tell Ralph that it's your turn." The teacher expanded her feedback to include specific words: "You can say, 'It's my turn now, Ralph.'"

**Feedback from Computers**   Interesting new research shows that children can get feedback from computers just as they can from teachers or parents. Bracken and Lombard's study (2004) examined the effect of praise from a computer on young children's learning. They found that children do have social responses to computer-generated praise and that their responses can lead to increases in recall and recognition in young children.

## Physical Environment

Adults influence children by setting up the physical environment of the classroom well and by providing clean, safe, and appropriate learning materials. Teachers also influence children by developing an appropriate time schedule and by developing appropriate classroom routines and structures. It is possible, for example, for children to learn social skills such as conflict resolution through direct instruction—skits and scenarios. Learning the skill, however, does not guarantee that children will use the skills on the playground, in the cafeteria, or in other places outside the lessons directly focusing on specific skills (Johnson, Poliner, & Bonaiuto, 2005). Children need to practice their new skills throughout the school day.

Effective teachers manage the environment so that children have opportunities to practice skills. They often use a morning meeting (Kriete, 2002), a structured beginning to each day, for children to get to know one another, feel welcomed, shape the classroom culture, and practice social skills. They value social interaction in learning activities and use learning centers. They reflect on routines like recess and lunch, and decide to change them to meet the needs of the children. For example, they might decide to switch recess and lunch, now having recess first and then lunch, so that children might unwind and have a quiet transition to afternoon activities. They plan transitions, realizing that good transitions reduce stress for children.

Such developmentally appropriate practices can improve children's achievement in urban settings (Huffman & Speer, 2000). Fawcett and Garton (2005) found that both social interaction and children's explaining how they solved a problem helped children develop better problem-solving skills. At-risk 5- to 6-year-old children in Hamre and Pianta's study (2005) improved in achievement scores and their relationships with teachers when they were placed in classrooms with strong instructional and educational support.

## Expectations

Teachers state expectations as part of scaffolding children's understanding of limits and interactions. Mr. Santini makes a conscious effort to define cooperative, helpful behavior. Authoritative adults like Patrick's teacher instruct by developing good rules or limits and then communicating them clearly to children. Authoritarian adults, on the other hand, tend to set too many arbitrary limits, and permissive adults may fail to communicate expectations at all.

## Change

Change involves encouraging children to modify (change) their attitude or understanding about something. A young child's brain enables him to process information and make sense of the world. Children can act cooperatively when someone takes the time to present them with additional or different information in a way that is appropriate to the child's particular level of development. Focus on teaching children to understand why they should or should not do certain things. Be gently firm about the need for the children to act more appropriately, and make it clear that there is a reason for acting more appropriately. Be kind at the same time, though. Authoritative caregivers are firm and kind.

An effective way to do this is to help a child become more empathic. The goal is to help a child to understand gradually how her actions affect others and to be able to take somebody else's perspective. Like most learning, this occurs gradually over several years and begins in infancy. The goal here is not to induce excessive guilt or to shame a child. A good way to arouse empathy is to describe another's situation in an open, direct way that still validates the other person and that does not accuse her.

> **EXAMPLES**   Mrs. Woodward said to Ralph, "I see from the job chart that it's your day to feed the gerbils. I'll bet that they're hungry. So get the gerbil food and I'll help you put it in their house."
>
> Mr. Lee, the third-grade teacher, said to Rory, "Name-calling hurts feelings, Rory. Remember our class rules? That's right. Treat each other with respect."

Each adult avoided sarcasm, threats, and accusations while focusing on how the other person or animal might have felt. Arousing a child's empathy—having her "walk a mile in somebody else's shoes or tracks"—is a powerful technique because it encourages the child to examine and begin to understand how her behavior might well have affected someone else.

A common thread linking different forms of antisocial behavior, including child abuse, is the perpetrator's inability to take another person's perspective (Chalmers & Townsend, 1990). Preventing abuse involves helping abusive adults learn social perspective taking. Helping children become empathic, to take the perspective of others, then, is an important task for teachers and parents during early childhood.

## :: FOCUS ON PRACTICE

This **Focus on Practice** activity is called *Constructivism in Guiding* Children. As you watch the video, notice how supportive the teacher is. Also note how the supportive teacher helps the girls change their understanding of the conflict.

### Cultural Scripts and Guiding Children

#### Understanding Your Own and Others' Cultural Scripts for Guiding Children

"**Culture** is a *shared* system of meaning, which includes values, beliefs, and assumptions expressed in daily interactions of individuals within a group through a definite pattern of language, behavior, customs, attitudes, and practices" (Christensen, Emde, & Fleming, 2004). The culture in which you grew up agreed on and then taught you that culture's shared beliefs, values, and behaviors. It is important for you to understand how your culture transmitted its beliefs and values about children and about how to guide them.

**Cultural Scripts Are Guidelines**   Cultural scripts give advice to members of a culture. When childrearing issues arise, for example, the members of that culture decide how to come to grips with the issue. For example, your culture, at some point, decided whether and how to state reasons for limits given to you as a child and then added this to the culture's set of values, beliefs, and behaviors regarding guiding children. The decision was communicated to everyone in your culture, your parents, teachers, and you through (most often) unwritten guidelines known as cultural scripts.

**Cultural Scripts Are Viewed as Undeniable Reality**   Teachers, their colleagues, and parents accept their own cultural scripts and rarely challenge what they believe about guiding children. Even if a person has never heard the term *cultural script*, she tends to view her beliefs about how to deal with things such as whether and how to state reasons for limits as the undeniably correct way to handle things. One person's cultural script for discipline strategies can easily clash with the script of a person from a different culture.

**Cultural Scripts Different from Your Own Are Comprehensible**   Begin understanding another culture's cultural scripts for guiding children by using your ability to take somebody else's perspective. Consider making a statement such as the following to yourself, "Some of the teachers and parents in this school come from a culture that seems to think it is not important to state reasons for limits. We have different perspectives and that is okay." Then, observe and listen carefully and without judging. You can just leave it at that for a while, but if and when it seems appropriate, ask questions about how other teachers or parents handle things without being rude or intrusive. It is one of those things that is "easier said than done," but making genuine and respectful attempts to understand a culture other than your own might well reduce the tension often existing between people from different cultures (Maschinot, 2008).

---

**WORKING
*with*
FAMILIES**    **FIND YOUR PARENTING STYLE**

Help parents understand the concept of different styles of parenting. This topic lends itself to parent education's many formats, including the following.

**Explain.** Give a handout about styles of caregiving or give the links to websites and handouts.

**Assess.** Find out (assess) parents' needs. Ask them what they want or need to know about caregiving styles. For example, do they:

- Want to know more about setting effective limits?
- Need tips on monitoring and supervising children?
- Need help in facing difficult issues with their child?
- Want to know how to give better explanations to children?
- Need help with communicating in a more open and validating way?

- Need to know what to expect from children of different ages?
- Want to learn about different discipline and guidance strategies?

**Plan.** Once you know what parents need or want to know about caregiving styles, develop an efficient plan to deliver the information.

**Deliver.** Get the information to parents via meetings, newsletters, the school website, handouts, and lists of resources.

### ADDITIONAL RESOURCE FOR PARENTS

Brooks, R., & Goldstein, S. (2009). *Raising a self-disciplined child.* New York, NY: McGraw Hill.

## ANALYZE A VIGNETTE

Refer to the vignettes at the beginning of the chapter and analyze them by answering these questions.

1. Both Blake and David's parents are permissive. Which child's parent is the *indulgent* parent? Which child's parent is *uninvolved*? Name at least two things that led you to this conclusion.
2. Patrick's father is an authori*tarian* caregiver.
   a. Cite at least three pieces of data that you can use to support this statement. Be sure to talk about this parent's demandingness and responsiveness.
   b. Then, from information in the chapter's examples, explain how the authoritarian style has affected Patrick.
   c. What do you think is the greatest obstacle standing in the way of Patrick's father making any significant changes in his style?
3. Leah's mother is an authori*tative* caregiver. Explain why her way of dealing with Leah's biting Robert so clearly illustrates the authoritative style.

## SUMMARY

Caregiving styles have two major components:

**Responsiveness.** This refers to how warm a person is and how he communicates and gives explanations as well as his knowledge of child development.

**Demandingness.** This involves how effectively and positively a person makes expectations clear to children and how she monitors and supervises children. It also refers to a person's way of facing issues with children.

The styles of caregiving include:

**Authoritative.** Positive and responsive; makes expectations clear; has a positive effect on children's development.

**Authoritarian.** Sets many rules but they are often unreasonable; communicates poorly; uses negative discipline strategies; often has a harmful effect on children's development.

**Indulgent/permissive.** Low in making expectations clear; highly responsive.

**Uninvolved/permissive.** Low in making expectations clear; low in responsiveness.

Adults use several methods to influence children's development and behavior:

Modeling desired behavior

Instructing and practice

Feedback

Physical environment: managing it well

Expectations: stating them clearly, kindly, and effectively

Change: refers to helping children look at things in a different way and build understanding of new ways of doing things

## APPLY YOUR KNOWLEDGE

1. You have read several examples of Mr. Santini's authoritative style in this chapter. One morning, he had invited the director of the local humane society to talk with the children about kind treatment of animals. The director brought along Hannah, a mellow golden retriever who was accustomed to such presen- tations. Patrick, happy about the dog, grew increasingly excited, causing Hannah to step away from Patrick and go to sit on the other side of the director.

   Role-play how you think Mr. Santini would guide Patrick in this discipline encounter, using information from the chapter on how he manages his classroom and deals with Patrick. He will *not* punish Patrick because you know already that he does not believe in punishment. What is he very likely to do instead?

2. Accentuate the positive! Do a real-world observation and find examples of positive authoritative caregiving. You should be able to see many good examples by visiting a variety of places in which you can observe adults and children interacting—for example, a grocery store, park, family reunion, laundromat, place of worship, or school. Briefly describe the setting and record the approximate age of the child(ren). Write a description of each interaction. Describe why you think this was an example of authoritative caregiving.

3. You are the leader of a parent education group. A frustrated parent of a 5-year-old child asks you what she should do to get her child to put her tricycle away and not leave it in the driveway. Use one or two of the basic processes of influence (modeling, direct instruction, practice with coaching, and others described in the chapter) as you offer this mother some simple, practical, and realistic suggestions for guiding her child. Be prepared to present your suggestions to your class.

# WEBSITES

*Center for Effective Parenting*
http://www.parenting-ed.org

A collaborative project of the University of Arkansas for Medical Science, the Arkansas Children's Hospital, and the Jones Family Center. This site has numerous links for parents and teachers.

*Educational Resources Information Center (ERIC)*
http://www.eric.ed.gov

This site is a digital library of education-related resources sponsored by the U.S. Department of Education. This is an excellent resource for teachers.

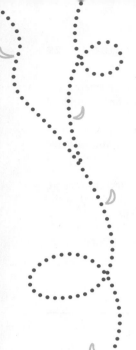

# CHAPTER 2
# Theoretical Foundations of Child Guidance

# Learning Outcomes

- Explain how theories about child development help teachers to guide children
- Describe theories focusing on the systems in which children develop and explain how they help teachers guide children
- Describe theories focusing on how children construct knowledge and explain how they help teachers guide children
- Describe theories focusing on psychological, emotional, and social learning needs and explain how they help teachers guide children

### VIGNETTES

#### TODDLER: JOSEPH CARRIES HIS BOWL

*It was lunchtime and Mr. Benson watched as Joseph, 2½ years old, finished lunch and then tried to pick up his bowl and spoon at the same time. When he could not seem to carry both, Joseph grew increasingly frustrated. "Here, Joseph, let's put the spoon in the bowl. Try holding the bowl like this" (the teacher demonstrated holding the bowl with two hands). He watched as Joseph started to the cart holding the bowl with the spoon in it. "Good, that's the way. Keep going."*

#### PRESCHOOL: EMILY COMES UP WITH AN IDEA

*Mrs. Johnson, the teacher, observed that 4-year-old Emily grabbed things from other children several times every day—for example, at the water table, in the book area, at the puzzle table. The teacher then observed as Emily and Aaron sat facing each other on the carpet and played individually, each with a pile of small plastic snap-together blocks. Emily soon ran out of a favored color and stared directly at Aaron's pile. Then, without a word to the other child, she reached over and took several blocks. After Aaron squealed in protest, Mrs. Johnson said, "Emily, Aaron was playing with those blocks. I'm going to give them back to him. What else could we do instead of taking Aaron's blocks?" Emily, looking directly at the teacher, replied, "Well, you could take Aaron's blocks and give them to me!"*

#### PRIMARY: LUCY CHANGES HER MIND

*Mr. Santini sat at one of the lunch tables with his class. Lucy, a first grader, sat across from him and announced, "I'm not going to eat!" The teacher replied, "Oh, you don't want to eat lunch today. That's okay. You can still have a good time talking with us." Lucy replied, "But, I really don't want to eat." Mr. Santini said, "So, you really don't want to eat." Lucy then stared at him, a look of surprise on her face. Lucy looked like she was trying to figure something out. The next day at lunch, Lucy started in on her "I-don't-want-to-eat" routine again but got quiet and looked at the teacher. Finally, she stopped talking and picked up her spoon, sighing audibly.*

## :: INTRODUCTION

Effective early childhood teachers, such as those in the chapter-opening vignettes, rely on theory to make decisions about guiding children. They use theories about child development as support for how to guide children effectively. This theoretical foundation is based on observations, facts, and research directly related to child development and early childhood education. **Theory** is not a hunch or a guess. Theory is an explanation about something in the natural world. For example, years of observation and research from different types of studies show that children can learn aggression by watching it.

In this chapter, we will focus on the theories that form a firm foundation on which we base many decisions about children, including how we guide them. First, you will study the theories that explain how children's behavior develops in different systems. Then we will look at theories focusing on how children construct ideas. Third, we will examine theories that focus on children's psychological, emotional, and social learning needs. For each group of theories, you will see that understanding and then using those theories in your work with children can help you guide children fairly and effectively.

**Theory**
Not a hunch or a guess; an explanation about something in the natural world, substantiated by observations, facts, and research

## :: THEORIES FOCUSING ON THE SYSTEMS IN WHICH CHILDREN DEVELOP

Some theories informing our work center on children within larger systems. We will look at two of these theories as a starting point because children develop in systems. These systems affect both children's behavior and our decisions about guiding children.

## Urie Bronfenbrenner

Urie Bronfenbrenner (1915–2005) was born in Moscow and moved to the United States when he was a child. He spent his career as a professor of human development at Cornell. We are indebted to him for his explanation of how children's families, homes, schools, and communities or societies affect their behavior and development. He also showed us that the economy, politics, and geography work together to influence children's families and neighborhoods and, by extension, children. This perspective was quite a departure from how researchers viewed human development. Until Bronfenbrenner disseminated this new perspective, researchers had studied each system's effect on children separately.

**Ecology of human development**
Concept that children grow up and develop in different systems, all nested within one another

**Ecology of Human Development**   Urie Bronfenbrenner explained the **ecology of human development**, which refers to the idea that children exist in several environments nested within one another (Figure 2.1). The environments are the microsystem, mesosystem, exosystem, macrosystem, and chronosystem.

- **Microsystem:** includes a child, her family, school, peer group, child-care center, and neighborhood. Relationships within families and the resources in a

Children exist in several *systems*, nested within each other. All of these systems affect a child's development. Systems closest to the child, such as family, school, and the child's neighborhood, have a more direct effect. Systems on the outer rings have a somewhat more indirect effect. For example, the society's views about children affect laws that are enacted, which, in turn, affect the child

**FIGURE 2.1**

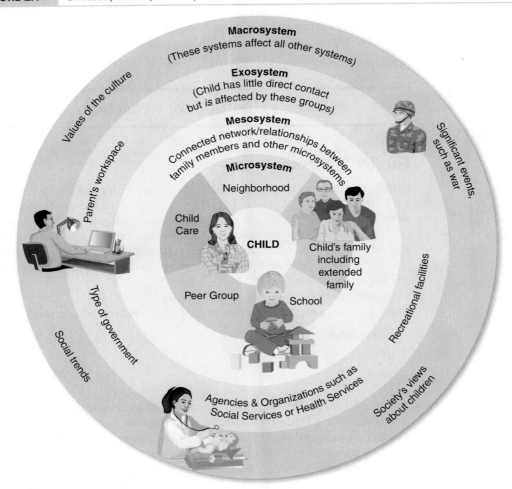

neighborhood all affect a child's development. Marta's parents, for example, get along well together and attend parent education classes at her school. The school believes that it has an obligation to develop partnerships with parents.

- **Mesosystem:** the connected network formed by the different microsystems. Children benefit greatly when the different systems function harmoniously.
- **Exosystem:** the groups farther away from the child but still affecting his development. For example, Marta's family has access to very good parks; thus, she gets to play and explore this type of environment.

- **Macrosystem:** a larger system comprised of the values of the culture, type of government, social trends, and major events such as natural disasters. These values and major events affect every other system. For example, societies valuing literacy will likely develop educational policies supporting literacy for all citizens.
- **Chronosystem:** the degree of change or consistency of various systems over time that, ultimately, affects children's development. For example, if a society experiences major economic upheaval, it might need to decrease funding for health care or education.

---

## :: *Question for Reflection*

---

## Family Systems Theory

Family systems theory explains that families are groups of interrelated people. Each family member affects and is affected by others in the group in predictable ways. For example, families have set ways of communicating with each other and tend to repeat the patterns over time. Children learn their family's way of behaving and communicating and bring those patterns to school. Teachers can guide children more effectively if they understand how a family system operates and affects children.

Family systems have many characteristics (L. G. Christian, 2006). Features of family systems particularly relevant to early childhood teachers are:

Boundaries

Rules

Roles

**Boundaries**    Teachers can use the concept of boundaries within a family system to understand how a family makes decisions. Boundaries refer to a family's ideas about separateness and togetherness. Some families favor a sense of each individual's autonomy and value independence. Other families seem to prefer less autonomy and greater control over members. A teacher might find that one family makes decisions about children together, and another set of parents do not consult each other about such decisions.

**Rules**    Rules are the traditions that families use to guide their interactions with each other. Rules also tell families how to deal with persons and systems outside their family. Observant teachers understand that children's behavior has developed, in part, from their family rules. For example, some boys might not understand that they should participate in cleaning up because their family rule is that "women do the cleanup work." When you hear a child calling teachers "Mrs. _____" or "Mr. _____," you are really hearing their family rules that call for addressing adults with their social title and their last name.

## Cultural Scripts and Guiding Young Children

### Understanding Poverty's Pathways to Destruction

**How Many Children Under 18 Live in Poverty?**   The data, from 2010, and presented below, shows rates of poverty for children living in the United States, where poverty exists in all groups (and cultures). The data reveal great disparities between poverty rates for different groups of children. Notice that the overall rate of poverty for children in general (22%) is much higher than the overall rate of poverty for all Americans (15%) (U.S. Bureau of the Census, 2011; Institute for Research on Poverty, 2013). As a group, then, nearly one-quarter of our children live in poverty.

- All children under 18, overall rate of poverty: 22%
- White but not Hispanic children under 18: 12.4%
- Asian children under 18: 13.6%
- Hispanic children under 18: 35%
- Black children under 18: 38.2%
- All Americans, overall rate of poverty: 15%

**Systems Overwhelmed by Poverty**   Bronfenbrenner's theoretical perspective helps us understand the real, poverty-plagued systems—family, neighborhood, schools—in which children living in poverty grow up. The environments in which a chronically poor child is nested are an almost incomprehensible world apart from those of a more affluent child and they have a devastating effect on all developmental domains of young poor children.

**Three Pathways to Damage**   There are three pathways through which poverty seriously diminishes a child's chances for a healthy, cognitively stimulating, and contented life (Evans & Kim, 2013). The first is an inadequately stimulating environment, for example, too much television watching combined with few chances for informal learning, developmentally inappropriate toys, a scarcity of printed material, and being read to by parents infrequently if at all. A second path through which poverty exerts its damage is harsher and less responsive parent–child interaction. Punishment tends to be harsh and children often do not get what they need from parents to develop the self-control, social, and emotional resources for healthy development. The third path is high stress that goes on and on, with no end in sight.

**Teaching and Guiding Children Living in Poverty**   Reflect on how you view children from poverty. See and treat each and every child as capable, especially as a child living in poverty brings his many needs with him every day. Expect, for example, to see a struggle for self-control and vow to help children from poverty write a different script on how to listen to others and control impulses. Expect a struggle to express herself because of less-than-helpful language skills, including a small vocabulary. Be determined to read and talk to children to help them expand their vocabulary and develop effective language skills. Expect a child to be confused by *your* professional cultural script for positive guidance strategies. Recall that she has likely experienced unhelpful, often harsh discipline. Vow to be unrelentingly positive when choosing guidance strategies.

**Roles**   A role is a responsibility or job that a family assigns to different members of the group. The roles include scapegoat (taking blame for things), peacemaker, helper, or savior. Families assign one of these roles to children and then encourage the child in that role. Some children are peacemakers, for example. They learn what the role entails and practice it in their family by trying to intervene when others are at odds. Their family system rewards them for acting out their assigned role. We should not be surprised, therefore, to see their assigned family role played out in our classrooms. The peacemaker might act as a mediator in classroom conflicts. L. G. Christian (2006) notes that such behavior might be commendable, but a peacemaker child also needs to know when *not* to act out his family's assigned role at school.

## Implications of Theories Focusing on Systems for Guiding Children

Understanding the theories focusing on systems can help teachers guide children more effectively. Acknowledging the influence of systems on children is a good starting point. How can teachers use ideas from systems theories in their work with children?

- Use the concept of systems to develop a fuller picture of the things affecting each child in a class. Yes, a child's family influences her but so does the neighborhood in which her family lives. Likewise, her neighborhood is influenced by larger systems such as her culture. Keep all these systems in mind when thinking about the children in your class.
- Realize that each child will view a teacher's or the classroom's rules and limits or boundaries through the lens of his own family's approach to rules, limits, and boundaries. Some children come to school prepared by their family to accept classroom limits and some children will need more of a teacher's help in learning to accept classroom limits and boundaries.
- Observe children's approach to interacting with other children and with the teacher. Can you detect a consistent *role* that a child assumes, such as peacemaker? Use observations as the basis for deciding how to guide a child. For example, if a child's family role is as the "smart" child, observe whether and how the child plays out that role in the classroom.

## :: THEORIES FOCUSING ON HOW CHILDREN CONSTRUCT KNOWLEDGE

The theories of John Dewey, Piaget, and Vygotsky focus not on systems in which children exist but on how children themselves construct or build knowledge. You will notice great similarities among these theories. All emphasize that children learn through activity and that interaction between a child and others is important.

## John Dewey

John Dewey, born in Vermont, lived from 1859 to 1952. As a teacher, philosopher, and social commentator, he committed himself to fostering the type of thinking that would help a democracy flourish. We in early childhood education are dedicated to many of the ideas that he put forward. Indeed, his influence has been as profound as Piaget's or Vygotsky's and we can use his ideas in guiding children.

**Four Primary Interests of Children** John Dewey identified four main interests of children. When we guide children, paying attention to these interests will help us be more effective.

- **Desire to investigate and discover things.** Children are interested in the process of inquiry to carry out investigations. Why, for instance, does Peter get so frustrated when he cannot find something in his locker?
- **Need to communicate.** Dewey believed that children are inclined to talk to teachers, to ask questions, and to discuss matters with other children.

  > **EXAMPLE** Sylvia, in third grade, had an assignment of writing the ending for her paragraph. She talked to her teacher about how to get started and then read her ending to another child at her table.

- **Joy in construction.** Children find pleasure in making and building things. They work industriously, for example, in constructing models of buildings that they have seen or that they imagine.
- **Artistic expression.** Dewey observed that children enjoy expressing themselves through the arts, such as drama, dance, art, and music.

**John Dewey believed that children find joy in constructing things.**

**Education, Including Guidance, Begins with the Learner's Curiosity** Children have questions about their world, including how to interact productively with others. Dewey believed that this curiosity is the sign of a child's intellectual power and increasing knowledge about the world. Observing children will give teachers clues about children's questions and interests, an idea from Dewey Pedagogical Creed (Dewey, 1897).

> **EXAMPLE** Mrs. Johnson noticed that Jenna watched Paul cry after another child hit him. The watchful teacher concluded that Jenna was curious about other children's emotions. She can use this knowledge to help Jenna learn about feelings and to think about other people.

**Creating Classroom Communities** John Dewey had a vision about democracy and viewed schools as the places where children could develop the thinking skills necessary for creating and sustaining democratic governments (Dewey, 1938). Teachers can create classrooms in which democratic values thrive. This calls for respect for everyone, collaboration, and joint decision making. It requires that communication be open and courteous. Children need to learn to resolve conflicts, not hide from them. Most of all, Dewey believed that children need to learn that they are linked to others and that their individual actions affect others.

## Jean Piaget

Jean Piaget was born in Switzerland in 1896 and died in 1980. He studied the natural sciences and published many papers in this area before concentrating on how children think and develop knowledge. Piaget's perspective on how children's knowledge develops is known as **constructivism**. Constructivism refers to how children build or construct knowledge and how they adapt to their environment.

**Constructivism**
Children's building or constructing knowledge

**Processes Involved in Adapting**    Two processes help children to build knowledge and to adapt to different environments, both physical environments and interpersonal environments.

***Interaction with People and Objects.***    Like Dewey, Piaget believed that children are curious and learn most effectively when they are actively involved in building knowledge. They learn about the properties of objects by manipulating them. Rocks, for example, are heavy; sometimes smooth, sometimes rough; and sink when dropped in water.

Children also learn about people by interacting with them. Other children cry when somebody hits them. Somebody gets upset when you take her toys. Other children do not see things in quite the same way that he does—that is, they have a different perspective, which is puzzling to a young and egocentric child. Children must learn to listen to adults who tend to set and maintain limits.

Teachers have a major role in helping children adapt to interpersonal environments, the environment of relationships with others. Teachers do this with appropriate guidance, in which they help them make sense of things that puzzle them about other people.

## :: FOCUS ON PRACTICE

This Focus on Practice activity is entitled *Children Benefit from Working with Other Children*. All constructivists in this section, Dewey, Piaget, and Vygotsky, highlight the beneficial effects of helping children construct knowledge. You will see, in completing this activity, that teachers can help children construct knowledge about socially appropriate behavior.

**Assimilation**
Process of incorporating new information into an existing concept

***Assimilation and Accommodation.***    **Assimilation** refers to *taking in* new information into an existing repository for such knowledge. The repository is a storage area for the child's ideas and grows over time as he takes in new information. For example, a child observes a butterfly and says, "Look, a birdie!" Why has he made such an obvious mistake? The child has an existing storage area or scheme for "things-that-fly." He puts anything that flies into this folder or scheme, even making mistakes upon encountering a new item, such as a butterfly. He has assimilated the butterfly into his things-that-fly scheme.

**Accommodation**
Process of changing an existing concept to include new information

**Accommodation** refers to the times when children *change* one of their existing ideas to make room for a brand new idea. In the butterfly example, the child observed something that did not fit easily into anything that he understood. It did not fit well with his existing ideas. His teacher explained that this thing was a butterfly and, yes, it does fly, but, no, it is not a bird. The child had to change his idea slightly to accommodate this new information. He formed a scheme (think of a scheme as a filing folder) for "things-that-fly-but-are-*not*-birds." He accommodated to this new information. He adapted.

# Stages of Cognitive Development

Piaget was a stage theorist: He believed in stages of development. He believed that children adapt to their environments gradually, over several years. They adapt as they interact with other people in different systems and as they assimilate and accommodate new ideas. Specifically, Piaget explained that children's thinking is qualitatively different at each of four stages. Figure 2.2 gives a brief overview of the progression through the stages. A somewhat more detailed explanation follows.

One thing to remember about Piaget's stages is that there are no abrupt changes from one stage to the next. Instead, there is a gradual change as children's cognitive structures develop. You will see this in the three stages presented here. At the end of the first stage, for instance, we see a new ability in which a child *begins* to think about things instead of having to perform actions on things. This new ability carries over to the second stage, where it blossoms and continues to develop. The same thing happens between the second and third stages, when new abilities *begin* to emerge and then continue developing.

**Sensorimotor Stage (Stage 1)**     According to Piaget, there is a predictable and gradual change in how infants interact with their world. Their perceptual and memory abilities help them to move through the sensorimotor stage.

- **Birth to about 4 months.** Infants use reflexive actions and actions centered on their own bodies to find out about the world—opening and closing fists, kicking at mobiles, and watching people.
- **4 and 8 months.** Babies start to focus on things other than themselves, and they seem to observe how their actions affect other events, such as crying bringing help from mother.
- **8 months to 12 months.** A baby has noticed many times when he has had an effect on things, such as being able to get mother to notice and play with him. Now, he acquires two new abilities. One is object permanence, the knowledge that things do not disappear when they are no longer visible. Dad, for example, still exists in the infant's mind, even if Dad is not present. Similarly, the baby can remember a toy even when it is in another room. The other new skill is goal-directed behavior, which refers to an infant's new and deliberate attempts to cause certain things to happen. Now, he wants to make things happen and uses previously developed skills to that end. For example, he uses his old ability to grasp things. He might want to interact with his mother. Therefore, he grasps his mother's ear or nose to start the interaction.
- **12 months to 18 months.** Piaget believed that infants were innately curious. During this part of the sensorimotor stage, infants display this inquisitiveness and rapidly increase their experience base by experimenting with objects. They are curious about the physical properties of the objects (hard, soft, and scratchy, for example). They also experiment on familiar objects.

  **EXAMPLE**  A baby presses a familiar soft cube on its corner, then on one of the edges, and finally right in the middle. She performs these actions repeatedly and this helps her figure out which of her actions causes changes in the cube, such as which action turns it over.

| FIGURE 2.2 | Piaget's stages of cognitive development |
|---|---|

**Sensorimotor Stage (from Birth to About 2 Years)**

- Babies center on their own bodies for the first 7 to 9 months.
- They gain information about the world mainly through motor activity and coordinating movements as well as through the senses.
- The ability to use *symbols* emerges at the end of this stage.

**Preoperational Stage (from 2 Years to About 7 Years)**

- Children can now use symbols to represent their experience and mental images: words, paintings, drawings, movements, deferred imitation (observing some action and imitating it later).
- They do not think as logically as they will in later stages.
- They are captured by how something *appears* and ignore other relevant information. For example, the same amount of water is poured into two glasses, one short and wide and the other tall and thin. The child will say that the tall, thin glass has more water because it appears that way to him. He cannot seem to take into account the idea that he watched you pour the same amount of water into each glass. This is called *conservation*.
- They cannot reverse things. They would not think about just pouring the water from our two different glasses into the original identical containers.

**Concrete Operations Stage (from About 7 Years to About 11 Years)**

- Children are no longer captured by the appearance in the conservation experiment.
- They can now reverse operations. They would say, "All you have to do is to pour that water from the tall glass and the short glass back into the first glasses. Then, you'd see that it's the same."
- They now think more logically but are limited to thinking about concrete objects.

**Formal Operations Stage (from About 11 Years Through the Rest of One's Life)**

- The child or adolescent can now apply logic to abstract ideas.
- They can now think through problems more efficiently.
- They can think about many possible reasons for an existing problem and many ways to solve problems.

- **18 months to about 2 years.** There is a change in how children can operate on the world. Now, they *begin* to use mental operations on objects, such the baby thinking about what would happen to that soft cube if she were to drop it. Now, the action can come first in the child's mind before testing out the idea. This is actually a major cognitive shift, involving the ability to imitate something later and representing things in the mind. We see how children in the next stage build on this new ability.

**Preoperational (Stage 2)**    This stage lasts from about 2 to about 7 years. The early childhood years are a time of positive intellectual accomplishment. Preoperational thinkers also have some major limitations on their ability to think. This section focuses on the major positive features and some of the limitations of preoperational thinking. These cognitive abilities and limitations influence the child's interactions with adults and the child's capacity for self-control.

***What Children Can Do in This Stage.***    One of the most significant changes in children's cognition from ages 2 to 6 years is the growing ability to **represent experiences**. That is, they can now use different types of symbols to represent or stand for an experience. Children symbolize their experiences, both good and bad, with deferred imitation, with language, and by using a variety of art media or technology.

**Deferred imitation** refers to delayed imitation. Children observe an event; form and hold a visual image of the event; and then often defer, or delay, imitating the action. Recall from Chapter 1 that children learn by observing models. Each of the children in the following examples has observed models and imitates them now for the first time. The models can be real people, either adults or peers, in person or on a screen. They learn from models in audio recordings or on computers. Children also learn from models in reading material such as books, pamphlets, or even billboards.

> **EXAMPLE**    Joseph swung his foot up martial arts style, and kicked another child. The model was an adult cartoon character in a video game. Sarah softly sang "Hush, little baby" as she cradled her doll in her arms. The models were Sarah's father and mother, who both sing to Sarah's new baby brother.

Talking about things or using language is one of the major ways that children represent their experiences. The major cognitive accomplishment of this stage is that children can use a symbol to represent something else; words are the symbols through which children represent experiences.

> **EXAMPLE**    Justine used words to tell Mrs. Johnson about the car crash that she had seen.

Children also represent their experiences through art media such as painting, drawing, or play dough. They use chalk, paint, play dough, markers, pencils, computers, and other media or technology to create an artistic expression that symbolizes, represents, or stands for an experience that they have had.

**Limitations of Preoperational Thinking**    A 4-year-old's cognitive skills seem so much more advanced than the skills of an 18-month-old because the older child can represent experiences. Nevertheless, a 4-year-old preoperational thinker still has a limited ability to think logically. Preoperational thinkers tend to judge things by

**Represent experiences**
Major cognitive accomplishment of preoperational thinkers; ability to describe an experience using a variety of means

**Deferred imitation**
Observing an action but delaying imitating it until later

how they look, focus on the before and after and ignore how things change (transformations), and have trouble reversing a process.

Preoperational thinkers are somewhat **egocentric**, or focused on their own viewpoint. You will be puzzled and charmed by preoperational egocentricity, as I was, in the following conversation with my 5-year-old niece, who wanted me to take her to get ice cream:

| | |
|---:|:---|
| **Marian (adult):** | "LiLisa, tell me how to get to the ice cream store." |
| **Lisa:** | "You go to the corner and then turn." |
| **Marian:** | "Which corner?" |
| **Lisa:** | "You know, the one with the trees." |

At the time of our conversation, Lisa was egocentric and not very good at perspective taking. She did not give me all the necessary information, largely because she did not understand exactly what I needed to know. Preoperational thinkers tend to think that the other person has the same information they do.

**Difficulty with Perspective Taking.**   Egocentric thinkers center on what they want or need, but this is not the same thing as being selfish. A selfish person understands somebody else's perspective and chooses to ignore it, but an egocentric thinker cannot take the other person's perspective; there is a blurring of his or her own viewpoint with the perspective of the other person. A preoperational thinker, such as Lisa in the example above, believes that everyone thinks the same way she does.

**Perspective taking** is a cognitive developmental skill, the ability to understand how another person views a situation. It takes several years, as a classic work from Selman (1976) explained, to develop and is first evident at the end of early childhood, as shown in Figure 2.3. We can expect that young children will not be able to take someone else's perspective. The ability to take another person's perspective is linked to a variety of abilities, including the ability to read effectively (discussed by Catherine Snow and Robert Selman, 2012, in a video at this website: http://ccdd.serpmedia.org/research-perspective-taking.php). Selman (2003) explained how understanding when children develop the ability to see things from another person's viewpoint is useful to teachers as they work with children.

**Fooled by Appearances.**   Picture two containers—one short, one tall—each holding an equal volume of water. Preoperational thinkers typically assert that the tall container has more water in it "because it looks like it has more." Appearances deceive them because they tend to judge something by how it appears on the surface.

**Focusing on the Before and After and Ignoring How Things Change.**   Preoperational thinkers ignore the process through which something is transformed or changed. For example, you show two cups of sand to a child and he says that the cups have the same amount in them. Then you pour the sand in one of the cups onto a cookie sheet. You ask which has more sand, the other cup or the cookie sheet, or if both have the same. Preoperational thinkers usually say that the cookie sheet has more sand. A child at this stage usually says that it looks like it has more. What is the problem?

A preoperational thinker focuses first on the equal amounts of sand in the two small cups (the before state). Then she focuses on the sand in one short glass and on the cookie sheet (the after state). She tends to ignore the pouring of the sand from the small cup to the larger surface of the cookie sheet. The pouring is the transformation.

**Egocentric**
Focused on one's own viewpoint

**Perspective taking**
A basic cognitive developmental skill; ability to see things from another's perspective

| FIGURE 2.3 | Levels of perspective-taking | |
| --- | --- | --- |
| **Age in Years** | **Level** | **Perspective-Taking Ability** |
| 3 to 6 | Level 0 | • Egocentric perspective<br>• No distinction between own and another's perspective |
| 6–8 | Level 1 | • Still not able to take another's perspective<br>• Believes that another, if in the same situation, will respond just as the target child would respond |
| 8–10 | Level 2 | • Can take another's perspective<br>• Sees self as others do<br>• Not everyone reaches this level |
| 10–12 | Level 3 | • Can take another's perspective but in a more sophisticated way than at Level 2<br>• Now aware of recursive nature of different perspectives: "Mom thinks that I think she wants me to." Not everybody reaches this level |
| Adolescence and Adulthood | Level 4 | • Very sophisticated in perspective-taking ability<br>• Believes that different perspectives form a network<br>• Has conceptualized society's viewpoints on legal and moral issues<br>• Not everybody reaches this level |

*Source:* Based on "Social-Cognitive Understanding," by R. L. Selman, in Moral Development and Behavior, by T. Lickona (Ed.), 1976, New York: Holt, Rinehart & Winston.

An older child, adolescent, or adult, aware of the pouring, would explain things by saying, "All you did was pour sand from one container to another."

***Difficulty Reversing a Process.*** Preoperational thinkers focus on one thing at a time, either the before or the after in any action. An older child, who can think about a couple of things at once, is not deceived by how things look. Adults and older children realize that they could quickly show that the volume of sand on the cookie sheet is equivalent to that in the small cup. They would simply transfer the sand on the cookie sheet into the small cup. They can reverse the process; young children, however, do not think so logically.

Just as there was a gradual shift from the first to the second stage of cognitive development, children begin a gradual transition from the second to the third stage at approximately age 6.

## :: *Question for Reflection*

**Concrete Operations (Stage 3)** The new, concrete operations stage lasts until about age 11. This stage occurs at the end of the early childhood years and the beginning of middle childhood. Several major changes occur in children's thinking for this stage.

***Children Begin to Think Somewhat More Logically.*** They begin to pay attention to relevant dimensions in different conservation tasks. Changes in appearances deceive them less and less. They begin to pay attention to transformations in matter, such as pouring water from one container to another or squashing a ball of dough into a seemingly larger flat shape. They now begin to understand that the apparent changes really do not change the basic nature of the material because the child can reverse the process. The changes do not occur all at once but gradually (Gallagher & Reid, 2002). This stage, however, is called *concrete* operations because children think about objects that they can see and touch, such as the ball of dough (University of Chicago Medicine, 2013).

Children classify things much more skillfully now. They use this cognitive skill in several ways. For example, children can understand that the category things-that-fly can be broken down into much more specific categories such as insects-that-fly or birds-that-fly. They can also seriate objects, meaning that they can arrange objects in a series.

> **EXAMPLE**   Mr. Santini put out 10 wooden dowel rods of varying lengths in the discovery/math center. He noticed that 8-year-old Celia easily put them in the correct order from the shortest to the longest.

**A Child Who Can Classify, Seriate, and Reverse Things Can Also Learn Mathematics.**   The limitation for children in this stage is that they can apply their new abilities only to real objects; hence, the name *concrete operations*. They cannot deal effectively with abstract ideas or hypothetical problems.

## Lev Vygotsky

Vygotsky, like Piaget, was born in 1896. Vygotsky was born in Byelorussia and graduated from Moscow University in 1917, just as the Russian revolution started. He died when he was only 37 years old.

Both Piaget and Vygotsky have had great influence on child development and education, although there are some central differences between their theories. Piaget lived much longer than did Vygotsky, and Piaget's writing, unlike Vygotsky's, was widely disseminated. Eventually, translations of Vygotsky's work, along with Piaget's, made their concepts more available to child developmentalists and educators. Educators quickly saw the value in his views, and they used Vygotsky's theory to inform constructivist curriculum and instructional. Adults can use concepts from Vygotsky's theory to help them make wise child guidance decisions, including the following (Vygotsky, 1978):

- Scaffolding
- Zone of proximal development (ZPD)
- Adult–child dialogue or discourse

**Scaffolding**
An adult's modifying support as children develop new knowledge or skills

Scaffolding   **Scaffolding** refers to a teacher's changing support as a child develops a new competency or skill. Think of it like this: A building under construction usually has a series of scaffolds, or platforms, that support construction workers. They are placed where the workers need them. Likewise, a child is like a building that constructs herself. Children are the main construction workers, constructing or building themselves, their knowledge, skills and competencies, views of morality, gender, self, kindness, and compassion. Adults help children in their construction by serving as guides, by scaffolding the child's learning. Other children, as well as television, influence the strength of the child's construction. A child who has supportive guidance and a nurturing social environment can forge ahead and build strong social competencies (Morrison, Brown, D'Incau, O'Farrell, & Furlong, 2005).

Scaffolding in child guidance is a teacher's changing support during a discipline encounter or series of interactions. For example, Mr. Santini notices that a child lacks a specific skill. He knows that the child could use support from somebody who possesses the skill (the teacher or a more skilled child). The more skilled partner provides help but tries to match the child's current level of ability.

Teachers usually offer more help when a guidance task is new. As the child gains skill in constructing the necessary knowledge, we can gradually step back, providing progressively less help. Scaffolding in child guidance helps children become autonomous and self-controlled. Here is an example of Mr. Santini scaffolding Rory's understanding of how speaking thoughtless words can hurt another person's feelings.

**EXAMPLE**   Rory had told Ellen, a skillful reader, that he did not want to be in her reading group anymore because of how she stopped to look at every picture. Ellen looked dejected and withdrew from her group, refusing to read aloud.

Mr. Santini noticed this interaction and talked with Rory in an effort to scaffold Rory's understanding of the effect of thoughtless statements on other people's feelings. Mr. Santini helped Rory by saying, "Sometimes people say things that make another person feel bad. They have not thought about how the other person will feel."

---

## :: *Question for Reflection*

---

### Zone of Proximal Development
The **zone of proximal development (ZPD)** is the space or zone where learning and development take place. At one end of the ZPD is a child's current ability, what he understands about some topic. At the other end of the ZPD is what the child can learn or accomplish with the help of an adult or more competent member of the culture. See Figure 2.4. Teachers can figure out where a child is in the ZPD by talking with the child and asking questions. The questions will help the teacher determine what the child already knows about a topic and what the child might be able to learn with the teacher's help (Learning NC, n.d.).

In the Rory–Ellen example, Rory at first did not really understand that thoughtless words born of frustration could hurt someone's feelings (Rory's current ability). Mr. Santini gave him some help, in a warm and supportive way (the expert help). Rory later demonstrated how much he had learned because of the dialogue with his teacher. He demonstrated the willingness and ability to acknowledge thoughtless behavior and its effect on another person.

**Zone of proximal development (ZPD)** Space in which learning and development occur

### Adult–Child Dialogue or Discourse
Any guidance strategy based on Vygotsky's theory relies heavily on adult–child dialogues, talking about tasks that a child can accomplish with adult help. Children gradually learn how to control their own behavior when adults scaffold their understanding of social interaction. This works by inducing children to use self-directed, private speech to guide their actions.

**EXAMPLE**   Mr. Santini and Rory talked (engaged in discourse) about the effect of Rory's words on Ellen's feelings (Mr. Santini's scaffolding through talking). When he was later alone, Rory's private speech helped him work through the problem. Essentially his private speech stated, "I said something mean to Ellen. I need to tell Ellen that I'm sorry. I will write a note and leave it on her desk."

| FIGURE 2.4 | Zone of proximal development (ZPD) |
| --- | --- |

This end of the ZPD is what the child can accomplish in reading with the teacher's help.

The arrow indicates the process of moving from one level of ability to a different, more sophisticated level of ability.

This is the child's current ability in reading without adult help.

## :: FOCUS ON PRACTICE

This Focus on Practice activity, *Teacher Child Conversations*, illustrates how helpful a conversation between a teacher and a child can be in helping the child learn. You will see the power of this strategy for helping children learn to get along with others.

## Implications of Theories Focusing on How Children Construct Knowledge for Guiding Children

Piaget's, Vygotsky's, and Dewey's theories are extremely useful in helping teachers guide children effectively. The core concept in these constructivist theories is that children construct or build knowledge. How can teachers use ideas from constructivists Piaget, Vygotsky, and Dewey in their work with children?

- Reflect on how you view young children. Constructivist theories view them as joyful and curious learners, eager to investigate and discuss their findings. Constructivists see children as competent, capable, and exceptionally curious, willing to learn how to link ideas to construct even bigger ideas. For example, you can help children learn how to make decisions when issues are shared by others. How long, for example, should one person have with the classroom computers when everyone wants to work in that center? From such a discussion on solving a problem, children do learn how to give computer time to everybody, but they also learn that they are connected to others and that they should consider others when making decisions.

- Provide plenty of opportunities for children to construct ideas about objects and materials. Provide materials for children to manipulate, whether you teach 3-year-olds or third graders. Preschool and kindergarten children need sand, paints, water, puzzles, rocks, and other similar materials. Primary grade children also need to manipulate objects as they learn specific mathematical, scientific, and social studies related concepts.
- Keep in mind that children learn through activity and social interaction. Use teaching strategies based on this belief. Active learners need large blocks of time for exploration, thinking, trying ideas, and discussing results. Young children need to talk to their teachers and to other children in order to learn. Provide the time and opportunity for children to work together. Be willing to discuss problems and ideas with children.
- Help young children learn about the perspective of others. This is a gradual process and does not happen overnight, but teachers can patiently and good-naturedly help children see the perspective of others. A teacher might lead a discussion, for instance, about how to listen to another child's story and how to ask questions about the story in a friendly way. A teacher might tell a child how another child feels when she is called a nasty name and then be firm about speaking to others with respect. Another teacher might emphasize every child's right to one of the snacks in a basket. Seemingly simple, everyday interactions such as these do help children gradually learn to take the perspective of others. Vygotsky would say that your role in initiating the conversations is very important for their learning. Children are active, curious information seekers. As you watch this **video**, focus on how active and curious the children are as they seek information. Notice how the children's teacher provides a learning activity that encourages children's desire to explore and make sense of their world.

## :: THEORIES FOCUSING ON PSYCHOLOGICAL, EMOTIONAL, AND SOCIAL LEARNING NEEDS

Some theories informing our guidance focus on children's emotional and social development and learning. You will see in each of the following theories that adults have an important role in guiding children's development and understanding of their world.

## Erik Erikson

Erik Erikson was born in Germany but attained U.S. citizenship after moving to the United States in the 1930s. He was a professor and a therapist. He developed a theory of psychological development describing human psychological growth from birth through death, which is a life-span perspective. Erikson proposed eight stages of psychological development, each presenting humans with a **psychosocial crisis**. The person's interactions with the social environment affect whether she resolves the challenge of each stage in a positive or negative way.

**Adult Influence**    Parents and teachers influence young children's resolution of the childhood challenges by using their knowledge of child development. For example, a

**Psychosocial crisis**
Challenges presented at different ages and resolved in either a positive or negative way

toddler has new motor and language abilities and wants to establish herself as an independent person. We can use this information when working with toddlers by encouraging their independence within limits.

Erikson's theory guides our relationship building with children at all of their different stages. Forming good relationships with young children is one of an early childhood professional's main responsibilities and the base for all of our developmentally appropriate practices. Erikson's theory is also helpful as we strive to develop good relationships with parents and other professionals, each of whom is going through one of Erikson's stages.

**Stages of Psychosocial Development**   Erickson identified eight stages of psychosocial development.

- **Trust versus mistrust: Infancy, birth to 18 months.** Children develop the positive trait of trust when their needs are met consistently.
- **Autonomy versus shame or doubt: Toddlers, 18 months to 3 years.** Encourage toddlers to do things by and for themselves when such independence is possible and safe.
- **Initiative versus guilt: Preschool and kindergarten, 3 to 5 years.** Encourage children's growing desire to explore and make sense of their world. Recall that Dewey also views children as active, curious information seekers, as do most of the other theorists.
- **Industry versus inferiority: Primary grades and part of elementary school, 6 to 12 years.** Children now operate in at least a couple of different systems, such as school, religious institution, or recreational groups. They need support as they face new challenges.
- **Identity versus role confusion: Adolescence.** This is a time when children must deal with the world outside their family on their own. Help them learn to deal with pressure from their peer group and to make good decisions.
- **Intimacy versus isolation: Young adulthood.**
- **Generativity versus stagnation or self-absorption: Middle adulthood.**
- **Integrity versus despair: Late adulthood.**

# Abraham Maslow

Abraham Maslow, born in New York in 1908, was one of several children born to his Russian immigrant parents. He earned all of his degrees from the University of Wisconsin—Madison and then taught in universities. He died in 1970. While a student at Madison, Wisconsin, Maslow had contact with Harry Harlow, who operated a research program with rhesus monkeys, which you probably studied in your basic psychology course. This work explained what happened when the baby monkeys were deprived of contact with and comfort from their mothers. Maslow noticed that some needs seemed to be very important.

Maslow (1954/1987) went on to describe and explain a hierarchy of human needs. This ladder of needs, shown in Figure 2.5, has been very useful to a variety of professions. This figure shows that a child's most basic bodily or physiological needs, such as for sleep and food, must be met before we can attempt to help her learn in school. They must also be met before we can think about guiding her or helping her

**FIGURE 2.5** Maslow's hierarchy of human needs

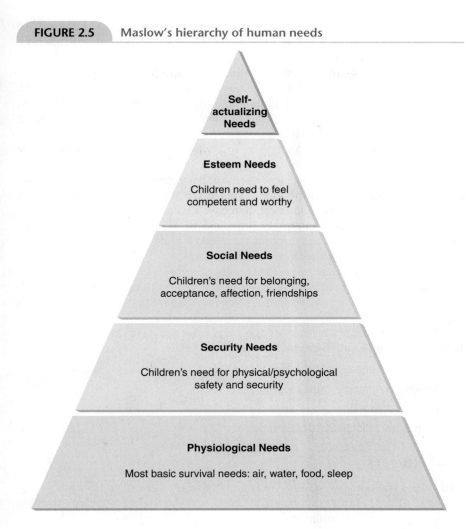

Self-actualizing Needs

Esteem Needs
Children need to feel competent and worthy

Social Needs
Children's need for belonging, acceptance, affection, friendships

Security Needs
Children's need for physical/psychological safety and security

Physiological Needs
Most basic survival needs: air, water, food, sleep

build ideas about getting along with others. Meeting needs for safety and security provides the foundation on which the social and esteem needs at the upper part of the illustration are met. Maslow's hierarchy is also useful in a teacher's work with colleagues and parents. We all have the same needs and have the right to feel like a valued member of a school or community.

In this video you will observe a preschool teacher helping children meet their social needs, including the need for belonging, acceptance, affection, and friendship. The teacher does this in an activity, circle time, an accepted part of preschool and primary grade classrooms.

## Alfred Adler

Alfred Adler was born in Vienna, Austria, in 1870. He was a physician with an interest in psychiatry. He was a contemporary of Sigmund Freud but broke with some of

Freud's main ideas. Adler believed that each person is primarily a *social* being. He maintained that a person's social environment and interactions, such as with teachers, heavily influence personality development. He believed that people actively, consciously direct and create their own growth. Notice that this is the same perspective that the constructivists hold—that we are active in building our ideas about the world.

This theory teaches us that children play a large role in their own development, that their interpretation or perception of their experiences is important. Adler thought that humans are social creatures who need to attain group membership. Children go about fitting into a group by following their own interpretations of the rules for group membership.

Some children are able to achieve a sense of belonging to their group by cooperating and making useful contributions. They make accurate interpretations of the rules of group membership. Other children have a pattern of misbehavior and noncooperation because they interpret events and people's intentions inaccurately. These children have a faulty perception, or mistaken goals, of how to fit into a group and use ineffective approaches to gain a place in it.

They base their behavior on their faulty perceptions of the world. To assist them, we must help them get a different perspective on things, to perceive events and people's intentions more accurately. Adlerians believe in thinking about what a child gets out of misbehavior, or what his mistaken goal is.

Table 2.1 explains the mistaken goals that drive some children's behavior. The faulty perceptions—mistaken goals—include the following:

Striving for undue attention from others

Seeking power over others

Hurting others through revenge

Displaying inadequacy or incompetence

## Carl Rogers

Carl Rogers was born in 1902 in Chicago. He was a teacher and an educational psychologist. Rogers counseled children and parents at the Child Study Department of the Society for the Prevention of Cruelty to Children. From 1940 to 1963, he developed and disseminated his views on counseling and therapy (Rogers, 1957). Rogers believed that individuals have the power within themselves to solve their own problems. A therapist or a teacher's job, therefore, is to help the person seek the answers.

Rogerian guidance strategies rest on the idea that children have the capacity for self-direction, that children can become increasingly able to control their own actions. Teachers and parents who use Rogerian guidance strategies believe that it is the adult's role to support children's efforts, to demonstrate acceptance and approval. Notice the fundamental similarity between Vygotsky's and Roger's theories. Both believed that children could develop or construct their own abilities and competencies. Both also believed that children need competent, warm adult support to do their constructing.

Carl Rogers had followers, professionals educated in his theory. One of these people, Thomas Gordon, developed a program of child guidance based on Rogerian theory. The program, Parent Effectiveness Training, is best known as P.E.T. (Gordon Training

| **TABLE 2.1** | Adler's Mistaken Goals | | | |
|---|---|---|---|---|
| Mistaken Goal | Child's Faulty Perception | What the Child Does | How Adults Feel and Tend to React | A Better Approach: Ignore First Impulses and |
| Attention (child seeks *undue* attention) | Try to make themselves the center of attention | Keeps adults busy, some through mischief, others through passivity or idleness | Annoyed Gives in to demands Scolds | Show how to join group appropriately Gently insist that passive children do their assigned work |
| Power (child struggles to get power) | My personal value comes from showing you that I am in charge | Develops techniques for getting power: Tantrums, disobedience, arguing excessively, stubborn defiance | Threatened or angry Tends to get drawn into a power struggle | Tell child you do not want to fight Refuse to argue |
| Revenge (child seeks vengeance) | Hurt and angry, the child essentially says, "I will get my recognition by hurting you or others through revenge." | Expends much energy convincing others that he is *un*likeable; gets even | Feels hurt Might back away Might retaliate Feeds into child's mistaken ideas Not at all helpful | Do not take things personally Help child feel valued Teach how to manage anger and anxiety |
| Incompetence (child displays inadequacy) | Defeated, the child's message is, "I will be a member of this group by taking the role of someone who can't do things well." | Acts as though he cannot do something, often when this is not the case | Frustrated, annoyed, confused Tends to give in and do work for child, then does not expect much | Inform child that you expect her to do the job Show confidence in her ability Give instruction if necessary in how to do the work Gently insist if child does not, at first, change |

International, 2011). He also developed a similar program for teachers, Teacher Effectiveness Training, or T.E.T. (Gordon Training International, 2005). Gordon's objective in starting the effectiveness training programs was to teach specific guidance skills to adults; these skills include the following:

Figuring out who owns a problem, adult or child

Listening actively when a child owns a problem

Delivering an I-message when the adult owns a problem

**Problem Ownership**    Problems, issues, or conflicts arise in all relationships. The first step in solving any problem requires figuring out if a problem even exists and, if so, who owns the problem—**problem ownership**. Figure 2.6 shows that, at times, an adult owns the problem and at other times, the child owns the problem. At other times, there is no problem (Gordon Training International, 2011).

Decide who owns the problem by looking at whose needs are thwarted. Who is upset? Who is afraid? Who is it that cannot do something? Who is frustrated?

**Problem ownership**
Concept from Rogerian theory referring to deciding who in a relationship has the problem

| FIGURE 2.6 | Problem ownership |
|---|---|

Child owns the
problem

Area of no problem

Teacher (or other adult)
owns the problem

**EXAMPLE** Mr. Santini (the first-grade teacher) noticed Vinnie and Susan sitting on the floor, a large sheet of paper between them. They had written one sentence and seemed stuck in the middle of the second. "How is it going?" asked Mr. Santini. The children said that they were trying to figure out how to spell *the*. This problem, the teacher quickly concluded, belonged to the children. They were the ones who were at a loss about the spelling. He suggested that they consult the list of frequently used words.

**EXAMPLE** Mr. Santini saw that Lucy was unusually quiet on Monday, hardly speaking the whole morning. He asked Lucy if she wanted to talk and found out that her grandpa had died. Lucy owned this problem.

It is important to decide on problem ownership because the guidance strategies that we choose depend largely on who owns the problem. Our goal is to *de*crease the number of problems owned by both adults and children and to *in*crease the area of no problems.

**Deliver I-Messages When an Adult Owns the Problem** Many questions raised in workshops on guidance and discipline center on problems in relationships with children, problems owned by the adults. Children sometimes behave in ways that interrupt an adult; cost the adult time, energy, or money; interfere with adult rights; or insult adults. For example, a child might consistently interrupt group time or might refuse to do an assigned job.

This theoretical approach advises adults to use I-messages when adults own a problem. The goal is to tell the child clearly that the adult has a problem with something that the child did. Another goal is to convey the adult's need for the child to do something to fix the problem. I-messages allow a child to make the change out of respect for the adult.

Good I-messages are simple statements of facts. A good I-message does not accuse a child of creating the adult's feeling (Gordon Training International, 2011). Good I-Messages include four elements:

- Give observable data (what you saw, heard, smelled, touched)
- State the tangible effects
- Say how you felt
- Focus on change. Give some ideas about how to change things or ask questions that prompt children to come up with solutions, a guidance strategy based on Vygotsky's theory, that will encourage the child to make a necessary change

Here is an example of how the first-grade teacher delivered an I-message when Ryan destroyed property (the teacher's problem).

**EXAMPLE** Ryan used a pencil to rip a jagged hole in a bottle of glue, not by accident. At first, Mr. Santini felt very angry. He turned away, took some deep breaths to calm himself, and then turned back to Ryan. He picked up the bottle and handed a towel to Ryan. "Clean up the glue, Ryan, before it runs off the table and onto the floor." When he and Ryan had cleaned the sticky table, he took Ryan aside and calmly delivered his I-message.

- Give data: "I picked up the bottle of glue and saw that glue was flowing out of the hole in the bottle. I saw that you were laughing about it."

- State tangible effects: "You and I had to clean up all the spilled glue, which took quite a long time. I will also have to get a new bottle of glue." Ryan responded, "So?" Mr. Santini ignored the attempt to deflect the conversation.
- Say how you feel: "When I saw all the glue, I was startled and then I got angry because I saw that you were laughing about it."
- Focus on change: "I want you to help me figure out how to fix this problem. How will you replace the bottle of glue?" This is only the beginning of a conversation on how to replace the bottle of glue.

Practice delivering an I-message in Figure 2.7.

**Listen Actively When a Child Owns the Problem**    Active listening is useful when children own a problem. (This process is similar to Vygotsky's idea of teacher–child discourse to solve problems.) Use this strategy when you want to help a child solve his own problem. In the example that follows, Jack, the child, makes a simple remark. The remark does not indicate that Jack has a problem, but Mr. Santini responds in a way that encourages Jack to get to the problem. Even when Jack first indicates that something is bothering him, Mr. Santini has no idea about what the real problem is. The teacher, however, communicates in a way that Jack felt safe enough to keep talking. He eventually gets to the real issue.

> **EXAMPLE**    Six-year-old Jack was playing a card game with Vinnie, who said, "I like playing cards!"
> Jack chimed in, "Me too! I like playing cards!" (At this point, the teacher did not see a problem at all.)

| | |
|---:|:---|
| *Teacher:* | Good. I'll make sure we always have cards in the room. |
| *Jack:* | I like playing cards at school. (He emphasized *at school*.) |
| *Mr. Santini:* | (attending more closely now) You like playing cards at school. |

| **FIGURE 2.7** | Practice sending an I-message |
|---|---|

- **Situation.** Jessica, in Mr. Santini's kindergarten, played in the sandbox outside along with several other children. Jessica took a hefty amount of sand and threw it in the air with both hands. She did not seem to be aiming at anyone but the other children had to dodge the sand shower. Mr. Santini's delivered this I-message:

  Give data: _____

  State tangible effects: _____

  Say how you feel: _____

  Focus on change: _____

- **Situation.** A rescue worker brought her rescue dog, Sarah, to Mr. Santini's K–2 class. Michael and Willis interrupted the beginning of the presentation twice by barking and then laughing. Sarah, the dog, never flinched. The presenter appeared to be upset but went on with the presentation. Mr. Santini's called Willis and Michael aside.

  Give data: _____

  State tangible effects: _____

  Say how you feel: _____

  Focus on change: _____

|  |  |
|---|---|
| *Jack:* | Yeah, but not at home. |
| *Teacher:* | . . . Not at home. |
| *Jack:* | Well . . . I like to play cards with my mom. |
| *Mr. Santini:* | (careful not to close down the conversation) You like to play cards with your mom at home. |
| *Jack:* | Yep, with my mom; not with Grandpa, though. |
| *Teacher:* | Playing cards with Mom is fun but playing cards with Grandpa isn't so much fun. |
| *Jack:* | Grandpa calls me a dummy if I count things wrong. (This is the real problem. Jack does not like it when Grandpa calls him names.) |
| *Teacher:* | When Grandpa calls you a name, you don't like it. Is that right? |
| *Jack:* | I don't like it. That's right. I don't want to play with him when he does that. |

Mr. Santini used Vygotsky's approach, too, by asking a question that prompted Jack to come up with a solution. "How can you let your grandpa know that you don't like to be called names, Jack?" Mr. Santini urges Jack now to solve the problem. He does not give a solution. Figure 2.8 lists guidelines for listening actively.

# Social Learning Theory

Social learning theory emphasizes social variables determining a child's behavior. It helps teachers understand that children are *not* just machines responding to stimuli. Social learning theorists believe that children are active in their own development, that they are affected by their environment, and that they contribute to producing their environment.

## Social Learning Principles and Child Guidance

- **Principle 1: Social learning theorists do not emphasize stages of development.** Some theorists view development as a series of phases or stages, each stage being qualitatively different from the ones before and after. In learning theory, however, development is not viewed as a series of stages but rather as a gradual accumulation of knowledge. Even though social learning theorists do not emphasize stages of development, they do acknowledge that a child's level of development plays a part in learning from models. For example, a child must have good enough perceptual

| **FIGURE 2.8** | How to listen actively |
|---|---|

| **Remember to** | **Avoid "roadblocks to communication"** |
|---|---|
| • Listen carefully. | • Avoid giving solutions. |
| • Try to figure out what the message means. | • Avoid interrupting the child. |
| • Listen for what the child is feeling. | • Avoid preaching or ordering. |
| • Suspend judgment (avoid judging anything about the situation). | • Avoid giving advice. |
| • Let the child finish speaking. Wait 1 or 2 seconds and then speak. | • Avoid trying to persuade the child to feel something else. |
| • Merely reflect back your perception of the child's feelings with words or body language. | These things close down communication. A person is not listening actively when she, for example, interrupts the child. |

skills to enable her to pay attention to the model. Similarly, a child must have a good enough memory to allow her to remember the model's actions or words.

- **Principle 2: Development occurs because of learning from the environment.** The major belief common to all branches of behavioral or learning theory is that human behavior is learned. All learning theorists believe that a child's behavior is gradually shaped as he interacts with his environment. For example, learning theorists believe that an aggressive child has learned the aggression.
- **Principle 3: Modeling influences much of children's learning.** Social learning theorists believe that learning takes place in, and cannot be separated from, a child's social setting. Children can learn new behavior by observing another person perform the behavior. A child who cooperates with classmates, the social learning theorists would say, has learned this behavior by observing different models' actions and words about how to work with others.

Children learn from a variety of models: a real person who is physically present; real persons on television, in movies, or in DVDs; cartoon characters; graphic representations of human figures in videogames; models in books; or audio models. Children become more and more accurate in their ability to imitate a model as they grow older.

The specific content that is demonstrated or modeled for a child depends on the child's social environment. All children learn simple things like vegetable preference, facial expression, and table manners by observing others. More complex social behaviors are also taught through modeling. Some social environments model behavior like respectful treatment of others and assertiveness, whereas other social environments model behaviors such as aggression and selfishness.

What accounts for a child's selectivity in what or whom they imitate? Children imitate models that are powerful, more skillful than the child, have a great deal of prestige, and who are nurturing and supportive.

- **Principle 4: Children learn complex behaviors in big chunks rather than in tiny steps.** Some learning theorists believe that children learn things in tiny steps, with each reinforced. However, social learning theorists believe that children learn complex behaviors in big chunks.

  > **EXAMPLE**  After a unit called "Showing Kindness to Animals," Nick demonstrated the kind behaviors that were shown on videos or demonstrated and described by Mr. Santini or by visitors to the classroom. He helped clean the hamster house, showing kindness to the hamster by handling it carefully.

- **Principle 5: Behavior can be changed if a child's social environment is changed.** Social learning theorists believe that the most effective way to change (modify) a child's behavior is to alter the child's environment. Because they believe so strongly in the effect of the social environment, they emphasize changing the social environment. In practice, this means that teachers in classrooms might need to change how they respond to a child's behavior if they think the behavior needs to change.
- **Principle 6: Children can learn behaviors with*out* reinforcement.** Children can learn many behaviors simply by observing a model perform the behavior (e.g., using a napkin properly during a meal, raking leaves, feeding the class pet). The learner's success might well be acknowledged by a teacher, but the

reinforcement can come after the learning took place. Teachers see the results of this type of learning in their classroom.

> **EXAMPLE**   Mr. Santini observed that three of the children were imitating the karate-chopping moves of the character they had watched on an action video. The character was the model, and they learned the movement simply by observing. Nobody reinforced them.

- **Principle 7: Reinforcement gives information to children.**

> **EXAMPLE**   After Nick cleaned the hamster's house, Mr. Santini acknowledged the effort, "You were very kind to Sunshine, Nick. I'm sure that she appreciates it." Vanessa heard Mr. Santini's words of encouragement and thought, "Hmm, Mr. Santini liked the way Nick acted with Sunshine."

We see reinforcement operating in Vanessa's learning. She learned how to be kind to the hamster from watching Nick as a model. Whether she actually imitates (reproduces) the behavior depends on how she looks at the consequences of that activity for Nick. Vanessa is highly likely to treat Sunshine kindly because she heard and observed Mr. Santini's words of appreciation (positive consequences) to Nick. Recall from Chapter 1 that appropriate feedback gives information to children about their behavior. Words of appreciation (reinforcement) are a form of feedback and a basic process through which adults influence children.

**Tokens: Tangible Positive Reinforcers**   Recall that authoritative adults have reasonably high expectations for and are highly responsive to what children need. Some authoritative adults make a deliberate attempt to modify a child's environment and therefore to help a child modify his behavior by using tangible rewards, or tokens, as positive reinforcement.

**Token**
An object that can be felt or held; therefore, it is tangible

- What is a token? A **token** is an object, so the term *tangible* is applied. Some examples are a sticker, smiley face, photo, star, checkmark, or plastic chip. It is best to use nonfood items as tokens.
- An adult who decides to use a token system targets a specific behavior that he wants to see, such as cooperation or carrying out some routine activity, like cleanup or tooth brushing. The child earns a token for demonstrating the targeted behavior. The adult often uses a chart like the one in Figure 2.9 to display the token.
- Tokens are a means to an end, not the end in itself. They are *merely* a way to remind adults to give a child feedback for her efforts to live within limits, to act responsibly,

**FIGURE 2.9**   Example of a token chart

| I want to remember to take things home! | Monday | Tuesday | Wednesday | Thursday | Friday |
|---|---|---|---|---|---|
| Week #1 | | | | No school | |
| Week #2 | | i forgot! | | | |

and to be a productive group member. Tokens are gimmicks, and the stickers or photos must be combined with social reinforcement. Tokens must be used *ethically*.

- Figure 2.9 shows a chart that Mr. Santini used to help Nick remember routine tasks. Mr. Santini encouraged Nick to decide how to mark each day's space, and he *decided to* use different ink stamps each day.

- What if a child forgets to perform the agree-upon behavior? After the first week, Mr. Santini reviewed with Nick the things that were helping him remember. Nick forgot to take some items home on Tuesday, Week 2. Mr. Santini said on Wednesday morning, "You know, you've remembered every other day so far. You can go back to stamping tomorrow." Mr. Santini did *not* take away any stampings for the other days as punishment for forgetting. Ethically and competently done token systems or charts focus on teaching, not on punishing.

- Fading out using a token chart. Mr. Santini faded out using the chart. All along, he had made brief comments acknowledging Nick's effort to remember. This social encouragement or reinforcer, combined with the token (Nick's stamping), was what Mr. Santini needed to do to really help Nick. The chart was a good way to remind the teacher how he interacted with Nick in this case. Like Vygotsky, social learning theorists believe that adults can help children learn appropriate behaviors through adult–child talking. The tokens are merely reminders that the adult needs to do his part.

**Effective Praise: Intangible Positive Reinforcer**   Early childhood educators raise some legitimate questions about using **praise**. Praise is an *intangible* form of reinforcement—it is not a thing that we can see. Praise can be used quite *ineffectively*. Some adults think that they can manipulate children with praise. Others think that praise is a good form of encouragement. There are some things to remember about praise in order to use it ethically and effectively.

**Praise**
A form of *intangible* feedback for children

- Be specific, descriptive, and appreciative but not gushy or mushy. When you praise, notice and then describe specifically what a child did. Describe what you saw, heard, tasted, or touched. Relate the praise directly to the event. Avoid judging (things such as the child's actions or character). Let the child know that you appreciate what she has done.

  **EXAMPLE**   Mr. Santini said to his class, which was assembled for a large-group lesson: "Thanks for putting all your writing notebooks in their bins with the spines facing out. That way, you can retrieve them easily tomorrow."

- Give praise as soon as possible after the event. Praise is most effective given immediately after the event. This requires that a teacher concentrate and make an effort to watch for, notice, and then immediately give the feedback. There is a good reason for reinforcing as quickly as possible. Words of encouragement give children information about the consequences of their behavior. Children make more accurate connections between their behavior and your feedback if the two happen close together.

  **EXAMPLE**   After the all-school assembly, Mr. Santini said, "This class was a good model for the younger children today. You listened to the speaker and showed respect."

- Praise sincerely and reward effort and small steps. If you choose to praise, use honest and sincere praise. Your firmly grounded set of values and ethical standards and your respect for children will forbid you from giving insincere, phony, or perfunctory praise. When you think feedback would be helpful for a child, try to find something in a situation that you can praise sincerely and honestly.

You can foster persistence in children by giving feedback about a child's effort to complete difficult tasks. Children need to know that they control the effort that they put into a task. Teachers can help them increase their effort by giving feedback, specifically about effort.

**EXAMPLE**    Several of the children seemed to be bored with the way they were practicing writing their weekly spelling words. Mr. Santini decided to use some different methods. One was for the children to write on a sheet of Plexiglas against a black background (like the menu boards in some restaurants).

**Pitfalls to Avoid: Ineffective Praise**    Several factors make praise or any type of reward ineffective. Authoritative teachers make an effort to avoid the following forms of ineffective praise.

- Avoid praising only perfection; do not combine praise with a negative comment. Some adults praise only perfection. Instead of noticing and praising a child's efforts to do something helpful, some adults attend only to something that the child is not doing.

  **EXAMPLE**    The playground aide said to Mr. Santini's class as they came in from recess, "You kids forgot again to put all the balls in the container." Rory, looking back at the playground said, "We put them in. Oh, there's one left." The aide replied, "That's what I mean. You left one out."

- Avoid praising only completion of a difficult task. Difficult tasks usually have a number of parts. Encourage children as they successfully complete each step in a difficult task. Some adults make the mistake of dismissing the effort it takes to do each part and to stay with a long-term task.

  **EXAMPLE**    Nick, bursting with pride about having written his first poem for a notebook of poetry, showed it to his grandfather. His grandfather responded, "Show it to me when you get all the poems written."

- Do not overdo praise. Children seem to adapt to a particular level of praise. An adult who uses praise indiscriminately will find it necessary to use even more praise because the child receiving such lavish praise becomes accustomed to it. Rewards given too frequently lose their value. Indiscriminately saying "Good job!" is an example.
- Do not give unnecessary praise. It is possible for praise and rewards to backfire and negatively affect a child's motivation. Children who are spontaneously interested in an activity but are then rewarded for practicing the activity might lose interest. They perceive the adult's praise as an attempt at control. The child's decreased interest is actually resistance to external control.

  **EXAMPLE**    The student teacher in Mr. Santini's classroom used praise with Nysha, who liked to read her math book and then do problems. Nysha made a face when she heard the praise, and the student teacher asked what was wrong. Nysha, not a shy child, said, "I like math and it makes me feel weird when you say 'Good job with the math, Nysha.'"

## Implications of Theories Focusing on Psychological, Emotional, and Social Needs for Guiding Children

We have discussed implications of theories focusing on the systems in which children develop and of theories about how children construct ideas. Both sets of theories are useful in a teacher's guidance of young children. In addition, theories focusing on the psychological, emotional, and social needs of children are also exceedingly useful as teachers guide children. Here are some major implications drawn from the theories targeting children's psychological, emotional, and social needs.

- Adopt the belief that positive, caring, respectful relationships are a necessity or precondition to guiding children effectively. We simply cannot guide children well if we do not have a good relationship with them. Take the time necessary and plan activities to establish good relationships. Consider it a priority, for example, to greet every child every day on his or her arrival at school and then say a simple and friendly good-bye to each and every child at departure time. This might be one small example, but it points to your need to focus sharply on doing specific things that develop a good relationship with children. No matter what else you need to do, your relationship with children should be your main concern.
- Relate to children in a way that helps them meet their basic needs for affection, friendly relationships, acceptance, and belonging. Consider emphasizing for example, not that "we are all friends in this room," but that friendliness to everyone is important, even if other people are not personal friends (friendship is a voluntary thing: we are not friends with everyone but we can be friendly in our dealings with others). Do one brief activity every day in which children greet one another. This is a regular feature of the morning meeting's greeting in the Responsive Classroom model and is an easy addition to one's plan.
- Keep in mind some children's mistaken ideas about how to fit into a group. Reflect on how you usually react to a child who acts on his mistaken belief and figure out a different way to respond to the child. Figure 2.1 will give you some ideas for this.
- Focus on problem ownership. When teachers have to make decisions about how to respond to a child's behavior, it is very helpful to work out who, adult or child, "owns the problem," a major concept in the theory of Carl Rogers. When you determine problem ownership, you can then choose an appropriate and helpful guidance strategy.

## ANALYZE A VIGNETTE

Refer to the chapter-opening vignettes, and then answer the following questions.

1. Joseph, the toddler in the vignette, is in the _____ of Erikson's stages of psychosocial development. How will the teacher's words and actions help Joseph resolve this crisis in a positive way?
2. Emily's preschool teacher used an appropriate guidance strategy. What is it about Emily's cognitive development that explains her solution to the teacher's question?
3. In the primary-grade vignette, how has the teacher demonstrated active listening?
4. In the primary grade vignette, which mistaken goal does Lucy seem to be showing? Explain your response. Also explain why the teacher's response was so effective.

## SUMMARY

Different theories inform our practice as teachers. Some focus on the systems in which young children develop and learn. These theories include the following:

- Urie Bronfenbrenner's ecology of human development, which describes the different systems in which a child and her family are nested
- Family systems theory, which examines stable patterns of interaction and communication within children's families

Other theories emphasize the processes that children go through in constructing knowledge. There are striking similarities among these theories, most notably the need for supportive interaction between adult and child and the need for active learning. We examined the theories of:

- John Dewey
- Jean Piaget
- Lev Vygotsky

Other theories helpful in guiding children are those focusing on their emotional and social learning needs. In this chapter, we have examined the theories of:

- Erik Erikson, who explained the stages of psychosocial development
- Abraham Maslow, who described and explained a hierarchy of needs that all humans have
- Alfred Adler, who identified mistaken goals that children might have as they seek group membership and acceptance
- Carl Rogers, who explained the concept of problem ownership and the guidance strategies to use when different people own a problem
- Social learning theory, which explains social variables influencing a child's behavior

## APPLY YOUR KNOWLEDGE

1. **Observe.** Observe young children in a classroom or some other setting. Find examples of adults using praise with children. First, judge whether the praise was necessary. Then decide whether the praise was effectively stated.

2. **Observe.** Observe in a preschool classroom. Find examples of children using different ways to tell about or represent their experiences. The chapter section on Piaget would be helpful here.

## WEBSITES

*Gordon Training International*

The website http://www.gordontraining.com/parent-programs/parent-effectiveness-training-p-e-t/ provides information about the organization based on Rogerian theory started by Thomas Gordon, who developed Parent Effectiveness Training (P.E.T.) and Teacher Effectiveness Training (T.E.T.).

*North American Reggio Emilia Alliance, Schools of Reggio Emilia, Italy*

The website http://www.reggioalliance.org/reggio_emilia_italy/infant-toddler_centers_and_preschools.php provides information about the preschools of Reggio Emilia, which embody principles of constructivist theory, focus on systems in which children develop, and pay attention to theories focusing on emotional and psychological development.

# CHAPTER 3

# Understand Child Development

## *A Key to Guiding Children Effectively*

## Learning Outcomes

- Explain why it is important for teachers to understand perceptual and memory development in young children
- Summarize the development of perception and memory during early childhood
- Explain how changes in perception and memory during early childhood affect a teacher's ability to guide children
- Explain the meaning of social cognition
- Explain differences in how preoperational and concrete operational thinkers differ in how they think about the behavior and motives of others
- Define self-control and explain how it evolves
- Define prosocial behavior and list and explain what children need to be able to do before they can help, cooperate with, or show compassion to others

### VIGNETTES

#### INFANT–TODDLER: PAUL REMEMBERS

*Mr. Bensen planned some "memory" games for 6-month-old Paul. He showed Paul a plastic block and then slowly covered it with a cloth. Paul grabbed the cover and pulled it off. Mr. Bensen encouraged his effort by saying, "You found the toy!"*

*On another day, Paul smiled when his teacher showed him his favorite stuffed bear, which had been lost for about 2 weeks. Then Mr. Bensen turned Paul away so he could not see it. When Paul turned his head back to look for the bear, the teacher praised his effort and helped him retrieve the toy.*

#### PRESCHOOL: MAYA DECIDES

*Mrs. Johnson and a small group were preparing to make fruit salad. Maya's eyes gleamed at the sight of the starfruit, something that she had never seen before. She ran her fingers over the smooth exterior, smelled it, and then stared at the fruit after the teacher sliced it. Mrs. Johnson usually encouraged children to taste things when they cooked. Today, however, she had a different goal in mind and deliberately set a limit that they could eat the fruit for a snack but that they would not sample the salad while making it. When the teacher turned aside to put the knife in a safe place, Maya stared into the bowl, at the starfruit. She reached for it, then hesitated, and finally pulled her hand away.*

#### PRIMARY: THOMAS SHARES

*Mr. Santini observed second graders Sean and Thomas in the coatroom getting ready for recess when Sean said, "Hey, where's my other glove? There's only one here." Thomas joined Sean in searching for the missing glove, but they did not find it.*

Thomas, "I have an extra pair in my locker. Do you want to wear them?"
Sean took the gloves, saying, "Yeah, okay. Thanks, Thomas."
As the boys zoomed out to the playground, Mr. Santini said quietly to Thomas, "I appreciated what you just did, Thomas."

## :: INTRODUCTION

All three teachers are warm, highly responsive, and supportive, and they also have high expectations of children. Skillful and kind teachers such as Mrs. Johnson, Mr. Bensen, and Mr. Santini did not just pull their guidance strategies out of a hat. They do not do the first thing that pops into their heads. Instead, they make deliberate and intentional decisions about their guidance strategies. They use developmentally appropriate child guidance so effectively because they have a solid foundation in child development. Their child development knowledge is not the only thing that they need, but it is one of the major elements in effectively guiding children, as shown in Figure 3.1.

In this chapter, you will read about what to expect from children of different ages in selected areas of development. We start with a brief outline of what to expect in general about the social and emotional development in children in the different phases of early childhood. Then, we shift to perception and memory, two parts of a child's cognitive development that are important in how children take in, organize,

**FIGURE 3.1** Teachers need three things before they can guide children effectively

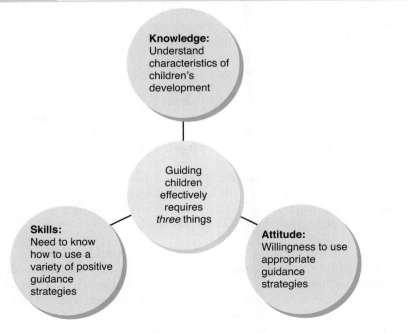

Knowledge: Understand characteristics of children's development

Guiding children effectively requires *three* things

Skills: Need to know how to use a variety of positive guidance strategies

Attitude: Willingness to use appropriate guidance strategies

and remember what they see and hear during interactions. Then, we will examine how children understand the behavior of others, how they view friendship, and how they understand accidental versus intentional behavior. Finally, we will look at how children build on perception, memory, and social cognition to develop self-control and to become compassionate and caring individuals. The rest of this book will help you understand how to use your knowledge of child development to guide children.

## ∷ SOCIAL EMOTIONAL DEVELOPMENT: WHAT TO EXPECT

This section will outline, briefly, the major facets of social and emotional growth in children during early childhood. This will be presented by age groups: birth to 8 months, 8 to 18 months, 18 months to 3 years, 3 to 4 years, 4 to 5 years, and 6 to 8 years (Center for Disease Control and Prevention, 2012; Healthy Children, 2011; Zero to Three, 2012).

**Birth to 8 Months**    Startles and gets frightened, learns to comfort self, shows feelings to caregiver with smiles, cries, frowns. By 6 months, might well show fear of strangers. Uses different cries and facial expressions to communicate things such as boredom or the need to play. Likes games like peek-a-boo and waves arms if he wants to continue playing.

**8 to 18 Months**    Enjoys interacting with caregivers: talking to, listening to, or playing with them and likes being cuddled. Since birth has had feelings (for example, anger, joy, distress, disgust) and can express them but does not understand feelings. Expresses feelings strongly and changes emotional states quickly. Does not yet know how to share, resulting in confusing interactions when this age child plays with others. Uses body to communicate feelings. Also uses words to communicate feelings but will get better at this with time and helpful interactions with teachers. Understands more than she can say.

**18 Months to 36 Months**    Independence is growing but still wants and needs parents and teachers. Can detect feelings in others and picks up on what others think about him—whether they think he is smart, for example, through words and tone of voice. Might have new fears, such as fear of the dark or of monsters but cannot tell the difference between what is real or not real. Learns about how to care about others by how she is treated and cared for. Likes playing with peers and is getting a little better at sharing but still has some growing in this area. Getting better at expressing herself and how she feels but needs teachers to be patient. Might need adult help in putting her strong feelings into words.

**36 Months to 48 Months (3 to 4 Years)**    Speaks much more clearly now and can make himself understood by others. Knows the names of some emotion words and can use them—mad, angry, happy, for example. Still might have difficulty telling the difference between reality and fantasy. Continues to like playing with other children and now cooperation is seen more often. Learning how to resolve conflicts but needs adult help to learn how and needs to be reminded. Now, might imagine unfamiliar items to be monsters, for example, the doorknob on his bedroom door when seen at night in the dark. Likes games with other children, such as simple circle games.

**48 Months to 60 Months (4 to 5 Years)**   Better language skills, such as ability to use sentences of more than five words. Likes to play with and just be with friends and wants to please them. Beginning to understand very basic rules and to agree to them. Shows greater independence and might be able during this period to begin telling fantasy from reality. Can now generate word labels for how she feels—"I am really *irritated!*"—if she has learned the word labels. Control of emotions getting better if she has been helped to express emotions in a way appropriate for a child her age.

**6 to 8 Years**   Cognitive and language skills advance enabling the child to think about people, time, and his place in the world differently. Can mask feelings now and can express feelings better because his list of word labels for how he feels is longer—that is, if he has been taught such words and then been encouraged to express his feelings in the way that his culture prefers. Likes being with friends and wants to be a good team member. Friendships are very important.

We now turn to some other aspects of child development that have a major impact on a child's social and emotional growth.

## :: PERCEPTION AND MEMORY

Many factors affect a teacher's guidance. Two such factors include how a child perceives things and whether he can remember what he perceives.

## Perception: What to Expect

When teachers use guidance, they need children to take in what they say, and observe and pay attention to other signals and cues in the environment, such as the facial expression that somebody makes. With guidance, teachers help children concentrate on learning activities and make choices about many things. Our real goal is to have children eventually *think* about choices.

**Perception** is one part of the whole process of cognitive development. It is the process of organizing information obtained through seeing, listening, touching, and smelling. First, children sense things. Then they perceive or organize the information, and eventually they think about it.

Infants take in sensations with their eyes, ears, noses, mouths, and hands, and they can organize the sensations from birth. For example, infants perceive the discomfort of needing a diaper change, needing food or water, and needing comfort and cuddling. They also feel and express basic emotions such as anger and contentment, even though they cannot understand or talk about the feeling.

Children continue to develop and refine perceptual skills as they get older. A 2-year-old, with many perceptual skills, improves on these abilities by age 4 or 5. However, there is room for more improvement. What you can expect is that preschoolers and kindergarten children will have some perceptual problems that keep them from paying attention. You can also expect additional changes in children's perception during the school years that will help them pay attention better.

**Perception**
Process that children use for organizing the information that they gain through sight, hearing, touch, smell

**Problems Affecting How Children Pay Attention**   The problems that young children experience with paying attention, which affect your guidance, fall into these areas.

- **Young children do not search or scan very well.**  Young children can search for something, but they are not systematic in their search. Their search is not as accurate or efficient as an older child's, and some children do not seem to realize that they should stop searching at some point.

    **EXAMPLE**   Robert watched Mrs. Johnson write his name on a nametag. Robert easily recognized his name when the teacher showed Robert his nametag along with three others. The next day, however, Robert's nametag was on the chart with 22 others. Robert looked for a long time, but became frustrated when he could not find his nametag.

- **Young children have difficulty ignoring irrelevant information.**  Young children have difficulty controlling their attention. They have difficulty tuning out (ignoring) meaningless information or stimulation. Their attention wanders when they hear or see some sudden, intense stimulus. Sudden changes or intense stimulation such as bright lights or loud noises will capture almost any person's attention for a short time. However, the issue with young children is that they have greater difficulty ignoring it.

    **EXAMPLE**   A new student teacher was frustrated when she read a story to a small group of 3-year-olds. A squealing sound from the parking lot and the squeaking from wheels on the lunch cart easily distracted them. Older children might also have noticed the noise, but they would have been better able to resume listening to the story.

- **Young children tend to focus on only one thing at a time.**  Young children tend to focus on one part of a problem at a time. For instance, show a 4-year-old two equally sized lumps of clay. Flatten one of the lumps in front of her. She will very likely say that the flattened mass has more clay. She has great difficulty paying attention to two things at the same time—the equal amounts of clay in the lumps and now the flattened state. Similarly, she will not be able to pay attention to her own viewpoint and to somebody else's viewpoint at the same time when they have a disagreement.

    **EXAMPLE**   Two of Mrs. Johnson's preschool children were playing at the sand table, constructing a tunnel. Then they had an argument about which way the tunnel should turn. Each child's focus was his own idea and neither could deal with the other child's suggestion.

- **Impulsiveness affects perception.**  Reflective children tend to be more accurate in their work because they proceed slowly enough to avoid major mistakes. Impulsive children tend to work too quickly, thereby missing important information and making unnecessary mistakes. Younger children tend to be impulsive, making it difficult for them to stop, look around, and think about choices.
- **Some disabilities affect perception.**  A characteristic of some disabilities, such as attention deficit hyperactivity disorder (ADHD) is impulsivity. ADHD is a problem with "inattentiveness, over-activity, impulsivity, or a combination"

to a degree that is not in the normal range of development for a child's age and development. Symptoms of impulsivity include shouting out answers before you finish a question, trouble waiting for a turn, and disturbing an ongoing activity or group, such as during a group time or when a teacher is talking to someone else (Ballas, 2009). Other factors place children with ADHD at even greater risk. For example, in one small study, abused children with ADHD had higher impulsivity scores than did children who were not abused but who did have ADHD (Becker-Blease & Freyd, 2008). Researchers also found that children with dyslexia were more impulsive and much faster in response time, during the testing phase of the research, than were children without dyslexia (Donfrancesco, Mugnaini, & Dell'Uomo, 2005).

**Changes in Perception Help Children Pay Attention Better as They Get Older**    Children in the primary grades have slightly more efficient memory, more mature language abilities, and more experiences to draw on. Listed below are three of the ways in which perception changes during the early childhood period. These changes will affect how you guide children.

- **Children get better at selecting between what they ignore and what they pay attention to.**  Child development researchers have known for over 40 years that even infants select—and seem to prefer—certain patterns (Fantz, 1966). A 2-year-old has the ability to attend selectively to stimuli, but this ability improves during childhood as she eventually learns to ignore distracting stimuli. Older children are much better than are younger children at selecting between what they prefer to attend to and what they ignore.

    EXAMPLE    Preschoolers in Mrs. Johnson's class looked up in surprise when they heard a helicopter flying over the school. Many jumped up from the group and ran to the window. The fourth graders in another part of the building heard the same noise. Several fourth graders simply said "Helicopter," and went right on with their work. The older children chose to ignore the intense, intrusive sound.

- **Children spend more time on task as they get older.**  Older children are capable of controlling the time that they spend on a task; they tend to stay with a task longer than do younger children. However, children also consciously spend less time on an activity that they think is boring or uninteresting, such as workbook sheets. Many programs such as High Scope in Ypsilanti, Michigan, use this information and plan learning environments and activities that are activity-based and interesting to children because children are more likely to start an activity in the first place if it captures their interest in some way.

    EXAMPLE    Mr. Santini set out small plastic tubs filled with damp sand in the writing center. Larry, a second grader, had seen this activity on arrival and zoomed to it at work time. He practiced writing his spelling words in the sand and willingly practiced incorrectly spelled words until he got them right, working industriously at smoothing sand, writing words, then smoothing sand again.

- **Children are better able to redirect their attention as they get older.**  Older children can more easily redirect their attention than can younger children.

When a task has a number of parts, the older child has an advantage because she is able to shift her focus from one aspect to another quickly. These children are better able to say, for example, "Okay, I'm done with that part. I can start on the next part and then I can finish with the third part. Whoops! I forgot something in part one." The next examples are from Mr. Santini's second grade.

> **EXAMPLE** Larry had to make a journal entry about the words he spelled correctly and incorrectly. After he finished with the sand, he started writing the list and then stopped suddenly. "I have to practice one more word," he said as he laid down his pencil and went back to the sand. After practicing, he went back to his list.

> **EXAMPLE** Almost all of Mr. Santini's second graders worked with several specialists at different times each week. This resulted in many interruptions in class work for individuals. The teacher noted that some children had problems shifting gears and redirecting their attention to classroom work when they returned.

## Memory: What to Expect

**Memory**
Process used to store information and later retrieve it

**Memory** is a basic cognitive process by which children store information and then later retrieve it. Children see and hear hundreds of bits of information each day, but they do not remember all of it. Their brain filters out some and stores only some in memory.

There are major and remarkable changes in how well children remember things during early childhood. Figure 3.2 shows the milestones in memory development, the slow and steady changes in the different types of memory. These changes allow a child to retain information pertaining to our guidance, such as the limit on staying inside the playground during recess or using words to tell somebody that you are irritated or upset.

**Forms of Memory**  Different forms of memory are important for early childhood teachers to understand because they affect how well children can remember what we say to them or what they remember from interactions.

**Long-term memory**
Storage site for permanently stored information

- **Long-term memory** refers to storage for the information that we perceive and then store as a permanent record. Most of us can call up information from long-term memory because we often have the memory stored as a strong sensory image of places and events, sometimes from years or even decades ago. For instance, I remember one sunny afternoon in my grandfather's garden whenever I smell basil because he crushed some of the fragrant herb that day and let me sniff it. Do you have a pleasant event from your childhood stored in your long-term memory?

**Short-term memory**
Temporary storage site for information with which a child needs to work. The child retrieves the information from long-term memory. Also called *working memory*

- **Short-term memory**, or working memory, is a storage site for temporarily placing new information or well-known information to which we need access. The lateral areas of the prefrontal cortex in a young child's brain are activated when she uses working memory, just as they are in an adult's brain (Tsujimoto, Yamamoto, Kawaguchi, Koizumi, & Sawaguchi, 2005). A child's space for short-term memory increases with age, allowing her to work with and process more information and to do so for longer periods (Eysenck, 2004).

> **EXAMPLE** "Oh, no," thought Thomas as the class got to the playground, "There's Patrick! He corners me every time he gets a chance."

| FIGURE 3.2 | Milestones: Memory development |
|---|---|

**Birth to 5 Months**
- Recognition memory is good. Infants habituate to—become accustomed to or bored with—a toy put in front of him several times. This boredom indicates that a baby remembers or recognizes the object.
- Recall memory: Very young infants *can* recall a memory but need to get a cue or reminder. An adult can encourage a 2- to 3-month-old infant to kick a mobile, then remind the infant several days later about the mobile by moving it while she watches. The infant will recall having kicked the mobile. However, notice that the adult had to give the baby a cue; the baby could not actively recall kicking the mobile on her own.

**Five Months to 1 Year**
- Recognition memory improves. Classic research on infants' memory showed that infants could recognize objects after seeing them only a few times. They also seem to be able to remember the object for several weeks (Fagan, 1984).
- Recall memory also improves. After about 6 months, infants do not need cues as often to remember things.

**One Year to 3 Years**
- Recall memory improves even more (Howe & Courage, 1993; Perlmutter, 1986). After about age 2, children can recall exciting events that happened some time before and occasionally even tell about the memory in the form of a story. By the time a child is 3 years old, he might be able to recall something that happened to him 1 year previously.

**Four Years to 12 Years**
- Memory improves remarkably during the preschool and middle childhood years.
- Pure recall memory: Four-year-olds can remember without cues *some* of the time, but 8-year-olds are even better at remembering something without a reminder.

  **EXAMPLE** Show a group of items to preschoolers. They will recognize almost all items but they would not be able simply to recall more than three or four. Third graders, on the other hand, would be able to recall about eight of the items (Baker-Ward, Gordon, Ornstein, Larus, & Clubb, 1993).

**Disabilities Can Affect Memory** (an example)

Recent research shows that the memory of children with autism is substantially different from the memory of children without autism. On one hand, children with autism had poor memory for complex verbal (stories) and visual (pictures) stimuli. On the other hand, recognition memory of children with and without autism was about the same (Williams, Goldstein, & Minshew, 2006).

---

- **Recognition memory** refers to a feeling of familiarity with a stimulus that we have seen or experienced and that we encounter once again. Ask a child, for example, to pick out pictures of her dog and the cat who lives next door from a small group of photos of cats and dogs. She probably will easily recognize her pet and the pet from next door. Recognition tasks are easier than are recall tasks, which are described next.

Recognition memory changes with a child's development. It is already good for infants birth to 5 months who become accustomed to or bored with an object placed in front of them several times. The boredom signals that the baby remembers or recognizes the item. Older research (Fagan, 1983) showed that between 5 months

**Recognition memory**
Feeling of familiarity with something that we know about from our past and that we encounter again

and 1 year, the baby needs to see the new object only a few times before recognizing it and now seem to remember the object for several weeks.

- **Recall memory** refers to memories for which a child has to retrieve or call up some information. There are different types of recall memory, and they are important when we look at the memory capacity of infants and young children. Cued recall memory involves using a visual, auditory, or olfactory (odor/smell) sense to remind someone about a memory. Thus, children would get a cue or something else to remind them.

> **Recall memory**
> Memories for which a child has to call forth information, either with or without a reminder or cue

   **EXAMPLE**   Mr. Santini made a list of the names of trees that the children have studied. He posted the list (the cue) at the children's level in the area where they worked on the tree project.

Recall memory also changes with a child's development. Very young infants can recall a memory but need to get a cue or reminder. For example, an infant's parent can remind the baby about a toy by moving it while she watches. The infant will recall having kicked the toy. Notice, however, that the parent had to give the baby a cue; the baby could not actively recall kicking the toy on her own. In 5- to 12-month-olds, recall memory also improves. After about 6 months, infants do not need cues quite as often to remember things. Again, older research (Howe & Courage, 1993; Perlmutter, 1986) showed that after about age 2 years, children can recall exciting events that happened some time before and occasionally even tell about the memory in the form of a story. By age 3 years, he might be able to recall something that happened to him one year previously. Four-year-olds can remember things without cues some of the time but 8-year-olds are even better at remembering something without a cue or a reminder. For example, 4-year-olds can recognize almost all items from a group of items shown to them but would be able to recall fewer than three or four. The 8-year-olds, on the other hand, would be able to recall many more from the array of objects (Baker-Ward, Gordon, Ornstein, Larus, & Clubb et al., 1993).

   Disabilities can affect memory. Recent research shows that the memory of children with autism is substantially different from the memory of children without autism. On one hand, children with autism had poor memory for complex verbal (stories) and visual (pictures) stimuli. On the other hand, recognition memory of children with and without autism was about the same (Williams et al., 2006).

**Explaining Changes in Memory**   Listed below are the four main reasons for the dramatic improvement in memory from ages 3 to 12:

1. **Changes in basic capacities.** Older children process information more quickly and manipulate information better than younger children do because they have more working memory (short-term memory) space in their brains. Third graders, therefore, can keep more information in their minds and can perform mental operations much more rapidly than can younger children.
2. **Changes in the strategies used for remembering things.** Older children will have learned a greater number of and more effective methods for getting information into their long-term memory and then for retrieving it later. Older children use memory strategies efficiently once they learn a strategy and understand why using it is helpful. A 12-year-old will rehearse something repeatedly until she remembers it. Preschool children generally do not use this strategy, and primary

children use it but not very effectively—adults have to prompt them to rehearse things. Older elementary school children rehearse lists very effectively (Flavell, Miller, & Miller, 1993) *if* they have learned about rehearsal or other strategies. Older children also use another memory strategy called organization more effectively than do younger children. For example, when confronted with a group of 12 items to remember, the older child will organize it into four groups, such as vehicles, animals, food, and clothing. Young children do not organize groups of items to make recalling the items easier. Older children do make these logical groupings and are therefore much better at recalling such lists.

3. **Changes in knowledge about memory.**  As an adult, you understand how and why memory strategies work and therefore perform memory tasks more effectively. This overall understanding of memory is metamemory. Children who are *at least* 10 years old seem to understand memory strategies, whereas younger children do not (Schneider & Pressley, 1989). Older children who understand why a memory strategy is helpful are much more likely to use such strategies in everyday life and in schoolwork (Brown & Campione, 1990).

4. **Changes in knowledge about the world.**  Younger children simply have been on the earth for a shorter time than older children and have not had the opportunity to acquire the wealth of knowledge that an older child has. Older children, having learned more, are familiar with a greater amount of knowledge, and therefore simply have more things *to* remember.

## :: SOCIAL COGNITION: HOW CHILDREN THINK ABOUT OTHERS

Piaget's (1970) theory described and explained the changes in children's cognitive development during childhood. Vygotsky's (1978) theory shows us that culture teaches children what to think and it affects how they think. Social cognition refers to how children think about the behavior, motives, feelings, or intentions of others.

**Social cognition**
How children think about how other people feel and about their motives, behavior, and feelings

### Preoperational Thinkers: Ages 2 to 6 Years Old

Teachers can use information about cognitive development to understand other domains of development. For example, a child's stage of cognitive development affects his social development, such as how he describes how others behave, whether he understands the difference between accidental and intentional behavior, and how he looks at the concept of friendship.

Describing Others   During the preoperational stage, children tend to describe another person by referring to the individual's physical qualities, such as "My Dad is big." They rarely describe abstract qualities, such as trustworthiness or honesty, because they are not cognitively equipped to deal with such abstract ideas. Occasionally, a young child will describe someone by using what seems to be an abstract term, such as "He's nice." Here, though, the child usually is describing something the other person has recently done rather than identifying a major psychological characteristic (Rholes, Jones, & Wade, 1988).

**Understanding Accidents or Intentional Behavior**    Up to about the middle of the kindergarten year, preoperational thinkers do not understand the concept of intentionality. Recall that they do not take another's perspective. This affects their ability to distinguish between an accident and something done intentionally. They cannot see that the other person intended to hurt them. Near the end of the preoperational stage, they begin to understand the difference between accidental and intentional injury.

**Viewing Friendship**    A child's level of development affects how she views friendship. Preoperational thinkers, somewhat egocentric, tend to describe a friend merely as someone who plays with her. Her egocentricity sets limits on how she sees the world in general, and the concept of friendship in particular.

## Concrete Operational Thinkers: Ages 6 to 11 or 12 Years Old

**Describing Others**    Children in this stage use fewer concrete terms and begin using broad psychological terms to describe other people. A young child in this stage might describe his friends by comparing their behaviors in some way: "Carl draws better than anybody in our class" or "Tyrone spells better than most of the class." Children usually use fewer and fewer such behavioral comparisons as they get older. Fifth graders—10-year-olds—would use broader psychological constructs in their descriptions: "Carl is very artistic"; "Cecil is one of the smartest people in class."

**Understanding Accidental or Intentional Behavior**    Children, with their egocentricity diminishing, now understand intentional behavior. For some children, this occurs during kindergarten, but others might take longer to understand the concept. Children move toward greater understanding of the meaning of intentional behavior, however, during this stage. They get more accurate in detecting when someone did something on purpose.

**Viewing Friendship**    As they mature, children's ideas about friendship change. They become less and less egocentric. Their sense of moral obligation blossoms, and they understand that they are responsible for themselves as they interact with others. Children become better at and more willing to share and take turns with age, and this enables them to bond with other children much more easily. Still later, in the next stage of cognition, a 14-year-old understands that friends support each other, a major shift in thinking about friendship. This is a more advanced view of friendship than the preoperational thinker's (young child's) observation that friends are merely momentary playmates.

## ∷ SELF-CONTROL AND PROSOCIAL BEHAVIOR

As teachers or parents, we want to help children develop self-control and become compassionate and caring, to develop prosocial behavior. All of the changes in cognition, including memory and perception, and in social cognition form a foundation for a child's ability to regulate his or her own behavior—self-control. These changes also make it possible for children to become compassionate and caring individuals.

## Self-Control: What to Expect

Self-control is the voluntary, internal regulation of behavior. It might well be one of the most significant changes during early childhood. Also known as self-regulation, it is an essential part of how children learn, is important in a child's growth and development, and is fundamental in preserving social and moral order. Figure 3.3 shows the milestones in the development of self-control.

**Self-control**
Regulating behavior internally and voluntarily

| **FIGURE 3.3** | Milestones: Development of self-control |
| --- | --- |

**Birth to Approximately 12 months**
- Infants are *not* capable of self-control (Kopp, 1981). The reflex movements of the first several months of life give way to voluntary motor acts such as reaching and grasping, but infants do not consciously control these movements.
- This is a time to learn that the self is separate from other people, the very first step on the road to self-control.

**Between Age 1 and Age 2**
- Children begin to be able to start, stop, change, or maintain motor acts or emotional signals.
- They demonstrate an emerging awareness of the demands made on children by caregivers.
- Communication skills become more sophisticated, enabling a child to understand another person's instructions and modeling.
- Caregivers usually discover that children this age are ready to follow an adult's lead.

**At Approximately 24 Months**
- Children can recall what someone has said or done.
- They can represent experiences.
- These new abilities help children make the transition to developing self-control.
- At this stage, however, children have only a limited ability to control themselves, that is, to wait for their turn or to delay gratification.

**At About 3 Years**
- Children can use strategies to help them delay gratification.
- These strategies set the stage for better self-control. Kopp (1981) did research with groups of 18-, 24-, and 36-month-old children to find out how they differ in their use of strategies to better tolerate delay. Researchers placed raisins under a cup, and the child being tested was told not to eat them. The older children spontaneously did things to distract themselves, such as singing, talking, sitting on their hands, or looking away. Younger children benefited from instructions on using delaying strategies, but they did not use them automatically.*

*Note:* Some disabilities can affect self-control. In one study, children diagnosed with autism showed more problems with self-regulation in very early childhood than did children not diagnosed with autism (Gomez & Baird, 2005).

**How Children Demonstrate Self-Control**    Children show self-control when they do the following:

- **Control impulses, wait, and postpone action.** A child would step back, examine a situation, and then decide how to act. He resists reacting impulsively.

  > **EXAMPLE**    Larry took a block from Jordan's structure. Jordan resisted his usual urge to slug Larry and used words as his teacher suggested: "Larry, I was using that block. Give it back!"

- **Tolerate frustration.** A child would be able to endure disappointment, irritation, or aggravation. We can help children with this in many ways, by giving them guidance with seemingly small things such as not finding one's favorite ice cream flavor or having to wait for a turn at the computer.
- **Postpone immediate gratification.** This refers to putting off a pleasurable activity, such as having coffee with friends, until after completing an important task, such as studying for an exam. Children are simply not as skilled at delaying gratification as are adults. They have to learn how to do it and then must want to try it. Even older children need help figuring out when it is important to put off until later something that they want right now.
- **Set a plan in motion and carry it out.** David and Michael, second graders, planned how to build a model of a farm, drew the plans, and then built their model. It took them several days to complete their project.

---

## :: FOCUS ON PRACTICE

This **Focus on Practice** activity is entitled *Observing Children's Self-Control.* Observe the ways in which the children demonstrate self-control and the strategies that the teacher uses to support the child in building self-control.

---

**How Self-Control Evolves**    Self-control emerges "from the outside to the inside," slowly, and haltingly.

- **Self-control evolves "from the outside to the inside."** Responsible adults actually perform most of an infant's or toddler's ego functions, such as remembering things for the infant and reminding a toddler to hold the kitten gently, thereby regulating the young child's behavior for her. In this case, the adult greatly controls a very young child's actions. The control is outside the infant; it is external. The infant *cannot* control herself.

  Nevertheless, teachers realize that a child can, and should, take more responsibility for controlling herself as she grows older and acquires greater cognitive skills. They expect children to begin to internalize the control taught by the adult. Responsible adults communicate this expectation when they gradually transfer executive control to children. The adult might expect, for example, a child to try solving a problem, with the adult observing and offering advice or help only when necessary. This is scaffolding, a concept from Vygotsky's theory.

Children need their teacher's help in learning about self-control. As you watch this **video**, you will observe very young preschool children, barely out of toddlerhood. Notice how Kia's teacher makes it clear, kindly and firmly, that she expects Kia to be able to show some self-control. Notice, too, how the teacher, realizing that it takes very young children quite some time to show self-control, calmly *re*states her expectation a couple of times.

- **Self-control develops slowly.** Children begin to develop self-control around the age of 2 (Figure 3.3). It takes several more years before this emerging ability fully develops. Children are better able to control themselves as they get older for a number of reasons. First, their cognitive, perceptual, and linguistic systems have developed, allowing them to understand things from a different perspective and giving them access to better skills for dealing with impulses. Control of the self also implies that a child realizes that a self exists; this knowledge develops during late infancy and early childhood.

- **Self-control evolves haltingly, in a "sometimes you see it and sometimes you don't" fashion.** Preschool children often astonish adults with remarkable self-control, but they demonstrate considerable lack of control at other times. Jackie, for example, controlled himself in the block corner, but on the same day, he shoved someone out of the way while rushing to the swimming pool. You will see the same thing in older children who have never learned to control themselves. Young children have to practice self-control, just as musicians have to practice their instrument-playing skills. It is reasonable to expect some measure of self-control in young children, but it is usually a mistake to expect perfect control.

As you watch this **video**, you will observe self-control in children who are now 6 years old and in first grade. Children this age need to be able to control themselves so that they can participate in normal, everyday activities at school, in this case, a math lesson. Notice how their teacher expects the children to be able to control themselves by waiting for each child to join the group during the math lesson. Notice how the teacher keeps things moving along but also makes statements reminding the children about staying where they are in their group.

---

## :: *Question for Reflection*

---

# Prosocial Behavior: What to Expect

**Prosocial behavior** is an action that benefits another person or animal. Altruism refers to unselfish, benevolent behavior. True altruism means that the person shares, helps, or cooperates with no thought about what is in it for him. Prosocial behaviors are intended to meet someone's needs, either physical, psychological/emotional, or both. Sarah's mother demonstrated compassion toward the family's cat. She modeled how to meet a creature's physical and emotional needs.

**Prosocial behavior**
Actions, such as sharing, helping, or cooperating, that promote the well-being of others

EXAMPLE    Sarah's mother attended to the cat's injured foot and cradled the cat, calming her down and telling her that she would be okay.

**FIGURE 3.4**    Prosocial behavior

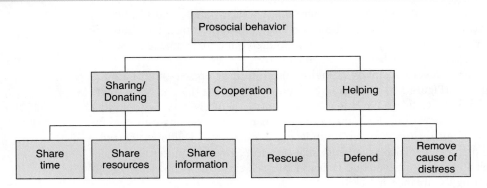

**Forms of Prosocial Behavior**    There are three major categories of prosocial behavior: sharing, helping, and cooperation (see Figure 3.4).

■ **Sharing** refers to dividing, giving, bestowing. A person owns something, or at least currently has possession of it, and decides to let somebody use the item or even gives ownership of the item to the other person. People can share or donate materials, information or time, as shown in Figure 3.4. Young children do share things with others. On some occasions, they share altruistically, such as moving over to make room at the lunchroom table, simply because they recognize that another person or animal needs something.

> **Sharing**
> Giving, donating; one type of prosocial behavior

On other occasions, children share something to initiate social contact and then keep the interaction going once it has started. Children might occasionally share as a way of meeting their own need for contact with others. Young children's sharing often takes the form of simply offering objects to other children or adults during social interaction (Eisenberg, Wolchik, Goldberg, & Engel, 1992).

> **EXAMPLE**    Patrick asked Vinnie to join him in play on the playground like this: "I have a hoop, Vinnie. You can roll it and jump through it. Wanna try it?" He offered something to initiate an interaction.

Whatever a young child's reason for sharing, he is usually not highly self-sacrificing; that is, he takes little risk. There is little risk in sharing extra mittens, for example, or sharing information on how to do something.

We see sharing, helping, and cooperation frequently in young children, even in children who are aggressive. Teachers need to notice and encourage such behavior in *all* children, including those with different levels of aggression. Unfortunately, some preschool teachers do not pay attention to positive behaviors such as sharing or helping in aggressive preschoolers, even if the aggression is mild (McComas, Johnson, & Simons, 2005). In this study, other children in the class paid positive attention to helping and sharing from their aggressive peers, but the teachers did not. Encouraging prosocial behavior is a good way to *decrease* aggressive behavior; therefore, a teacher who ignores a child who shares or helps misses an opportunity to support that child.

- **Helping** involves performing simple everyday acts of kindness and rescue (as did the rescue workers after Hurricane Katrina struck New Orleans in 2005). It also includes defending others, as when a bystander in a bullying incident intervenes and helps the victim. Helping also includes removing the cause of someone's distress, as when Sean's Dad removed a splinter from Sean's foot.

    All children are capable of sharing and helping, but a variety of factors influence their actual level of prosocial behavior. For example, children's willingness to help or share is heavily influenced by whether their teacher and parents value prosocial behavior (Eisenberg et al., 1992). A child might also share or help more easily if important adults have modeled the behaviors.

    > **EXAMPLE**   Thomas's father *helped* a neighbor fix the neighbor's gate. Thomas watched as his dad *shared* his tools.

**Helping**
Assisting, performing acts of kindness, rescuing; one type of prosocial behavior.

- **Cooperating** refers to working together willingly to accomplish a job or task. The motive for working together is altruistic.

    > **EXAMPLE**   Pippin, Tom, and Janet cooperated to clean the gerbil's house. Pippen cleaned and filled the food and water dishes, while Tom and Janet washed the inside of the house. Then, they all checked off completion of this task.

Many children play cooperatively (Anderson, Hilton, & Wouden-Miller, 2003; Parten, 1932). In cooperative play, children follow one another around and make mutual suggestions about what to do next. Such budding interest in others and in playing and working cooperatively is prosocial behavior when the cooperation benefits someone or a group, as Pippin, Tom, and Janet's cleaning the gerbil house did.

**Cooperating**
Working collaboratively to complete a job or task; one type of prosocial behavior

**Children Need Specific Competencies to Act Compassionately**   Sharing or helping seems like such a simple thing. However, several events must occur during a child's first several years of life before he becomes capable of compassion and generosity. Most significantly, he needs to be securely attached to his parents, which boosts compassion as a child grows older (Mikulincer, Shaver, Gillath, & Nitzberg, 2005). He also needs a very specific set of competencies: cognitive and emotional. In addition, he needs specific skills (Zahn-Waxler, Radke-Yarrow, Wagner, & Chapman, 1992). A child can show compassion only when he has all three abilities (see Figure 3.5). Having one or two of these abilities is not enough.

**FIGURE 3.5**   **Three competencies children must have to act compassionately**

*Cognitive Competencies*
(e.g., I can make things happen.
"I can share my book.")

+

*Emotional Competency*
(e.g., I am *beginning* to understand what somebody needs.
"Jessie does not have his book. He needs a book.")

+

*Specific Skills*
(e.g., I have some "sharing" skills.
"I know how to ask Jessie if he would like to share my book.")

=

*Prosocial Behavior*
Ryan shares his book with Jessie.

**Cognitive Competencies**    Children need specific cognitive competencies before they can share, help, or cooperate.

- **Sense of self.** A child needs to know that she is an individual and separate from other individuals (Bengtsson & Johnson, 1992). This occurs in infancy.
- **Identify needs.** The child must be able to recognize what somebody needs, such as understanding that a friend who lost some lunch money needs a small loan.
- **Make things happen.** A child must be able to see himself as a person who can make things happen (for example, "I can help John by sharing a little of my lunch money with him"). This ability arises in infancy and continues to develop throughout childhood.
- **Language.** Children need good enough language skills to describe how others might be feeling and to describe how they themselves feel (for example, "John lost his lunch money and needs to eat").
- **Memory.** A child's memory has to be sophisticated enough to allow him to keep somebody's need in mind long enough to act on it.

All of these abilities have their roots in early childhood. Glimmers of these abilities appear in older infants and toddlers, allowing the youngest children to begin to act in ways that appear to be helpful or cooperative. These cognitive competencies are not fully developed, however, in very young children. For instance, young children can often tell that someone needs something, but they are not very good at reflecting on another person's or animal's inner experience based on the need. Recall that they tend to focus on people's readily observable, external characteristics. As they get older, children tend to focus more and more on another person's internal psychological perspective (Bengtsson & Johnson, 1992).

**Emotional Competencies**    Children also need to have specific emotional competencies, which seem to develop quite slowly in order to respond to another's needs or distress.

- **Decoding emotion in another person's face.** This is the ability to look at a person's or animal's face and make sense of his or her facial expression. High-prosocial children seem to be much more accurate than are low-prosocial children in decoding emotion in other children's faces (Greener, 1998). This ability *begins* in infancy and continues to develop.

  Even adults can learn how to better read another person's emotions through training (Klinzing, 2003). Some children, as teachers quickly realize, are better at decoding emotion or "reading faces" than are other children. For example, children with Asperger's syndrome (AS) had more difficulty decoding facial expressions than did children without AS (Lindner & Rosen, 2006). A child who decodes emotion very well has a far better chance of understanding how another child might be feeling.

  > **EXAMPLE**    Mr. Santini discussed a playground incident with his class. Thomas responded, "Jason was mad!" "How do you know he was angry?" asked the teacher. Thomas: "His face looked mad."

- **Responding to the emotions of others.** Classic research demonstrated that a very young baby responds to emotions in other people (Sagi & Hoffman, 1976) and seems to be able to discriminate among her mother's different emotions; in some cases, the baby can imitate these emotions (Cohn, Campbell, Matias, & Hopkins, 1990). Some children do not learn to read emotions very well and become adults who do not read or deal with emotions well. Hildyard (2005) found that mothers who neglected their children could not discriminate emotions in their children very well and did not know many labels for emotions. Recent research highlights the important influence that imitation plays in human development (Hurley & Chater, 2005).

## :: *Question for Reflection*

- **Demonstrating empathy.** **Empathy** is the ability to participate in another person's or animal's feelings; one person's emotional state is similar to the other person's emotional state. Hoffman (2005) calls empathy the "glue" that holds a society together.

**Empathy**
Vicariously understanding the thoughts or feelings of another

> **EXAMPLE** Mr. Santini realized, on the first day of school for his first graders, that they would probably be anxious. He has good perspective-taking skills (Figure 3.6) and is able to feel what children might be feeling.

Like most other aspects of development, empathy develops slowly and starts in infancy (see Figure 3.7). Researchers have thought for a long time that human children are biologically prepared for empathy (Hoffman, 1975) because they respond to another person's emotional state. However, the budding ability to recognize another person's emotional state is not real empathy.

| FIGURE 3.6 | Levels of perspective-taking | |
|---|---|---|
| **Age in Years** | **Level** | **Perspective-Taking Ability** |
| 3 to 6 | Level 0 | • Egocentric perspective.<br>• No distinction between own and another's perspective. |
| 6–8 | Level 1 | • Still not able to take another's perspective.<br>• Believes that another, if in the same situation, will respond just as the target child would respond. |
| 8–10 | Level 2 | • Can take another's perspective.<br>• Sees self as others do.<br>• Not everyone reaches this level. |
| 10–12 | Level 3 | • Can take another's perspective but in a more sophisticated way than at Level 2.<br>• Now aware of recursive nature of different perspectives: "Mom thinks that I think she wants me to." Not everybody reaches this level. |
| Adolescence and Adulthood | Level 4 | • Very sophisticated in perspective-taking ability.<br>• Believes that different perspectives form a network.<br>• Has conceptualized society's viewpoints on legal and moral issues.<br>• Not everybody reaches this level. |

*Source:* Based on "Social-Cognitive Understanding," by R. L. Selman, in *Moral Development and Behavior*, by T. Lickona (Ed.), 1976, New York: Holt, Rinehart & Winston.

| FIGURE 3.7 | How very young children are likely to show prosocial behavior |
| --- | --- |

**Up to Approximately 12 Months**
- Pats or rubs. Almost all babies will pat or rub a person who appears to be upset or hurt.
- Gives an object. Some young infants will try to offer an object to someone who appears to be upset.

**14 to 20 Months**
- Kisses or hugs.
- Gives some object.
- Might try to protect someone.

**20 Months to 2½ Years**
- All of the above, plus the following:
  - Gives physical assistance.
  - Tries to get help from a third person.
  - Asks questions indicating concern (e.g., "Does your finger hurt?").
  - Gives advice to a person who is upset or hurt (e.g., "Tell your mommy").
  - Might offer reassurance to person or animal (e.g., "It's OK").

*Source:* Based on "Roots, Motives, and Patterns of Children's Prosocial Behavior," by M. Radke-Yarrow and C. Zahn-Waxler, in *Development and Maintenance of Prosocial Behavior*, by E. Staub, D. Bar-Tel, J. Karylowski, and J. Reykowski (Eds.), 1984, New York: Plenum Press.

It takes many years for children to develop empathy, to share another person or animal's emotional state.

High-prosocial children score significantly higher on self-reports of empathic response (Greener, 1998). In a study of prosocial behavior in 10- and 11-year-olds, Bengtsson and Johnson (1992) found that some children had a high level of empathy for a victim. They were able to take both the victim's and the victimizer's point of view, as shown in the next example from the research.

A young girl was turned away by force when entering a room where her older sister and a friend were playing. Some children showed extended empathic reasoning by showing empathy for the little girl as well as understanding of the victimizer: "I didn't like the way they pushed the little girl out of the room, but I can also understand that they wanted to be left alone while playing."

Children who reasoned like this about another person's situation showed the highest levels of prosocial behavior. These were 10- and 11-year-olds, not young children. We know that children in the early childhood stage are not capable of reasoning like this. It takes several years to develop high-level empathy and the ability to think about the perspective of both a victim and a victimizer. Some children never develop this high level of empathy. Growing older is an important element in developing empathy but growing older, by itself, is not enough.

## Cultural Scripts and Guiding Children

### Acknowledging Different Beliefs of Individualistic and Interdependent Cultures

**A Culture's Values, Beliefs, and Goals for Children**   A culture's values and beliefs are given voice when adults describe their goals for children. The values and beliefs find their way into the sets of guidelines, cultural scripts, given to members of the culture. Cultural scripts guide family beliefs and behavior for many issues, such as how early to provide a child with stimulation, how to talk to a child, how to interact with a child during mealtimes, or whether to let a child make choices and explore the environment. These beliefs and behaviors influence the development of children growing up in that culture (Maschinot, 2008).

**Individualistic and Interdependent Cultures Provide Different Cultural Scripts**   The goal in individualistic cultures is individual gratification and fulfillment. To this end, an individualistic culture encourages children to make choices and function on their own as early as possible. In interdependent cultures, the goal is group harmony with cultural scripts encouraging putting the needs of the group before individual needs. South America, Africa, and Asia tend to be interdependent cultures and many immigrants in the United States come from these areas. The Native American and the Alaska Native cultures are also interdependent. Mainstream U.S. culture tends to be quite individualistic.

**Both Cultures Are Represented in a Classroom**   Some of the children in a class will be growing up in families encouraging children to make choices, to speak up for themselves, to explore the environment, to select her own toys, and to participate in conversations with adults as equal partners (individualistic culture). Other children's families do not emphasize children's choice-making, focus somewhat more sharply on direction-giving instead of seeing children as equal conversational partners, and focus on seeing the group's needs as more important than one's own needs (interdependent culture).

**Teachers Have Cultural Scripts**   An early childhood teacher, with her own culture, has beliefs about many things, including providing stimulating learning activities, having conversations with children, and using discipline strategies. Her cultural scripts are very likely to be different from the scripts of some of the families. A child's ability to understand a teacher's expectations is affected by the experience that he has lived in his culture. For example, children from interdependent cultures that tend not to emphasize expressing strongly worded opinions. Teachers from an individualistic culture tend to value speaking up and expressing an opinion. They might have unrealistic expectations for children from cultures different from theirs if they are not aware of the values and beliefs of the child's culture.

## :: FOCUS ON PRACTICE

This **Focus on Practice** activity is entitled *Children's Perspective Taking Influences Their Behavior.* Note how the teacher's strategy can help children learn to share.

| WORKING *with* FAMILIES | RAISING A COMPASSIONATE CHILD |
| --- | --- |

Here are some tips that you can give parents for encouraging kind and compassionate behavior in their child.

- Observe children sharing and helping. Encourage parents to watch their child closely, in school if necessary, for times when their child does share and help. Consider sitting with the parent during the observation.
- Provide cooperative games and play materials. Tell parents that these games, and not competitive games, encourage sharing, cooperation, and helping. Make children's books focusing on prosocial behavior available to parents and emphasize the value of such stories in developing sharing, helping, and cooperation.
- Encourage children to watch television shows and movies containing prosocial content. Label examples of sharing, helping, and cooperating (Rosenkoetter, 1999). Plan a parent meeting or write a brief handout on how to choose appropriate videos, show clips of good videos, and give parents a list of suggested movies and videos showing prosocial behavior. Encourage parents to look for advertising that emphasizes prosocial behavior and teach parents to make appropriate comments about the helping, sharing, and cooperation in such ads.
- Have children participate in prosocial behaviors. The idea here is not to force altruism but for the child just to observe and participate with a parent who shares, helps, or cooperates but does not preach. For example, encourage children to choose cans of food for a food pantry. Tell parents to make the whole process low key and tell them not to preach.
- Give children appropriate and manageable household responsibilities. Help parents understand how meaningful such work is in fostering sharing, helping, and cooperation. Immersion in a family in which all members do their fair share of the work is an extremely effective strategy.
- Recognize and encourage the results of this teaching. Bolster a parent's confidence in encouraging kind, compassionate behavior. For example, give parents three specific ways of showing or telling their child that they recognize the child's efforts. "You were very helpful when we made cookies today, Amanda" or "It was kind of you to share your sand toys with Jess."

**Skill Development**    Children need to know how to help, share, or cooperate; they need specific skills. If Moua, for instance, wants to share something, he must have the social skill of approaching another child and must know what to say as he offers something. Zahn-Waxler et al. (1992) believe that young children have a better chance of developing such skills if they have a firm attachment to their primary caregivers and if their parents or caregivers shared, took turns, and cooperated with them.

## ANALYZE A VIGNETTE

Referring to the chapter-opening vignettes.

1. The memory games that Mr. Bensen planned for 6-month-old Paul were appropriate for this age child because _____.
2. In the preschool vignette, the focus was on self-control. From your perspective, which aspect of self-control was the teacher working on? How do you think that the teacher's limit setting in this case would help a child develop self-control?
3. Explain the emotional competencies that Thomas needed before he was able to share his extra gloves with Sean.

# SUMMARY

Knowing about perception and memory can help teachers choose appropriate guidance. Infants are born with perceptual abilities that continue to develop throughout childhood. For example, children spend more time working on tasks as they get older and can ignore intruding stimulation. However, we can expect that young children will have problems with perception that make paying attention difficult at times. Some of these problems include the following:

- Trouble ignoring extraneous information.
- Difficulty scanning and searching.

Children's memory improves significantly during childhood. For example, children need fewer cues or reminders in order to remember what they need. These changes are explained by

- Growth in children's brains, which provides more storage
- Better methods for remembering things
- More knowledge about the world

As children get older and as their cognitive skills change, they also change *how* they think about and understand other people.

- Younger children tend to describe others in a very concrete way, while older children make a gradual transition to using psychological constructs.
- Younger children do not understand the difference between accidental or intentional behavior. Older children do understand the difference because they have developed the necessary cognitive skills.
- Somewhat egocentric young children view friendship quite differently than they do when they are older. An older child begins to understand the give-and-take nature of true friendship. Self-control evolves during early childhood. It develops slowly and allows a child to control impulses and to plan and carry out projects. Prosocial behavior is any action that benefits somebody else and includes sharing, helping, and cooperating.

# APPLY YOUR KNOWLEDGE

1. **Self-control:** Observe how adults seem to behave in terms of expectations for self-control for children of three different ages.
    a. **Infants:** Observe an adult–infant interaction. Look for evidence that the adult does not expect the infant to control himself, For example, the adult does not expect the infant to remember things, to manage his emotions, or to complete tasks on his own. Describe specific things an adult does for the infant (rocks him to sleep, calms him down, burps him, wipes his mouth, and changes his diaper).
    b. **Toddlers–older preschoolers:** Now look for evidence that an adult expects these children to show some measure of self-control. For example, does the teacher expect the children to remember to wash their hands after using the bathroom, or to manage feelings by saying, "Use words to say that you are upset"?
    c. **Kindergarten and primary school children:** What evidence do you find in a classroom for 5-

to 8-year-olds that teachers really do expect older early childhood children to be better able to control themselves?

2. **Sharing and helping:**
    a. Present this short puppet story about helping or cooperation. One puppet, Sam, has trouble placing paper on an easel.

    *Amanda:* What's the matter, Sam?

    *Sam:* I can't reach the clip for the paper.

    *Amanda:* Maybe I can reach it. (She clips the paper onto the easel.) There, it's done.

    *Sam:* Thanks for helping.

    b. Place the puppets in a learning center after this demonstration. Encourage children to practice what they observed. Encourage them to take both roles—helper and the one helped—so that each has a chance to practice helping.

# WEBSITES

*Centers for Disease Control and Prevention*
http://www.cdc.gov/ncbddd/child/development.htm

A division of a federal agency, Health and Human Services. Reliable and accurate information on child development. Many good links to information for yourself as well as for parents.

*Child and Family Web Guide*
http://www.cfw.tufts.edu/

An excellent site. It is "a directory that evaluates, describes and provides links to hundreds of sites containing child development research and practical advice."

*Educators for Social Responsibility*
http://www.esrnational.org

Based in Cambridge, Massachusetts. Mission is to teach social responsibility in education.

# "Direct" and "Indirect" Child Guidance

This book describes positive ways of guiding children, *only* positive approaches. The National Association of the Education of Young Children (NAEYC) Code of Ethics states that the most important part of the Code is that we do nothing to harm a child. To help you learn a positive constructivist approach, you will study three factors: the value of a well-constructed physical environment, how to use positive guidance strategies, and how to use observation in guiding children.

## Chapter 4   Supportive Physical Environments: Indirect Guidance

This chapter explains the concept of *indirect guidance*, strategies that we occasionally forget to think about as sources of guidance. The adult using indirect guidance might actually say little to the child; for example, a teacher who develops an appropriate time schedule with as few transitions as possible prevents or minimizes the stress and anxiety-based behavior that unfortunately and frequently accompany too many or poorly done transitions.

You will read about the major indirect guidance strategies of designing and managing the physical environment effectively, setting up and managing your room well. This information is presented for both infants and toddlers and for preschool through third grade. When reading the section on infants and toddlers, you will learn about how important appropriately timed sensory stimulation is for the youngest children. The other major categories of indirect guidance include an appropriate time schedule, curriculum and activities based on the learning needs of young children, and competent management of materials. Chapter 4 gives several examples of practical ideas for indirect guidance that can be adapted for any early childhood setting.

## Chapter 5  Positive Guidance and Discipline Strategies: Direct Guidance

You will read about the special nature of guidance for infants and toddlers and then for preschool through primary grade children. Chapter 5 emphasizes *direct guidance*, specific positive guidance strategies. Setting good limits, redirecting behavior, delivering an I-message: these are just a few examples of direct guidance in this chapter. These strategies involve a child or group of children directly. Your confidence in dealing with day-to-day discipline encounters will grow as you learn about, practice, and experience success in using these and other positive discipline strategies. The feature on culture for this chapter describes how beneficial just a little "extra talk" is when stating limits for children. After reading Chapter 5, you will know exactly how to use a great many positive, specific, and practical discipline strategies.

## Chapter 6  Using Observation in Guiding Children

Children tell us what they need in so many ways and their behavior alone can communicate curiosity, disappointment, happiness, or even great anger. Chapter 6 will help you understand the value of observation as the first step in reading children's behavior. We will deal with the important role of assessment in today's schools. You will learn some specific methods for observing children's behavior, including using portfolios in assessment and how to achieve greater objectivity in your observations. The feature on culture for this chapter emphasizes the role of the teacher's culture in his or her choice of what to observe.

# CHAPTER 4

# Supportive Physical Environments

*Indirect Guidance*

## Learning Outcomes

- Explain how early childhood theory helps teachers arrange classrooms to support children's development and behavior
- Recall guidelines for developmentally appropriate room design in an early childhood classroom
- Summarize basic elements of schedules, curriculum, activities, and materials in a developmentally appropriate early childhood setting.
- Point out major differences in classrooms designed for infants and toddlers and for 3- to 8-year-old children
- Explain the value of sensory experiences for infants and toddlers

NAEYC
Standards

---

### VIGNETTE

#### PRESCHOOL: MRS. JOHNSON'S PRESCHOOL CLASSROOM

*Mrs. Johnson, the preschool teacher, and her assistant teacher use the Project Approach (http://www.projectapproach.org/) to curriculum development, working closely with the children, observing, and consulting with them, to determine children's interests. The current project started with a trip to the hardware store to get a gallon of paint mixed for the tricycle storage shed (the trip was a shared experience for every child in the class). Mrs. Johnson had visited the store ahead of time and talked with the person who would mix the paint, giving the store employee suggestions on what she might say to the children.*

*The "paint lady," as the children called her, opened the can and showed the light base color, almost white. She showed the paint chip with the color the school needed. Then she used the rotating device holding concentrated colors and carefully added the three different colors they needed to the base color, showing and naming each new concentrated color. "I need a teeny-tiny bit of black," she said, using her thumb and forefinger to illustrate such a tiny amount, "but we need a lot more blue (space measured by finger and thumb widened). Here's the gray—only four drops. Count with me!"*

*. She showed them the base color, now with the dark spots of coloring agents. When she put the paint can on the shaker, she asked, "What do you think is happening to the little spots of paint now? Why do we need to shake the can?" In addition, she said, "What do you think the paint will look like after it has been shaken?" When she opened the can, the children confirmed their hypothesis about a new color, and she made a color chip for each child. The teachers decided that a project centering on color and color mixing was appropriate and practical, as well as interesting to the children.*

*Mrs. Johnson and her nineteen 4-year-olds investigate things from their classroom base, a busy but calm place. She has organized the classroom into activity areas. The activities in small-group learning centers, for example, reflect the principles of developmentally appropriate practice (DAP) and current projects under investigation. On arrival each day, children find areas ready for work and play, and Mrs. Johnson encourages each child to choose an area. On Monday, the children worked in different areas on the following activities.*

## Art Area

*"Squish-squash, closely watch," said Mrs. Johnson as four children joined her around a small table. She had placed one lump of smooth, white play dough that the children had made on Friday in front of each child. Today's focus was to add one drop of blue food coloring to a little depression in each lump of white dough and to encourage squishing, squashing, predicting, observing, and describing color changes. Investigating color changes continued at the finger-painting table, where blue and yellow paints were available, and red and white paints waited at the easel. (The play dough, finger painting, and easel are all art and science activities in this integrated curriculum.)*

## Library Area

*This is a serene, quiet, enticing area, with good lighting and high-quality books displayed on the rack. One of the books was about mixing colors, the current topic for the investigators of color in Mrs. Johnson's class. She put out the flannel board with figures for retelling the story of Little Blue and Little Yellow, and put out the tape recorder and headset, along with a set of pictures illustrating a story on the table.*

## Writing Area

*This is also a high-interest area. Mrs. Johnson set out transparencies of the color of the paints mixed for the shed. Children placed the transparencies on top of each other to approximate the new color of the shed. Two children dictated a summary of that process just as the entire group had dictated a thank-you note to the paint lady at the store. Now, some of the children wrote notes to parents about the trip, attached their notes to the paint chip, and took the notes home. Two other children wrote in their trays of damp sand with a stick.*

## Science/Math Area

*Today, the children made a graph showing the proportion of each color in the paint for the shed. Mrs. Johnson also placed three ice cube trays with clear water in each compartment on a separate table. Next to each tray were two eyedroppers, one with blue dye and one with yellow, for a color-mixing experiment. The parents have helped the teachers develop many homemade math materials (these items are packaged, labeled, and stored for easy retrieval). Two boys used some of the materials to work on the concept of larger and smaller "sets" on the table. Three other math-related games rested on shelves in the math area.*

## Dramatic Play Area

*Dramatic play center activities usually stay set up for several days. This week, girls and boys working in the "fix-it shop" wore special "inspector" shirts. They checked books and puzzles for needed repairs, inspected tricycles for squeaks needing oiling, examined dolls for necessary bathing and washing of clothing, determined whether blocks had splinters and needed light sanding, and inspected animal housing for required cleaning and repair. They dictated needed repairs to a teacher, who wrote them in a notebook. Then, over several days, and with teacher supervision, they completed two tasks per day from the notebook, checking off completed jobs.*

### Block Area

*To follow up their one-half-block walk to watch the traffic signal change colors, Mrs. Johnson set out a model traffic signal the children could operate to change its colors. Several of the children worked on building a replica of the street outside the school, with their traffic light at the intersection.*

### Puzzle and Manipulatives Area

*The school has a large collection of well cared for puzzles and other manipulatives. On Monday, Mrs. Johnson placed three old, frequently used but well cared for puzzles on the table and set two tubs of small, interlocking blocks on the floor. The children could also choose from among seven or eight other manipulative toys stored neatly in clear plastic containers on low, open shelves.*

This early childhood classroom, the physical environment, the learning opportunities, and the time schedule, were designed and based on theory and research in child development and early childhood education. This type of environment sends messages to all who enter, including children (National Association for the Education of Young Children, 2008; Tarr, 2001):

> You are *safe* here.
>
> You can learn many things here.
>
> You can play and work with other children in this room.
>
> You can make many choices here.
>
> You can work on many different projects.
>
> When you finish your work in one area, you can go to a different spot and work there.
>
> When you want to, you can work by yourself.

## :: INTRODUCTION

We guide children both directly and indirectly. A teacher who states a limit, "Please use the sponge to wash the paint drips," uses *direct* guidance (verbal). A teacher who provides clean sponges and water near the project table uses *indirect* guidance. This chapter focuses on **indirect guidance**, that is, using room arrangement, the schedule, materials, and the structure of learning opportunities to guide children.

An essential part of indirect guidance includes designing the physical environment of a classroom. We will start by using theory as a guide to room design. Theory is not just a bunch of guesses or hunches but a powerful guide for teachers. Theory gives us a framework for all of our work. We will examine appropriate room design

**Indirect guidance**
Influencing children's behavior through environmental design, appropriate curriculum, activities, and materials management

and the power of sensory stimulation for infants and toddlers, but this chapter emphasizes arranging a developmentally appropriate classroom for 3- to 8-year-olds. This will include an overview of developmentally appropriate room arrangements and their effects on children's development, and specific guidelines for designing good learning environments for young children.

Appropriate room arrangement is only one aspect of indirect guidance. We will also examine, briefly, the role of appropriate time schedule, curriculum, activities, and materials in indirectly guiding children.

## :: THEORETICAL FOUNDATIONS FOR EARLY CHILDHOOD CLASSROOM DESIGN

Model programs in early childhood education, such as the programs of Bank Street, High/Scope, Montessori, Reggio Emilia, and Responsive Classroom, have some obvious differences. More importantly, however, they share a theoretical orientation. Every one of these programs is premised on children's need for:

An active approach to learning

Collaborating with others

Working with real objects

Talking with adults skilled in mediating learning

There are three categories of theory relevant to our practice as educators. We rely on these perspectives here to design physical environments, time schedules, and learning opportunities that meet children's needs for activity and collaboration whether the child is an infant or a third grader. A developmentally appropriate physical environment is a major—*indirect*—part of a teacher's guidance plan.

### Theories Focusing on the Systems in Which Children Develop

Bronfenbrenner's (1979) theory explained the ecology of human development. It helped educators to understand that the many systems in which children exist affect their development, learning, and behavior. Classrooms are part of the microsystem of child, family, peers, and school in Bronfenbrenner's theory. This theory posits that every system, including a child's classroom, time schedule, and learning opportunities, affect a child's behavior.

### Theories Focusing on How Children Construct Knowledge

The theories of Dewey (1938), Piaget (1970), and Vygotsky (1978) have informed early childhood practice for many years. They focus not on systems in which children exist, but on how children themselves construct or build knowledge. There are differences, of course, among these theories. However, we find that the great similarities are very good guides to our practice. All emphasize that children learn through activity and that interaction between a child and others is important. Program models based on these constructivist theorists design classroom spaces so that children are active in their learning, can collaborate with others, work with real objects, and talk with teachers as they learn.

## Theories Focusing on Psychological and Emotional Needs

Other theories focusing on children's psychological and emotional needs inform our practices. Erikson (1950), for example, discussed stages of psychosocial development; the first three or four stages are especially important in an early childhood teacher's work. Each of these stages can be resolved in either a positive or a negative way. Teachers who design developmentally appropriate classrooms help children develop trust during infancy; autonomy during toddlerhood; initiative during the preschool and kindergarten years; and a sense of industry during first, second, and third grades.

Maslow described and explained the human's hierarchy of needs. Figure 4.1 presents Maslow's 'triangle' showing the different levels of needs and then explains a

**FIGURE 4.1**    Maslow's hierarchy of needs: Implications for teachers

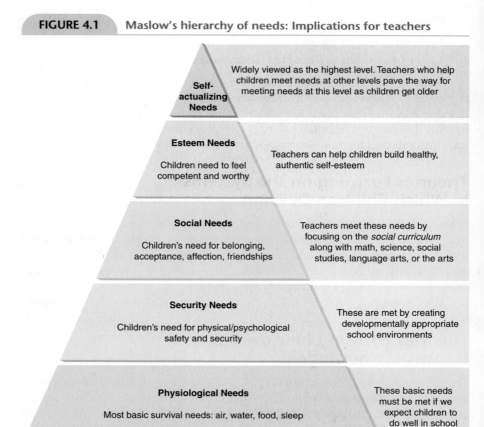

**Self-actualizing Needs**
Widely viewed as the highest level. Teachers who help children meet needs at other levels pave the way for meeting needs at this level as children get older

**Esteem Needs**
Children need to feel competent and worthy
Teachers can help children build healthy, authentic self-esteem

**Social Needs**
Children's need for belonging, acceptance, affection, friendships
Teachers meet these needs by focusing on the *social curriculum* along with math, science, social studies, language arts, or the arts

**Security Needs**
Children's need for physical/psychological safety and security
These are met by creating developmentally appropriate school environments

**Physiological Needs**
Most basic survival needs: air, water, food, sleep
These basic needs must be met if we expect children to do well in school

teacher's role in helping children meet needs at each level. The classroom that you develop can help children feel safe and secure. It can also help children meet their needs for friendships and feeling confident and competent.

---

## :: FOCUS ON PRACTICE

This **Focus on Practice** activity is called *Maslow's Hierarchy of Needs and Early Childhood Classroom Design*. Teachers can help children meet their psychological and emotional needs, such as for friendships and feeling confident and competent. Notice in the video how a well-designed classroom supports children's psychological and emotional needs.

---

## :: PHYSICAL ENVIRONMENTS AND SENSORY STIMULATION FOR INFANTS AND TODDLERS

This section focuses on basic elements of developmentally appropriate physical environments for infants and toddlers. It also features information on the power of sensory stimulation for infants and toddlers, a type of learning opportunity especially relevant to this age group.

### Child Development Theory Supports Effective Teaching and Room Design

Infants and toddlers are in Piaget's first stage of cognitive development, the sensorimotor stage (Piaget 1970). They take in information and act on their world through sensory and motor schemes, learning through experimentation and repetition, for example, swinging their hands over and over at a mobile. They also learn by interacting with teachers who provide a safe and stimulating physical environment, who observe an infant or toddler's play and base responses on the child's actions. For example, teachers can intentionally scaffold a young child's understanding of spatial language or terms such as *in, on, under* during regular play activities, following information from Vygotsky's theory about scaffolding. When an infant plays with nesting blocks, for example, a teacher might scaffold understanding of the word *in* by saying, "You put the block *in* the basket." Similarly, as a toddler puts a doll to bed, a teacher observes and might say, "The baby is *under* the covers" (Schutte et al., 2011).

From Maslow's (1954/1987) theory, we have learned that infants' and toddlers' basic physiological needs and security needs must be met for optimal development. From Erik Erikson's (1950) theory, we have learned about how important it is to develop trusting relationships with infants and toddlers so that infants can build a sense of trust and toddlers a sense of autonomy. They need a classroom and a teacher supportive of their needs and budding abilities. For example, once infants discover that they can climb, they need to do so without hearing their teacher saying "no" to them constantly. If we want to help infants and toddlers develop a sense that they can do things, then their environment should be designed to encourage their need and craving to practice new abilities. We need to be intentional and design an infant or toddler room, for example, with specific structures designed for safe climbing (Torelli, 2002).

**Room Design for Infants and Toddlers**   Well-designed infant and toddler rooms contain activity areas but are not just scaled-down versions of classrooms for children age 3 to 8 years old. A well-designed infant and toddler room is clean and has spacious bathing and dressing areas. It encourages crawling, scooting, and walking in safe, open areas. It inspires pushing, pulling, rolling, emptying, and filling safe, clean toys; and climbing on safe structures. A developmentally appropriate infant or toddler room encourages children to gaze at objects at their level and to do messy, active things such as finger painting (SERVE Center of UNCG, 2013; Torelli & Durrett, 1996). The website from Grossmont College, http://www.pitc.org/pub/pitc_docs/grossmont.html, one of the PITC sites, shows a developmentally appropriate environment for infants and toddlers. This site shows before and after photos of the remodeling project and its move to a more developmentally appropriate physical environment for this age group. Additional websites at the end of the chapter depict equally appropriate infant toddler spaces.

## Sensory Stimulation: A Powerful Avenue for Infant–Toddler Development

Being able to coordinate all the information flowing in from our senses is an essential building block of perception and cognition. Understanding the importance of this aspect of early development and then developing learning opportunities appropriate for infants and toddlers is an important aspect of the job of a teacher of infants and toddlers.

**Infants Can Coordinate Information from Different Senses**   Do babies gradually develop this ability or are they able to coordinated and use sensory information? Research in infant development from the past 30 years revealed that even young infants could coordinate information from different senses. Young infant brains are already organized so that they can then use coordinated sensory information. For example, a young infant sees, hears, smells, and touches her mother. She is able to put all the information from these senses together and us it to recognize and respond to her mother quickly (Lickliter, 2011).

**Sensory Stimulation Benefits Infant Sensory Coordination and Brain Development**   Research reviewed by Lickliter (2011) also showed the plasticity of an infant's brain, that being deprived of stimulation of one of the senses, such as vision, or receiving sensory stimulation, can change the infant's brain. The message from this research for teachers of infants is that sensory integration is a developmental issue that they should attend to. They need to keep in mind that they can enhance a baby's brain development and sensory coordination abilities by deliberately providing the baby with appropriately timed sensory stimulation.

**Provide Appropriately Timed Sensory Experiences for Very Young Children**
Honig (n.d.) outlined excellent suggestions about providing sensory experiences for infants. Teachers can plan specific stimulation for each of the senses—vision, hearing,

olfactory (sense of smell), touch, and taste. Honig notes that appropriate sensory stimulation, such as gentle stroking of the baby's skin or other gentle and loving touch, not only stimulates the senses but also helps the baby feel lovable and relaxed and secure. So, sensory experiences benefit a baby's brain development and sensory coordination, but also help meet emotional and social needs. A few examples of stimulating one sense include the following:

- **Vision:** For newborns to about 4 months, babies usually turn their face to one side. Therefore, present items to look at to the side. Examples: your face or a soft toy. Mobiles are fine even then, but are much more useful for stimulation when an infant is about 3 to 4 months old.
- **Touch:** Babies revel in contact comfort and are comforted by it. Softly pat or stroke the baby's skin.
- **Hearing:** gentle voices, soft music, reading or crooning a tune to an infant. Avoid harsh or loud noises.

Combining stimulation of a couple of senses is also possible and desirable at times. For example, sing softly to an infant as you hold him and stroke his arm or play music as a toddler works with blocks. Be cautious and observe children's reactions carefully. Consciously avoid excessive stimulation, which can overwhelm a child's capacity to cope. Our goal is to gently stimulate the senses, either singly or in combinations manageable by infants and toddlers. We have to guard against the mistake of presenting a jumble of stimulation that unnerves and overwhelms a toddler's ability to cope.

Most teachers have also have seen 3- to 8-year-old children overwhelmed by clearly too much stimulation: excited by an upcoming holiday perhaps, excessive screen time, harsh lighting, or music that is too loud. The principle of appropriate amounts and appropriately timed sensory stimulation also applies to 3- to 8 year-old children. They, too, need proper amounts of sensory stimulation. We now turn to environments for children beyond toddlerhood, those who are from 3 to 8 years old.

## :: DEVELOPMENTALLY APPROPRIATE PHYSICAL ENVIRONMENTS FOR 3- TO 8-YEAR-OLDS: INDIRECT GUIDANCE

Three- and 4-year-old children are in preschool; 5-year-olds are generally in kindergarten; and 6-, 7-, and 8 year-olds are in the primary grades. Each of these groups needs a classroom designed for the specific developmental level of that group. However, based on sound early childhood theory, preschool, kindergarten, and primary classrooms, whatever their differences for the different age groups, should be structured to offer children an active approach to learning, opportunities to collaborate with others, and plenty of chances to work with real objects. Any classroom for young children, whatever the age of the children, should also make it easy for children to talk to adults skilled in facilitating learning. The designs of the classrooms in Figure 4.2, a preschool classroom, and Figure 4.3, a primary grade room showing children working collaboratively, are arranged appropriately for the age groups using them, and they have a positive impact on children's behavior.

**FIGURE 4.2**    Floor plan of Mrs. Johnson's preschool classroom

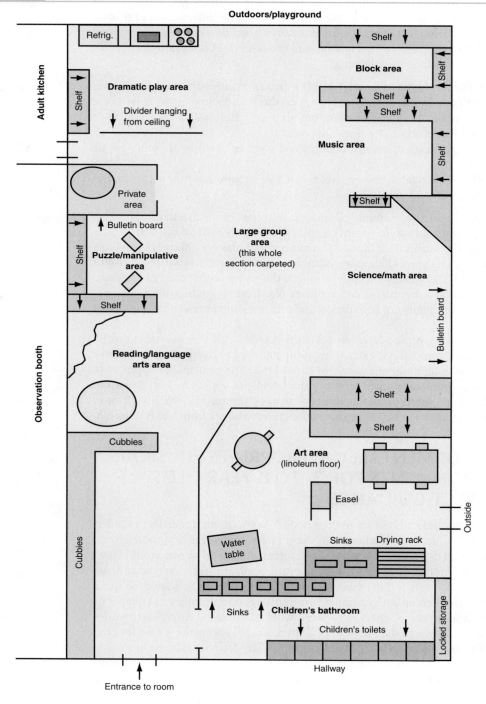

# Room Design Based on Theory

Both rooms in the figures are appropriate for young children because they demonstrate a teacher's respect for and knowledge of how children develop and learn. The teachers practice what they believe about children. The arrangements tell us that the teachers believe that children are curious, resourceful, and competent, just as John Dewey (1897) advised and as schools such as Reggio Emilia or the Bank Street programs for children put into action. Each conveys a sense order, offers chances for social interaction and making choices, and active learning.

**FIGURE 4.3** Children collaborate with others and learn actively in this classroom

**Sense of Order**   Each room conveys a sense of order and provides a comforting place for work and play (Greenman, 2005; National Association for the Education of Young Children, 2008). The rooms are well arranged, tidy, and organized. Children know that items have their own place in the room and that the basic structure will be the same from day to day, even though the teacher might change materials and activities in centers.

**Social Interaction**   Classrooms need to be set up so that children can interact easily with other children as well as with their teachers. Teachers have set up the learning centers deliberately and intentionally to foster working and playing together. Such interaction gives children the opportunity to confront other children's ideas and to clarify their own viewpoints.

**Making Choices**   Children need to learn how to make wise choices, and these rooms give them good practice. Consider the learning centers and materials. During choice time, children work alone or with other children. Each center has a variety of materials directly related to that center, and children choose from available materials. For example, children in the primary grade classroom can write after choosing from among computers, small and large chalk or whiteboards, colored pencils, markers, or even trays of damp sand. Over time and in a supportive environment, children can learn to make wise decisions and choices.

**Active Learning**   Classrooms should encourage active learning. Whether in preschool, kindergarten, or the primary grades, children learn actively in centers, through discovery and working with real objects, and through projects. Children develop physical knowledge when they manipulate real objects such as blocks. Children can also learn actively when teachers initiate a learning activity, such as second graders working on simple machines. When children manipulate physical objects and gather data, they develop new ideas or deepen their understanding of older ideas. For example, preschool children can extend their understanding of colors in the art area by mixing two colors of paint. Second graders working with levers and pulleys can extend any existing knowledge about simple machines with their teacher's support.

## :: FOCUS ON PRACTICE

This Focus on Practice activity is entitled *Constructivist Principles of Designing Early Childhood Classrooms*. Note that active learning, collaboration, and making choices benefit children's learning.

## Benefits of Well-Designed Spaces for Children

Children benefit in many ways when their teachers design developmentally appropriate classrooms such as those in Figures 4.2 and 4.3. They have lower levels of stress and far fewer discipline problems. They interact with other children in a more positive way than do children in inappropriately structured classrooms (Hart et al., 1998; Nicholson, 2005; Steinhauer, 2005).

Well-designed spaces help children to be more independent and self-controlled. They display greater feelings of competence and confidence, both of which are elements of positive and healthy self-esteem. Therefore, a well-designed physical environment supports children's efforts to meet the higher order needs, such as the esteem needs, in Maslow's (1954/1987) hierarchy. They also develop better decision-making skills and better ability to take initiative and engage in more sophisticated dramatic play than children do in poorly designed rooms. The research in these areas is not new. We have known about the benefits of good design for decades, and later researchers continued this work (Charlesworth, Hart, Burts, & DeWolf, 1993; Howes, 1991; Johnson & Duffek, 2008; Petrakos & Howe, 1996; Stallings, 1975). The research base has been applied in a very practical way by writers of articles urging teachers to design their rooms to foster active learning and social interaction (Shalaway, 2013).

The years of research on brain development have significantly affected how teachers understand children, their development, and how they learn. Teachers can use this research-based information as support in making decisions about setting up classrooms, deciding on time schedules, and even on the learning opportunities and materials that they choose. Rushton, Eitelgeorge, and Zickafoose (2003) described a constructivist classroom environment likely to foster brain development as a well-structured, an enriched environment where children do real learning by working with hands-on materials and through social interaction with other children and with their teachers.

The schools of Reggio Emilia, Italy, citing children's need for beauty, simplicity, and challenge (Gandini, 1993; Reggio Children, 2013), have added to our renewed interest in classroom design. I participated in a study tour in Reggio Emilia in May 2008 and was struck by the beauty of the classrooms. Children and teachers were calm and engaged. Children were busy learning through focused and enjoyable activities. They worked and played freely with other children, with the room designs fostering their engagement.

**Effects of Poorly Designed Classrooms**    Poorly designed schools send quite a different message of expecting failure and lacking respect for children in the schools (Nicholson, 2005). A poorly designed space for children's classroom or program can contribute to poor academic achievement and behavioral problems. Higher levels of stress behavior occur in inappropriately versus appropriately designed preschool and kindergarten classrooms. The stress in poorly designed classrooms contributes to some of the discipline problems (Hart et al., 1998; Steinhauer, 2005).

## :: GUIDELINES: DEVELOPMENTALLY APPROPRIATE ROOM DESIGN FOR 3- TO 8-YEAR-OLD CHILDREN

A big part of early childhood classroom management is managing the physical environment of the classroom as well as the time schedule, curriculum, activities, and materials. There are several practical things to consider when setting up or designing the physical environment in early childhood classrooms. We will consider the guidelines for designing a supportive physical environment, including the following:

Organize the classroom into activity areas and develop enough of them.

Arrange activity areas logically.

Create attractive and sensory-rich areas.

Use a variety of indirect strategies to make it easier for children to work and play in the classroom.

## Organize the Classroom into Activity Areas

Appropriately designed classrooms are organized into areas or zones of activity. A good classroom arrangement of areas embodies the principles of movement, active learning, social interaction, and working with supportive adults. Effective teachers develop and arrange **activity areas** that support the overall curriculum goals for the children in that classroom (Michigan Department of Education, 2013).

There are several different types of classroom activity areas. Some of the areas are small, some large; some have seating, others do not. Specific materials are stored

**Activity areas**
Zones designated for supporting children's development and learning

in some areas, but other areas have no materials stored there. Well-designed class-rooms usually contain individual or small-group learning centers, a large-group area, and some sort of private area. Most early childhood teachers provide a writing center with a variety of writing instruments and surfaces for writing. However, it is beneficial for children's literacy development to provide writing materials in all centers (Clark & Kragler, 2005). These researchers found that having writing materials in not only the writing center but also the music, art, math, blocks, and other centers enhanced the children's literacy development.

**Small-group learning center**

Space large enough for five or six children; center has a specific function, such as art or discovery

**Learning Center: Small Group**   A **small-group learning center** refers to a permanent or semipermanent space large enough for five or six children. Well-designed small-group learning centers serve a specific function reflecting the age of the children in that class as well as each school's curriculum goals. Examples of well-defined small-group areas include the following: math and science, manipulatives (puzzles and other small-muscle equipment), library and writing, dramatic play, block center, and creative arts (see Figures 4.4 and 4.5 for examples).

Teachers in developmentally appropriate classrooms create the types of centers that meet the needs of the children in that class. Therefore, *not* all classrooms will have the same small-group learning centers. One teacher might emphasize writing and math with permanent, well-stocked centers for each. Another teacher might provide those centers but with far less emphasis, stressing instead art, blocks, and music.

- **Seating arrangement.** The seating arrangement varies with the purpose of each center, making this type of center quite flexible. Some centers call for a table and chairs, as in Figure 4.5. Some small-group learning centers do not require a table and chairs, such a preschool's block area. You may also decide to arrange a center so that children can work either at a table or on the floor, a good way to help children practice good decision making. Small-group learning centers should be well separated from other areas, which clearly communicate each area's function.

  Primary grade classrooms arranged in activity areas encourage active learning. Children work with other children in classrooms set up to foster collaborative work and learning. The Dartmouth Early Learning Center (n.d.) describes a primary grade classroom's learning centers and routines set up to help children be responsible for themselves and to take good care of the classroom.

**FIGURE 4.4**   **Dramatic play small-group area**

- **Materials for the center.** Store materials related to the activity in the area. Avoid storing materials not related to the function of the area in that location. Guide children indirectly by storing materials within their reach when you want them to have easy access to the materials; store other materials out of their reach.

Our goal in managing an early childhood classroom is to be helpful to children. One study (Cameron, Connor, & Morrison, 2005) examined the effect of good classroom organization and clear teacher instructions for activities. It found that children in well-organized classrooms could manage their own activities well as the year progressed. We can manage the classroom, for example, so children have an easier time cleaning up in any center. We can manage group time so that it is an easier activity in which to participate. We can manage schedules so that all children can choose their next activity effortlessly. We can help children by using indirect guidance in the physical environment in many ways. Table 4.1 shows several ideas. For each suggestion, state the possible benefit to the child.

Learning centers for small groups change over time, as the needs, interests, and abilities of the children change and as they engage in different projects. In well-designed classrooms, teachers evaluate learning centers for needed modifications. They regularly add materials for new activities, rearrange the seating of a center as needed, reorganize materials as necessary, and remove materials no longer required.

| FIGURE 4.5 | Dramatic play area (a small-group learning center) |

| **TABLE 4.1** | Indirect Guidance in the physical environment |

| Indirect Guidance Strategy | What Is the Benefit to the Child? |
|---|---|
| Paint block shapes on the shelf where blocks are stored. | |
| Music instrument shapes are painted on the pegboard for hanging instruments. | |
| Transparent storage tubs are used for art or writing materials. | |
| Attach a sample item from a box of art supplies to the end of the tub facing the room. | |
| Apron is placed on the back of a chair for messy activities. | |
| Picture choice cards are available for activities; they are used by the teacher in transitions or by children throughout work time. | |
| Day planner: index card on which a young child draws or writes a daily plan for activities. | |
| Carpet squares are arranged in a specific pattern before group activities: semicircle, cluster, lines, circle. | |
| Pictures of children properly washing hands are placed over the sink. | |
| Song about playground limits is provided. | |

**EXAMPLE** At the beginning of the school year, Mrs. Johnson arranged a play sink, refrigerator, and stove along with a table and chairs and dress-up clothes in the dramatic play area. The children enthusiastically used the center for a while, but then Mrs. Johnson noticed less and less play there, even though she had added different items of interest. Mrs. Johnson concentrated on changing the area to rekindle interest in dramatic play.

She recruited parent volunteers to develop prop boxes and collected some great dress-up clothes. The "office," the "backyard," the "gardening center," and the "fix-it shop" were all hits. In the "backyard," children used a small picnic table, umbrella, toy lawn mower set on a green carpet, and hand gardening tools, along with a planting tray for starting plants from seeds in the outside garden.

**Individual learning center**
Space for one child to work

**Learning Center: Individual** Figure 4.6 shows several examples for creating **individual learning centers** or work centers. This is a flexible area because the same comments about seating arrangements and materials for the small-group learning area also apply to individual learning centers. These centers block some stimulation,

**FIGURE 4.6** Individual learning centers. There are many easy and inexpensive ways to create individual centers

*Source:* Marion, 2011

| FIGURE 4.7 | Early childhood classrooms have a large-group area where everyone can gather at one time |
|---|---|

allowing a child to concentrate on a specific activity. They also give children a chance to work alone in a busy classroom.

> **EXAMPLE**   Mr. Santini, the teacher in the mixed-age K–2 classroom, developed three individual learning spaces in one corner of his room. When children chose their activity, he often asked them where they would like to work. "Where would you like to write your story, Philip? You can sit at the big table with the other boys or you can pick one of the one-person workstations. There is still a space open in the one-person workstations. Which would you prefer today?"

**Large-Group Area**   A **large-group area** is a space large enough to accommodate most or all of the children for large-group activities or several children during a work period. This space should be large, open, and flexible to accommodate group activities such as music, language arts, creative dramatics, stories, nutrition education, dance, and other activities that a teacher thinks would be appropriate to do as a group. See Figure 4.7.

**Large-group area**
A space in which a whole class can gather for a variety of learning activities

- **Seating arrangement.**  This depends entirely on the activity that takes place in the area. Some teachers have a permanent large-group area in their rooms. Some teachers move a table or two to make room for a large-group activity.
- **Materials for the center.**  The large-group area serves many purposes. Therefore, specific materials are not stored in the large-group area but are brought there by the teacher. Mrs. Johnson, the preschool teacher (see Figure 4.8), has brought items for an obstacle course to the large-group area.

Many teachers do store items in the large-group area that help them manage the space well. For example, individual pieces of carpeting can be arranged in seating

**FIGURE 4.8**  Large-group area in a preschool classroom

patterns and indicate to children where they are to sit before group begins. Some teachers keep items in the large-group area that are used in transitions out of the large group (picture cue cards or printed names, for example, or the puppet that introduces the activity for the day).

**Private Space**  A **private space** is a small, partially enclosed space with room for only one or two children. A teacher would be able to monitor and supervise this area easily, but it should be visually isolated from other children (Marion, 2011). There are no chairs, tables, or special materials in the private area. Figure 4.9 shows the private space for Mrs. Johnson's classroom. A teacher would follow the same principles for developing a private space for a kindergarten or primary classroom.

**Private space**
Place of refuge and relaxation, large enough for only one or at most two children; must be easily monitored by the teacher

We provide a private space because healthy systems acknowledge the right to privacy and the right to choose or limit contact with others. Teachers in appropriately designed classrooms pay attention to the needs of both the entire class and of individuals. Like adults, children need breaks from large groups. Well-designed private spaces can help us make a special effort to teach children how to take these breaks and to pace their interactions.

Manage this part of your classroom well by clearly defining how everyone—teachers and children—may use the private space. Make sure that every adult who works in your room knows that the private space is a place of refuge and relaxation. Never use the private area as a punishment area. Make sure each child knows that she can retreat to this spot to be alone and will not be disturbed. Teach each child the strategies for politely telling another person that he does not wish to be disturbed when in the private area. Be sure to set limits about the number of children who may use the private space.

| FIGURE 4.9 | Private space in a preschool classroom |

## Develop Enough Activity Areas

The principles of designing early childhood classrooms call for children to have choices; to move about the classroom; and to be actively involved with materials, other children, and adults. Thus, a classroom needs enough activity areas so that children do indeed have choices, are actively involved, and can easily move from one activity to another.

**Age and Number of Children**   Figure 4.10 shows how many of each type of space is useful. Consider two factors, the age and number of children when making decisions about the number of centers. Kantrowitz and Evans (2004) found that some classrooms do not provide enough centers for the number of children in a classroom, which led to discipline problems. Having enough centers, then, is important in helping children choose well and stay focused. Provide one-third more spaces than there are children so children can change activities without having to wait.

**General Formula**   The general formula is $x = n + (n \div 3)$, where $x$ = number of spaces needed and $n$ = number of children in a classroom. A kindergarten classroom for 21 5-year-olds would need 28 workspaces: $x = 21 + (21 \div 3) = 21 + 7 = 28$ spaces, or one-third more spaces than children. This means that any child who completes a project in one area can move to another activity because there are always more workspaces in the classroom than there are children.

> **EXAMPLE**   Mr. Santini's mixed-age class has 18 children. This classroom has six learning centers based on the needs of his children—reading, social studies, math, art, science, and writing. Applying the formula here, we have $x = 18 + (18 \div 3) = (18 + 6) = 24$ spaces.

| FIGURE 4.10 | Number of areas needed based on ages and numbers of children in class | | | |
|---|---|---|---|---|

| Area | Ages of Children | Number of Children in Class | | |
|---|---|---|---|---|
| | | Up to 9 | 10–14 | 15–24 |
| Private area | 3–4 | 1 | 1 | 1 |
| | 5–6 | 1 | 1 | 1 or 2 |
| | 7–9 | 1 | 1 | 1 or 1 |
| Small-group area | 3–4 | 1 | 3 | 4 or 5 |
| | 5–6 | 2 | 3 | 4 or 5 |
| | 7–9 | 2 | 3 | 5 |
| Large-group area | 3–4 | 1 | 1 | 1 |
| | 5–6 | 1 | 1 | 1 |
| | 7–9 | 1 | 1 | 1 |

It is possible to create a classroom that is too cluttered, so it is wise to avoid filling your classroom with so many activity areas that children are overstimulated, frustrated, and unable to move around easily.

## Arrange Activity Areas Logically

Another important step in designing a supportive physical environment is to arrange activity areas logically. Do this by thinking about the type of work or play in each center, by separating centers from each other, and by regulating the flow of traffic in the classroom.

**Type of Work and Play in Each Center**    Design centers that are both stimulating and peaceful. Supportive classrooms contain quiet, purposeful, enthusiastic, and even vigorous interaction, but they are not excessively noisy.

- **"Quiet" learning centers.** Some learning and play centers lend themselves to relatively quiet, less vigorous work or play. Children tend to sit or stand and work quietly on projects or activities in these centers even if they work with several other children. This does not mean that children are silent in these centers. On the contrary, children in supportive classrooms talk quite a bit as they work together on math, at the computer, or on puzzles. The overall tone of these quiet centers is simply more subdued. The quiet centers typically include:

    Private space

    Library/writing centers (reading, writing, listening)

    Science

    Math

    Puzzles and other small-table toys

    Computer center

- **"Less quiet" learning centers.** Other learning and play centers lend themselves to somewhat noisier, more vigorous work or play. Children seem to move around more in certain centers because the nature of the work or play encourages a lot of movement. As they move around, children engaged in these centers tend to talk to each other. Activity in these centers is less subdued than in the quieter centers, but it is still not excessively noisy. This movement and talk is what makes certain centers into less quiet learning centers, and the activities there typically include:

> Dramatic play
>
> Blocks
>
> Physical education
>
> Music
>
> Arts
>
> Water or sand table
>
> Play and/or work in a large-group area

Logically arrange areas so that quieter areas are placed near other quiet areas and so that they are well separated from areas encouraging active play.

> **EXAMPLE**    Figure 4.2 shows how Mrs. Johnson appropriately placed the dramatic play area near the block area; both are high-activity areas, and dramatic play flows so easily from one to the other. She wisely placed the language arts center close to the puzzles/manipulatives toy center, with both of these centers well separated from the noisier areas.

She also developed and clearly stated limits on noise level. Children in her class work and play together without disrupting other people, and she emphasizes everyone's right to a quiet place in which to work. The children are learning that one of their basic classroom values is respect for the rights of others, including the classroom animals.

**Create Physical Boundaries for Areas**    Supportive systems have appropriate boundaries. Here, you will learn why they are necessary and how to create good **physical boundaries for activity areas**. Creating proper physical limits for activity areas is not trivial. It is both age and individually appropriate. Creating good boundaries among areas is age appropriate because all children need to know how to function in the physical environment, and good boundaries give them useful cues. Creating good boundaries—with shelving and partitions of various types—is individually appropriate because some children especially need help understanding limits and boundaries.

**Physical boundary for activity areas**
Partition separating one activity area from another

Creating good boundaries may well be one of the most appropriate things you do for children from chaotic, disorganized homes. People in unhealthy systems tend to violate the psychological and physical boundaries of others. One of the clearest marks of a healthy system, however, including a developmentally appropriate classroom, is the idea of clear and distinct boundaries. These boundaries include psychological boundaries, such as keeping people safe through rules about no hitting and no name-calling, and the physical boundaries within the classroom itself.

**FIGURE 4.11** One example of how to create boundaries between activity areas

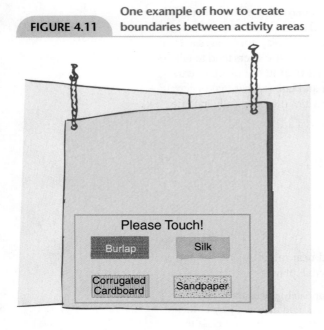

Please Touch!

Burlap

Silk

Corrugated
Cardboard

Sandpaper

**Traffic pattern**
Flow of movement in an
early childhood classroom

We teach the concept of boundaries by clearly separating one area from another. Children tend to be more cooperative and far less disruptive when they understand where one area ends and the next begins. Clear physical boundaries, along with well-organized materials, also help children know where each piece of equipment belongs and encourage them to put things in their proper areas. Figure 4.11 shows one idea for practical and efficient boundaries.

This **video** depicts a preschool classroom that exemplifies appropriate room arrangement for three to five-year-old children. Notice that the areas are arranged logically, that there is a large group area and that there are a number of small group learning centers.

**Create Good Traffic Patterns in a Classroom**
Classrooms that have well-arranged activity areas and good physical boundaries give children cues about the traffic pattern in the room. The **traffic pattern** refers to the flow of movement in an early childhood classroom. Children should be able to move about the room through logical traffic patterns. Create good traffic patterns with open pathways that clearly lead to areas and that make it easy for children to move between areas.

- Pathways should be wide enough for wheelchairs.
- Pathways should be long enough to make moving among areas easy.
- Pathways should not be so long that they encourage running—avoid zoom areas.
- Regulate traffic by making only one entrance to a center.
- Make sure that the circuit around the room allows children to stop off at each center if they wish.

---

:: *Question for Reflection*

---

## Create Attractive, Sensory-Rich Activity Areas

Children need a clean, attractive, and sensory-rich space (Torelli & Durrett, n.d.). The design of the room does not have to be extravagant, and furnishings need not be expensive. However, a children's classroom should be aesthetically pleasing and serene. One good way to create such an environment is to pay attention to seemingly commonsense matters such as lighting and the sensory environment. Several specific and practical suggestions are discussed in the following subsections.

**Strive for a Sensory-Rich but Clean and Uncluttered Classroom**   Many early childhood teachers do a good job of adding interesting items to the classroom, but it is also important to weed out items that have served their purpose. A cluttered, disorderly, or dirty room is unpleasant and distracting. Eliminating clutter helps children focus on new material because the number of stimuli to which they must attend is decreased.

> **EXAMPLE**   For a project on butterflies, Mrs. Johnson added a book on butterflies, two large color photographs, and several real butterfly models to the science area. So she was puzzled by the children's lack of interest. A close look at the discovery area showed that it was cluttered with old cups of seeds, the rock collection, a magnet, and a magnifying glass. The pictures had been pinned to a somewhat cluttered bulletin board, the butterflies dwarfed by a large, green plant.

Mrs. Johnson cleared the table and the bulletin board, and then set out only "butterfly" things—the collection of butterflies, books, and the magnifying glass. She arranged the pictures of butterflies attractively on the bulletin board so that they were the central focus. She also placed a picture of butterflies on the door of the classroom with a note to parents to "join us in learning about butterflies."

**Modify the Lighting**   Skillful use of lighting is an indirect method of guidance. Many schools are equipped with bright lights, and although it is desirable to have adequate lighting, it is boring, stressful, and overly stimulating to be in harsh bright light for an extended period. Classrooms are often equipped with only one or two light switches, giving adults only two options: all the harsh lights on or all off. Installing dimmer switches is quite inexpensive and enables teachers to control the intensity of lighting in different sections of the room.

**Modify Ceiling Height or Floor Level**   Create safe, cocoonlike spaces that define the areas in a classroom. Many schools, for example, build a safe, inexpensive platform to give some dimension to the room. Children use platforms for a variety of activities.

Consider defining an activity area by draping strips of cloth across and between dowels hung from the ceiling. This strategy softens an area and room and actually makes the ceiling appear to be lower, especially useful when children need a private, quiet, partially enclosed activity area. This idea can be applied to almost any area in the room.

> **EXAMPLE**   Mrs. Johnson, in her first year at her school, was disappointed that the children did not seem to enjoy the reading area. She assessed the area. She drew a floor plan of the reading area and decided that she needed to make some changes:
>
> - Use bookshelves to better separate the reading area from other areas.
> - Add a fluffy carpet.
> - Place large pillows against a wall.
> - Suspend cloth across two rods hanging from the ceiling.
> - Occasionally, but not always, play soft classical music in the area.

The children loved their new area and reading activity soared. They even made special requests for specific music while they read.

**Modify the Sensory Environment**   Well-designed classrooms are pleasant and attractive because the teacher has created visual, auditory, olfactory, and textural interest.

- **Create visual interest.** Enhance the aesthetic appeal of your early childhood classroom by keeping it clean and tidy. Make a real effort to keep clutter to a minimum. Judiciously add well-chosen, inexpensive items such as paintings; posters; safe, green plants; photographs of the children; cloth hangings; and artwork. Do not feel compelled to fill every square inch of wall space with these things, though. Leave some blank space where children get relief from stimulation.

- **Create auditory interest.** We have already discussed the importance of a calm and peaceful environment where children are free to move and to talk but not to make excessively loud noise. It is much easier to use sound to create a pleasant environment in such a calm environment. How pleasant and relaxing it is for children to be able to hear their favorite composer's music when they arrive at school! Other sounds help create this kind of atmosphere if the children are tuned in to the sounds and are not distracted by unnecessary noise. Examples include musical instruments or a tinkling mobile (available periodically).

- **Create olfactory interest.** Exquisite fragrances, such as lilac shrubs in bloom, the garden after a rainfall, homemade bread, and fresh oranges often call forth joyful memories. Other odors trigger unpleasant memories (the disinfectant odor of a hospital, the skunk odor reminding us that one of those critters sprayed the dog). Here are some easy ways to make a classroom pleasant through fragrance. First, eliminate unpleasant odors by maintaining cleanliness. Add pleasant aromas from safe sources:

   Bake bread, muffins, or cookies.

   Vary ingredients in baking, urging children to identify scents.

   Add food-grade extracts such as peppermint or orange to play dough.

   Place inexpensive scented soap in the bathroom on occasion. Introduce this at group time with reminders about hand-washing procedures.

   Occasionally place safe (real) flowers at the snack table or in the library (in a plastic vase).

   Place safe, fragrance-filled plants in the room or yard.

- **Create textural interest.**

   If appropriate, install carpet on selected sections of the floor. Carpet on certain sections of the wall is also a nice touch.

   Cover bulletin boards with cork or burlap.

   Hang a children-created large collage of cloth scraps.

   Create a touch wall with an expanse of corrugated paper and other materials. See Figure 4.11 for an example.

   Clear one wall of all signs and pictures and put up a fabric wall hanging.

   Make it a custom in your classroom to hang a differently textured fabric in a place where children are likely to see and want to touch it—for example, near lockers or cubbies. You will have created a way to start conversations with children who touch the fabric; you can ask, "How did the new fabric feel when you touched it? Did it feel the same as the strip of burlap we had up last week? How did it feel compared to the silk?"

We turn now to other essential methods of indirectly guiding young children, the time schedule, the curriculum, learning activities within the curriculum, and materials.

## :: TIME SCHEDULE, CURRICULUM, ACTIVITIES, AND MATERIALS: SOURCES OF INDIRECT GUIDANCE FOR 3- TO 8-YEAR-OLDS

At first glance, these might seem to have little to do with guiding children. Each, though, can support teachers in guiding children effectively. Each is an indirect way of guiding children.

## Schedule

A good time schedule refers to the sequence of activities for a classroom's day and guides children indirectly by structuring the day in a way that benefits children. Scheduling things with children's needs in mind is a sign of respect for them. If our goal is to help children gradually learn to control themselves and to make choices, then their daily schedule should enable them to practice these two skills, such as making a choice between the discovery and art centers during work time. If our goal is to foster children's ability to work well either alone or with others, then the schedule should be set up for these purposes. For example, during self-selected center time, a child should be able to choose between reading by herself in the library area or working with other children in a center. If our goal is to help children avoid unnecessary frustration and stress, then the daily schedule will only contain transitions that are absolutely necessary. If we believe that children need to have enough time with learning opportunities instead of hurrying through the day, then the daily schedule will show large chunks of time devoted to learning opportunities.

**Intentional Scheduling**    Teachers, then, need to be intentional about the time schedule, deliberately and consciously structuring the day to meet children's needs, whether the child is an infant or a second grader. Essential elements of a developmentally appropriate schedule for young children include built-in structure, flexibility, and balance.

- **Built-in structure** is the teacher's vision for the flow of the day. Preschool and kindergarten classrooms usually include time for group meetings or circle time and center-based learning time, outdoor learning and play, small group, and teacher-led learning focusing on children's knowledge about music, math, and other curriculum areas. The integral or built-in structure also includes appropriate but not excessive time for routines such as clean-up, resting, and snacks or lunch. Appropriately developed primary classroom schedules are similar but reflect the different learning needs of first-, second-, and third-grade children.

- **Flexibility** is evidence that the teacher sees the need for some "give" in the schedule, as when he lengthens the center time to accommodate intense interest in the current day's work. I observed a first-grade teacher, in a large-group setting, discuss the trees outside. She stopped to say to her class, "You know, why don't we just stop talking about the trees on the playground and grab out clipboards and pencils and go out there and draw them?" She was flexible about how the large-group, circle time discussion might benefit the children's understanding about trees.

- **Balance between more and less vigorous activities** is evidence that teachers think that children need both. An appropriately structured schedule would never require young children to sit quietly for extended periods. Instead, it would focus on learning that one has the capacity to listen quietly to a story for short and manageable periods and that the teacher will segue or move smoothly into equally beneficial hands-on, spirited, energetic activities.

- **Balance between child-initiated and teacher-directed activity** are necessary for all children—preschool, kindergarten, or primary. For example, a second-grade child might be good at and like writing haiku poetry, so she writes a collection of these poems (child-initiated activity). A second-grade teacher might schedule language arts instruction to teach children about writing haiku poetry (teacher-directed activity). Constructivist theories of Dewey, Vygotsky, and Piaget theory have informed us that children need to learn from expert others such as peers and teachers, and need time on their own to build ideas.

**Schedule for Preschool**    The following schedule presented by the Center on the Social and Emotional Foundations for Early Learning (2007) is typical of an appropriately structured daily agenda for preschool and kindergarten children. It reflects the built-in structure, flexibility, and balance that young children need. An appropriately structured schedule for young children reflects the goals of that school for children's development and learning (Dartmouth Early Learning Center, n.d.). The following schedule is for a half-day preschool or kindergarten.

- 20 minutes—Arrival Time
- 15 to 20 minutes—Group Time
- 60 minutes—Activity Time
- 15 minutes—Story Time
- 30 minutes—Outdoor Time
- 10 to 15 minutes—Snack Time
- 10 to 15 minutes—Closing Activities and Dismissal

**Schedule for Primary Grades**    The following schedule (Arizona Department of Education, 2013) is for a primary classroom and reflects the built-in structure, room for flexibility, and balance characteristic of developmentally appropriate time schedules in classrooms. The schedule allows for learning in math, science, social studies, language arts, for example, but does not chop up the day into these areas. The teacher would plan for math, science, and other areas mandated by state standards throughout the day.

Math, for instance, can be taught and learned during opening activities, group times, center work time, or even during quiet time. A third-grade teacher might use her afternoon whole-group time to focus on the math concept of graphing by involving every child in building a graph. The next day, the same teacher might use a small part of the opening activities to show the graph constructed by the class and then tell the children that one of the small group teacher-directed activities would be to develop another graph but this time the children would be graphing the degrees of 'roughness' in samples of sandpaper.

- 15 to 20 minutes—Opening Activities
- 20 to 40 minutes—Group Time (large and small group)
- 45 to 60 minutes—Work Time in Learning Centers
- 5 to 10 minutes—Clean Up/Prepare for Snack
- 10 to 15 minutes—Snack Time
- 20 to 30 minutes—Outdoor Activity Time
- 30 to 45 minutes—Shared Reading Experience
- 20 to 30 minutes—Lunch
- 15 to 20 minutes—Quiet Time
- 40 to 50 minutes—Special Activities (such as Art, Music, Physical Education)
- 15 to 20 minutes—Journal Writing
- 20 to 40 minutes—Group Time (whole- and small-group instruction)
- 45 to 60 min—Work Time in Learning Centers
- 15 to 20 min—Closing Activities and Daily Reflections

**Effective Use of Schedule**   A teacher can go beyond just developing a good schedule and intentionally teach children about it and then give reminders about the flow of the day at school. This strategy treats children with respect and acknowledges their need to understand the schedule.

Effective teachers plan teacher-directed activities aimed at helping children learn about the schedule and then emphasizing its role in the day's learning. They often do this at a group meeting and might give a copy of the daily schedule to parents. Teachers also post the schedule, in writing for older children and a picture schedule for younger children or any child needing additional cues for remembering the schedule. Teachers refer to the daily schedule often and this reinforces its importance, especially at the beginning of the year or when a new child joins the class. At the start of the afternoon story time, a kindergarten teacher might, for example, say, "Here is our schedule and here we are in story time (she points to the picture of children listening to a story). What comes after story time?"

When schedule changes are necessary, a teacher using a picture schedule might briefly discuss this at morning meeting or circle time and involve children in moving pictures around to accommodate the modest change in the day. A teacher who uses a plain printed schedule can do the same thing by printing each segment of the schedule on magnetic strips so that changes for a given day will be clearly stated. This is an excellent way to guide children indirectly because it tells the child, indirectly, what will happen that day. Advance knowledge of schedule modifications prevent the rise of anxiety about "What happens next?" that anybody, including a child, feels when they are not sure about the order of things.

# Curriculum

The main objective in this section is to explain how a developmentally appropriate curriculum for children is an indirect part of guidance. You will study curriculum and instructional strategies more thoroughly in other texts and other courses. The National Association for the Education of Young Children (2009) notes that indicators of an effective curriculum for young children are the following.

- Children are active and engaged
- Goals are clear and shared by all
- Curriculum is evidence based
- Valued content is learned through investigation and focused, intentional teaching
- Curriculum builds on prior learning and experiences
- Curriculum is comprehensive
- Professional standards validate the curriculum's subject-matter content
- The curriculum is likely to benefit children

An appropriate curriculum for young children builds on how young children think and learn (Copple & Bredekamp, 2009), implying that children are themselves a source of the curriculum. Effective teachers observe and assess children's needs, interests, and abilities, and then develop a scope and sequence of activities supporting children's development and learning (Helm & Katz, 2001). They *use* their knowledge about development and theory. They know that children learn in an active, not a passive, way. They believe that young children construct or build knowledge as they interact with people and things (Piaget, 1952; Vygotsky, 1978).

Effective teachers offer options to children. They encourage children to participate in ways that best suit each child's learning style (Ogu & Schmidt, 2009). They integrate the curriculum rather than chopping it into separate content areas such as math, science, and language arts. Teachers provide concrete experiences that actively involve children. They value play as an integral part of the curriculum as well as outside the classroom (Nell & Drew, with Bush, 2013).

**EXAMPLE**    Mrs. Johnson focuses on literacy in her integrated preschool curriculum. She wants her children to know that reading and writing, as well as listening and speaking, are useful. Her encouragement of literacy pervades the curriculum and is evident in every part of the room. Here are just a few examples:

- Paper and pencils for writing and dictating stories about play are placed in block and dramatic play, discovery or science, block, home living, and all other areas.
- Several types of paper, markers, and pencils are always available for drawing, writing, copying, inventing, and spelling.
- Charts, such as the arrival chart with the printed name of each child, are displayed and changed when appropriate. Next to the printed name is a space for a child to copy his or her name with a dry-erase marker. Parents sometimes help.
- Menus for each day's food (snack and lunch) are displayed near cubbies. Parents and children read the menus.

- Large recipe cards for one or two items are occasionally displayed during snack or lunch. Children and teachers read the recipes, and then recall the steps in preparing the food when they eat.
- A chart with pictures of all the new vegetables and fruits that the class has tried is displayed. Words describing each item are next to the picture, for example, for the raw carrot—*crunchy, orange, sweet, hard,* but for the cooked carrot— *soft, smooth, orange, sweet.*
- An "emotions" chart, with a drawing of a happy face on one side of the chart, is displayed. Children and teacher generate several synonyms for *happy* and list them on the other side of the chart.
- Tickets are issued to watch a video. Tickets display the name of the video.

## Activities and the Project Approach

The curriculum focuses on accepted content areas such as math, science, social studies, language arts, music, foreign language, and other areas from a state's learning standards. In addition, early childhood educators look to children as a major source of the curriculum. Children are curious, have many questions about their world, and are eager to investigate things to get answers to their questions. Within the curriculum, teachers develop learning activities that support children's search for answers to their questions and that deal with content areas.

In selecting the specific activities worthy of children's time, many teachers use the Project Approach to decide on some of the activities to be included in the curriculum Teachers and children go through two phases in deciding on activities that will be part of the investigation (Project Approach, 2013; Helm & Katz, 2001).

**Project Approach: Phase One of Projects and Investigations**  The first step in developing a project is usually a common experience. This shared experience triggers interest in a topic and then becomes a project. Teachers lead children in asking questions about the event—that is, the children generate questions about "What we want to know." The teacher creates a web of the questions (Helm & Katz, 2001).

EXAMPLES  A kindergarten class generated questions about a recycling truck that they had seen when they were on the playground. Their teacher created a web of questions about the truck, as shown in Figure 4.12a.

Mrs. Johnson's preschool class generated questions about colors after the shared experience of the trip to the paint store (in the chapter-opening vignette). Mrs. Johnson created a web of their questions. See Figure 4.12b.

**Project Approach: Phase Two of Projects and Investigations**  This step involves deciding on activities that would help children answer their questions. The investigation of the topic with different activities spans several days (Helm & Katz, 2001).

EXAMPLE  The kindergarten teacher arranged the following activities to help the children answer some of their questions about the recycling truck:

- **Day 1.** Visit from recycling truck and driver. Children observed, and asked questions of the driver. Back in the classroom, they dictated their observations to the teacher, who listed the observations on a chart.

**FIGURE 4.12a** Web of questions about the recycling truck that the kindergarteners created and the teacher recorded

Wheels
- How many wheels?
- Why are two wheels right next to each other? (double wheels)
- Why are the wheels bigger than the ones on my dad's car?

Back of Truck
- Does it go up and down like a garbage truck?
- What is that screen for? (the mesh covers for containers)

Next Stop
- Where do the drivers take all the bottles and cans?

Recycling Truck

Compartments
- Why are there so many compartments?
- How do the compartments get emptied?

Drivers
- Why are there 2 people riding in the truck?
- Do the drivers have to wear the same clothes? (uniforms)

Doors
- How many?
- Why aren't there any doors on the containers?

**FIGURE 4.12b** Mrs. Johnson used the children's questions to create this web of questions about colors

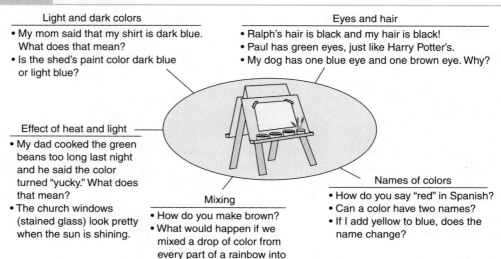

Light and dark colors
- My mom said that my shirt is dark blue. What does that mean?
- Is the shed's paint color dark blue or light blue?

Eyes and hair
- Ralph's hair is black and my hair is black!
- Paul has green eyes, just like Harry Potter's.
- My dog has one blue eye and one brown eye. Why?

Effect of heat and light
- My dad cooked the green beans too long last night and he said the color turned "yucky." What does that mean?
- The church windows (stained glass) look pretty when the sun is shining.

Mixing
- How do you make brown?
- What would happen if we mixed a drop of color from every part of a rainbow into a tray of white paint?

Names of colors
- How do you say "red" in Spanish?
- Can a color have two names?
- If I add yellow to blue, does the name change?

- **Day 2.** Children began constructing their own recycling truck from cardboard and other safe recycled items. They put together a driver's uniform from clothing in the dramatic play area, and they printed a sign for their truck. The teacher showed a film about recycling trucks.
- **Day 3.** Construction of the recycling truck continued. One of the fathers brought his heavy-duty pickup truck to school to show the double wheels. Children asked questions about double wheels. They doubled the wheels on the back of their mock-up of the recycling truck.
- **Day 4.** Children collected classroom items for recycling, placing them in the recycling bins of their truck. They made up a recycling song to the tune of "Bingo."
- **Day 5.** The children dictated a letter to parents about their project in progress. The teacher documented the project with photos, which she placed on a photo board in the classroom. The teacher also printed and duplicated the children's letter and sent it home with each child.
- **Day 6.** The children invited the principal to see their truck and the photo display. They talked to him about their project, teaching him the recycling song.

## Criteria for Developmentally Appropriate Activities

Early childhood activities, whatever the project and whatever the questions investigated, are developmentally appropriate when:

- There are many, but not an excessive number, of age-appropriate activities that occur throughout the day.
- Children know that some activities will occur at the same time each day.
- Children are actively involved and engage in concrete experiences.
- Children choose their own activities from among the large number of activities set up by the teacher.
- Children have options about when and how to complete activities.

## Materials: Choosing and Managing

Teachers in supportive environments provide appropriate materials with which children work and play. Appropriate materials refer to a moderately rich assortment of exploratory and safe items that encourage competent, independent behavior in children. These materials reflect the needs, interests, and abilities of the children. Figure 4.13 is a rating scale for managing classroom materials.

*:: Question for Reflection*

*:: Question for Reflection*

**FIGURE 4.13**    Rating scale: Managing classroom materials

Use this rating scale to evaluate classroom management of materials and equipment in this early childhood classroom. Rate each item using the scale. "1" indicates the lowest rating you can give. "5" is the highest rating you can give. A space is provided for comments.

| | Lowest Rating | | | | Highest Rating |
|---|---|---|---|---|---|
| The teacher has taken leadership in *gathering materials*. | 1 | 2 | 3 | 4 | 5 |
| All materials needed for an activity are there. | 1 | 2 | 3 | 4 | 5 |
| Materials appear to have been gathered well in advance of the activity. | 1 | 2 | 3 | 4 | 5 |
| Equipment is correctly sized for children using it. | 1 | 2 | 3 | 4 | 5 |
| Equipment works well. | 1 | 2 | 3 | 4 | 5 |
| Children will be able to use the materials without a lot of adult help. | 1 | 2 | 3 | 4 | 5 |
| Equipment is clean. | 1 | 2 | 3 | 4 | 5 |
| Materials are organized logically. | 1 | 2 | 3 | 4 | 5 |
| Items within centers are stored so that they are easy for children to get to and then to put away. | 1 | 2 | 3 | 4 | 5 |
| If children are expected to clean up after any activity, this teacher appears to have thought it through and has provided necessary items. | 1 | 2 | 3 | 4 | 5 |
| If children are expected to set up an activity, necessary materials are available. | 1 | 2 | 3 | 4 | 5 |
| Materials not intended for children's use are stored out of their reach. | 1 | 2 | 3 | 4 | 5 |

**Comments and suggestions:**

# ANALYZE A VIGNETTE

Refer to the chapter-opening vignette. Then answer these questions.

1. Mrs. Johnson has developed activities based on principles of developmentally appropriate practice. Find examples of how her preschool classroom meets the criteria for developmentally appropriate activities.
2. Explain how there is a wide, but not overwhelming, variety of age-appropriate activities that occur throughout the day.
3. Give examples of how Mrs. Johnson schedules activities so that they occur at the same time each day.
4. How does she emphasize concrete activities that actively involve the children?
5. Explain how she encourages children to choose their own activities.
6. How do the children have options about when and how to complete activities?

# SUMMARY

Major theories of child development and early childhood education guide a teacher's practice in guiding children. We use theories from the following categories of perspectives:

- Theories that emphasize systems in which children develop
- Theories emphasizing how children construct knowledge and skills about getting along with others
- Theories focusing on children's psychological and emotional development

Early childhood theories can guide teachers in designing classrooms that put theory into practice and that have clear benefits for children. Such classrooms convey or encourage:

- A sense of order
- Social interaction
- Making choices
- Active learning

Guidelines for designing supportive physical environments for young children include the following:

- Organize the classroom into activity areas and develop enough of them
- Arrange activity areas logically
- Create attractive and sensory-rich areas
- Use a variety of indirect strategies to make it easier for children to work and play in the classroom

Other indirect guidance includes the time schedule, curriculum, activities, and materials in a classroom. Effective early childhood curriculum is integrated rather than segmented into separate curriculum areas. Effective learning activities indirectly guide children because of the following:

- How the activities are organized
- The number of activities
- Children's active involvement
- The choices offered to children

# APPLY YOUR KNOWLEDGE

**Observation: Recognizing Appropriate Practice in an Early Childhood Classroom**

*What You Will Be Doing: Observing and Suggesting Change*

Observing. Request permission to visit an early childhood classroom for preschool, kindergarten, or primary children. As a guest in the classroom, your goal is not to criticize; it is to look at how the teacher has designed activity areas, how the areas are bounded, the traffic patterns in the classroom, and the management of materials in the classroom.

Suggesting change. Practice professionalism by making suggestions for change after you leave the classroom. Keep information on the classroom confidential. If you share information in one of your courses, remove information that could identify the teacher, class, and school from your work. Present any suggestions in a positive way so that you are merely suggesting ideas that would make a good classroom even better.

1. Observing:

   **Activity Areas**
   Draw a simple floor plan of the classroom that you have observed. Include the toilet area for children, doors to the outside and to hallways, small-group learning centers, large-group area, private areas, and boundaries among areas. Label each area clearly. Use the floor plan in Figure 4.2 as a guide. Then analyze the activity areas in this room:

   - **Private area.** Explain whether and how the private space in this classroom meets the criteria for private spaces.
   - **Large-group area.** Explain whether and how the large-group area in this classroom meets the criteria for large-group areas.
   - **Small-group learning centers.** Number of centers: _____. Explain whether and how the small-group learning centers in this classroom meet criteria for this type of activity area.

- **Individual learning center(s).** This classroom does (or does not) have individual learning centers. If it does, explain how these centers meet the criteria for this type of activity area.

### Boundaries

Describe the boundaries used to separate activity areas from one another in this classroom.

- Which areas were especially well bounded? Why?
- Which areas would benefit from having more effective boundaries?

### Traffic Pattern

Use a contrasting color and draw arrows from the entrance to the classroom and around the room to each center.

- Describe the traffic pattern in this room using information on good traffic patterns from the chapter.
- Suggest how to make the traffic pattern of this room even better.

### Management of Materials in the Classroom

Use the rating scale (Figure 4.14) to evaluate classroom management of materials and equipment in this early childhood classroom. After you are done with the rating scale, name three ways in which this classroom's management of materials would most benefit from a change in how materials are managed.

2. Suggesting change: Working by yourself or with another student or even a small group, make suggestions for change based on your observation. Choose a method for presentation. Here are a few suggestions:

- Draw a second floor plan for this classroom. Clearly show your suggestions for change in your drawing. If, for example, you note that the classroom does not have quite enough small-group learning centers, decide where you would put them and draw them on your second floor plan. Indicate changes with a colored pencil or pen.
- Make a table or chart listing the changes.
- Prepare a PowerPoint set of slides on the changes needed.
- Present your ideas verbally to your classmates.

# WEBSITES

*Bank Street*
http://www.bankstreet.edu
Home page for the Bank Street College of Education. The college has an old and respected children's program.

*Program for Infant/Toddler Care (PITC)*
http://www.pitc.org/pub/pitc_docs/home.csp
Home page for the State of California's concerted effort to attain high-quality care for infants and toddlers.

*Grossmont College*
http://www.pitc.org/pub/pitc_docs/grossmont.html
Home page of Grossmont College's infant and toddler center, near San Diego. It offers suggestions for creating a developmentally appropriate physical environment for infants and toddlers.

*Spaces for Children*
http://www.spacesforchildren.com/
Home page for Spaces for Children. An architectural firm specializing in designing developmentally appropriate spaces for children's centers and schools sponsors this excellent site. You can view centers for infants and toddlers as well as schools for older early childhood children.

*Reggio Emilia Preschools*
http://www.reggiochildren.it/?lang=en
Home page for the Reggio Emilia approach to early childhood education. Reggio Emilia is a municipality (city) in Italy. This approach is named after the city. Look at the website for links to the beautiful and appropriately stimulating physical environments for young children.

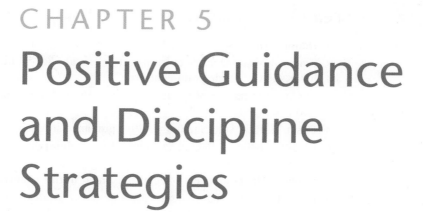

# CHAPTER 5

# Positive Guidance and Discipline Strategies

*Direct Guidance*

# Learning Outcomes

- Define terms associated with guidance and discipline
- Predict how a teacher's culture and beliefs about children might affect how he or she will guide young children
- Explain the nature of guidance for infants, toddlers, and older early childhood children
- Describe and explain major positive guidance strategies
- Predict the likely effect of a teacher's beliefs about discipline on choices about guidance strategies
- Explain why guidance strategies presented in this chapter are positive
- Defend the idea that using positive guidance strategies creates a warm, supportive relationship between children and a teacher

## VIGNETTES

### INFANTS AND TODDLERS: LOOKING AT BIRDS, SINGING ABOUT LUNCH, AND SPEAKING UP FOR BLUE

*In the infant toddler room of a preschool, 11-month-old Paul grabbed his teacher's hair. Mr. Bensen, the teacher, removed Paul's hand, picked him up, and turning to the window, said, "O-o-o-h! Look at the birds, Paul." Paul brightened when he saw birds at the feeder.*

*Fifteen-month-old Jada scooted across the room toward the kitchen, and Mr. Bensen scooped her up and carried her back to a small table, singing, "Jada, Jada, lunchtime, lunchtime. Let's have lunch." "Lunch, lunch" returned Jada, in singsong style.*

*Alex, 2 years old, banged his hands on the play dough table while his teacher turned around to get the dough. The teacher placed his hands lightly on Alex's small hands, showed him two lumps of play dough, and said, "Listen carefully, Alex. Tell me whether you want white play dough or blue play dough." Alex piped up cheerfully, "I want BLUE!"*

### PRESCHOOL: JERRY DRIZZLES SAND

*Four-year-old Jerry stood at the sand table and scooped up a handful of sand. He looked at the sand and then at the floor. He then slowly drizzled sand onto the floor next to the sand table. He bent over to examine the little pile of sand on the floor. Mrs. Johnson watched for a few seconds and then decided that Jerry seemed to be doing an experiment with the sand. She said, "You're dropping the sand very carefully." Jerry replied, "Yeah. It goes straight down and doesn't fly around like snow." Mrs. Johnson said, "It's great to experiment but dangerous to put sand on the floor. I have an idea. Here is a towel to put on the floor to catch the sand. Then you can just lift the towel and put the sand right back in the sand table when you're done."*

### PRIMARY: HANNAH ASKS FOR A LUNCHBOX

*Hannah, 6 years old, and Mom went to the store to buy a backpack for Hannah. They were in a hurry and had just enough time to pick out the backpack and still get to a doctor's appointment. Mom could afford to buy only a backpack. At the store, Hannah started the "Look-Mommy-I-want-that-WHY-can't-I-have-it" game. "Mom, can I get the lunchbox, too?" "No, Hannah. No lunchbox." "But Mom, I want the lunchbox. It's purple, just like my new backpack!" "Hannah, stop it. No lunchbox." "Why, Mom?"*

## :: INTRODUCTION

All of the adults in the vignettes faced typical interactions calling for guidance. The teachers have responded with positive guidance, but Hannah's mother has responded in a far less helpful way. A chief part of your professional role lies in helping children become compassionate and competent people. You will do this by guiding children effectively, whatever their age.

Effective teachers use **positive guidance strategies**. We will first look at guiding infants, toddlers, and 3- through 8-year-olds. We always guide children, but the guidance must be based on a child's level of development, his capabilities and limitations. This chapter's central focus is to describe and then to explain each of the major positive guidance strategies that teachers and parents have used successfully with 3- through 8 year-old children. We need to have access to many good strategies because we cannot rely on only one or two methods. You will learn about each strategy and read a number of real-life examples for each.

> **Positive guidance strategies**
> Methods that rely on teaching

## :: THE CONCEPT OF GUIDANCE AND DISCIPLINE

### Culture and Socialization

How a society guides children reflects the values and beliefs of its **culture**. Culture refers to the values, beliefs, or traditions of a group of people, which they give to the next generation through language, interactions, and relationships. Culture provides a setting or context in which the contacts with others, the relationships, take place. The members of the society gradually learn the culture's values and beliefs (Lewis & Ippen, 2007). Different systems affect children's development, and children, families, schools, and communities reside in their culture, each system affected by the culture (Bronfenbrenner, 1979).

Each culture has values and beliefs about many things, including how it should take care of and socialize children (Wise & daSilva, 2007). Suppose, for example, that one of a society's main values was the protection of children. Suppose that democratic society also valued and believed in freedom of speech, which includes the freedom to make many types of movies, some of which contain violence. This free society would not ban unsavory movies. It would put its protection-of-children value into action in this case, however, by limiting access to such movies to older members of the society and by teaching parents how to minimize their children's exposure to the violence in movies.

> **Culture**
> Beliefs, values, and traditions of a group of people, transmitted to the next generation through language, interactions, and relationships

**Socialization**
Process through which children learn the values and traditions of their culture

**Socialization** refers to the process through which children acquire their culture and learn the values and habits that will help them adapt to it. Children acquire their culture's values as they observe and interact with other members of that culture, with adults and peers modeling and directly or indirectly teaching the culture's beliefs and values. Older members of the culture gradually lead a child to understand and accept culturally approved behaviors and values. A society believing that children should show respect for elders, for example, would transmit this belief to children in many ways, such as through words, interactions, books, and stories. Here is another example from Mr. Santini's primary classroom, this time with Caitlin, age 6½. The teacher helps Caitlin learn about the culture's value of treating other people with respect and *not* manipulating them.

> **EXAMPLE**  Caitlin wanted a turn with the headphones and the story on tape, but it was near the end of choice time and Jerry had already sat down and started to put on the only remaining headset. Caitlin sidled up to him, a sad, sad look on her face. "I really wanted to listen to the story, Jerry—really, really," she whined as she started to gulp. Jerry looked startled by all of her emotion and handed over the headphone. As she put it on, she smirked to the others at the table, "Pretty good, huh?"

The next example illustrates the teacher's socialization through guidance—his deliberate, firm, positive, and intentional teaching of the culture's belief in showing respect to others.

> **EXAMPLE**  Mr. Santini interrupted her, "Caitlin, put the headphone on the table and come with me." Away from the others, he said to her, "I watched you cry when you talked to Jerry and he let you take his place, which was a nice thing for him to do. However, I then saw you smile and make your eyes go like this (he demonstrated the smirk) and heard you say "Pretty good, huh?" That was a very mean thing to do to Jerry. We do *not* treat other people like that. It is not respectful and we've talked about showing respect to others. We have the headphones almost every day and you'll get a turn, but not today."

Teachers use guidance—that is, positive discipline—to teach the culture's beliefs directly, as Mr. Santini did with Caitlin, and indirectly. Their guidance is one part of the process of socialization.

## Discipline, Guidance, and Punishment

These three words are confused by many people. Do they all refer to the same thing? Can one be substituted for the other? One way to reduce the confusion is to define and or give the root for each word. Then, when talking about discipline, keep in mind the differences among the three words and be precise in your choice of words.

**Discipline**
Teaching or learning

The word **discipline** is derived from the Latin *disciplina*, "teaching, learning," and *discipulus*, "a pupil." You can see, then, that *discipline* refers to *teaching, and learning.* However, adults have different ideas from their culture and smaller social group within their culture about *the type* of discipline to use and what to teach with discipline. Some adults are not even aware that discipline teaches something. There are different forms of discipline.

Some forms of discipline are positive, such as those explained in this chapter. Limit setting, maintaining the limits, teaching appropriate behavior, encouraging children's efforts, for example, teach children how to control themselves. Positive strategies do not coddle children but they do help children learn from firm but kind adults that their culture expects them to be cooperative, kind, and assertive but not aggressive. Positive discipline teaches self-control and helps children develop self-esteem that is positive and realistic.

Other forms of discipline are, unfortunately, negative. Some forms of negative discipline are just plainly unhelpful and irritating to children, but they do not hurt the child's body. For example, nattering and nagging do not teach anything helpful to the child and are irritating at best. This does not make nattering and nagging acceptable. Adults who blather and nag often started out not knowing about discipline and then went sliding down the slippery slope of falling into nagging a child. The danger with these unhelpful, irritating, and negative strategies is what might well happen when the strategy does not work. The adult is then left with no other avenue in guidance and might then pump up the volume of the negative strategies into something more hurtful. They would benefit from learning more positive strategies and are generally willing to learn. Other forms of negative discipline are clearly hurtful to a child in some way. These forms of negative discipline fall into the punishment category, discussed below.

**Guidance** as a word has a number of different roots, but all refer to *pointing out*, *showing the way*, *leading*, or *directing*. Guidance is definitely a category of discipline and, from its meaning, you can infer that guidance has a positive connotation. An adult using guidance searches for and uses positive strategies so that he can indeed stop children from hurting others (a child who uses cyberbullying to hurt others, for example) if that is the case and so that he can teach, show the way, and lead when working with children, as Mr. Santini in the example above shows. Using guidance takes a lot of thought and energy and commitment.

**Punishment** is also a form of discipline. The word is derived from the Latin *punire* (Harper, 2013) and means rough treatment, to rebuke, impose a penalty on, or take vengeance on. Thus, if an adult uses punishment, she will reprimand or impose a penalty on a child, such as time-out or taking away recess. Some punishments involve taking something away, such as time-out or withholding food (a more extreme punishment). Some punishments are psychological, such as refusing to talk to a child, while others punishments are physical, such as hitting. Some punishments, as you know, can be very hurtful. Therefore, any supposed teaching through punishment is likely to be done in a punitive and often combative way.

**Focus of This Text**   This text advocates positive forms of discipline only. It presents guidance strategies that focus on teaching children what they need in order to develop self-respect and self-control along with respect for other people and animals. This text does *not* advocate punishment.

## :: GUIDING INFANTS AND TODDLERS

Early childhood professionals need to know about children's development as it changes over the early childhood years. Effective teachers understand that guidance looks different for a group of infants than it does in a first-grade classroom. However, an authoritative, positive approach to guidance is always based on respect for children whatever phase of early childhood they are in. The respect shows up as a teacher's willingness to learn about guidance, for example, for infants and toddlers and for

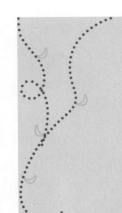

### Cultural Scripts and Guiding Children

#### Using the "Extra Talk" Cultural Script to Help Children Construct Understanding

"Extra talk" refers to going beyond giving directions to highlighting an experience and expanding or elaborating on it (Maschinot, 2008). One teacher might simply say, "No talking when we walk to the library," and not say why, even when the limit is first stated. Another teacher does some "extra talk" with a discussion the first time the class goes to the library. He asks "wh" questions: Which classrooms will we pass on the way? What would happen if we were noisy?

**Cultures Differ on the Need for "Extra Talk"**   Teachers follow their own culture's values and beliefs about extra talk, some having a script that does *not* favor extra talk, instead focusing on a "just the facts" approach. A teacher using this script would very likely give to-the-point directions, seeing no need for elaboration or discussing things with children. Other teachers have a cultural script favoring extra talk, evident, for instance, in asking "wh" questions or giving reasons for limits. Both kinds of teachers see their approach to extra talk as valid and might be puzzled about their colleague's different style.

**Children Benefit from Hearing Limits Stated as Well as from Extra Talk**   Any cultural script favoring clear limits for children guides that culture's adults in a direction of helping children learn that limits are a necessary part of life. Maschinot's (2008) review also identified clear benefits to children from a script favoring some extra talk. Elaboration of events through extra talk benefits a child's vocabulary size, her receptive language ability, and the child's amount of speaking. Children whose culture emphasizes extra talk are accustomed to hearing questions asked of them and are better able to answer questions, an important school-success skill. Children with better language skills are also better able to "use words" when angry or irritated.

**Build on the Foundation of Concern for Children's Learning**   How are the two cultural scripts similar? They both value and believe in setting limits for children and both value a direct and clear statement of a limit. The goal in both cultures is for children to do well in school and with friends. How are the two scripts different? One sticks to stating a limit while the other does extra talk, believing that the extra talk will help the child construct understanding. Teachers who reflect on the benefits to children from extra talk can easily learn this skill and then add it to their storehouse of teaching strategies. They will be building on the firm foundation of their culture's script about stating limits.

older early childhood children. Caring teachers realize that guidance teaches and they want to make their teaching through guidance as effective as possible.

## Guidance for Infants

Erikson's (1950) theory discusses an infant's need to develop a sense of trust. Maslow's (1954/1987) theory tells us that an infant's basic physiological needs for food, shelter, and clothing and for a feeling of safety and security must be met.

Piaget's (1970) theory informs us about the infant's sensory motor way of understanding the world. Infants are not capable of self-control because their cognitive, physical and motor, and linguistic abilities do not support self-control. Infants cannot be expected to understand the needs of other people. Infants are limited to crying as a means of communicating their needs. Infants are utterly dependent on adults to meet their needs. Therefore, our guidance for infants must take all of this into account.

The goal in guiding infants is to help them feel safe and secure and to develop a sense of trust. We do this by developing a loving, kind, gentle, and caring relationship with them and by meeting the baby's needs. We start out realizing that the infant cannot really do much for herself and we willingly and ungrudgingly give the baby what she needs. When she cries, we keep in mind that she is communicating with us: "I am hungry" or "I need you to hold me. I am lonely." We help parents understand infant development and why infants cry, and that they can learn to guess with some accuracy what the different cries mean.

Do infants need guidance? Infants do not need the same type of guidance that we use with older children. Infant "guidance" consists of understanding their developmental level, developing a positive and loving relationship with them, and then meeting their needs as quickly as possible. Infants fare much better as they develop when their infant needs have been met and when they have a good relationship with caregivers.

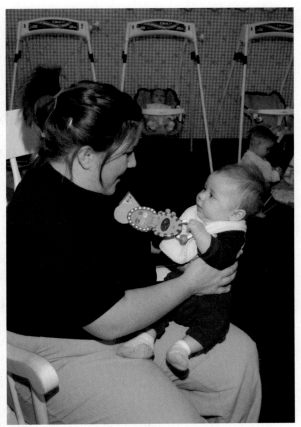

**Infants who have their needs met quickly, and who are held and comforted when they cry, develop a strong sense of security and well-being and actually may cry much less later on.**

## Guidance for Toddlers

Erikson's theory tells us that 18- to 36-month-old children, toddlers, need to develop a sense of autonomy. Maslow's theory tells us that toddlers continue to need the basic physiological necessities and to feel safe and secure, but that their social needs are also important. Toddlers are beginning to enjoy playing next to or with other children, and they like their teachers as well. They have a need for acceptance, affection, and friendship. Vygotsky's (1978) theory underscores the importance of adult–child, and in this case, adult–toddler talk. as a way of helping the toddler build understanding about himself and getting along with others.

Toddler language development enables the child to communicate his needs a bit more effectively. Toddlers are making strides in all other domains of development as well—physical, emotional, and social. However, they are still very young children and are not capable of self-control. They are still egocentric and not really capable of focusing on the needs of others without adult help.

The goal in guiding toddlers is to continue to help them feel safe and secure and to maintain their sense of trust. We do this as we did for them during infancy—by developing a good and caring relationship with them and by meeting their needs. We then build on this base by keeping toddler capabilities and limitations in mind.

Do toddlers need guidance? Yes, but we need to tailor our guidance to their abilities and limitations. First, show respect for a child's temperament, his way of approaching things. Some toddlers will stand back and observe before doing things, but others barrel right on in to an activity. Some toddlers have quiet responses to new activities while others have vigorous responses, whether positive or negative. Help toddlers build that sense of autonomy, that they can do things for and by themselves, when such independence is safe and possible. Help them build healthy self-esteem—that is, the idea that they are worthy of your time and are competent. Use modeling with toddlers, demonstrating how to perform an activity for them. For example, model or show them how to place the paintbrush back in the paint cup. Simple? Yes, but it is guidance for a toddler. Tell a toddler what you consider to be acceptable by labeling a behavior, "Put the book back on the shelf." Encourage toddler efforts, but avoid heaping on too much praise. Encouragement is a better approach: "Okay, you put the book on the shelf!"

## :: GUIDING 3- THROUGH 8-YEAR-OLDS

A child's development during preschool, kindergarten, and the primary grades calls for guidance appropriate for their new capabilities.

### Guidance for 3- Through 8-Year-Olds

Erikson's theory informs us that children this age need to develop a sense of initiative (3 to 5 years of age) and then a sense of industry (primary grades and into middle childhood). Maslow's theory tells us that children this age can now build on their base of feeling safe and secure and on having their basic needs met. They can now concentrate on meeting social needs for belonging, acceptance, affection, and friendships and on meeting esteem needs or the need to feel competent and worthy. Their development in language skills, cognition, emotional competence, and social skills advances makes meeting higher level needs possible.

Some of the goals in guiding preschool, kindergarten, and primary grade children include helping them to develop healthy self-control, to manage emotions well, to foster good social skills and relationships, and to foster healthy and positive self-esteem as well as respect for others.

**Guidance or discipline encounter**
Interaction between a child and an adult in which the adult helps the child to alter his behavior

### Guidance and Discipline Encounters: 3- Through 8-Year-Olds

A **guidance or discipline encounter** is an interaction between an adult and child, and often includes helping the child understand and alter her behavior in some way. For example, the adult can help a child stop doing something harmful or destructive, treat someone with respect, or take responsibility for cleaning up. Mr. Santini stopped Caitlin from treating someone disrespectfully. Discipline encounters occur frequently in early childhood, even in classrooms and homes where adults are warm and supportive. These interactions occur so that we can help children learn the culture's beliefs and values and to understand their obligation to respect the rights of others and to comply with legitimate authority (Baumrind, 1996). Each of the adults in the following examples faced typical discipline and guidance encounters.

**EXAMPLES**  Mrs. Johnson, the preschool teacher, watched as Calvin threw sand onto the tricycle path. She heard Nellie and Justine squabbling over the jar of paste at the collage table. She turned quickly when she heard someone banging on the hamster's house.

Several of the second graders in Mr. Santini's class left their backpacks on the floor instead of putting them in lockers.

The third-grade teacher noticed that two boys were bouncing their basketball on the wall right next to a classroom window.

Teachers deal with discipline encounters every day. Some include everyday concerns such as disturbing group time or not putting things away after using them. Others deal with serious issues, such as a child's endangering an animal or rude treatment of other children, as when Caitlin manipulated Jerry to get her turn with headphones. All, however, are discipline encounters.

Managing discipline encounters is a big part of a teacher or parent's role. First, adults have to help children learn to control their short-term behavior—for example, to stop banging on the hamster's house. Second, adults want to influence attitudes, values, and long-term behavior, which are part of the child's culture. They might want to help them understand, for example, about developing a humane attitude toward and kind, compassionate treatment of animals, a cultural value in many societies. They know, however, that they cannot fully determine attitudes or long-term behavior. They can only influence them.

**EXAMPLE**  Mrs. Johnson has faced several discipline encounters with Zeke over aggressive behavior. Because she is responsible for the safety of all the children in her class, she must help Zeke control his aggression for the short term—stop him from threatening or hurting other children and the classroom animals. She is also concerned about Zeke's long-term attitude and behavior. She knows that he will have an increasingly difficult time getting along with other children if he is aggressive, so she wants to help him willingly learn better social skills.

## Guidance Strategies

**Guidance strategies** refer to specific positive actions that adults use in managing guidance encounters. This chapter explains the major guidance strategies. Authoritative, trust-building adults use positive strategies, focusing on teaching and not on punishment. For example, they explain limits, redirect behavior, and teach behaviors that are more helpful. They give information that children need for learning and practicing behavior beneficial to the child.

**Guidance strategies**
The actions that we use in managing guidance encounters

**EXAMPLE**  The third grade teacher managed the discipline encounter with the boys who were bouncing the basketball on the wall near the window by reminding them firmly but kindly to throw the ball only at the basketball backboard. His action, restating a limit, was positive and gave information while maintaining a limit.

Other adults use negative strategies, focusing more on punishment. They might write the names of children on the board when children have violated a limit, which is public humiliation. Some adults isolate children, use physical punishment, are sarcastic, or even refuse to speak to a child (love withdrawal). Still other adults use strategies that are simply unhelpful, such as nattering and nagging. The idea of even thinking about negative or harsh discipline strategies repulses some early childhood teachers because they know that negative discipline harms children.

However, our goal is to guide all children effectively. "All" in this case means *all,* including children whose families use negative, harsh discipline. Our practices must be individually appropriate and we need to acknowledge that some children experience harsh discipline at home. This will help us understand their experience and then to use this information to develop appropriate guidance plans. All children benefit from positive discipline strategies, but children who have experienced harsh discipline at home need these strategies most desperately.

## :: FOCUS ON PRACTICE

This Focus on Practice activity is entitled *Characteristics of a Positive Guidance Strategy.* In completing this activity, you will notice that positive guidance strategies are beneficial for *all* children.

## :: *Question for Reflection*

## :: POSITIVE GUIDANCE STRATEGIES: DESCRIPTION AND EXPLANATION

This chapter describes and explains the major positive guidance strategies (Figure 5.1). Learning how to use these strategies makes it possible for you to meet the needs of individual children and choose the most effective strategy in a variety of discipline encounters. The appendix also lists these strategies and outlines how to use each. These strategies differ in how much direct teacher control is involved and how much direct teaching is involved, as shown in Figure 5.1 and in Table 5.1, which comes at the end of the chapter.

## :: FOCUS ON PRACTICE

This Focus on Practice activity is entitled *Identifying Positive Discipline Strategies.* Completing this activity will help you understand that effective teachers need to know about and know how to use a variety of positive guidance strategies.

Authoritative adults know how to use many positive guidance strategies. Some strategies, pink colored balloons, involve greater direct teacher control and teaching. Other strategies, yellow colored balloons, involve far less direct teacher control and teaching

**FIGURE 5.1**

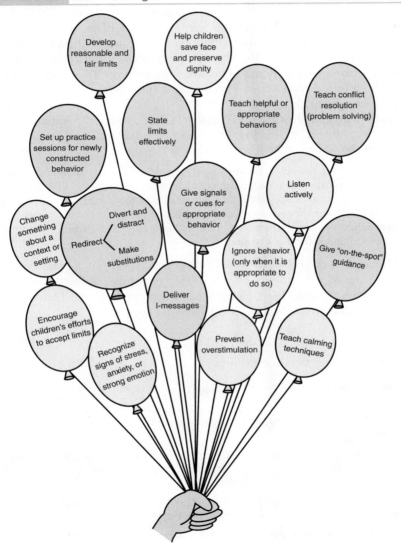

## Use Limits Effectively

Adults spend a lot of time helping children understand boundaries or limits. Doing this effectively involves four factors:

Developing reasonable limits that focus on important things

Stating limits effectively

Helping children accept limits

Communicating limits to others and reviewing limits periodically

**Develop Reasonable Limits That Focus on Important Things**   Adults influence children by stating their expectations for desired behavior and helping children understand that there are boundaries, or **limits**, on behavior. Authoritative caregivers understand the importance of proper boundaries in relationships in general, and appropriate limits in an adult–child relationship in particular. They figure out and clearly communicate limits that will be most helpful in encouraging children to behave appropriately. They understand what a good limit is and what benefits appropriate limits have for children (Marion, Swim, & Jenner, 2000).

Authoritative adults work with children in developing some, but not all, limits. For example, Mr. Santini, the first-grade teacher, led a discussion about classroom limits at the beginning of the school year.

> **EXAMPLE**   Mr. Santini started by first stating, "The most important rule in our classroom is that we treat each other and our animals with respect," as he wrote on a large sheet of paper. Mr. Santini then described what that might mean and elicited the children's contributions—for example, "The gerbils get scared when they hear loud noises. What would be a good rule about noise around the gerbils?" He printed limits and posted them as a reminder.

Mr. Santini's class is much more likely to take ownership of limits because the children have helped to develop them. Highly responsive, authoritative adults set and maintain reasonable, fair, developmentally appropriate limits. Their limits focus on important, not trivial, factors, as explained in Figure 5.2.

**Limits**
Boundaries; in guiding children, refers to boundaries on children's behavior communicated by a teacher or parent

---

**FIGURE 5.2**   Classroom limits: Focus on significant things

| Reasonable Limits | How Limits Can Help | Example |
|---|---|---|
| Help children learn self-control | Limits clearly communicate appropriate behavior and reasons for the behavior | "Scoot back to your spot on the carpet, Jack. Vinnie can't see if you sit in front of him." |
| Protect physical health | Limits specify procedures that keep disease from spreading | Limits about thorough hand washing or sanitizing toys, using tissues, proper toileting and diapering routines |
| Ensure physical safety | Limits govern safe use of equipment and physical space | "You can pour and dump sand in the sand box, but not on the tricycle path." |
| Ensure psychological safety | Good rules let everyone know that they are safe | Teacher to second-grade child, "You are angry, and that's ok, but I want you to tell Ryan that you are upset. Use words to tell him that you want your book back." |
| Help make the classroom a caring community | Focuses on respect for others and on humane treatment of animals | "Hold the kitten gently, like this." (teacher demonstrates). "Mitchell's name is on the list before your name. He goes first." |

**State Limits Effectively**   Authoritative caregivers have a clear, direct, and validating communication style. If a goal in guiding children is to help children, we can best help them understand necessary limits by stating these limits effectively.

**Speak Naturally, but Speak Slowly Enough That the Child Hears Everything You Say; Use Concrete Words and Short Sentences When Stating Limits**   "Put your puzzle in this first slot of the puzzle rack." This limit tells a child exactly where the finished puzzle goes. It is more effective than saying, "Put it over there." Avoid using abstract words or phrases such as "in a little while," "be a good boy," or "knock it off."

Good limits, such as telling the children, "Be gentle when petting," teach them about respectful treatment of other people and animals.

**Tell a Child Exactly What to Do Rather Than What Not to Do, and Be as Positive as Possible**   It is more helpful to say, "Use this tissue to clean your nose" rather than "Don't pick your nose!" We do need to be clear about what children may not do, but it is most helpful to focus on what we want children to do.

**Use Suggestions Whenever Possible**   Suggestions are persuasive statements. Suggestions describe an acceptable behavior to a child in an appealing way; they do not order a child to do anything. Children cooperate more frequently and willingly when adults use suggestions (Baumrind, 1996). Ty's teacher makes a suggestion in the next example.

> **EXAMPLE**   Ty and Daniela's teacher said to the two 4-year-olds, "Hmm, two children and one rocking chair (adult-size chair). I wonder if you could figure out how two children could sit on that chair at the same time."

Use direct, self-responsible statements when you think it is necessary to make a reasonable request.

Authoritative adults do occasionally have to state a very direct request, but their style is highly responsive.

> **EXAMPLE**   Mrs. Johnson had given an appropriate warning about cleanup on the playground, but Jackie was still zipping around on his tricycle. "Whoa, there!" said the teacher as she signaled Jackie to stop. "I gave the signal for cleanup and now I want you to park the tricycle." Then she put her hand on the handlebars, pointed to the row of tricycles parked against the shed, turned Jackie in that direction, and said, "There's a spot for your tricycle right next to the yellow tricycle. Let's go and fit it in that space."

This limit is stated directly, firmly, and kindly. This authoritative teacher relies on persuasion, not force. She has acted self-responsibly, and the child is very likely to cooperate. Consider how a different, more authoritarian teacher would have stated the limit—by ordering, "Jackie, put that tricycle away now!" Ordering others around is a power-based way of speaking and it stirs up anger and resistance, not cooperation (Baumrind, 1996).

**Give Choices Whenever Possible**   Children face so many important choices as they grow up. One of our goals, then, is to help children learn to make wise choices, a skill that we have to teach. A good way to start is by offering manageable choices to children.

> **EXAMPLE**   Mrs. Johnson first used a when-then statement to communicate clearly that the limit was that children had to wear paint aprons when painting: "When you put on your paint apron, then you may paint at the easel."
>
> Then she gave Ralph a choice: "Do you want to wear the green or yellow paint apron?" Alternatively, she could have given a different choice: "Would you like to snap the Velcro pieces together yourself or do you want me to help you?"

**Avoid Giving a Choice When the Child Really Has No Choice**   For example, avoid saying "Do you want to wear a paint apron?" or "Do you want to go home now?" A logical response from a child to these questions is a yes or no answer because this is a closed type of question. It is unfair and confusing to give a child a choice when she really does not have one. You also set yourself up for an argument with a child who says no to such questions because then you must backtrack and tell her why she really has no choice.

**Issue Only a Few Suggestions at a Time; Avoid Giving a Chain of Limits**
It is difficult for children to keep a string of limits or suggestions in their minds. If a child cannot remember part of your string of limits, chances are good that he will not comply with all of the limits. Children comply more easily with limits when we state them in small chunks, small enough for children to remember. For example, "Use the clothespins to hang your painting." "Good, it will dry nicely. Now, wash the part of the table where you worked with this sponge." "Okay, nice and clean. Now, wash your hands and hang up your apron."

**Avoid Rushing**   Allow time for the child to process information and complete a task before issuing another suggestion (Schaffer & Crook, 1980); repeat a limit if necessary, but do it effectively.

Suppose that a child ignores your request. Frustrating? Yes, but do not take it personally. Avoid getting angry and remember that your job is to help this child accept a simple limit. You will be most effective if you manage your emotions well, repeat the limit calmly and with goodwill, call the child's name again, pick up the item, and hand the item to the child. Repeat the request. Avoid simply restating the limit in a snappish, peeved way because your irritation will show and will likely bring out anger and stubbornness from the child; then you will have a full-blown argument on your hands. See Figure 5.3 for guidelines on setting limits.

**Help Children Accept Limits**   Authoritative caregivers and teachers help children willingly accept good limits. They do several things to set the stage so that children will accept legitimate boundaries on behavior. Here are some practical ways to get you started on helping children willingly accept limits.

Researchers demonstrated many years ago how important it is to set the stage so that children can accept a limit (Schaffer & Crook, 1980; Stayton, Hogan, & Ainsworth,

| FIGURE 5.3 | Guidelines for limit setting |
| --- | --- |
| **Things to Remember about Stating Limits** | **Avoid These Behaviors When Stating Limits** |
| • Involve children in developing some limits in a classroom or other setting.<br>• Tune in, help children focus on the task, and give good cues.<br>• Speak naturally but slowly enough that a child hears the limit clearly.<br>• Use concrete words and short sentences.<br>• Use natural, normal sentences—for example, "It's time to put away the teacups."<br>• Tell a child exactly what to do—for example, "Take small bites of your bread."<br>• Be as positive as possible and give choices when appropriate.<br>• Give short, clear, fair reasons for limits.<br>• Issue only one or two suggestions at a time.<br>• Give a child enough time to carry out the limit or to complete something else before she carries out the limit.<br>• Restate limits appropriately. Restate limits when it is necessary to do so. | • Avoid giving choices when children really do not have a choice—for example, "Do you want to go to the library?" when the whole class goes to the library.<br>• Avoid giving a chain of limits.<br>• Avoid using "cute" reasons; for example, avoid saying things such as "I think that the teacups want to be put away now." This makes a teacher sound silly.<br>• Avoid telling children only what not to do—for example, "Don't take such big bites of your bread!"<br>• Avoid vague limits—for example, "I'm not sure that you should be doing that."<br>• Avoid stating arbitrary or trivial limits.<br>• Avoid arguing or playing the "why game" about limits.<br>• Avoid complex or excessive reasoning about limits. |

1971). Adults who effectively help children accept limits believe that children are naturally compliant (Haswell, Hock, & Wenar, 1981). Authoritative adults tune in to a situation, help children focus on the task at hand, and give good cues.

*Tune in to the Context.*   Effective teachers pay attention to the context or setting. They focus on what children are doing and what is going on in the setting before telling or asking a child to do something. Here are some specific and practical things to remember about tuning in to the context.

**Observe What the Child Is Doing Before Stating a Limit**   Be responsive and take into account what a child is doing because her activity is important to her. If Moua is putting together her favorite puzzle when the cleanup signal is first given, she will very likely try to finish her work before putting materials away.

**Give Children a Reasonable Amount of Time to Complete Their Work**
Consider cleanup in a classroom. Before officially beginning to clean up, announce cleanup quietly to the whole group, to small groups, or to individuals, and then allow the children a bit of time to finish their work.

*Decrease Distance Between You and a Child.*   Avoid calling out limits from across the room. Decrease horizontal distance by walking toward a child. Decrease vertical distance by bending or stooping so that you can talk directly to a child.

***Get a Child's Attention Politely.*** Touch a child on the arm or say her name quietly. Using nonthreatening verbal or nonverbal cues and appropriate physical contact is essential with toddlers and is highly recommended with preschoolers, especially those who have not learned to live with reasonable boundaries and limits at home.

***Help Children Focus on the Task at Hand and Give Cues.*** Direct a child's visual attention to a specific object or task. "Here's one of the puzzles that you worked on, Moua," you say as you show her the puzzle you are holding and then point to the puzzle table. This is orientation compliance; its purpose is to orient the child properly (direct her attention toward something) before stating a limit or making a request.

***Have the Child Make Contact with a Specific Object.*** For example, place a puzzle with which a child has worked in her hands and say, "Please hold the puzzle while we walk over to the puzzle table." This is contact compliance; its purpose is to help the child tune in to the task at hand before she is asked to do anything specific.

***Make Your Specific Request (Ask for Task Compliance).*** A child is much more likely to comply with your request when you have properly oriented her. It is much easier for a child to accept the cleanup limit when she is at the puzzle table holding the puzzle rather than when she is sitting in another area listening to a story when you announce cleanup.

***Give Reasons for Rules and Limits.*** Children accept limits much more readily when they understand the rationale behind them (Baumrind, 1996). Three practical suggestions will help you use reasons well.

- Give short, simple, concrete reasons along with a limit. An example is "Put the lid on the paint cups" (the limit). "It will keep the paint fresh" (the reason).
- Decide when to state the reasons. One choice is to state the rationale *before you give the limit*: "We need tables cleared of toys before we can have guided reading" (the reason). "Put each puzzle back in the rack" (the limit). Some children tend to argue less about a rule if they hear the reason first and the limit second. Another choice is to state the reason *after you state the limit*. "I want you to put the puzzles away" (the limit). "Then the table is clear for snacks" (the reason). A third option is to state the rationale *after the child complies with the limit*: "The puzzle table is clear! Now we can do guided reading there."
- Decide whether you need to repeat the rationale if you restate the limit. Repeating the rationale is a good idea when you want to emphasize the reason for the limit, perhaps when children are first learning a limit.

  > EXAMPLE  Mrs. Johnson said, before going out to the playground on the second day of school, "Tell me our safety rule about how many children are allowed on the sliding board at one time. . . . That's right, only one at a time so that nobody gets hurt." She also showed a picture of one child on the slide.

Be aware, however, that some children might try to distract you from carrying through with a limit by playing the why game, repeatedly asking, "Why?" Ignoring their "Why?" is one of the most helpful things you can do for them. You can also say, "I think you're having fun asking me why and I'll tell you why one more time and then the game is over" (Seefeldt, 1993).

## :: FOCUS ON PRACTICE

This Focus on Practice activity is entitled *Was this Limit Communicated Clearly?* Note that it is imperative to use this strategy in matters of health and safety.

**Communicate Limits to Others; Review Limits Periodically**   It is important that everyone who works in your classroom, however short the time, understands and uses the same limits. This includes but is not limited to parents, other volunteers, specialists, the principal or director, children from upper grades, college students in a practicum, and persons invited to do a presentation. Some children are confused when adults in the same classroom use different limits.

> **EXAMPLE**   Mrs. Johnson forgot to tell a new volunteer about some of the classroom rules. The volunteer told two boys that they could just leave the blocks out and that she would put them away. The classroom rule is that children put away things that they have used.

Communicate classroom limits by posting them conspicuously. Point out the list when a visitor first comes to the classroom. Or have a number of copies of a handout titled "Classroom Limits" ready to give to anyone who works in the room. Talk with all classroom workers and visitors about how important it is for all adults to use the same limits. Demonstrate limits when necessary, as with proper hand washing.

You can make classroom limits even more effective by telling parents about the limits. First, this highlights limits for parents and reassures them. Second, communicating effectively with parents tells them that you think they are worthy of your time. This will help you develop a good working partnership with parents. Third, talking with parents about limits might help some parents ask questions about limit setting at home.

Parents like the topic of how to set and maintain reasonable limits when offered as a parent education topic. Communicate information to parents about setting limits in a variety of ways: with handouts, newsletter write-ups, appropriate articles, formal parent meetings, and videos/DVDs either used in meetings or borrowed by parents. See the Working with Families feature and the list of websites at the end of this chapter. You will find many handouts and other free or inexpensive material about guidance and discipline to use with parents.

## :: *Question for Reflection*

## COMMUNICATING WITH FAMILIES ABOUT GUIDANCE STRATEGIES

Teachers must clearly communicate school or center policies, including discipline policies and strategies, to parents. You will have to think through this issue and be able to articulate the policy without insulting parents who believe in using physical punishment such as hitting (spanking) (Socolar,1995). Your goal is to establish rapport and then maintain a good relationship with parents so that you can work effectively with each family and child. You can take several steps to explain school policies about positive discipline strategies to parents.

### Write It Down!

Let parents know about the child guidance policies of the school. Use the NAEYC Code of Ethical Conduct and Statement of Commitment (National Association for the Education of Young Children, 2011) as a base and draw your own center or school policies from that. Incorporate your guidance policies in a policy manual written just for parents. Then it will be clear to parents that the school has a guidance policy, that it is based on a professional group's guidelines, and that it is positive in nature.

### Focus on Teaching

If you plan to do home visits, you can, as a small part of your visit, talk with each parent about a few of the specific positive strategies that you use. Does your school have a newsletter? Write a brief article explaining a specific discipline strategy. Does your school have a parent's bulletin board? Use this space to display information about a specific strategy. Are you having a group parent meeting? Explain the guidance policy along with all the other policies and highlight one or two positive discipline strategies.

For example, explain how you set limits and how you restate them if a child does not seem to listen the first time. Many parents react almost reflexively with spanking when their children do not obey immediately. Explain how you use redirection.

### Do a Needs Assessment

Effective teachers work as partners with parents. Make a list of the many positive discipline strategies that your school uses and ask parents to check off the ones about which they would like to know more. Work with parents by giving them information on the strategies that they have identified as areas of need. Do this through an early childhood family education program that includes one-on-one interaction with parents as well as more formal methods such as group meetings.

### Listen with Respect, Avoid Being Judgmental, and Don't Argue

Some parents ask questions that simply call for clarification of a specific policy. A few parents challenge a policy. Some might even want to engage you in a protracted debate about controversial discipline strategies such as spanking that they see as acceptable. In all cases, you help parents best by remaining calm and professional; do not argue with a parent.

Suppose a father says, "I was spanked when I was a kid and it never hurt me!" You can neutralize such a statement and avoid arguing by not taking his statement as an attack and by saying respectfully, "Yes, lots of people were spanked and believe in spanking. Our school does not want to force ideas on anybody. But we do want parents to know that we guide children with positive discipline strategies."

## Teach Helpful or Appropriate Behavior

Help children build self-control by teaching them about helpful behaviors. Children must learn so many behaviors that they do not know automatically. Here are just a few examples:

How to ask for something.

How to listen when others talk, and not interrupt them.

How to join a play or work group.

How to put things away when children complete a project.

How to participate in a group, such as where and how to sit, how to listen, how to offer an idea, and how to get the teacher's attention.

Mealtime manners, such as passing items and waiting their turn.

Plan lessons to teach the skills. Choose from your large collection of teaching strategies and incorporate them into your regular teaching plan. Teach individuals, small groups, or large groups. Use songs, stories, finger plays, flannel boards, demonstrations, films, DVDs, guest speakers, or other methods.

**EXAMPLE**    At the beginning of the school year, Mrs. Johnson observed that several of the children did not understand the concept of passing items. For instance, the children seemed confused about how to pass baskets with snacks, and they did not know how to pass pitchers with juice or milk. Here are two examples of the lessons through which she taught the children how to pass things.

- Lesson 1: Large group. Mrs. Johnson held a basket filled with colored squares of paper. She said, "I'm going to take one of these squares from the basket. Then I'm going to pass the basket to Nellie" (who sat next to the teacher). Nellie takes the basket. "Now, Nellie will take one square out of the basket and pass the basket to Ralph. Ralph takes a square and passes it to Justine." After all the children had a chance to pass the basket, Mrs. Johnson showed them a basket used at snack time. She said, "We will pass baskets like this one when we eat our snack."
- Lesson 2: Snack time. "Here's the basket that we will pass! I'll start today." Mrs. Johnson softly chanted as she took a cracker and then passed the basket:

  "Mrs. Johnson takes a cracker and passes them to Jerry.
  Jerry takes a cracker and passes them to Chelsea.
  Chelsea takes a cracker and passes them to Ralph."

They continued singing until every child had passed the basket.

Determine which skill you need to teach by observing. Consider using checklists, anecdotal records, or rating scales to assess the needs and abilities of children in your class as described in Chapter 6 of this text. Then, observe again to assess a child's understanding after you have taught a skill. Mrs. Johnson noted that Calvin had learned how to pass the basket from the demonstration.

## Set Up Practice Sessions and Give "On-the-Spot" Guidance

Give children a chance to practice what you show or tell them, as Mrs. Johnson did when they practiced passing baskets. Mr. Santini had observed that Willis did not wait his turn for the computer stations in the K–2 classroom. Consequently, he had taught Willis the steps in getting a turn (putting his name on the list if necessary, checking the list and waiting, and working somewhere else until his name was next). He knows how important it is for children to practice what they have learned, and so he planned a simple practice session for Willis about waiting for a turn.

Mr. Santini started the practice session (Mr. Santini worked with Willis individually) by saying, "Let's practice waiting for a turn at the computer, Willis. You already know the main things that you have to do. Please tell me the first thing."

| | |
|---|---|
| *Willis:* | I have to put my name on the list. |
| *Mr. Santini:* | That's right. Write your name now on this list. (Willis prints his name at the bottom of the list.) Good. Now, check to see how many children are ahead of you. |
| *Willis:* | Sandi and Michael. That's two. |
| *Mr. Santini:* | Right again! You won't have to wait very long at all. What would you like to do while you wait? |
| *Willis:* | Work on my math. |

**On-the-spot guidance**
Helping children through direct coaching in daily guidance situations

The next day, Mr. Santini introduced a new math game to use at the computer, and Willis was eager to get a turn. Mr. Santini gave **on-the-spot guidance** to Willis. He quietly reminded him about how to get a turn and used this real-life situation as another practice session. Willis did very well. He had learned the steps, had practiced them with the teacher individually, and finally had practiced them in the classroom.

## Give Signals or Cues for Appropriate Behavior

**Cues**
Verbal, nonverbal, pictorial, or written reminders about limits

**Cues** are hints or suggestions that remind children about a limit in a low-key way. The signals or cues can be verbal, nonverbal, pictorial, or written (for older children). Good cues are developmentally appropriate; they are age and individually appropriate for a variety of children—typically developing children, children with disabilities, and children who are learning English. Recent research with a child with autism used pictorial cues or symbols to help him understand words that a teacher used in describing an action. Supporting this child with visual cues resulted in fewer behavior problems (Mirenda, MacGregor, & Kelly-Keough, 2002).

**EXAMPLE**    At the end of group time, Mrs. Johnson verbally reminded the children to wash their hands for snack time. The group sang their "action" song, and then she sent them to the bathroom (the song was the cue or reminder).

**EXAMPLE**    Shortly after the children went to the bathroom, she showed one of the pictures of a child washing her hands to the group. "Where can we hang this picture so that it reminds us to always wash our hands after going into the bathroom?" (The picture is the cue.)

Cues are helpful to all children, but some children might benefit from them even more. For example, many children in classrooms are learning English, and using cues is one of the research-based methods found to help them in literacy instruction (Linan-Thompson & Vaughn, 2007). Visual types of support are also useful in guiding English language learners. Picture cues can help children with limited English understand limits, schedules, and transitions.

**EXAMPLE**    At transition from work and play time to large group, for instance, Mr. Santini showed each child two picture cues, one of a child playing and the other of the child in a circle with other children. At the same time, the teacher described moving from play to large group. (The pictures are cues.)

Children with an autism spectrum disorder (ASD) tend to have well-developed visual skills, while their skills related to hearing are less well developed. A problem arises for children with ASD when we guide them. We tend to set limits and give other guidance suggestions with words, which often makes it difficult for a child with ASD to remember and comply. Supporting this child with a **visual support**, such as pictures, in the environment keeps the limit and/or guidance fresh for the child long after you have stated a limit or suggestion with words (Illinois State University, n.d.).

**Visual support**
Pictures, photographs, or drawings intended to help children remember the messages implied in the image

## Encourage Children's Efforts to Accept Limits

Children need more than limits—they also need encouragement for their efforts to accept limits and to behave in a prosocial way, cooperatively or helpfully. There are many ways to encourage children's efforts.

Promote new behavior that is "self-encouraging." Think of ways to set things up so that a child will find a new behavior so attractive that he will eagerly comply.

**EXAMPLE**   Larry did not wash his paint smock when he painted. Mrs. Johnson made a new job for the job chart and assigned that job to Larry for 2 days. The new job entailed being the person who ran the paint smock wash. This person wore a special hat and smock, was in charge of checking all the smocks to make sure they were clean, and was responsible for the new sponge and bucket.

Observe children to determine whether they have learned what they need to learn and whether they have complied with a limit. For example, Mr. Santini wanted all children to use a tissue when sneezing and wiping their noses. He taught them how to use the tissue with a demonstration. Then he used a simple checklist to document learning.

In another example, the principal visited Mr. Santini's room to read a story for the class. The children had just cleaned up after their morning work period and they sat on the floor for the story time. Mr. Santini introduced the principal. He showed a large photo of the entire class with the label "We are good helpers!" He said to the principal, "We have lots of children in this class and we are all good helpers." He then noted how every child had helped during cleanup.

## Change Something about a Context or Setting

Behavior communicates. Behavior does not occur in a vacuum—it happens in a context or setting. The context of a behavior has an effect on that behavior. With these statements in mind, consider reframing or rethinking the concept of a discipline encounter by asking a question. "What can I do about this context, this situation, that will help this child be safe or help her choose a different behavior more helpful to her?" For example, "Do I want to keep telling these two children to stop arguing over the blocks, or can I change something to help them accept the idea of cooperating?"

Three major ways to change a situation to be helpful and to prevent or stop potentially dangerous or inappropriate behavior include changing the physical environment or the time schedule, increasing options, and decreasing options.

### Change the Physical Environment and/or Time Schedule If Necessary
You can easily change something about a situation by evaluating how you have structured the physical environment. You can then decide that a slight change might be very

helpful to children. Do children run, not walk, from one center to another? Then check for zoom areas, which are tunnel-like spaces that invite running. If any exist in the classroom layout, then rearrange the room to eliminate the zoom area(s). You can also adjust the schedule to help children, as Mr. Santini has done for his large-group time.

> **EXAMPLE** Mr. Santini's student teacher found that his opening large-group time was almost unpleasant because of all the talking and squirming. Mr. Santini, during the evaluation of group time, asked the student teacher to reflect on how long the lesson had been. The student teacher discovered that the group time was too long and made a simple adjustment. The adjusted schedule resulted in a much shorter, more productive, and more peaceful group activity.

**Increase Options Available to a Child** Authoritative adults closely supervise and monitor activities. They recognize when children need more options from which to choose. They realize that children might be stuck on a nonproductive course of action and require additional information or choices. Here are three practical ways to increase options for children.

***Prevent Predictable Problems.*** Prevent problems whenever possible. Young children have a difficult time controlling themselves. Observe the group for signs that adult intervention is necessary. One way to do this is to identify the times in a group's schedule when things could go wrong and prevent these problems. Transitions are troublesome and stress inducing for children. Prevent problems by having as few transitions as possible in the schedule. Observe and identify the times when transitions are difficult for children, for example, nap to waking activities or from large group to outside play. Reflect on the transitions and alter them to make them more appropriate.

> **EXAMPLE** Transition from nap to waking activities: Some children awoke from nap before the others but still had to be quiet. Instead of just asking them to sit quietly, the teacher prevented the potential problem by using toys and books for quiet play. This was a special group of items used only after nap and before everyone was awake.

> **EXAMPLE** Transition from large group to outside play: The teacher cut out and laminated simple squares of different-colored construction paper and kept them in a basket in the large-group area. At the end of the activity, each child took one square from the basket. She then sent the five children with blue squares to put on coats, and continued with the other colors in turn. This simple method helped children focus on the transition and seemed to decrease anxiety about it.

***Introduce New Ideas to Children Engaged in an Activity.*** Our goal is to let play sessions unfold and not to dominate play. Occasionally, however, children benefit from getting ideas from adults. Offer a new idea when it would extend the play or help children get beyond an argument. Sometimes children will use the idea, and sometimes they will not.

> **EXAMPLE** Mrs. Johnson noticed that some of the children had worked cooperatively on building a train from large blocks for about 10 minutes. When she heard an argument about who would be the driver of the train, she said, "Here is that book about trains. Look here [points to passengers]. We do need a conductor but we need passengers, too. The conductor helps passengers find a seat on the train." Ralph immediately shouted, "I want to be the passenger!"

***Introduce New Materials into an Activity.*** Assess the situation and decide whether new materials would be helpful. Then decide how to present the new materials to the children. One way is to add the new item, simply and quietly, without comment. Another way is to introduce the new materials in work sessions as needed.

> **EXAMPLE** Mrs. Johnson gave red or blue tickets and small suitcases to the train "passengers." She also gave the conductor a hat and a hole puncher with which to punch one hole in each passenger's ticket. Another time, she brought out plastic farm animals and placed them near the children working on building a farm. A final example took place at the play dough table. After children had worked with dough for one day, she brought out new rolling pins, taught them the term *rolling pin*, and asked them how they might use the new item with play dough.

**Decrease Options Available to a Child** Occasionally, the problem is not that children need new ideas or materials, but that they need fewer options. Too many choices can easily overwhelm children, especially impulsive children. Guide children effectively by limiting choices or changing activities.

***Limit Choices.*** Making wise choices is a skill that develops over time. Helpful adults teach young children how to make choices from only a few alternatives.

> **EXAMPLE** Mr. Santini knew that Pae (pronounced "pay") had great difficulty zeroing in on one activity. He helped Pae focus attention and he limited his choices by asking, "You said yesterday that you wanted to write a story about your kitten and you wanted to make labels for your leaf collection. Which of those two things would you like to do first today?"

***Change Activities.*** Authoritative caregivers understand that a variety of things might affect children's attention or behavior. They are skillful enough and have enough confidence in their ability to modify plans or to abandon a plan if necessary.

> **EXAMPLE** Mr. Santini had just gathered the entire group for story time when the roaring noise started. The earthmovers had come onto the school grounds to start digging the swimming pool. "There goes group time," he thought, but he remained calm. To the children he said, "Let's walk outside and stand out of the way so that we can watch for a little while. Then I'm going to tell you the story of an earthmover!'"

# Ignore Behavior (Only When It Is Appropriate to Do So)

Teachers **ignore behavior** when they stop paying attention to a specific action. You can safely ignore some behaviors but not others. The ignore strategy is appropriate for the following categories of behavior:

> Whining or arguing about limits.
>
> Any other effort to distract you from following through on a limit.
>
> Efforts to pull you into an argument.
>
> A child's efforts to make you angry.

It is safe to ignore these behaviors because they are not hurtful, not destructive, not disrespectful, and not dangerous. In fact, it is a good idea to ignore them because

**Ignore behavior (only when appropriate to do so)**
Stop paying attention to a specific action

paying attention makes them worse. Giving attention to whining, for example, rewards the child's whining. The following guidelines will help you use the ignore strategy effectively.

**Guidelines for using the ignore strategy**

- Tell the child that you will ignore a specific, targeted behavior. Suppose that you decide to use the ignore strategy when a child argues about limits. You know that telling the child about the strategy will make things easier. Therefore, you politely but clearly tell the child that you will stop paying attention to her when she argues about something that she has to do: "Nellie, I've made a mistake and paid attention to you when you argue about some things, such as cleaning up. From now on, I will not pay attention when you argue with me. I won't look at you, and I won't talk to you when you argue about cleanup."

- Take enough time to use the ignore strategy effectively. Adults usually give a lot of attention when they need to ignore. Paying attention has caused problems for the child. When an adult decides to use the ignore strategy, a child who has received so much attention for unhelpful behavior, such as arguing or whining, will be surprised and is likely to increase the intensity of the arguing or whining. Essentially, her behavior says, "Look here, you've always argued back when I argue. Now you're ignoring me. Looks to me like I have to argue more loudly. Maybe that will get your attention!"

   Consider how you are now ignoring Nellie's arguing. She will not stop after you first ignore her, even though you have politely alerted her. Like most children whose irritating behavior is ignored for the first time, she will try even harder to recapture your attention by arguing even more insistently. You should expect and be prepared for the "bigger and better" arguments. You will have to carry out the procedure at least one or two more times before Nellie finally realizes that you have resolved to stop paying attention to her arguing.

- Decide to ignore the behavior completely. Give *no* attention. This is difficult because the adult has decided to change her own customary behavior. To refrain from paying attention to and encouraging the arguing, the teacher wrote the following list of prompts:

   "Resist the urge to mutter to myself under my breath."

   "Resist the urge to make eye contact."

   "Resist the urge to communicate with this child, either with words or gestures."

- Teach and encourage more acceptable behavior. Go beyond ignoring a behavior to teaching children some other, more appropriate behavior. Mr. Santini ignored Vinnie's whining but also remembered to teach Vinnie how to ask for things in a normal voice. Mr. Santini modeled the "normal" voice.

**Do Not Ignore These Behaviors**  Figure 5.4 explains the types of behaviors that we should *not* ignore because they are clearly dangerous, destructive, or hurtful. Ignoring some behaviors endangers people or animals. This figure also illustrates an appropriate teacher response to the behavior.

**FIGURE 5.4**    **Do not ignore these behaviors**

| Do *Not* Ignore These Types of Behaviors | Example and/or Comment | Teacher Responds |
|---|---|---|
| Treats someone rudely; embarrasses someone; is intrusive and/or disrespectful; causes an undue disruption | Tyler said to a volunteer, "You're not the teacher. I don't have to listen to you."<br><br>Teachers can help children learn civility. Teach specific skills and state expectations. | "It is disrespectful to speak to a helper like that. It was his job to remind you about lunch." |
| Endangers anyone, including herself, as well as animals | Jack poked a stick into the rabbit's house.<br><br>Ignoring dangerous behavior gives approval for it; increases it. | "In this classroom, we take care of the rabbits. They were afraid when you poked the stick into their house." |
| Damages or destroys property or acts in a way that *could* damage something | Lori jams her binder into the storage shelf forcefully because the shelf is full.<br><br>Ignoring it conveys approval. | "That will damage binders. What can you do to store your binder without damaging it or the others?" |

## Redirect Children's Behavior—Divert and Distract the Youngest Children

**Diverting and distracting** is a form of redirection in which an adult immediately does something to distract a child from the forbidden or dangerous activity. The adult then gets the very young child involved in a different activity.

**Diverting and distracting**
Useful with toddlers; redirection in which an adult sidetracks a toddler from one activity and steers him to a safer activity

Authoritative, responsible caregivers perform most of an infant's or young toddler's ego functions. For example, they remember things for the child and keep him safe because an infant's or young toddler's concept of danger is just emerging. Authoritative adults accept responsibility for stopping very young children from doing something by setting limits that discourage certain behaviors, but they do so in a helpful way.

Diverting or distracting the youngest children accomplishes both of these tasks. An adult can be most helpful by immediately doing something to distract the child from the forbidden activity and steering her toward a different activity.

> **EXAMPLE**    Mary, 16 months old, walked over to the bowl of cat food, picked up a piece, and started to place it in her mouth. Her father said, "Put the cat food back in the bowl, Mary" (a short, clear, specific limit). Then he picked up Mary and said, "You know, I think it's time for us to take a walk!"

## Redirect Children's Behavior—Make Substitutions with Older Children

**Substitution** is a form of redirection in which an adult shows a child how to perform an activity or type of activity in a more acceptable and perhaps safer way. Substitution is an excellent strategy to use with children who are at least older toddlers or young preschoolers. Substitution is a good strategy to use with older children because it acknowledges the child's desire to plan and engage in a specific activity. The adult

**Substitution**
Useful with preschoolers and older children; redirection in which a child learns how to do an activity in a safer, more acceptable way

**Active listening**
An adult listens reflectively and carefully to a child; does not offer solutions and does not criticize; useful when the problem belongs to the child

**The teacher used diversion and distraction when she scooped up Sam to get him away from the outside door. "Look, Sam, I have a toy!"**

**Redirect by using substitution. "You can play in the water in the water table, Jack, instead of at the sink. Other children need to use the sink."**

must accept the responsibility of developing safe substitutions to demonstrate the first step of problem solving.

**EXAMPLE** Mrs. Johnson saw Justine aim her paintbrush at Calvin's picture. The teacher stepped in and said, "Paint on one of these pieces of paper, Justine, not on Calvin's. Which size do you want to use?" She then led Justine to the other side of the easel.

Children may test adult commitment to substitution by trying the inappropriate activity again—later in the day, the next day, or with a different person.

**EXAMPLE** Justine swung around from her side of the easel to try to paint on Calvin's paper. The teacher stayed calm and simply said, "Paint on your paper, Justine." Justine eventually accepted the substitution because the teacher resisted the power struggle that would have occurred had she become angry about Justine's challenge. She continued to make the substitution quietly and firmly but with goodwill.

## Listen Actively

**Active listening** is a positive strategy that is useful when a child "owns" a problem. The adult focuses on what the child says, not interrupting, not offering solutions, but listening for the feelings in the words,

# ANALYZE A VIGNETTE: REDIRECTION

### Redirect by Diverting or Distracting

The teacher in the infant and toddler room redirected by diverting or distracting (see the chapter-opening vignette). Answer the following questions about his strategy.

1. Focus on the child's actions. Which behavior did Mr. Bensen need to stop for Paul; for Jada; and for Alex, the toddler?
2. The teacher used diversion and distraction three times. From your perspective, was he effective all three times? If he was, explain your reasoning for your decision. If he was not in any of the three situations, state why.
3. Suppose that Mr. Bensen used diversion and/or distraction effectively. Explain what you would do to make the strategy even more effective in one or more examples.

4. Explain how redirecting with diversion and/or distraction is developmentally appropriate for infants and toddlers.

### Redirect with Substitution

1. Explain how Mrs. Johnson redirected Jerry successfully. Consider noting when she showed Jerry how to perform the same activity in a more acceptable way. Did Jerry test this substitution? If he did, explain how the teacher effectively dealt with Jerry's testing of the substitution.
2. Think about the differences between diversion/distraction and substitution. Why do you think that substitution is especially appropriate for preschoolers and older children?

---

suspending judgment, avoiding preaching, and then feeding back perception of the feelings. Mrs. Johnson watched Ralph try to mix colors to get orange paint. He forcefully jammed one brush in the cup, clenching his jaw at the same time, twisted his face in a frown, and blew out a deep breath.

|   |   |
|---|---|
| *Mrs. Johnson:* | Looks like you might be tired of dealing with that paintbrush! |
| *Ralph:* | Yeah, I want to make orange. |
| *Mrs. Johnson:* | You want orange but could not get orange? |
| *Ralph:* | I got pink! |
| *Mrs. Johnson:* | I see that you mixed red and white and got pink. (Ralph turned back to the easel and looked at the two paint cups. Mrs. Johnson continues.) So, those two colors together don't make orange. |
| *Ralph:* | Can I get another cup of paint? (He points to different colors.) |
| *Mrs. Johnson:* | Sure. Here's an idea. Keep your red paint and put the white away. Get one different color to mix with red. (Ralph got blue paint. When that did not work, he tried yellow with the red.) |

Ralph had a problem and the teacher used active listening to help him work through it. An authoritarian caregiver would have dealt with Ralph's rough use of a paintbrush differently, very likely by punishing Ralph. Authoritarian teachers do not take the time to find out what a child is feeling and thinking, or what is bothering the child. They miss the chance to "hear" what a child's behavior says. Children often communicate their deepest fears or try to tell adults through their behavior that something is wrong. Adults discover what is wrong only if they take the time to listen actively.

Active listening, then, is the skill that responsible adults use when something is troubling a child—the child is afraid, is angry, is jealous, cannot do something, or is frustrated. The adult can best help a child by listening actively and responding to the feelings implied in the child's words or actions.

# Deliver I-Messages

**I-message**
Self-responsible behavior
useful when the problem
belongs to the adult

An **I-message** is a positive, self-responsible strategy useful when the *adult* "owns" the problem in a relationship with a child. An adult owns the problem when a child has done something that interferes in some way with that adult's needs. Here are some examples:

The child does not clean up after an activity.

The child interrupts group time frequently.

The child curses at the teacher.

The child takes scissors and cuts into the glue bottle.

The child tosses library books on the floor.

Adults who see these kinds of behaviors usually feel afraid, irritated, or annoyed—all normal, natural feelings because the behavior usually tangibly affects the adult in some way. For example, a teacher would have to spend her time cleaning brushes and aprons left by a child; the teacher would have to use her own money to replace the ruined glue bottle.

I-messages are easy to learn to use. It is difficult, however, to use an I-message if an adult has not experienced hearing them. The key to using I-messages well is to acknowledge the feelings of irritation, annoyance, sadness, anger, or fear. Adults who use I-messages well fully realize that a child has done something annoying that has cost them time, energy, or money, but they know that they are the ones experiencing the feelings. They avoid accusing the child of causing these feelings. They simply take responsibility for communicating the feelings to the child in a firm but respectful and nonaccusatory way.

> **EXAMPLE**    Mrs. Johnson had a discipline encounter with Madelyn, who immediately left a center when the signal for cleanup was given and left whatever she had been working on to somebody else (usually the teacher) to put away. Mrs. Johnson knew that she owned the problem, that she was annoyed, and that she should tell Madelyn in a nonaccusatory way. She used an I-message.

I-messages have four parts.

**Give Data**    I-messages give data about the child's behavior but avoid accusing the child. The message tells the child what the adult saw, heard, smelled, touched, or tasted. These are facts, not opinions, and are stated as facts.

> *Mrs. Johnson:*    Madelyn, when I gave the signal for cleanup, I saw you leave the block area and go to another center. (Data: Teacher saw something; the child left the area without cleaning up. Mrs. Johnson told Madelyn what she saw, but did not accuse.)

**Describe the Tangible Effect**    I-messages tell the child how her behavior tangibly affects the adult, such as how the child's behavior has cost the adult time, effort, and/or money.

> *Mrs. Johnson:*    That means that I would have to pick up the blocks. (Madelyn's behavior tangibly affected the teacher because the teacher would have to do the extra work of straightening the block area.)

| **FIGURE 5.5** | Practice delivering an I-message |
| --- | --- |

Discipline encounter: Mr. Santini observed Reese walk away from the writing center, having left markers, paper, pencils, and rulers strewn over the table. Moua wanted to use Reese's spot at the table but would have to straighten up first. Mr. Santini decided to use an I-message with Reese. Practice writing an I-message by filling in each part.

Give data: (what did you see, hear, touch, taste, smell?)

Describe the tangible effect: (avoid telling about your feelings here)

State feelings: _____

Tell how to change things: _____

Reflection: Adults are important models for children. What has Mr. Santini modeled for Moua by delivering an I-message to Reese?

**Communicate Feelings**   I-messages tell the child how the adult feels.

> *Mrs. Johnson:*   I get frustrated when I have to pick up things that somebody else has worked with. (Teacher states the feeling but clearly says that she has the feeling. Mrs. Johnson did not accuse Madelyn of causing that feeling.)

**Tell How to Change Things**   If you, an adult, heard an I-message, you would likely know what to do to change things. A child, however, most often does not know how to do this. In the example above, a child would hear that her teacher was irritated and that the teacher had to do some extra work. The child would not necessarily know what to do to correct the situation. The teacher can follow up an I-message with a simple statement telling a child how to change things: "I want you to come with me to the block area and put away the blocks." Practice writing an I-message in Figure 5.5.

# Teach Conflict Resolution (Problem Solving)

Madelyn and Ralph had been working in the block corner, building a road and a yard with a large building. Then Mrs. Johnson heard the shouting.

> *Madelyn:*   It's a barn!
> *Ralph:*   No! It's my garage!
> *Madelyn:*   It's a barn! It's for the tractor.
> *Ralph:*   It's for the cars!

Madelyn stuck the tractor into the building and Ralph thrust it aside, putting his cars into the building. Madelyn, face red, grabbed one of the cars. Ralph grabbed it back and shouted loudly.

> *Ralph:*   Put it back, Madelyn!

**Treat Conflict as an Opportunity to Teach a Skill to Children**   This teacher knows that conflict is inevitable and not necessarily bad. She believes that relationships can become even stronger when people resolve conflicts peacefully and with goodwill. She believes in supporting children in learning how to recognize and manage conflict. She takes the stand that everybody in the conflict can "win," that there do not have to be any "losers."

Some teachers might simply punish Madelyn and Ralph by taking away all the blocks or by placing each child in time-out. Teachers who use the red light–green light strategy would probably change each child's light to yellow or red. All of these strategies are forms of punishment and do not teach anything positive. The bickering might irritate the teacher, but she realizes that her job is to support children in learning a brand-new skill—conflict resolution (Clark, 1999).

You will find that you use other guidance strategies along with the steps described for conflict resolution. For example, you will very likely use calming techniques, active listening, or I-messages when you teach children how to resolve conflict.

Adults who teach conflict resolution acknowledge that children's needs are important, and they communicate trust in their ability to construct and carry out decisions. Using this method, therefore, requires that adults truly accept the child's feelings and needs as valid and important. This is not a strategy that an adult can fake.

**Teaching Conflict Resolution**   Mrs. Johnson heard the argument and walked quickly to the block corner. "We need to talk, but first, let me just move the car and tractor over here for a minute." She unobtrusively took the car and the tractor and set them aside, then turned to both children. "It sounds as though you have a problem. Two children, one building."

|  |  |
|---:|:---|
| *Madelyn:* | It's a barn! |
| *Ralph:* | No, a garage! |
| *Mrs. Johnson:* | First, let's take a slow breath. (She does deep breathing with them, a calming technique. She then continued, after checking to see that both children were calm enough to talk.) Okay. Listen carefully. You have one building. Madelyn, you want it to be a barn. Ralph, you want it to be a garage. Is that right? (The children nod.) I see. We do have a problem then. Two children and one building. (She then looked at both children.) Let's think for a minute about how to fix the problem. Do you have an idea? |
| *Madelyn:* | Make another building? |
| *Ralph:* | Make this building bigger! |
| *Mrs. Johnson:* | Two ideas! Do you have any other ideas? |
| *Ralph:* | Make a wall right here. (points to the middle of the building) Then we can have a garage and a barn together. (The children had generated these three ideas.) |
| *Mrs. Johnson:* | Good ideas. Do you have enough blocks for another whole building? (The children decide that they do not have enough blocks.) |

| | |
|---|---|
| *Madelyn:* | We can't make another building, huh? |
| *Mrs. Johnson:* | Probably not. Do you think that there are enough blocks to make the building bigger? |
| *Ralph:* | (looking at the supply of blocks.) Yes. |
| *Mrs. Johnson:* | How about enough blocks to make a wall to divide the building? (Both children vigorously nodded.) |
| *Mrs. Johnson:* | Which idea do you want to try—making the building bigger or dividing it to make two parts? |
| *Ralph:* | Let's make it bigger! |
| *Mrs. Johnson:* | Is that okay with you, Madelyn? |
| *Madelyn:* | Uh-huh. If we make it bigger, then we can have a wall, too. |
| *Mrs. Johnson:* | What do you think about that, Ralph? We could use two of your ideas together. (Ralph nodded, indicating that he agreed.) Tell me the first thing that you can do to get started on making your building bigger. (They discuss this a bit more.) Okay. Start making the building bigger. Then make the wall and we'll look at how things work out when you are done. We will check to see how this works. |

Figure 5.6 shows the steps in teaching conflict resolution.

---

**FIGURE 5.6**  Steps in teaching children conflict resolution

✓ **Identify the problem and define it as a shared problem.**
Young children do not take the perspective of others very well. Adults have to help them understand that they can share a problem with someone else. Children will likely see the problem mainly in terms of what they want (Ralph wanted a garage, Madelyn a barn). How has the teacher carried out this step?

✓ **Invite children to participate in fixing the problem.**
Children think about what they want, not about solutions. Teachers or parents must get and keep them focused on moving toward solving the problem together. A good, constructivist approach is to invite their participation. How did Mrs. Johnson do this?

✓ **Generate possible solutions as a group.**
This is brainstorming. Encourage a variety of solutions. Do not evaluate solutions at this stage. You might have to teach children not to evaluate now. When did Mrs. Johnson do this?

✓ **Examine each idea for its merits or drawbacks. Decide which idea to try.**
Encourage children to think through each idea. Facilitate an evaluation of each idea and let the children decide which idea to try. Acknowledge the children's participation and thank them for working together. How did Mrs. Johnson do this?

✓ **Work out ways of putting the plan into action.**
Children need help in taking action after coming up with ideas. They do not automatically move from the problem to working on a solution. How did Mrs. Johnson help Madelyn and Ralph start to put their plan into action?

✓ **Follow up. Evaluate how well the plan worked.**
Children need to learn that some plans work nicely and some do not work at all. Teachers have to help them through this process. Children who are just learning how to resolve conflicts might get frustrated when a new idea does not work for some reason. Teachers can then step in and help them figure out why the plan did not work and anything else they might do to create a better plan. The children learn about fine-tuning a plan. When did the teacher do this?

*Source:* Based on *Before Push Comes to Shove: Building Conflict Resolution Skills with Children,* by N. Carlsson-Paige and D. Levin, 1998, St. Paul, MN: Redleaf Press.

# Prevent Overstimulation and Teach Calming Techniques

Many times, the best thing that we can do for children is to look beyond the behavior that we see. Children often have difficulty controlling themselves when they are under stress or when they are anxious. Children often lose control because they are under so much stress (Goleman, 1995). At these times, children have difficulty thinking clearly, and adults need to help them. We help them best, not by punishing, but by doing the following:

Recognizing signs of anxiety and stress.

Preventing overstimulation.

Teaching calming techniques.

> **EXAMPLE**   Mr. Santini noticed right away that first-grader Gene was acting differently as they talked about the visit from the firefighter. Gene bit his lip and was very agitated. Mr. Santini recognized the signs of anxiety and stopped talking about the visit. Instead, Mr. Santini and the children did their favorite "rubber-band" exercise. They stretched out both arms and stretched one as far as they could. Then they slowly brought the arm back to its original position. After this, they did slow, deep breathing with their eyes closed. Only then did the teacher proceed with talking about the firefighter's visit. Later, Mr. Santini discovered that Gene's family home had burned the year before and that several fire engines had responded to the fire.

Mrs. Johnson knew that some holidays are stressful for many people and wanted to prevent overstimulation (Greenberg & Berktold, 2006). She realized that many of the children would become overstimulated if she stressed the holiday too much, and the effect would last for several hours or days. She approached holiday seasons carefully. She did nothing to whip the children into a holiday frenzy. They proceeded with the curriculum, bringing in the holiday only when it seemed relevant to a project at hand, and then in a low-key way.

> **EXAMPLE**   One of the few things that the children did for Valentine's Day was to bake a heart-shaped cake with red frosting. This was part of an ongoing project about creating colors and color mixing, and was done to focus on helping the children remember the list of ingredients and the steps in preparing the cake.

# Help Children Save Face and Preserve Their Dignity

Our culture values children, and one of its beliefs is that adults should protect children. Our responsibility, then, is to examine, critically and unemotionally, any strategy that somebody tries to get us to use. Some strategies that you will see on the Internet or in a teacher workshop come complete with teacher recommendations, but you still need to ask yourself, "Is this disrespectful or psychologically harmful to children?" Consider, for example, something called the red light–green light strategy. (This strategy is *not* recommended.) A child starts the day with a green light. His first or second infraction earns him a warning and a yellow light. Still another infraction earns him a red light and he loses 5 minutes of recess (This is a form of punishment.

It is response cost—your inappropriate behavior will cost you 5 minutes of recess.) Still another infraction earns a *double* red light. The child loses the entire recess and the teacher sends a note home.

Think critically. Be compassionate. Put yourself in the child's place. How would *you* feel if your instructors used the red light–green light method in your classes? What if you turn in a paper late? How would you *feel* if the teacher used this system and changed your light to yellow? I would feel humiliated if my dean or department chair used such an outrageous method. Children have the same feelings that we have, and so it would undoubtedly be degrading and humiliating to them as well. This system and others like it should be rejected. *We should not use them.*

This chapter presents many positive strategies. We do not need punishment such as the red light–green light strategy. We reject such strategies because our ultimate responsibility is to help children save face and preserve their sense of dignity, no matter what positive guidance or discipline strategy we use. Authoritarian adults degrade children by using negative discipline strategies. Some continue to humiliate a child; they might tell others about what the child did in front of her (double red light), or they might humiliate her by saying "I told you so," or "No recess for you" to the child.

Use your perspective-taking skills and put yourself in a child's place. Think about how it would feel to have an adult changing that light from green to yellow, and then to red. *You,* an adult, would probably not like it at all and would demand that the other person treat you in a dignified way. Children also deserve dignified treatment.

---

## :: *Question for Reflection*

---

# :: BELIEFS ABOUT DISCIPLINE INFLUENCE CHOICES ABOUT GUIDANCE STRATEGIES

## Beliefs and Practices

Early childhood professionals study developmentally appropriate practices. They must examine their own practices and their beliefs about those practices. For example, a teacher attends a series of workshops on appropriate guidance and discipline. She learns the strategies. She does not use the new strategies in her classroom, however. In this case, the teacher's cultural scripts, past experiences, and beliefs about discipline more strongly affect her practices than anything that she learned in formal classes. She strongly believes, for example, that time-out is acceptable and uses it even after learning that it is a form of punishment.

This teacher's "memory" of past experiences, then, "believes" some things about inappropriate discipline; these inappropriate beliefs will be difficult to modify. To make any real changes, this teacher will have to examine her beliefs about discipline before she thinks about specific strategies (Haupt et al., 1995).

## An Opportunity to Examine Your Beliefs about Discipline

Take the time to examine what you really believe about discipline. What did you experience as a child? If you are already a parent, what have you tried with your own children? Which strategies have you used as a teacher? It is important to reflect because your experiences strongly affect what you believe about discipline. One of my students, as a childcare aide, had been told to use the "sad pad." The sad pad is a carpet square with a sad face drawn on it. A child is sent there when she is angry. This is *not* a very good strategy because it confuses two emotions and is often used in place of a time-out chair. Whether one uses a sad pad or time-out chair, it is still a form of punishment and *not* a positive form of discipline. We should question any form of discipline that comes our way.

This chapter described many positive discipline strategies. When a person is confronted with such a large number of possibilities, there is a tendency to feel overwhelmed. Avoid this feeling by looking at things differently. Adopt an optimistic perspective by keeping three things in mind.

**Knowledge Base**   At this point, you should be able to describe each strategy and state why it would be effective in some cases. That is a knowledge base, the beginning of expertise.

**Skill Building**   Second, you will have a chance at the end of this chapter to build your professional self-esteem by doing some skill development in the Apply Your Knowledge section. You will have an opportunity to use several positive guidance strategies. Then, as you work with children in classrooms, you will practice using these strategies—you will become more skillful over time.

**Decision-Making Approach**   Third, this text teaches the decision-making model of child guidance. It teaches how to make decisions about which strategy to use in specific discipline encounters. You will be able to do this because you have learned and practiced the strategies. You will work through the decision-making model of child guidance in a systematic fashion and learn how to make wise decisions about which strategy to use.

## ANALYZE A VIGNETTE

Hannah's mother (in the chapter-opening vignette) was embarrassed and angry and used a negative discipline strategy. Boost her confidence as a parent by teaching her more positive ways to deal with the same discipline encounter. Teach the skills that will enable her to use positive strategies.

1. Set Limits
   - Show Hannah's mother how to set a limit, before going to the store, on what they will buy. (Be specific and follow the guidelines for limit setting.)

- Suppose that Hannah's mother simply forgot to state a limit. Then, in the store, Hannah started whining. Tell Mom how she could state the limit in a direct, nonaggressive way by saying:

2. Teach and Cue More Appropriate Behavior
   - Show Hannah's mother how to teach Hannah a new behavior that is different from whining, such as asking for things in a normal, conversational tone of voice. Show her how to model and give direct instruction.

- Show Hannah's mother how to use a cue to remind Hannah about the limit. Explain why it is best to cue her daughter in a matter-of-fact, low-key way in a public place. Be prepared to role-play what this would look like.

3. **Ignore Behavior**

- Demonstrate how to use the ignore strategy effectively in this case. List the essential things that you would tell Hannah's mother to do—or not to do.

- How do you think Hannah's mother might feel when Hannah reacts with a bigger and better whine? Give her some hints on how to cope with the feeling and with other adults in the store who say, "She should do something to that kid to stop her squealing!"

## SUMMARY

How we guide children is based on what we value and believe as a culture. A culture has specific beliefs about how it should care for children. We help children acquire the beliefs of their culture through the process of socialization. We adults help children understand what the culture values through our teaching and our interaction with them.

- Discipline refers to guidance and teaching, *not* punishment. Adults help children make better choices about behavior through guidance and discipline encounters, and dealing with guidance or discipline encounters is a big part of a teacher's professional role.

- We use *positive* guidance strategies in guidance or discipline encounters. The strategies are the actions that we use in managing the encounter.
- There are many positive guidance strategies, and it is a good idea to know about all of them. Knowing about and being able to use a group or cluster of positive strategies allows teachers to meet the individual needs of children. Table 5.1 summarizes the major positive guidance strategies.

Our beliefs about guidance grow out of our experiences in our culture. Believing that positive guidance is preferable to punishment makes it easier for teachers to learn and then use positive strategies presented in this text.

## APPLY YOUR KNOWLEDGE

### Discipline Encounters and Appropriate Solutions

Each adult in the following vignettes faces a discipline encounter. Help the adult deal effectively by offering advice on how to use the specific strategy mentioned. Refer to information in this chapter when writing your solution.

1. **Discipline encounter:** Maricela walked over to the piano and started to bang on the keys. Her teacher called out, "Stop banging on the piano!"

   **Appropriate strategy**
   I think that this teacher would be helpful and effective by telling Maricela what *to* do instead of what not to do. The teacher can be positive, polite, and firm as she says, "_____."

2. **Discipline encounter:** Ed and Jim rode their tricycles at breakneck speed and their teacher said, "Stop driving so fast!"

   **Appropriate strategy**
   This teacher would be more helpful and effective by telling the boys what to do rather than what not to do. I would advise that she say, "_____."

3. **Discipline encounter:** Tim's parents had been sitting in the booth at a fast-food restaurant for 15 minutes. Both parents had cellphones out and used them as they ate. Three-year-old Tim wiggled off the bench, ran around, and then crawled under the table. His dad scooped him up and told him, "Now, you sit here and be quiet," and went back to his phone. Five minutes passed, and Tim, who had missed his morning nap, started screaming in frustration. His dad grabbed Tim's arm to try to quiet him, but Tim continued screaming.

   **Appropriate strategy**
   I would change this situation by _____. (*Note:* Tim must be supervised constantly, so sending him to the

| TABLE 5.1 | Summary of major positive guidance strategies |
|---|---|
| **Guidance Strategy** | **Purpose or Benefit of This Strategy** |
| **Greater Direct Teacher Control and Teaching** | |
| Use limits effectively | Helps children understand boundaries |
| Teach helpful or appropriate behavior | Fosters children's self-control |
| Set up practice sessions and give on-the-spot guidance | Practicing new behaviors and skills is important for children |
| Give signals or cues for appropriate behavior | Reminds children about appropriate behavior |
| Redirect with diversion and distraction or with substitution | Diversion and distraction is helpful for younger children; substitution is beneficial |
| Use I-messages | Useful when the adult "owns" the problem for older children |
| Teach conflict resolution | Teaches skills for solving interpersonal problems |
| **Less Direct Teacher Control and Teaching** | |
| Encourage children's efforts | Lets children know that you appreciate their effort to behave prosocially |
| Change something about the context | Context affects behavior; changing context helps children choose a different behavior |
| Ignore behavior (only when it is appropriate to do so) | Decreasing our attention for a behavior helps children decrease that behavior |
| Prevent overstimulation; teach calming techniques | Children need to learn to deal with stress and to calm themselves |
| Help children save face and preserve their dignity | Children *always* have the right to dignified treatment, including the use of positive guidance strategies |

restaurant's playground is not an option unless the parent goes with him.) Start your solution by stating whether you would increase options, decrease options, or change the physical environment or time schedule, and then state exactly how you would proceed.

4. **Discipline encounter:** Dad was frustrated when 10-month-old Richard kept crawling right to the uncovered electrical outlets. He said "No-no" every time his son approached an outlet.

   **Appropriate strategy**
   I suggest that Dad change this situation by _____.

5. **Discipline encounter:** John, 4 years old, has been working for 20 minutes in the sand pile constructing a "canal" for water (he has no water yet). You glance over and notice that he is tossing sand into the air.

   **Appropriate strategy**
   In addition to stating a safety rule, I would change this situation by _____.

6. **Discipline encounter:** Sylvia finger-painted on the window because she likes how the sun shines on the colors.

   **Appropriate strategy**
   I would use this substitution: _____.
   (*Note:* The substitution must be appropriate and safe for the child and acceptable to you.)

7. **Discipline encounter:** Pat wiped his nose on his sleeve.

   **Appropriate strategy**
   I would use this substitution: _____.

### Should I Ignore This Behavior?

Look over this list and decide which of the behaviors you should *not* ignore. Which could you safely ignore? Give a rationale for your choices.

- One child tells another child, "You're stupid!" Ignore?

  Yes _____    No _____    Reason: _____

- A 3-year-old girl smashes her play dough creation. Ignore?

  Yes _____    No _____    Reason: _____

- The same child smashes another child's play dough structure. Ignore?

  Yes _____    No _____    Reason: _____

- One of the children in your group forcefully splashes water from the water table onto the floor. Ignore?

  Yes _____    No _____    Reason: _____

- Josie shoves Kyle as they walk to the bathroom. Ignore?

  Yes _____    No _____    Reason: _____

- "You clean up! I don't want to clean up. Why do I have to clean up?" a 7-year-old said argumentatively to her teacher. Ignore?

  Yes _____    No _____    Reason: _____

# WEBSITES

**ACT (Act Against Violence)**
http://actagainstviolence.apa.org/index.html

Home page for this organization whose mission is to prevent violence through publishing information on discipline, resolving conflict, managing anger, and other related topics. Printable handouts and other resources useful to teachers and parents are available.

**Association of Professional Humane Educators (APHE)**
http://aphe.org

Main website for the organization. Good materials for helping children learn about humane treatment of animals. Helps teachers state limits about treatment of animals to children.

# CHAPTER 6
# Using Observation in Guiding Children

## Learning Outcomes

- Define terms related to the process of observation and assessment in guiding children
- Explain the central role of assessment in modern schools
- Describe the nature of appropriate assessment in early childhood education
- Summarize the goals of assessment in early childhood education
- Recall reasons for observing children's behavior
- Describe and explain the major practical and effective methods that teachers find useful in observing children's development and behavior
- Point out circumstances when each observational strategy would be appropriate
- Explain a portfolio's utility in observation and assessment

### VIGNETTES

#### INFANT-TODDLER: ENRIQUE TRIES MITTENS FIRST

*Mr. Bensen recorded this observation of Enrique, 2½ years old, as the toddlers prepared to go outside.*

*Enrique shook his head vigorously, saying, "No!" as his teacher took his coat off the hook. Instead, Enrique put his hat and gloves on first and only then picked up his coat. He struggled to get the coat on over the gloves, then took off his gloves, and finally put on the coat.*

#### PRESCHOOL: JERRY MAKES AN OFFER

*Mrs. Johnson has been observing how Jerry works with other children. Today in the discovery/science center, she watched as Jerry and Sarah, both almost 5 years old, collaborated on making shapes with rubber bands stretched around nails, which were hammered into squares of wood. Sarah needed another big rubber band and Jerry responded, "Here, I have one," and offered it to Sarah. Later, at story time, the teacher noticed that Sarah made room next to her on the carpet for Jerry.*

#### PRIMARY: SANDI FINDS A SOLUTION

*Mr. Santini assessed each child's social skills. Here is one of his notes about Sandi's interaction with three other children in a small, first-grade reading group. Bert finished reading; Alicia started her turn. Dave yelled, "It's my turn!" Sandi looked at each child in the group as if figuring out something and then said, pointing at Bert, "Uh-oh! Bert just read. Alicia is sitting next to him, so she goes next." Then Sandi beamed at Dave and chirped, "You go right after Alicia!" Dave said, "Oh, yeah. Okay."*

## :: INTRODUCTION

All three of the teachers in the chapter-opening vignettes are committed to using constructive guidance. As effective teachers, they monitor and supervise children well, which implies that they *observe* children's behavior as they have done with Enrique, Sarah, and Sandi. This observation is a part of the larger process of assessment of the children's development and behavior.

Assessment drives *everything* that we do with children, from curriculum to room arrangement to guiding them. Assessment is not a luxury, something that you do if you have the time. Instead, it is a requirement growing in importance and it is what you do first so that you can make wise decisions about everything else. School districts, Head Start, child-care centers, and preschools are accountable to different accrediting bodies, state agencies, or professional organizations for demonstrating progress in meeting agency, state, or federal guidelines. Schools and teachers, therefore, use appropriate assessment to demonstrate to these bodies that they have met specific requirements, that they have demonstrated accountability. Assessment drives virtually every aspect of modern school life.

Observation is an essential component in assessment, and this chapter focuses on observation's role in assessing and mainly in guiding children. Effective teachers use observation to crack the code, or unravel, and assess the meaning of children's development and behavior. This will make it possible for them to guide the children effectively. In this chapter, we will briefly examine the meaning of assessment in early childhood education, keeping in mind that assessment drives almost every decision that teachers make. The focus, however, is on the role of **observation** in guiding children. First, we will examine the role of assessment, and then we will focus on reasons for observing children's behavior. A major part of the chapter emphasizes practical methods for observing young children with an eye toward achieving objectivity in observation. You will also read about the effect of culture on choosing what to observe.

**Observation**
Systematic study; in guidance refers to watching, recording, and reflecting on children's behavior

## :: ASSESSMENT IN EARLY CHILDHOOD EDUCATION

**Assessment**, which drives teacher decisions, involves gathering and recording information about young children's development and learning appropriately and ethically. Teachers use assessment to make a variety of decisions affecting children, such as developing plans for individual children or for groups of children. Appropriate assessment involves many sources of information about young children's development and it is appropriate for *all* children, including those with disabilities or children from diverse backgrounds (National Association of the Education of Young Children, 2003a, 2009). An even more child-centered view of assessment comes from Heritage (2013). She notes that appropriate formative assessment of course gives teachers information on which to base decisions, but also includes the child in the process. Heritage sees appropriate assessment in the

**Assessment**
Systematic procedure for obtaining information from observations, interviews, portfolios, projects, tests, and other sources that can be used to make judgments about characteristics of children or programs

framework of a child's educational rights, that children have a right to appropriate assessment and they have a right to have some say in decisions coming out of any of their own assessments.

The major overall goal of assessment is to identify and build on children's strengths; appropriate assessment, therefore, is strength based. It is important to assess all domains of development because we take a whole-child approach and because all domains are the basis of state learning standards. In addition, how a child develops in the domains, including the social and emotional, is related to outcomes such as school success. Social and emotional competence includes skills such as regulating emotions and getting along well with others. Assessing children's social and emotional strengths yields information teachers can use to support development in these domains (Scott-Little, Kagan, & Frelow, 2006; Snow & Van Hemel, 2008).

Appropriate assessment benefits children, teachers, administrators, and parents. Parents benefit because ethically done assessment gives them a full, rich picture of their child's development and learning. They also benefit from being a member of the assessment team. Children benefit when teachers use assessment to plan effective environments and curriculum. Children also gain when they learn how to evaluate and reflect on their own work. Teachers and administrators benefit from effective assessment because they get a good picture of a child's development, which helps them perform their roles more effectively.

**EXAMPLE**   Mr. Santini observed how a second-grade child new to the classroom reacted to the morning meeting. He recorded the child's ability to join the group on the very first day, not seeming to be afraid at all. He noted, however, that she did not know the greeting. This reminded him to make sure that she had a friend to help her learn the greetings used in their meetings.

Assessment in early childhood education has several purposes. It allows teachers to plan so that they can meet *all* children's developmental and learning needs. "All" refers to every child, without exception, having a right to appropriate assessment, including those with disabilities and those who are homeless as well as young children who are learning English. First, young English language learners have a right to be assessed so that teachers can make informed decisions about how to assist them. Second, they have a right to be assessed in ways that support their development (National Association of the Education of Young Children, 2009). Good assessment also allows teachers to identify individual children who might need focused programs or interventions. A third purpose for assessment is to evaluate the effectiveness of programs and services.

As you watch this **video**, notice these things about the teacher's observations: how she uses observation to assess children's development and skill level, how she sets up for observation, and how she asks questions appropriately during observations.

There are many good ways to assess young children. **Authentic assessment** is performance based, with children applying their skills and knowledge in a real-world setting. Examples include their work samples, interviews with children, and *teacher observation* (National Association of the Education of Young Children,

**Authentic assessment**
Children apply their skills and knowledge in a real-world setting

2009b). This chapter emphasizes observation, an essential part of effectively guiding children. We will examine reasons for observing and will look at what we can learn about children's behavior with systematic study. You will also learn about several practical and efficient methods for observing children's behavior and development.

## :: REASONS FOR OBSERVING CHILDREN'S BEHAVIOR

Observation helps teachers gather information that they need in planning for children. In guiding children, the major reasons for observing are as follows: children communicate with behavior, we can discover and build on their strengths, and we can assess individual needs.

### Children Communicate with Behavior

Perceptive teachers know that behavior has meaning, that it is a code. For example, a 3-year-old whirls with delight, trying to catch snowflakes. Another child's face turns red with anger as he strikes out at a classmate. A 5-year-old twirls her hair tightly around her finger as she sits hunched over a workbook page. A boy in the same class lowers his head until it nearly touches his workbook and turns his head from side to side, eyes darting to the other children's pages. Finally, a tear drops onto his page. A first grader, head thrust forward slightly, one hand scratching his head, eyes open wide in wonder, and mouth making a little O-shape, stares at the gorilla mother and her baby in the zoo.

Head scratching, wide eyes, worried looks, tears, twirling, smiling, a red face, and a fist that smashes—not one of these children uttered a word, but they all communicated eloquently. Their hands, feet, facial expressions, and body movements communicated just as well as words could. Of course, young children *do* communicate with words. They are just as likely, though, to tell us what they are experiencing, how they feel, and what they think through their behavior.

Their words and behavior give clues about what happened, who was involved, when things happen, and where things take place. Reflecting on these "W" questions often helps teachers to figure out the final "W" question, which is *why* some behaviors occur. See Table 6.1 for an explanation of the five "W" **questions about behavior.**

**"W" questions about behavior**
Questions that observers can answer with well-planned observations. They include What? Who? When? Where? and Why?

## :: FOCUS ON PRACTICE

This Focus on Practice activity is entitled *Answering the 5 W Questions about Children's Behavior.* Note how this strategy yields information that helps teachers plan for children.

| TABLE 6.1 | The 5 "W" questions about children's behavior |
|-----------|-----------------------------------------------|

| The Question | Ask Yourself |
|--------------|--------------|
| Who was involved? | Was only the one child involved, or were others involved? |
| | If there were others, were they adults, children, or both? |
| | Did the behavior involve animals? If this is a recurring behavior, are the same children, adults, or animals generally involved? |
| What happened? | Note the *precise* nature of the behavior. |
| | Record what happened before and after the behavior. |
| | Note how long the behavior went on. |
| When did the behavior occur? | Does it occur at the same times during the day or at different times? |
| | Only on certain days of the week or every day? |
| | What type of activity is going on at the time—for example, is the child arriving at school; is it naptime, large-group time, during transitions or throughout the day? |
| | Be specific. |
| Where did the behavior take place? | Does it happen only in certain areas of the classroom or school, or just about anywhere? |
| Why did the child behave this way? | This requires you to reflect and interpret the behavior, which is difficult. |
| | Reflect on answers to the other four questions. |
| | Decide if you have enough information for interpreting. |
| | Do you even need to interpret this behavior? |
| | Do you need more information before you can make an accurate conclusion? |

The teacher has observed that the children in this class seem to prefer working with other children.

## Discover and Build on Children's Strengths

Ethical professionals observe behavior to discover children's preferences and what they can do successfully. We also use observations as a logical step in helping children with challenging behaviors and identifying strong points, as well as areas in which the child needs help. For example, a teacher might observe that a child, cheerful and well liked, does have some trouble when interacting with others because he occasionally interrupts them. Teachers observe a child alone or as she works with others. See the examples below.

> **EXAMPLES**   Mr. Santini discovered that Jim often took on a leadership role when he collaborated with other children in small-group activities, which is a strength.
>
>   Mrs. Johnson observed Jerry's social skills because some of the children had been rejecting his bids to play with them (he needed help with some social skills).

---

:: *Question for Reflection*

---

## Observe Individual Needs for Possible Further Screening

When teachers observe children, they occasionally notice, just as parents do, that a child's pattern of development might be outside the normal range of development for his age. A vague sense that something is amiss with a child's development is a red flag for a teacher and should be noted and discussed with parents. Teachers and parents are *not* responsible for making an official diagnosis. It is important that special needs such as autism spectrum disorder (ASD) be identified by qualified professionals as early as possible, and getting help for a child with ASD often begins with those observations by teachers or parents.

Formally diagnosing ASD is a process carried out only by professionals qualified to screen, do additional formal assessment, and diagnose (National Institute of Mental Health, 2011). Teachers are not usually educated as therapists, psychologists, or psychiatrists but they are teachers. Therefore, they never make a diagnosis. They may, however, provide observations of a child's behavior to professionals qualified to formally assess the child. That is all that teachers are to do. They do not diagnose. With that caution in mind, Figure 6.1 lists the three major categories of indicators of ASD.

**Objectivity**
Impartiality, detachment, and fairness in recording observations

## :: ACHIEVING OBJECTIVITY AND AVOIDING SUBJECTIVITY IN OBSERVING

**Objectivity** refers to impartiality, detachment, and fairness. Observations are more influential and useful when they are truly objective. **Subjectivity** refers to bias or preconception. Observations are meaningless and, more important, can actually harm children when they are subjectively recorded.

**Subjectivity**
Bias or preconception in recording observations

| **FIGURE 6.1** | Indicators of autism spectrum disorders |
| --- | --- |

Social skills
- Content being alone
- Ignores a teacher or parent's bid for attention
- Seldom makes or asks for eye contact
- Does not respond when someone calls his name
- Problems with joint attention or sharing interest in an object or event with someone and looking back and forth between the other person and the object (seen very early, at about 10 to 12 months)
- Problems making friends

Communication deficits
- Lacks speech, important when coupled with
- No apparent desire to talk
- No compensatory skills such as using gestures
- Parroting of speech of others; should not be confused with advanced speech

Repetitive patterns of behavior
- Nonfunctional and recurring behaviors such as twirling, rocking, hand flapping
- Might not advance beyond a sensory motor type of play with objects, such as repeatedly opening and closing snaps on a doll's dress, rather than playing with the doll

*Source:* Based on Johnson, Myers, & Council on Children with Disabilities (2007), and National Institute of Mental Health (2011).

# Teachers Are Responsible for Recording Observations Objectively

The most important part of the Code of Ethical Conduct from NAEYC is that we do nothing that harms or has the potential to harm children. Carelessly recording a child's behavior or letting one's bias or preconception infiltrate our observations has great potential to harm children. Therefore, we strive for as much objectivity as possible. We make it a priority and we intentionally, consciously, and deliberately produce objectively written observations. We do this to honor children because observations and assessments are increasingly used to document children's development. Assessments are also increasingly used to analyze the function of challenging behaviors. Therefore, teachers have a professional and ethical responsibility to strive for and maintain objectivity in recording observations whether using anecdotal notes, checklists, event sampling or any other observational strategy.

# Practical Suggestions for Achieving Objectivity in Observing

Here are two versions of the recording of the same event in a preschool classroom. We will use these examples to focus on two practical strategies for achieving greater objectivity in recording observations.

**EXAMPLE 1, TONY AND JOE:** Joe and Tony sat next to each other on the outside of the cluster of children listening to a story. Joe leaned back on his hands, listened to the story, and did not turn to or talk to anyone. His eyes were focused in the direction of the teacher holding the book and they stay focused like that. Tony assumed the same pose, both boys listening for the first part of the story. Then Tony's right hand started inching slowly toward Joe. Tony's hand jerked sideways, Tony then falling onto Joe. Joe moved aside, keeping his eyes on the book, and continued listening to the story. Tony glanced at Joe, narrowed his eyes, smiled, and then poked Joe's shoulder. Joe called out, "Hey!"

**EXAMPLE 2, TONY AND JOE:** Tony and Joe are friends and were happy to sit together. Tony wiggled around, annoying the teacher. Both boys enjoyed the story until Joe rudely interrupted the reading. He was angry and shouted, "Hey!"

**Use Descriptive Phrasing**   Descriptive phrasing simply records observable behavior, behavior that you or any other observer can see or hear. Observable behavior can easily be verified by another observer. Sticking to describing only what you see or hear, just the facts, yields a more objective observation. It is not open to much interpretation at all. Some instances of observable behavior from Example 1 include the following:

- "Tony's hand jerked sideways, . . ." (Observable behavior? The hand moved. The hand moved sideways.)
- "Joe leaned back on his hands, . . ." (Observable behavior? His body moved backwards. He leaned. He leaned on his hands.)
- "His eyes were focused in the direction of the teacher. . . ." (Observable behavior? Eyes pointed forward. Eyes pointed in the direction of the teacher.)
- "Tony's right hand started inching slowly toward Joe." (Your turn—observable behavior?)
- ". . . narrowed his eyes, smiled, and then poked Joe's shoulder." (Your turn again—observable behavior?)
- "Joe called out, 'Hey!'" (Observable behavior?)

**Avoid Using Subjective Phrasing**   Subjective phrasing is "slanted" writing, phrasing shows the observer's bias and opinion. Subjective phrasing cannot be verified by another observer. For example, it is not possible for a different observer to verify a subjective phrase such as "He was mean!" How would a person ever be able to corroborate such a statement? Subjective phrasing interprets a scene rather than just reporting the facts. Subjective phrasing gives little or no observable behavior or data. It makes observations unusable in making sound decisions about children and can even be dangerous if important decisions are made based on such inadequate reporting. Some illustrations of subjective phrasing from Example 2 include the following. Again, you will have a chance to make some judgments about how certain phrases are subjective.

- "Tony and Joe are friends . . ." (Subjectively phrased because there is no way to verify from the data that they are friends)
- "Tony and Joe . . . were happy to sit together." (Subjectively phrased because this is an interpretation with no observable data to back up the statement.)
- "Tony wiggled around, annoying the teacher." (Subjectively phrased because there is no evidence that the teacher was annoyed, just the observer's opinion.)

- "Both boys enjoyed the story. . . ." (Your turn—subjectively phrased because _____.)
- "Joe rudely interrupted. . . ." (Your turn—subjectively phrased because _____.)
- "He was angry and. . . ." (Subjectively phrased because _____.)

We now turn to methods for observing children's behavior and development.

# :: PRACTICAL AND EFFECTIVE METHODS FOR OBSERVING CHILDREN'S DEVELOPMENT AND BEHAVIOR

Constructive positive guidance rests on observing, reflecting on what you see, and then wisely using the information to make decisions about children and, for this text, about guidance decisions. This part of the chapter focuses on practical information that teachers need to observe well. There are several major methods for observing, and you will learn how to choose the format best suited to your needs. Whichever method you choose, remember that objectivity is the goal with all methods. The rules for remaining objective—using descriptive and avoiding subjective phrasing—apply to all observational strategies.

**Narrative method**
Observation that tells a story

Choosing the most helpful format for observing depends on whether you need to tell or narrate a story. If you need to tell or narrate a story, then you would choose a **narrative method**, such as anecdotal or running records. If you do not need to write an account, then you would choose a **non-narrative method**, such as a checklist or rating scale. You could also choose a sampling format such as time sampling or event sampling.

**Non-narrative method**
Observation method that does not tell a story

**Mrs. Johnson has concluded, after several observations, that Brian, (far left) works very well with other children.**

## Anecdotal Records

**Anecdotal record**
Brief written notes about an incident; like a snapshot; gives less information that the longer running record

An **anecdotal record** allows a teacher to observe an incident and then to tell about it in brief notes that form a snapshot of the incident. There is just enough detail to describe the incident accurately and to recall it later. Teachers can use this method to observe a variety of behaviors or any aspect of children's development or learning. The observations can be spontaneous or planned. For example, a primary grade teacher might plan to record anecdotal records on every child's social skills. He might then make a few unplanned entries about how other children react to a child's improved social skills.

Using anecdotal records provides clear advantages. Teachers write anecdotal records while they teach; therefore, they do not have to take time away from the children. Anecdotal records are easy to learn to use and take very little of a teacher's time. Anecdotal records also have two disadvantages. The first is that there is very little information given—an anecdotal record is, after all, a snapshot, a very short story. Another is that an observer might come up with conclusions unsupported by data presented in the notes.

Figure 6.2 shows the format for anecdotal records. Some teachers duplicate the form and make several copies readily available. They file completed forms in a child's folder. Some teachers use sticky notes instead of the form and place these very brief entries in the file. Still other teachers prefer to use a digital voice recorder, with a file for each child, or they like recording anecdotal records on a computer or other electronic device. Taking a digital photograph of a child during an episode about which one is writing is an effective addition to the file. Whichever format they choose, teachers are responsible for maintaining files in a confidential manner and guarding the child's privacy.

## Running Record

**Running record**
A longer narrative method for observing; tells a longer story; gives more detail than an anecdotal record

A **running record** is like the anecdotal record in that it tells a story, but it is also different because it gives more detail. Greater detail gives more information that should

**Anecdotal record format. Fill in the comments section only when you have detected a pattern after several observations. Do not feel obligated to comment on every anecdote**

| FIGURE 6.2 | |

**Goal for this observation:** Jerry's social development

**Date/day:** Thursday, May 20

**Time of day:** 8:00 a.m.

**Focus child, if appropriate:** Jerry (J)

**Other children involved?** Sarah (S)

**The anecdote:** S had gone to the art center immediately after putting things in her cubby. She asked Jerry to play there, too. He walked over to the center but just stood, watching as Sarah chose a marker. She turned to him, offering a marker. He smiled and took it, and then they worked on drawing together.

**Comment:** Jerry often, but certainly not always, hesitates before beginning to play, even when another child has issued a clear invitation. He seems to be very cautious but also seems to enjoy playing with others, and he usually responds in a very positive way.

help a teacher understand some developmental issue, such as how a child expresses feelings. Having a clear focus is important here. For instance, a teacher might focus on one child's attempt to enter an ongoing work group, or on the class's general reaction to a classroom rule after the class discusses an issue.

Running records take only about 5 to 10 minutes and tend to produce much usable information if the observer sticks to objective, descriptive phrasing. They allow a teacher to see an incident in detail. For example, in a 5-minute segment of observing on the playground, Mr. Santini watched Hector as he was greeted by four other children and all five approached the climbing wall. Mr. Santini documented Hector's continued positive interaction with the others. A clear drawback is that a teacher cannot interact with the children in his class while observing.

Figure 6.3 shows the format for running records. There are three columns. Use the Context/Background/Time column to record brief notes on the setting: Where did the incident take place? Was there something going on that affected the context? For instance, were there sirens blaring outside? Did the mood of the group seem important for this observation? It is a good idea to record the time you begin to take notes and the time you end.

| FIGURE 6.3 | Running record format. Do not feel obligated to comment on every item |
| --- | --- |

| **Focus:** Jerry/social development | **S** = Sarah |
| --- | --- |
| **Date:** May 15 | **J** = Jerry |

| Context/Background/Time | Intensive Observation | Comments/Reflections |
| --- | --- | --- |
| 8:00 a.m.<br><br>Arrival time: children arrive, put things in cubbies, and then go right to a chosen center. Today, the teacher had placed a very large piece of paper on a wall—a mural-size piece of paper.<br><br>Sarah's mother drove both Jerry and Sarah to school.<br><br>Jerry and Sarah live next door to each other and have a good relationship.<br><br>She has helped Jerry gain new social skills, but they occasionally have arguments. | S & J put things in cubbies, S surveying the room. J continued to organize his cubby.<br><br>S, "O-o-o . . . look, J! A BIG piece of paper. J glanced at the paper as S speed-walked to the paper, set up for mural drawing. S looked at the baskets on the floor, picked up a marker, and ran her hands over it, smiling. S dropped the marker, and scurried back to Jerry.<br><br>S whispered to J, "I saw *new* markers in the art center. They're big and fat! Let's go *there*." S hurried back and grabbed a marker.<br><br>J walked slowly to the mural, watching S for about 15 seconds. He moved closer and looked in the basket of markers.<br><br>S looked up at him, "See? Really fat markers!" She held one out to him. J *smiled at her, nodded,* and then slowly folded a hand around the marker.<br><br>S smiled back, relinquished the marker, picked up another, saying, "Come on. Let's draw!"<br><br>(Observation lasted 5 minutes) | S indicates that she wants to play with J.<br><br><br><br>J seems curious. As usual, is cautious. Other observations reveal his trust in S.<br><br>J's smile/nod: nonverbal positive interaction. Tentative in accepting even S's offer.<br><br>S responds positively. Issues another invitation to work together. |

Most of the writing takes place in the second, the Intensive Observation, column. Here, a teacher gives an objective and somewhat detailed account of the episode, and records both the child's speech and action. It is important to use descriptive phrasing to record only observable data—facts, what you saw and heard—not your opinion. In the next example, the observer has stated an opinion—that is, used subjective phrasing, which cannot be backed up by what she has recorded. Teachers should refrain from making such judgments.

**EXAMPLE**   "Sammy was selfish. He took the last piece of fruit." This is an opinion.

First, we do not have the right to judge others and there simply is not enough information presented for the teacher to conclude that Sammy is "selfish." This is one observation, and it is not ethical to draw conclusions on such an unconvincing amount of data.

It is advisable to record only what you see or hear, as the next example shows.

**EXAMPLE**   "Sammy had eaten two apple slices already when John joined the group. There was one slice left, Sammy watching it closely. Just as John reached for the plate, Sammy swept the plate over to his spot at the table, seized the remaining fruit, popped it into his mouth, and turned to John, grinning. He said, "Two points!"

This record gives better data. We have a better picture of Sammy's actions and words. The observer has not stated an opinion. However, we still do not have enough data to make conclusions. We would need more data, such as what happened before snack time, whether John had done something that upset Sammy before snack, and whether Sammy does this sort of thing with other children and in different places. One observation, however clearly written, is not enough data for making judgments.

The third column, Comments/Reflections, is for brief comments and reflections after completing the intensive observation. It is not necessary to comment on or interpret every observation. Writing comments or reflections is very helpful if we detect a pattern, but even then your comment must be made with utmost care. Even though you might think that you have enough information and know the facts, you might well have missed important information. Regarding Hector, Mr. Santini commented, "Same thing yesterday . . . lots of children greeted him [Hector] . . . demonstrated good social skills." For the apple episode, the teacher simply said nothing in the reflection column but vowed to observe further.

## Checklists

**Checklist**
Non-narrative method for observing; an inventory of characteristics or behaviors that can be checked as observed

A **checklist** is a list of characteristics or behaviors. A teacher observes an individual child or a group of children and notes whether each child does or does not show that behavior. The teacher records a check if a child shows the behavior or leaves a blank space if a child does not show the behavior. Checklists are an efficient way to determine the presence or absence of behaviors. For example, which children wash their hands correctly? How do children react to anger-arousing interactions? What social skills does the child demonstrate most of the time?

A checklist is a shortcut method because so little detail is given and it takes so little of a teacher's time. The teacher does not need to tell or narrate a story; thus, a checklist, like rating scales, and the sampling methods described in this chapter, is a non-narrative method. For a hand-washing checklist, for example, a teacher would know only whether a child had demonstrated the skill but would not know if he had to be reminded to wash his hands. You would choose a checklist approach if you only needed to know whether a child can or cannot do something. You would choose another method if you needed more detail.

Figure 6.4 shows the format for one type of checklist. It is McClellan and Katz's (2001) Social Attributes Checklist, which assesses social development. This checklist should be used several times to get as accurate an idea as possible. The developers of this checklist believe that a child's social development is adequate if he *usually* shows many of the attributes in the checklist.

Checklists have several benefits or advantages. They are extremely easy and quick to use for behaviors requiring only a check to determine their presence or absence. Checklists are flexible, meaning that teachers can choose when to complete the checklists and can use them to observe for the presence of specific social and emotional skills, such as using a word label for emotions. The drawbacks for checklists include lack of information about the quality of the behavior or the *how* of the behavior. It tells an observer whether a child approaches a group, for instance, but does not indicate *how* she approached: fearfully? joyfully? cautiously? Checklists give no information on how frequently a child shows a behavior. Does the child who approached a work group do this every day? Only when encouraged by the teacher? Only when specific children are in that group?

Increase the power of any of the non-narrative methods by combining them with anecdotal or running records, thus giving the detail missing in checklists. Some teachers insert a comment section on a checklist so that they can record their reflections or comments. This allows the teacher to give a bit more detail on the checklist. Here, remember that you need to use descriptive phrasing in the comments section and avoid writing subjective comments.

## Rating Scales

Teachers use a **rating scale** to *summarize* observations and to make a judgment about a child's performance. This implies that the teacher has already been observing with some other method. A rating scale is a shortcut method because the teacher does not present the original data, but it does allow teachers to organize information quickly and in an easy-to-read format. A rating scale, in general, is not very helpful at all unless it is preceded by other observations. A rating scale is somewhat useful in summarizing observations.

Teachers can develop rating scales that give them information for making guidance decisions. Figure 6.5 is a rating scale on Jerry's peer relationship attributes. These attributes were also checked in the sample checklist, but they are now evaluated using a rating scale instead. Note the section for comments, which allows a teacher to add brief notes on how she arrived at the judgment shown in the rating scale. The teacher has also added a section on how she intends to use the information to guide the child. Once again, to reiterate, it is essential to use descriptive, objective phrasing and avoid subjective phrasing in the comments section.

**Rating scale**
Non-narrative method for observing; a listing of activities or characteristics; calls for a summary judgment

**FIGURE 6.4**      A sample checklist.

**Social Attributes Checklist**
**Child's Name:** _____          **Date:**
**Observation number (circle one):** 1   2   3   4

**I. INDIVIDUAL ATTRIBUTES**
The child:
_____ Is *usually* in a positive mood
_____ Is not *excessively* dependent on the teacher, assistant, or other adults
_____ Usually comes to the program or setting willingly
_____ Usually copes with rebuffs adequately
_____ Shows the capacity to empathize
_____ Has positive relationships with one or two peers; shows capacity to really care about them, miss them if they are absent
_____ Displays the capacity for humor
_____ Does not seem to be acutely lonely

**II. SOCIAL SKILLS ATTRIBUTES**
The child *usually:*
_____ Approaches others positively
_____ Expresses wishes and preferences clearly; gives reasons for actions and positions
_____ Asserts own rights and needs appropriately
_____ Is not easily intimidated by bullies
_____ Expresses frustrations and anger effectively and without escalating disagreements or harming others
_____ Gains access to ongoing groups at play and work
_____ Enters ongoing discussion on the subject; makes relevant contributions to ongoing activities
_____ Takes turns fairly easily
_____ Shows interest in others; exchanges information with and requests information from others appropriately
_____ Negotiates and compromises with others appropriately
_____ Does not draw inappropriate attention to self
_____ Accepts and enjoys peers and adults of ethnic groups other than his or her own
_____ Interacts nonverbally with other children with smiles, waves, nods, and so forth

**III. PEER RELATIONSHIP ATTRIBUTES**
The child:
_____ Is usually accepted versus neglected or rejected by other children
_____ Is sometimes invited by other children to join them in play, friendship, and work
_____ Is named by other children as someone they are friends with or like to play and work with

*Source:* This is from an ERIC DIGEST. You may duplicate it without permission but must give credit to the developers: McClellan & Katz (2001).

**FIGURE 6.5**    A sample rating scale. Use rating scales after doing other forms of observation, which yield enough information on which to summarize with a rating scale

### Rating Scale: Peer Relationship Attributes

Reflect on your observations of this child, and rate his or her peer relationship characteristics. For each statement, choose the rating that best describes this child and circle the appropriate spot on the scale. Write a brief narrative in the Comments section. Use this information when you think about how to guide this child's peer relationships.

**Child's Name:** Jerry

**Date:** May 20

| | Usually | Only Occasionally | Never |
|---|---|---|---|
| Accepted by other children | ✓ (circled) | ✓ | ✓ |
| Neglected or rejected by other children | ✓ | ✓ | ✓ (circled) |
| Invited by other children to join them in play, friendship, and work | ✓ (circled) | ✓ | ✓ |
| Named by other children as a friend | ✓ (circled) | ✓ | ✓ |
| Named by other children as someone they like to play and work with | ✓ (circled) | ✓ | ✓ |

**Comments:** Jerry is well liked and, like all the children his age, has learned quite a lot about managing emotions and about social skills this year.

How I will use this information in guiding this child:

## :: FOCUS ON PRACTICE

This Focus on Practice activity is entitled *Methods for Observing Children's Behavior.* Note that each observation method is useful for teachers.

Some of the same advantages found in checklists exist in rating scales, too. Rating scales are easy to use and do not require much training. Observers tend to like using rating scales because they get to make a judgment and do not generally show the other observations on which the rating scale is based. Disadvantages include the great possibility of personal bias because the observer does not give supporting data. Many observers tend to rate every child at the middle of a rating scale, effectively rendering it useless.

Teachers should use rating scales only after they have observed a child in some other way and then want to make an overall statement about some aspect of guidance. For example, if a teacher has completed several objectively written anecdotal records about a child's peer relationship attributes, then a rating scale on the same topic would be a good way to present the data. The teacher could use the rating scale when talking with parents, saying that it was completed only after observing carefully using other methods. The teacher might show the rating scale along with captioned photos showing the child in thoughtful work groups with others, playing a board game with a friend, or greeting another child during morning meeting.

## Event Sampling

**Event sampling**
Formal method for identifying specific categories of behavior

**Event sampling** is a good way to observe one particular aspect of a child's development or learning. An observer identifies a specific target, such as "positive nonverbal interaction with other children." An important step is to define the category precisely. For instance, the teacher defines *positive nonverbal interaction* as "nodding; smiling; waving; or giving thumbs-up, a high-five, or other positive gesture of greeting." Then the teacher observes the child and records instances only of the defined behavior, nothing else.

Event sampling is a very focused type of observation and is quite useful (Brassard & Boehm, 2007). Suppose that a teacher, when using the Social Attributes Checklist, did not check an item such as "usually approaches others positively." The teacher wants to know more about this social skill for the child and decides to do an event sampling, which would zero in on that aspect of behavior. The major advantages of event sampling are that the focus is on something so specific and that a bit of detail is encouraged. A potential drawback would arise if the teacher did not define the behavior well. Figure 6.6 is an example of an event sampling form. In addition to the information about the date and child's name, you will see that there are three essential things to record. First is what happened right before the event, such as Sarah's observation told to Jerry that there were brand new markers in the writing center. Second is the event itself. Third is what happened after the event, such as Sarah's statement that there were many markers.

| **FIGURE 6.6** | **Event sampling form** |
| --- | --- |

**Focus of the observation:** Social skills, positive nonverbal interaction

**The event that I am looking for is as follows:** Interacts nonverbally with other children with smiles, waves, nods, a thumbs-up, a pat on the back

**Day of week/date:** Thursday, May 20

**Time:** 8:00 a.m.

**Child:** Jerry

| | |
| --- | --- |
| **Antecedent event:** What happened before the event? | Sarah whispered to Jerry, "I saw *new* markers in the art center. They're big and fat!" |
| **Describe the event** | Sarah went to the art center and stood at the mural paper on the wall. Jerry watched for about 15 seconds and then approached Sarah. She looked up at him and said, "See? Really fat markers!" and held one up for him to see. *He smiled at her and nodded.* |
| **Results:** What happened after the event? | Sarah smiled back and said, "Come on. Let's draw." |

## Cultural Scripts and Guiding Children
### Recognizing Culture's Potent Effect on Choosing What to Observe

**Remember Cultural Scripts about Childrearing**  Your culture's views on childrearing are a powerful influence on how to think about guiding children. These cultural scripts influence your beliefs and values even when you are unaware of the effect. If you grew up in mainstream American culture and your family has lived in this extremely individualistic setting for a long time, then you have likely absorbed the culture's value about asserting one's own rights.

**Teacher's Culture May Affect Choices in Observing**  Objectivity is a key issue in observing children's development. Eliminating bias is probably not entirely possible, given the power of culture over a person's belief system. Perhaps a more realistic view of objectivity in observing is to be as objective as possible, given the power and influence of one's culture, for example, in choosing what to observe in the first place. Suppose that you are selecting a behavior to observe with event sampling, and that your culture has taught you that asserting one's own rights is important. Therefore, you are likely to view observing this behavior as acceptable, even for children from more interdependent cultures *not* valuing the behavior.

**Scan Your Thinking When Choosing What to Observe**  Just as you run a spelling check when writing, consider running a "bias check" when choosing what to observe with event sampling and other observational strategies. Is the child you intend to observe from the same culture as you or is she from a different culture? Do not be afraid to reflect on whether your cultural scripts are influencing your choice of what to observe. Conscious reflection is appropriate and alerts us to take great care in our choices.

**Choose What to Observe with Different Cultures in Mind**  Is it ever acceptable, then, to choose to observe a behavior when your culture values the behavior and a child's culture places far less value on it, such as asserting one's own rights? It depends on your approach and your respect for a child. For the example given, parents in all cultures quite likely do not want their children to be victimized by bullies and would want to teach their children when and how their culture allows asserting the right to safety and freedom from being hurt. Our choice of what to observe will be more culturally sensitive if we embed our choices in knowledge of a different culture's beliefs. In the case of protecting children from bullying, a teacher could ask parents how their culture feels about bullying and about how they teach children to avoid being a victim of a bully.

## Time Sampling

**Time sampling** allows teachers to observe small samples of a child's behavior. It is useful in guiding children because teachers often use it for recording children's interactions. Time sampling is different from event sampling because it does not record every instance of a behavior, but instead records only a *sampling* of the behavior.

Figure 6.7 shows a time sampling form. The observer has to choose the total amount of time for observing and then divides the total time into equal intervals. The observer also decides the length of each interval. Finally, the observer chooses how long he will observe during the interval, for example, the first or last minute of a 3-minute interval.

**Time sampling**
Observes for a limited time period; focuses on a precisely defined behavior; records whether that behavior occurred

**FIGURE 6.7**    Time sampling form

**Observer's name:** C Johnson
**Child's name:** Jerry
**Date:** May 20
**Start time:** 8:00 a.m., beginning of center time
**Behavior observed:** Positive nonverbal interactions with another child, for example, smiles, nods, thumbs-up, waves

| Total Observation Time: 15 Minutes | How Long Is Each Interval? 5 Minutes | When and for How Long Will I Observe in the Interval? 1½ Minutes at the Beginning of the Interval |
|---|---|---|
| Interval | Did the behavior occur (yes if the behavior occurs; no if it does not); number of times that it occurred | Total number of times that the behavior occurred for this observation time period |
| 1 | Yes, one time in the 1½-minute interval | |
| 2 | Yes, one time | |
| 3 | No | Jerry showed positive nonverbal interaction with another child 2 times during the first 15 minutes of center time. |

There are benefits in time sampling. It requires observers to write less than in anecdotal or running records or even event sampling. Observers do not have to record every example of the behavior, only those behaviors that occur in the designated interval. A disadvantage is that some of the target behaviors do occur but outside the interval designated for monitoring.

---

## :: *Question for Reflection*

---

The next section focuses on portfolios, not an observational strategy, but a way of storing and documenting development and learning.

## :: PORTFOLIOS IN OBSERVING AND GUIDING CHILDREN

In this section, we will focus on how to use portfolios in the observation and assessment.

**Portfolio**
Collection of a child's work and the teacher's observation reports and selected observations

### What Is a Portfolio?

A **portfolio** is a collection of a child's work and of the teacher's observation report and selected observations about the child portfolios are a way for teachers to pull together meaningful documents and observations for each child. A portfolio is a convenient and logical method to collect, store, and document information about a child's progress throughout the year. The teacher uses such documentation to assess development and progress, making decisions about guidance and curriculum based on the analysis (Spinelli, 2008).

A portfolio is *not* a haphazard pile of items thrown into a folder or box. Teachers do not just collect everything that a child produces and they do not just throw all of their observations into a heap. Portfolios are collections, but they are thoughtfully constructed, discarding items that are not useful in assessing a child's learning and development and retaining items that clearly show a child's status. For example, Mr. Santini's set of event sampling observations showed that.

Portfolios are viewed as authentic or performance-based assessment. Authentic assessment involves items such observations and other forms of documentation to demonstrate a child's ability to function in real situations and not in artificial testing situations. Portfolios are a developmentally appropriate method for documenting and assessing children's development.

## Benefits of Portfolios for Children, Teachers, and Families

There are great potential benefits to children when teachers use portfolios well. Children's self-esteem—that is, their sense of competence, control, and worth—is enhanced when they learn about how they are progressing in academic work, social skills, and emotional development through the portfolio process. Giving children some say in what goes into the portfolio enhances their sense of control; feelings of competence grow when a child sees clear evidence of what he *can* do; a sense of worthiness, that feeling of being liked and appreciated develops on realizing that the teacher sees children worthy of teacher time necessary for portfolio development.

Teachers benefit from using portfolios well. Portfolios serve as an organizing force for developmentally appropriate practice. Portfolios are also an excellent starting point for talking with parents about a child. It is much easier, for example, to show a parent three paragraphs, one from September, one from October, and the third from November, that show clear progression in this writing skill than to just talk at the parent with no visuals.

Parents also benefit when teachers use portfolios well. Early childhood educators know the value of developing reciprocal and positive relationships with parents. Portfolios, when done well, helps teachers build such a relationship. Parent's understanding of their child's development grows upon examining a carefully constructed and informative portfolio. Parents understand academic performance after examining authentic assessments, such as progressively more skillfully written paragraphs or examining a progression of name-writing cards from a preschooler's portfolio. Parents better understand their child's social and emotional development when they read the teacher's observation report—not the original observation notes, but a report generated by using all observational strategies. Parents are much more likely to understand the goals of their child's school by examining the contents of a portfolio. For example, suppose that a school's website says that the school focuses on social skills and that children learn by interacting, at least some of the time, with other children. Then, a kindergarten teacher focuses on a child's social skill development in observations and in the portfolio (in addition to documenting academic work). When meeting with parents, she shows the parents the photos with captions showing their 5-year-old son working cooperatively with other children in several different settings. She points out the summary statement about their son's ability to work cooperatively with others. Thus, this teacher has brought the school's goal of fostering social skill development and cooperative learning to life for the parents.

## Efficient Use of Portfolios

Keep in mind that portfolios are repositories for data, observations, and other documents. Portfolios can be electronic or hard copy. Electronic portfolios are mandated by some schools, but other schools prefer using a hard copy portfolio. The format is not as important as how a teacher approaches the chosen format. Here is some information on using your time efficiently in working with children's portfolios, this example referring to hard copy portfolios.

- **Organize materials as simply as possible.** For example, use low-cost, sturdy boxes. Label each child's box clearly. Organize the group of boxes simply, such as alphabetically by child's last name. Place the set of boxes, the portfolios, in an easy-to-get-to spot. Figure 6.8 shows boxes serving as the portfolios.
- **Date observations and samples of work.** It is easy to forget when an item was created. Dating everything prevents frustration. Write the date on every item and in the same spot on every item, say, in the upper left corner. Making dating items a habit increases your efficiency and makes the portfolio much more useful.
- **Place items in the portfolio sequentially.** Store older items in front, more recent items behind the older. This saves your time. It also acts as an assistant. When you look at a portfolio, you will already have done much of the organizing work and you can move on quickly to thinking about what the progression shown in the organized items tells you about some aspect of the child's development. For our purposes, the progression would tell you about the child's progression in social and emotional development.
- **Organize by creating categories for different items.** This really depends on the age of the children and what a school is mandated to assess or what a school and each teacher chooses to assess. If teaching preschool, for example, categories might include *visual arts*, either originals or color photographs of easel paintings and drawings, for example. Samples, not every painting or drawing, from beginning to end of year, show a child's progress. Another would be *writing samples*, such as how the child progresses in writing her name or letters of the alphabet or numerals. Making guidance assessments is easier with documentation of a child's progress. Therefore, create a category *observation notes and observation reports,* which would have anecdotal records, checklists, or whatever specific observational methods are

**FIGURE 6.8**   Example of portfolio organization in an early childhood classroom

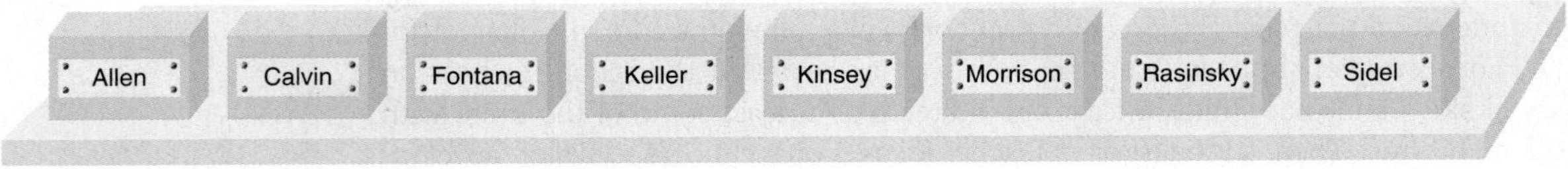

Allen   Calvin   Fontana   Keller   Kinsey   Morrison   Rasinsky   Sidel

## FAMILIES AS PARTNERS IN OBSERVING

Invite parents to form a partnership with you. Working together, you and the parents will guide children in your class even more effectively. Here are some ideas for helping parents understand the importance of observation.

- **Explain.** Give a handout or a website about why it is important to observe. Tell parents that you will be observing in the classroom to learn more about their child. Explain that you will use your observations to better plan for individual children.
- **Illustrate.** Show an example of a real observation form (one that is blank) and describe how you will complete it. Mrs. Johnson showed an anecdotal record form to a group of parents.

- **Request.** Tell parents that you will be observing emotional and social development, and request examples of their child's reaction to a happy emotion. Ask that they write this down or simply verbalize it. Tell them that you will be looking for similar examples of this and other parts of emotional development or social skills.
- **Invite.** Give parents two or three anecdotal record forms and urge them to observe how their child gets along with other children over the next couple of days. Request that they let you know about their observations.
- **Report.** Merge your and the parents' observations for your final report. Discuss both sets of observations with parents when you meet with them.

used. Also stored here would be photographs focusing on the child's social and emotional development—for example, working with one or more other children on a project or photo of child carrying out a required classroom job.

- **File items promptly.** Schedule this time; avoid letting things pile up. File things right away or at the end of every day. Older children can file their own work after a teacher has dated it and has taught them the chronological system.

## ANALYZE A VIGNETTE

Refer to the chapter-opening vignettes and to Table 6.1. Answer the following questions.

1. Answer as many of the first four "W" questions (Who, What, Where, When) as possible for each vignette.
2. The "Why" question—Toddlers: Enrique insisted on putting on mittens before his coat. Why might such a young child behave in this way? What does it tell us about normal toddler development?
3. The "Why" question—Preschool: Jerry shared something with Sarah and later she made room for him in group time. In your view, is it possible that the two events are connected? If so, then how?
4. The "Why" question—Primary: Sandi had a positive approach and was cheerful. Why does this sort of interaction usually work for children? What do you think would have happened if she had *ordered* Dave to wait his turn?

## SUMMARY

Assessment drives nearly every aspect of modern school life and is used to demonstrate a school's having met accountability requirements from a variety of agencies. Assessment is increasingly being used to document chil-

dren's development and to figure out the function of a child's difficult behavior. Assessment involves using a variety of methods to gather and record information about young children's development and learning. Appropriate assessment is done ethically, and teachers use assessment to make many different decisions that affect young children. Observation is one method of assessment. Key ideas about assessment include the following:

- Appropriate assessment is strength based, which means that it focuses on children's strong points, not their weaknesses.
- Appropriate assessment benefits children, teachers, parents, and administrators.
- One of the major purposes of assessment is for teachers to plan for meeting children's individual needs.

Observation, a form of authentic assessment, helps teachers plan for children. There are three main reasons for observing children's behavior:

- Children communicate with behavior. Observing helps teachers answer the 5 "W" questions about children's behavior.

- To discover and build on what children know and can do well.
- To assess individual needs.

Teachers have access to several realistic and efficient methods for observing. Some of these tell a story and other methods do not. Teachers choose the method best suited to their needs. The methods include the following:

- Anecdotal and running records.
- Checklists and rating scales.
- Event sampling and time sampling.

Portfolios provide a way for teachers to document children's learning and development. A portfolio is a thoughtfully constructed collection of children's work samples and teacher observation reports. This collection or portfolio, when carefully put together and analyzed, can clearly demonstrate a child having met learning standards and having grown in social and emotional as well as other domains of development.

## APPLY YOUR KNOWLEDGE

1. Suppose that you wanted to know more about the social skills, particularly turn taking, of the children in your kindergarten. Which of the following observational methods do you think would be the most powerful for getting this information? Why?
   a. Anecdotal records alone.
   b. Checklist alone.
   c. Anecdotal records plus checklist.

2. You decide to observe how a child reacts to anger-arousing events. Which of the formats for observing described in the chapter would work best for you in this case? Why?

## WEBSITES

### Center on the Social and Emotional Foundations for Early Learning (CSEFEL)
http://csefel.vanderbilt.edu/

Home page for CSEFEL, a federally funded, national resources center. Excellent resources in general, including on using observation. For example, take a look at the "What Works" link on the left side list on the home page. You will see in the *What Works Brief, Number 9*, one example of how observation is used, along with other sources of information to help children with challenging behaviors.

### High Scope Foundation
http://www.highscope.org

Several good links. Find the "Assessment" link and look for the Child Observation Record (COR). There is an Infant-Toddler COR and a Preschool COR. These are excellent observational assessment tools that chart a child's development and progress over time. Combines rating scales with anecdotal records. Highly recommended.

# Special Topics
# in Child Guidance

Each of the five chapters in this part of the book is designed to help you apply your knowledge to a specific special topic in guiding children.

**Chapter 7**   Self-Esteem and the Moral Self

Developmentally appropriate child guidance helps children develop a healthy and balanced sense of self and self-esteem that is firmly rooted in a strong set of personal values. Chapter 7 gives you several practical suggestions on how to use guidance to support children in developing healthy self-esteem and a moral identity.

**Chapter 8**   Feelings and Friends: Emotional and Social Competence

Effective teachers support children's social and emotional competence. Children begin to develop these competencies in infancy and continue to develop them through childhood. We will examine the "essential topics" in Social Emotional Learning (SEL), and will learn about specific ways in which you can teach these topics. In addition, we will examine practical strategies for helping young children deal with disappointment and anger and for developing skills in forming friendships.

**Chapter 9**   Resilience and Stress in Childhood

Chapter 9 explains the concept of resilience and concentrates on the positive when describing children and stress. You will read about the nature of stress and how stress affects children. The main focus in this chapter is to help you develop knowledge and skills for assisting children in coping with specific stressful events, with one major stressor emphasized as an example.

### Chapter 10   Aggression and Bullying in Young Children

You will study two topics in Chapter 10: aggression and bullying. The chapter describes and explains different forms and purposes or goals of aggression. The focus then shifts to a topic of great concern to teachers—bullying, which is a type of aggression. We will examine cyberbullying and skills that children need for dealing with a bully, such as a bully who teases and taunts. The chapter explains how children gather information on how to be aggressive from different systems and the feature on culture focuses on helping children acquire new cultural scripts that prevent aggression, which includes bullying.

### Chapter 11   Minimizing Challenging Behavior

All teachers are puzzled and frustrated at times when our positive guidance strategies do not seem to work. Chapter 11 will help you understand the nature of challenging behaviors and the major roots of challenging behavior. You will learn about how useful it is to figure out the function that a child's challenging behavior serves—that is, the purpose of the behavior. We will examine the process of functional behavioral assessment (FBA), through which a behavior's function can be revealed. Then, we will use FBA to learn how to deal with several specific challenging behaviors, such as interrupting, teasing, biting, aggressive behavior (for example, throwing things, kicking objects and people, or damaging and destroying things), whining and pestering, and tattling. Once you know how to identify the function of a child's challenging behavior, you will be in a better position to begin to deal with it effectively.

# CHAPTER 7

# Self-Esteem and the Moral Self

## Learning Outcomes

- List and explain the parts of the self
- Explain why each part of the self is important in a child's development and behavior
- Label the building blocks of self-esteem
- Outline the development of self-esteem in early childhood
- Define authentic self-esteem
- Explain how teachers can help children develop authentic self-esteem
- Define moral identity
- State reasons for helping children develop a moral identity

### VIGNETTES

#### INFANT-TODDLER: PLAYING THE "POINT TO" GAME

*Mr. Bensen sat facing 15-month-old Jamal, who had just pointed to his nose. The teacher said, "Now, point to your arm." "Arm!" squealed Jamal. They continued Jamal's favorite game, with the toddler pointing to his feet, legs, head, and eyes.*

#### PRESCHOOL: SHOWING KINDNESS TO SQUEAK

*Mrs. Johnson, the teacher, was leading a discussion on making rules for the classroom and wanted the children to help design the limits. "We need a rule about how to show kindness to Squeak, our hamster. What do you think that we should say?" Sarah said, "Don't drop Squeak. Don't squeeze him. Hold him like this." She demonstrated gentle holding and stroking. Jerry added, "Yeah, and be quiet when you're near his house."*

#### PRIMARY: GRAPHING GROUP INFORMATION

*Instead of doing an "all about me" chart for each child, Mr. Santini's class did an "all about us" chart. He explained this different approach. "I was trying out this idea to get the children away from focusing so much on themselves as individuals. It's Katz's (1993) idea, really. We gathered information about each child: number of teeth, eye color, number of lost teeth, shoe size, current weight, birth weight. Then we pooled all the information on each item and made graphs. What you see on the wall chart is information—for example, on how many children in the class have brown, blue, or green eyes, or the average weight of first graders in our room. This way, we did not single out any one child."*

## :: INTRODUCTION

The children in the chapter-opening vignettes are learning about themselves and will eventually develop self-esteem and a moral identity. Building self-esteem is an active process that continues throughout a lifetime (Mruk, 2013). The wonderful thing about working with children is that we are present as children start to evaluate themselves, and we can help them construct a healthy and balanced view of themselves. Children's initial self-esteem develops slowly in early childhood and tends to be positive and stable (Robins & Trzesniewski, 2005). Authentic self-esteem—positive, healthy, earned, and balanced—provides a secure foundation for further growth and development. Negative, unhealthy, unbalanced self-esteem, on the other hand, provides a shaky foundation for a child's development. Some children with damaged self-esteem make a negative evaluation of their competence, control, or worth. This negative evaluation stays with a person for many years or even decades, and affects many aspects of a person's life.

In this chapter, you will learn about the four parts of the self. We will then focus on the building blocks of self-esteem and how self-esteem develops. Then, because children need a strong moral compass as much as they need positive self-esteem, we will examine moral identity and what it means to a child's sense of self. Then you will study practices that help children develop positive, authentic, earned self-esteem.

## :: PARTS OF THE SELF

The **self** is a mental structure, a set of ideas that humans gradually construct or build (Harter, 2006; Mruk, 2013). Children need to develop a stable sense of self so that they understand themselves, and like all humans, they need to set goals, regulate thoughts and emotions, find out what they enjoy doing, and be able to persevere in meeting goals. The starting point to this understanding is in knowing one's self (Brown, Mangelsdorf, Neff, Schoppe-Sullivan, & Frosch, 2009).

Children begin to construct their sense of self during infancy and continue to develop this concept throughout their lives. The four parts or components making up a child's self are:

Self-awareness

Self-concept

Self-control

Self-esteem

Figure 7.1 illustrates each of the four parts and Figure 7.2 gives examples of each.

**Self**
A concept that a child produces in his or her mind; ideas are constructed gradually; consists of four components: self-awareness, self-concept, self-control, and self-esteem

## Self-Awareness

**Self-awareness** refers to the idea that a child views himself as separate from others. For example, a child might say that his mother is a person and that he is separate from her. Infants gradually learn that they are separate from other people as the perceptual system develops during the first year of life. Self-awareness emerges during infancy and toddlerhood and continues to develop during early childhood. Self-awareness also

**Self-awareness**
Child sees himself as separate from others

**FIGURE 7.1**   There are four parts to a child's self

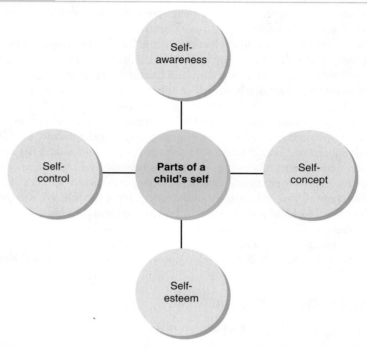

means that a child realizes that he can make things happen. For example, an infant learns that when he cries, someone will pick him up. A preschool child knows that he can get the teacher's attention by asking for help.

A child must be aware of her self as separate from others and as capable of causing things to happen before she can develop self-esteem.

## Self-Concept

**Self-concept**
The accumulation of knowledge that a child gathers about herself

**Self-concept** is the knowledge that a child acquires about herself. Children go through a long process of learning about the self. They gradually gather information about their physical appearance, physical abilities, gender, intellectual abilities, and interpersonal skills. Gathering such knowledge occurs at about the same time as more general changes in cognitive development, as shown in the next examples.

> **EXAMPLE**   Six-year-old Joe participated in one of the classic Piagetian conservation experiments with Mr. Santini and said, "You have the same amount of water in that short glass as you have in that tall glass because the short glass is so wide that it holds just as much as the tall glass." Conservation is one of the general changes in cognitive development.

During that same week the teacher heard Joe say to his friend Reese, "Yeah! We're boys and we'll always be boys. They're girls (pointing to a group of girls) and they're always going to be girls." This is called gender constancy, and children

| FIGURE 7.2 | Observe to discover what children are constructing about the parts of the self |

Children gradually build ideas about the self and their current knowledge reveals itself in simple everyday statements that they make to other children or teachers. They also reveal their current knowledge about their self through behavior. Here are a few examples.

**Self-awareness** (child knows he is an individual and can influence events)

"Mommy! (toddler points to his mother). "José!" (toddler points to himself).

"When I curse, everybody looks at me and then they giggle or laugh" (preschool child's behavior indicates this).

"We have five people in my family: Mommy, Dad, John, Sarah, and me" (kindergarten child says this when he and Mr. Santini looked at pictures of families).

"When I call my dog, she trots over to me and then I pet her or give her a treat" (primary child).

"I swing at the mobile and it moves" (infant's behavior).

**Self-concept** (child learns things about herself)

"My grandma told me that I look like my aunt Gail."

"Sam and Ralph like me" (child learns that others like him).

"I am a girl" (child learns that her gender is female).

"I can run fast. I'm still learning how to swim" (child learns about athletic ability).

"I can speak Spanish and English!" (child learns about ability to speak languages).

**Self-control** (children use these behaviors to regulate impulses, tolerate frustration, and delay immediate gratification)

"I used WORDS to tell Pete that I wanted my book back."

"I wanted to tell the teacher something, but he was talking with Susan, so I waited."

"I'd better look at the list to see who is next at the computer."

**Self-esteem** (child evaluates the "self" she has come to know)

"My dad called me a dummy this morning. I feel bad."

"My uncle helped me with my math last night and said that I'm a 'natural-born' mathematician."

"My brother and I finally figured out how to attach the wheels to the car. Mom said that we are persistent and that is a good way to be."

"My teacher told the class that we work well together. We are a class full of helpers."

understand that gender remains the same when they understand the concept that some things remain the same despite apparent changes.

A child's set of ideas about himself affects how he behaves. Because 7-year-old Melanie thinks that she can run fast, for example, she is much more likely to enter races than her friend who does not think that she can run fast.

## Self-Control

Self-control, also called self-regulation, refers to controlling impulses, tolerating frustration, and delaying immediate gratification. The means of this control lies deep within us and is the basis of our intentional and deliberate behavior. In acquiring self-control, children must learn how to *stop* a behavior, such as blurting out questions during a large group. They have to be able, then, to *inhibit* (stop) a behavior. They must also be able to *do* something that they are supposed to do even if they do not want to comply such as cleaning up a play or workspace after using it. Therefore, they must be able to initiate or start a behavior (Bedrova & Leong, 2005).

Milestones in self-control show the beginnings of self-control at about 24 months and children become better able to use certain strategies to regulate their own behavior as they get older. Self-control or regulation enables children to stop themselves from hurting somebody, to think before acting, and to use words instead

**Self-control**
A child's ability to put off gratification until later, to put up with some frustration, and to keep impulses under control

of hitting. Developing good self-control depends on a number of factors, among them how a child's brain processes information. Recent research (Hackman & Farah, 2009; Kishiyama, Boyce, Jiminez, & Knight, 2009) identified disparities in processing of information in the brain between high socioeconomic status (SES) and low SES children. A child whose brain does not process information well will be at a disadvantage in developing self-control.

How important is it for children to develop self-control? Does higher level self-control have any significant impact on a child's success in life? The answer is decidedly yes. We can see differences in self-control between children during early childhood. In a large study that followed the same children from very early childhood to adulthood, researchers found that self-control predicted wealth, crime, and health for both boys and girls and over a 30-year span. Self-control stood out as the thing that best predicted a child's future health, wealth, and crime and the researchers were able to separate self-control from a child's level of intelligence, social class, or their family's circumstances (Moffitt et al., 2011).

Moffitt et al. (2011) advise that prevention of future difficulties starts with helping children develop self-control and advise that developing self-control be the lynchpin in any such prevention effort. Effective and positive child guidance is one of the best ways to help children develop their ability to regulate their own behavior. Setting up a classroom where the child safely practices self-control, is required to be responsible for his actions, and where he finds friendship, acceptance, and a warm and nurturing teacher who also makes reasonable demands is an excellent roadmap to self-control. For example, we now know that high-quality imaginative play in which children have to develop props and stop and think teaches them to attend to changes and to adjust to the "twists and turns" of such play (Valentine, 2008). Adjusting to daily twists and turns in interactions and in the classroom is one of the things that will help children gain better self-control. Everyday interactions between a teacher and a child are another way to help children learn about regulating their behavior on their own. In the next example, Mr. Santini helps Clayton with inhibiting or stopping a behavior, and then intentionally doing something more productive instead.

**EXAMPLE** "Remember what we practiced yesterday?" Mr. Santini asked Clayton when he greeted him in the morning. "That's right. Listen to others during large-group lessons."

## Self-Esteem

**Self-esteem**
A child's overall judgment of the self about which he is aware, knows about, and regulates

**Self-esteem** refers to how a child evaluates the self about whom she has learned (Coopersmith, 1967; Harter, 2006; Mruk, 2013). A child pays attention to information that she has gathered about herself and judges the self. A child who evaluates herself as competent, in control, and worthy will likely develop healthy, balanced judgment; she is likely to have predominately positive self-esteem. A child who evaluates herself as unworthy, unloved, and not competent will likely develop a negative view of the self; she will very likely have predominately negative self-esteem.

Others have a positive view of their abilities, but are conceited, arrogant, self-absorbed, and egotistical at the same time (Mruk, 2013).

A brief note on the term *high self-esteem*, which is a heterogenous term consisting of varied parts. We get an interesting picture when we examine the term *high self-esteem* more closely. Some people with high self-esteem simply and gratefully acknowledge their abilities, such as a talented speller who is humble. High-self-esteem people can also include another type, however, such as those who are conceited, narcissistic, self-absorbed, egotistical, and arrogant (Baumeister, Campbell, Kreuger, & Vohs, 2003; Mruk, 2013). For example, another child is a good mathematician but sneers at others with less math ability.

---

### :: *Question for Reflection*

---

## :: BUILDING BLOCKS OF SELF-ESTEEM

What is it in the self that a child examines and evaluates so that she can develop her self-esteem? Self-esteem is not just one overall global concept; it can be broken down into distinct parts (Coopersmith, 1967; Harter, 2006; Mruk, 2013). As shown in Figure 7.3, the parts or dimensions of self-esteem are:

Competence

Control

Worth

---

## :: FOCUS ON PRACTICE

This Focus on Practice activity is entitled *Physical Activity and Development Can Influence Children's Self-Esteem.* Notice how play can have a positive influence on how children form self-esteem.

---

|  |  |
|---|---|
| **FIGURE 7.3** | Competence, control, and a feeling of worthiness are the building blocks of a child's self-esteem |

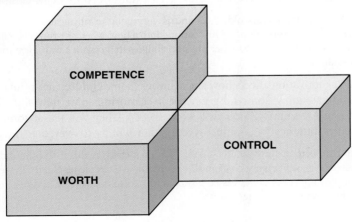

# Competence

**Competence** is the ability to meet demands for achievement, growing over time and with effort (Dweck & Molden, 2005) along with support from a nurturing parent or teacher (Tafarodi, Wild, & Ho, 2010). Children earn authentic, healthy self-esteem. People with healthy self-esteem have learned that they cannot just wish for competence, but that they must work for it. They understand that they have to make things happen through their own effort rather than trying to force or manipulate others into doing things for them. Successfully planning and doing hard work tends to result in healthy self-esteem, an earned and positive self-evaluation, which increases feelings of competence.

Children congratulated for mediocre work do not develop healthy, earned self-esteem. Giving good feedback means that teachers give positive feedback, as well as suggestions for change when appropriate. Failing to give suggestions for change or implying that everything a child does is excellent is highly inappropriate.

It is important to help children develop self-esteem that is realistic, positive, and healthy. It is highly *in*appropriate to hollowly boost children's view of themselves artificially. Artificially boosting self-esteem gives children inflated self-esteem and an unrealistically positive view about the self (Baumeister et al., 2003). Children who have a balanced sense of self can look at themselves in several dimensions and make realistic judgments about how they are doing in a particular area. It is possible to feel extremely competent in one area and only moderately competent in another, and still have positive self-esteem.

> **EXAMPLE**   Sandi, a child in Mr. Santini's first grade, is 6 years old and is very competent socially; she gets along well with adults and other children. She makes friends easily and knows how to get her parent or teacher's attention without whining. She deals with angry feelings in a positive way. She is only moderately competent in physical skills but seems to enjoy them anyway because her mother and father have never made physical skills an issue.

Other children have a far less balanced view of themselves. They might not recognize their competence in an area and might even dwell on poor performance in some other area. Children with a negative view of their competence might have had their lack of ability pointed out by adults. Some children are humiliated for being competent.

> **EXAMPLE**   Celia, 5 years old, likes and is very good at physical activities. Her mother, however, teases Celia about "turning into a boy" when she runs and climbs. Celia has begun to think about her physical abilities in a negative way, even though she is skillful.

A child's motivation affects how she achieves. Some children are primarily interested in understanding something new or in acquiring some new skill. They are oriented toward learning (Elliott & Dweck, 1988). They will fail at some tasks or make mistakes, but they will not just give up; they will try to overcome the problem.

> **EXAMPLE**   Pete, a third grader in Mr. Santini's class, realized that he did not understand the new science concept about a pulley as a simple machine. He seemed puzzled but not upset about his confusion and said to his teacher, "I don't understand this. Can you help me?"

Other children, motivated differently, go to great lengths to avoid unfavorable judgments about their competence. They dread mistakes and often react to them by giving up a project instead of trying again, practicing, and overcoming the difficulty.

> **EXAMPLE**  Eight-year-old Karim went to a day camp during the summer and one of the projects was to collect, preserve, and identify a variety of leaves. Karim forgot to press the leaves and ended up with crinkled, dry leaves that cracked when he put them in his book. When the camp counselor offered to help Karim gather new leaves, Karim started crying. He refused to go back to camp the next day.

Some children have confidence that they can achieve their goals, whereas others expect that they will not be able to achieve their goals even when they have the capacity to do so. Children who expect to perform well on challenging tasks are able to analyze the skills needed for effective performance. Children who expect to be able to perform well realistically analyze tasks. They are not overly optimistic, but they do not overestimate the difficulty of a task or say, "I can't do it" (Dweck & Leggett, 1988; Elliott & Dweck, 1988). They also tend to deal well with failure or minor setbacks.

## Control

Control is the degree to which a child thinks that he is responsible for how things turn out. Control is a lifelong issue, and a child's sense of control is a critical aspect of self-esteem. Some children believe that they do have a measure of control, that they can "get things done," and that their actions influence whether they achieve a goal. They also believe that they can decide how much effort to expend in achieving goals—that they have control over their effort. They have a positive and healthy view of control, as 4-year-old Nellie does in the next example.

**Control**
The extent to which a child thinks that he can influence outcomes of events

> **EXAMPLE**  Nellie was doing a science experiment—adding food coloring to white play dough to change the color of the dough. She tried to match a light blue color on a chart but added far too much coloring. Her teacher said, "You have a problem. What do you think would happen if you took this big glob of white dough and mixed it with your small glob of dark blue dough? It will take a lot of squishing and squashing!" Nellie pummeled and pushed the dough until she got the light color that she wanted and said, "Look! I made the color of the sky!"

Nellie had had a minor setback. Something had not gone well for her and she essentially failed at what she had set out to do. It is important for children to learn to deal with such minor setbacks if they are to develop authentic self-esteem (Katz, 1993). Hundreds of such interactions with adults who help them deal with setbacks teach children that they can control many of the outcomes in their lives.

Many children have been discouraged from viewing themselves as "in control." *Authoritarian* teachers and parents, for example, exert a great deal of arbitrary control over children, discouraging them from making decisions and from engaging in appropriate verbal give-and-take with adults. Some parents are abusive or neglectful, which very possibly has long-term negative effects on children's development (Child Welfare Information Gateway, 2013). For example, some abusive parents model an extremely rigid, external type of control. It is difficult for children from these types of families to evaluate themselves as controlling anything that happens to them. The children tend not to think that their own actions influence whether they achieve goals, and this contributes to negative self-esteem.

## Worth

**Worth**
A child's view about how significant he is to others

**Worth** refers to a child's general sense of his own social value, of his significance to others. He evaluates how much he likes himself and whether he thinks that others like or love him. Whether a child judges himself worthy also grows from feeling accepted by and deserving of attention from others. Children who feel accepted, well liked, and deserving of others' attention are likely to evaluate themselves as worthy. Others see themselves as unloved and unworthy of attention, and are likely to evaluate themselves as unworthy.

## :: SELF-ESTEEM DEVELOPS IN A SOCIAL CONTEXT

Any child's view of herself develops in a social context or setting. Infants are born with a basic temperamental style and certain physical, psychological, and emotional characteristics. These characteristics influence that baby's behavior as well as adults' reactions to the infant. An infant's self depends on both factors—the child's characteristics and

The "self" that an infant comes to know depends on the infant's characteristics *and* the behavior of other people.

interaction behavior with other people (Kernis, Brown, & Brody, 2000; Mruk, 2013). This implies that both the child and the adult have an active role in a child's developing sense of self; a child's sense of self is not just a mirror image of the adult's attitude toward that child. However, *adults always have a greater share of responsibility in any interaction with a child.*

> **EXAMPLE**   Mr. Bensen, the infant teacher, noticed that Amelia, 5 months old, cried a lot in spite of loving and appropriate caregiving. The teacher thought that something was bothering Amelia, that Amelia needed something. The caregiver thought, "Hmm, how can I help Amelia?"

To this caregiver's credit, he recognized his responsibility to figure out how to mesh his responses with the baby's style.

## Adults Influence a Child's Self-Esteem: Garbage In, Garbage Out (GIGO)

Teachers, parents, grandparents, brothers, sisters, and others make up a child's social environment; a child's opinion about her competence, control, and worth develops out of close involvement with them. Adults observe children, have attitudes about them, interact with them, and interpret a child's behavior and characteristics. Adults reflect their attitudes about children to children. Children evaluate the self and develop self-esteem, to some extent, because of the attitudes of others important to them. Parents and teachers affect children's self-esteem because young children believe that adults possess a superior wisdom and because children tend to rely on adult judgments.

Computer programmers use an unusual term, *garbage in, garbage out*, to describe the effect of feeding nonsensical or invalid data into a computer. What comes out is often a huge pile of equally nonsensical or invalid output. The process that adults use to influence children's self-esteem is similar to the process that a computer programmer employs to develop information "output."

Significant adults feed data to the child through words, facial expressions, and actions, which essentially outline the adult's attitude toward the child. The adult "data" say things such as:

"You sure have lots of friends!"

"You're so gentle with Sam [the puppy]. I'll bet he feels safe with you."

"I like being with you."

"It's okay to feel angry when somebody takes something that belongs to you and you remembered to use words to tell him that you were upset."

"It was thoughtful of you to whisper when you walked past the baby's crib when she was sleeping."

"It was fun to play the video game with you. Let's do that again sometime."

"This class really works well together on projects."

"You tell funny jokes. Let's call Grandma so that you can tell her!"

Unfortunately, adult data can also bruise self-esteem with hurtful statements such as these:

"No wonder nobody plays with you!"

"You're really a lazy person."

"Yuck! What muddy colors you used for painting."

"Don't bother me. Play by yourself."

"Grow up! Stop whining because she took your puzzle."

"Why don't you stop cramming food into your face? You're fat enough already."

"You know something? I wish you'd never been born."

Computer scientists emphasize that if input is garbage (harmful data), then we can expect output to be garbage as well. Adults who degrade a child with rubbishy messages should realize the harmful effects of their practice: garbage in, garbage out.

Other relationships, such as those with other children, can also affect children's self-esteem.

## Bullying and Self-Esteem

Bronfenbrenner's theory reminds us that the systems in which children live include other children, for example, a child's peers and siblings. Interactions and relationships with other children can affect a child's self-esteem. Some interactions, such as bullying, are problematic.

**Bullying**
Intentionally and repeatedly hurting or humiliating someone. Bullying takes different forms and is done in different ways

**Bullying**, discussed in greater detail in another chapter, is a form of aggression in which a child intends to humiliate or hurt the victim. Bullying involves repeated negative acts in which the bully enjoys hurting the victim and the victim feels oppressed. Bullying can be verbal, psychological, or physical, and it can be done face-to-face or more underhandedly such as through gossip or through social networking—that is, cyberbullying. For example, a bully might hit or punch his victim or might call him names. The bully might tease his victim or spread rumors. Many bullies use some form of technology, such as cell phones, the Internet, or interactive and digital devices. As technology advances even farther, we can predict that some child and adolescent bullies will use the new devices to torment a victim.

Recall that it is possible to have high self-esteem and still be arrogant and mean-spirited. More than two decades ago, Olweus (1993) found that bullies very often, but not always, have high self-esteem. A later review of research noted that some bullying prevention programs were based on the idea that all bullies had low self-esteem but that this assumption was in error. Instead, later work found that high self-esteem, in a subset of people, tends to be associated with narcissism (egotism and self-absorption) and possibly aggressive behavior (Mar, DeYoung, Higgins, & Peterson, 2006), such as bullying. This is a subset, not everybody with high self-esteem, and means that having a high self-esteem score does not necessarily go hand-in-hand with being a nice person. Some child bullies fall into this category—high self-esteem and willing to hurt others.

Some child bullies, on the other hand, have lower overall self-esteem than children who do not bully (O'Moore & Kirkham, 2001). What about victims of bullying? Does getting bullied damage self-esteem? It would be reasonable to hypothesize that being bullied—for example, hit, gossiped about, made fun of, and humiliated—would bruise self-esteem, but what does the evidence from research tell us? Bullying does seem to have a negative effect on children's self-esteem. The victims in O'Moore and Kirkham's study (2001) had the lowest scores on self-esteem.

## :: THE MORAL SELF

It is not enough to help children develop knowledge about themselves and positive self-esteem. Children certainly need positive self-esteem, but each child also needs to embed his or her self in a strong ethical and moral framework because their world is filled with moral issues and they need to be able to deal with these effectively as they get older. A child needs to develop a moral self or moral identity.

### What Is Moral Identity?

The work of Narvaez and Lapsley (2009) guides this section. A person may define and describe him- or herself in many ways. One way is to use concepts such as caring, compassionate, fair, friendly, generous, helpful, hardworking, honest, and kind. Thus, a person who uses such words to describe his self is referring to his **moral identity** or moral self. His view of himself focuses closely on the ethical and moral part of a person's self and involves a willingness to see things from another's perspective as well as behaving compassionately and doing work that matters (Coles, 1986, 1997; Damon, 2009; Lapsley, 2008; Narvaez & Lapsley, 2009). Although every person has a moral identity, people differ in the degree to which they use moral principles to define the self. Words used to describe oneself, therefore, give clues about that person's moral identity.

**Moral identity**
Describing oneself by using moral principles such as honesty, kindness, and fairness

> **EXAMPLE**  Alex uses words such as "fair when I work as an umpire" and "kind to my pets" to describe himself. Alex's friends use words such as "nice" and "kind" to describe him because he will help anybody with math.

Just as a compass indicates direction, Alex has a strong *moral compass* guiding his behavior. Suppose that he did not have such a guide and approached things differently, such as refusing to help others or even laughing at them, or feeding and playing with his pet only when it was convenient to Alex. With such egotistic, arrogant behavior, it would be unlikely that he would describe himself as kind. Children need to feel good about themselves, but they also need a strong, objective moral compass to help them acquire a stable sense of right and wrong.

### When and How Does Moral Identity Develop?

We tend to think about morality as an issue for older adolescents and adults, but realize that the beginnings of a moral self have their roots in very early childhood, for example, in toddlers. The progress made by toddlers in all the developmental domains is the foundation of their emerging moral capabilities. When they are about 18 months old, toddlers seem to have a good idea of the way that people are supposed to act. They have a sense of what adults expect and a general sense of responsibility. Furthermore, each child's temperament, level of self-control, and understanding of other people are a part of the foundation for developing a moral self. Kochanska's research, cited by Narvaez and Lapsley (2009), explained how children build on these capabilities to develop their moral self, their moral identity. There are two basic steps involved in developing a moral self in which a toddler becomes a caring, compassionate, fair, friendly, generous, helpful, hardworking, honest, and kind individual.

**Quality of Adult-Child Relationship and Developing a Moral Self**
Bronfenbrenner's (1979) theory informs us that children exist is several "nested" systems—family, peers, school, neighborhood, larger culture—and is affected by all of the systems. Within their families and other caregiving settings, a very young child experiences relationships with adults. The quality of the relationship between a very young child and adults who care for her is a major factor in a child's developing a moral self. Such a relationship has to be a two-way street, with caregiver and child responding to one another willingly and quite often joyfully. Both the caregiver and child are willing to start interactions, the contacts are positive, and they have a great time together. Both caregiver and very young child cooperate in these interactions.

**Compliance and Moral Internalization**    This type of a relationship indicates a secure attachment, and makes it possible for a child to willingly accept the parent or caregiver's values and beliefs. The child is then ready to comply with parent's wishes willingly; the child's compliance is given freely. This gives rise to the child's moral self and it is this moral self that regulates moral behavior in the child's future. A child's moral identity, first of all, governs his view of the right thing to do. Alex, 16 years old, knows that the right thing to do is to help others, whether it is his pets or other students needing help with math. Second, moral identity also determines *why* a child should take a specific course of action (Damon, 2004). Alex takes his friends' perspective and understands their frustration when they have trouble with math because he also experiences frustration even though he excels in math. He reasons that he can and should help them learn math, just as others have helped him.

At age 16, Alex's moral decision making is more sophisticated that it was when he was a very young child, but the foundation for his 16-year-old moral decision-making ability started in early childhood, specifically with a loving relationship with parents. Alex willingly accepted and later internalized his parent's values. Other children with a less secure attachment to parents and more authoritarian parenting tend not to self-regulate their behavior very well and have less advanced moral reasoning (Piotrowski, Lapierre, & Linebarger, 2013).

## Theoretical Perspectives on Moral Identity

Many theorists have contributed to understanding moral and character development. Lawrence Kolhberg's cognitive developmental approach described a lifespan view of moral development. He named six stages in moral development and maintained that the stages were universal. Each stage, he believed, was qualitatively different from stages either before or after it (Kohlberg, 1958, 1981; Power, Higgins, & Kohlberg, 1989). However, Carol Gilligan noted that Kohlberg's work was based on research involving boys only, not girls. She believes that his work, therefore, was fundamentally flawed. Her research went beyond that of Kohlberg to describe and explain girls' moral development (Gilligan, 1993, 2008; Snall, 2007).

Robert Coles, a child psychiatrist, wrote extensively about the moral life of children (Coles, 1986, 1997). He was particularly interested in how some children living under the most extreme stress could show grace, psychological strength, and moral clarity. He described the experience of Ruby, an African American child who integrated a school in the American South in the early 1960s and who displayed a remarkably calm approach to dealing with her harassers.

John Dewey, a philosopher, believed that children, such as Ruby in Robert Coles's work, gradually understand the moral resources of the culture. Dewey also believed that schools should work with parents in terms of moral education. He believed that children develop moral understanding as they work and learn with others in school (Dewey, 1897).

Constructivist theorists, such as DeVries and Zan (1994) or Hildebrandt and Zan (2008), believe, as Dewey did, that teachers can help children build their own ideas about the right thing to do. Among the many strategies that they advocate is discussing moral issues. Children can, for example, come up with classroom rules or limits. Many of these are based on moral principles and topics about which children care, such as how animals are treated or how we treat others in embarrassing situations. Note this classroom rule suggested by a first grader and reported by Hildebrandt and Zan (2008): "Don't laugh when people pass gas. It might hurt their feelings." Even though this child was only 6 years old, he was concerned about the possibility of causing embarrassment to others.

## :: PRACTICES THAT HELP CHILDREN DEVELOP AUTHENTIC SELF-ESTEEM

Adults use specific practices that affect a child's self-esteem. Author*itative*, supportive adults use strategies that help children develop authentic—healthy, positive, earned, and realistic—self-esteem. Nonsupportive adults use strategies that degrade or humiliate children, thus contributing to the development of negative self-esteem (Pawlak & Klein, 1997). Other adults focus on activities that ultimately foster narcissism or excessively self-centered views of the self.

### Believe in and Adopt an Authoritative Caregiving Style

Authoritative caregivers are demanding in an appropriate way. They are also highly responsive to what children need. The authoritative style helps children comply with (obey) reasonable limits and assists them to be more helpful and cooperative and less aggressive. Authoritative adults also help children develop positive self-esteem (Kernis et al., 2000; Pawlak & Klein, 1997). Parents and teachers are most likely to help children develop healthy self-esteem by combining acceptance, affection, high but reasonable expectations, and limits on children's behavior and effort. Children also have a better chance of developing healthy self-esteem when parents have little conflict in their marriages. It appears that excessive conflict between parents spills over into the relationship between a parent and child. Parents having difficulties in their marriage may not be as responsive to their child as they would like to be (Day, Hair, Moore, Kaye, & Orthner, 2009).

## Plan Appropriate Activities That Are Deserving of Children's Time

You really do not need to plan "cute activities" intended to boost self-esteem. In fact, cute activities are frequently developmentally *in*appropriate. One of the leaders in our field explained quite a while ago that children are most likely to develop authentic self-esteem when they participate in activities for which they can make real decisions and contributions, such as the graphing of information in the chapter-opening vignette for the primary grade (Katz, 1993). The project approach, for example, helps children focus on real topics, environments, events, and objects that are deserving of a young child's time and effort. Developmentally appropriate activities help a child see herself as connected to others, as a hard worker, as kind and helpful, and as a problem solver. These are enduring traits that will help children develop a healthy sense of self and self-esteem and a moral self.

As you watch this **video**, identify the real topics that the children's painting were based on. How would this activity, the painting, and then the discussion lead these children to seeing themselves as connected to others and as a hard worker?

Organize a classroom so that children play and work collaboratively, which allows for the give-and-take that helps children understand that others have ideas, too. Self-esteem and moral identity grow in classrooms where children take responsibility for keeping the room tidy, for how they speak to others, for how they work with others, and for how they treat animals.

## Express Genuine Interest in Children and Their Activities

Engage in joint activities willingly. Show an interest in children and their activities whether the child is playing with measuring cups, finger painting, playing computer games, building a campsite, or playing in sand. Spend time with children willingly. Genuine adult interest tells the child that her interests and activities are valid and interesting. You will communicate your belief that a child is worthy of your adult attention. Children tend to be competent, both academically and interpersonally, when significant adults communicate genuine interest in them (Heyman, Dweck, & Cain, 1992).

## Give Meaningful Feedback to Children

Vygotsky's (1978) theory highlights the value scaffolding—that is, giving assistance to children as they are learning something and then gradually withdrawing or

**Developmentally appropriate activities help children build competence and confidence.**

decreasing the adult help as the child demonstrates understanding. Teachers do this in a number of ways, including giving feedback. Giving feedback is one of the basic ways through which adults influence children. Information from adults about how a child has performed a task is an important source of information about the child's competence. Kernis et al. (2000) found that children with unstable self-esteem had fathers who were critical and who gave unhelpful feedback.

We can help children learn to acknowledge what they do well without bragging—to take credit gracefully. Adults who encourage humility focus on what a child has done well, thereby helping her recognize her competence, one of the dimensions of self-esteem.

**EXAMPLE**  Mrs. Johnson knew that Justine recognized and could name a square and a circle. From her checklist, she also realized that Justine did not know the name for a triangle. Consequently, she placed a large square, circle, and triangle on a bulletin board and had the same shapes in a box. "You know the names of some shapes, Justine. Please reach into this box, take out one shape, and put it on top of the same shape on the board." When Justine correctly matched squares, the teacher said, "You're right! This is called a square." When Justine matched the triangular shapes, Mrs. Johnson simply said, "You've matched the *triangles*!"

## Use Encouragement and Appreciation and Avoid Empty Praise

Empty praise or flattery, such as constantly saying, "Good job! (Kohn, 2001), does not boost self-esteem. It seems that the opposite is the case, that empty praise is related to problems such as narcissism (Mruk, 2013). We are most likely to help children develop a healthy sense of self and self-esteem when we express **appreciation**

**Appreciation**
Encouraging children with appropriate comments based on a child's effort

and use encouragement. This is meaningful positive feedback directly related to a child's effort or interest. Expressing encouragement or appreciation is an appropriate practice that will help a child build a healthy view of her competence (Erikson, cited in Coles, 2001).

> **EXAMPLE**    Bennie was working on a project about mammals and had a specific question. Mr. Santini had a book at home with some information in it that Bennie needed. The teacher brought the book to school the next day so that Bennie would have a good reference.

This teacher was helping Bennie develop healthy self-esteem based on increased understanding of a specific concept. It is also possible that Bennie would view himself as worthy of the teacher's time because Mr. Santini took the trouble to search for the book.

> **EXAMPLE**    Carl, a third grader, finished his homework. His grandmother said to him, "You really concentrate well, Carl. You had homework to do and did it in spite of all the noise outside."

Practice expressing appreciation and encouragement instead of empty praise. Change each of the following examples of empty praise into a statement of encouragement.

- Your professor says, "You wrote a wonderful observation!" (Change this to a statement of encouragement:_____.)
- Teacher says to child, "Good job with the new puzzle." (The child had put together her most intricate puzzle to date.) (Change this to a statement of encouragement: _____.)
- Child helps a child new to the class get to the lunchroom and teacher says, ". . . such a good helper, Henry!" (Change this to a statement of encouragement.)
- Jimmy helps a friend pick up the hundreds of Legos, after the friend had dropped his container onto the floor. The teacher says, "Way to go, Jimmy!" (Change this to a statement of encouragement:_____.)

## Acknowledge Both Pleasant and Unpleasant Feelings

A child is jealous of a new baby brother. Another child feels guilty about having hit someone. Another feels great anger when an older child takes his lunch money. A primary grade child envies the children who have a swimming pool. A preschooler is worried about his puppy that needed surgery. Still another child is angry with a grandfather who makes fun of him. These children are all experiencing unpleasant emotions or feelings.

The real test of support for children comes when they are sick, hurt, unhappy, angry, jealous, fearful, or anxious—when they have unpleasant feelings. It is difficult at times for adults to acknowledge unpleasant feelings. Some adults tend to focus on a young child's behavior that often results from these feelings. They become so upset themselves with the child's behavior that they forget how to or refuse to deal with whatever brought on the guilt, anger, or sadness.

# :: FOCUS ON PRACTICE

This **Focus on Practice** activity is entitled *A Teacher's Role in Helping Children with Challenging Behavior*. As you complete this focus activity, notice how the teacher helps young children deal effectively with unpleasant or confusing emotions.

## Demonstrate Respect for All Family Groups and Cultures; Avoid Sexism and Judging Physical Attributes

Convey, with words and actions, your abiding belief that all children are valuable, *all* children. It is important that children observe adults demonstrating authentic respect for both genders, for children with different abilities, and for various family groups and different cultures.

> **EXAMPLE**   Mr. Santini knows his class well. Several children live in single-parent families, and one child lives with her grandmother. When discussing the topic of families, he showed digital photographs on a large screen of each child's family taken at the school picnic. He acknowledged that each group was indeed a family. He said, "We all live in families. Some families have lots of people in them and some families are small."

> **EXAMPLE**   Moua's mother and aunt do intricate embroidery on cloth, producing beautiful and complex geometric designs. The children, other faculty members, and administrators have admired the wall hanging that they produced and that Mr. Santini placed in the classroom.

## Teach Specific Social Skills

Some children have poor social skills; for example, they might interrupt others, hit when angry, tattle, refuse to help others, call others names, or not know how to join others in play. Children with serious deficits in social skills are likely to view themselves as incompetent with others and in many social situations. They are also likely to evaluate themselves as having little control over anything. Consequently, they are likely to develop negative self-esteem.

Avoid the attempt to artificially boost self-esteem. Instead, consider teaching children real skills as a way of to give them positive social experiences with others. For example, they might need to learn how to take turns, how to ask for something, how to enter a group, or how to respond to someone's anger. Mr. Santini, in the next example, teaches a 7-year-old how to wait his turn.

> **EXAMPLE**   Mr. Santini observed one of the second-grade children trying to push his way into the line at the slide, only to hear other children shout, "Hey, wait your turn!" The teacher walked over and asked the child in private, "Would you like to take a turn on the slide? . . . Okay, I guess that you've noticed that others don't like it much when somebody crashes into the line. If you want a turn, go to the end of the line and wait until it's time for you to go up the ladder."

To summarize, many appropriate practices are available for you to use to guide children toward a healthy and balanced sense of themselves and self-esteem. Many children, however, come from families using inappropriate and even hurtful practices. Such practices do *not* help children gain accurate self-knowledge or self-control. Hurtful, inappropriate practices batter and bruise children's self-esteem by degrading and demeaning them.

---

## ∷ *Question for Reflection*

---

## ∷ PRACTICES CONTRIBUTING TO UNHEALTHY SELF-ESTEEM

This brief section describes these degrading practices so that you will know just how some of the children you teach have been treated. Children incorporate negative adult opinions into their sense of self; you will likely see a child's negative view of herself reflected in her behavior. Your job with these children will be to keep this in mind as you reflect a more positive view.

### Lack of Warmth and Genuine Acceptance Toward a Child

Positive and healthy self-esteem requires loving acceptance and adult warmth toward a child. When loving acceptance and warmth are missing, self-esteem suffers. One likely outcome of an adult lack of warmth toward a child is that the child is likely to look to external things as the marker of her worth. This might be evident in her intense focus on her appearance, grades, or athletic performance as the base of her sense of worth (Mruk, 2013).

### Child Abuse or Harsh Discipline

There are several forms of child abuse. Child abuse can be mild, moderate, or severe. It can be a one-time event or the abuse can be chronic, a continuous assault on the child. When abuse is severe and ongoing, a child's self-esteem is likely to be damaged (Bolger, Patterson, & Kupersmidt, 1998). Harsh discipline, even when it is not physical—for example, sarcasm, threats, and humiliation—hurts and degrades children. Harsh discipline has a negative effect on self-esteem. It leaves children lacking in self-confidence, feeling inadequate and incompetent, and belittling themselves.

### Failure to Emphasize Self-Responsibility

Some adults do not know how to or do not take the time necessary to help children assume responsibility. Chores are not specified, or if they are, there is no penalty for failing to do them. Nonsupportive adults also often fail to require children to take responsibility when they have hurt another person or an animal, or damaged property.

## Unhelpful, Overly Critical, Negative Style of Communication

Constant negative feedback is degrading because it communicates the adult's belief that the child is incompetent and unworthy of better feedback. Younger children, who rely heavily on adult opinion, feel incompetent when they are constantly criticized. Children who are criticized by adults and who live in a negative verbal environment tend to judge themselves negatively, including judgments of their goodness (Kernis et al., 2000). Adults who are unresponsive and disapproving foster poor self-esteem in children (Leary & MacDonald, 2003).

## Denying Unpleasant Feelings

Denying feelings is akin to denying a child's self because even unpleasant feelings are real and are part of the child. The implication is that "if my feelings are bad, then maybe I'm bad, too." An accepting adult, on the other hand, thinks that it is important to accept a child's whole being, including her weaknesses and strengths. A child can be a very friendly person but still get upset at times with another child. A child can be primarily cheerful in nature but might get irritated when someone takes her toys. A child might be very kind most of the time but more irritable at other times. A child might really dislike another child in the class. Accepting these children's feelings, the unpleasant as well as the more positive emotions, is genuine acceptance of that child. Such a balanced view of a child is associated with positive self-esteem (Mruk, 2013). Consider an adult's reaction to Lily's dislike of a game she played.

**EXAMPLE**  "Lily! You're not angry. You really like the new game, don't you?"

Lily obviously did not like the game and was angry, but this adult is denying her right to her feelings. Question: What would be a better way to show acceptance for Lily's right to dislike a game?

## Ignoring Children or Spending Time with Them Grudgingly

Consistently ignoring children is one of the classic forms of psychological child abuse. Ignoring children sends them the message that they are essentially unlovable and unloved, that they are not worthy of an adult's time. Some adults do not ignore children, but they are irritable more often than not when they interact with their children. They give their time grudgingly more often than not.

**EXAMPLE**  Marty asked his father to show him how to dribble a basketball. Feeling obligated, Dad did teach him. However, he clearly communicated resentment, annoyance, and irritability by talking quickly and answering Marty's questions abruptly. It is quite possible that Marty will conclude that he cannot be very likable because his own father does not like to do things with him.

# Acting in a Judgmental or Sexist Way, or Showing Contempt for Some Families or Cultural Groups

Judging, such as "Where did you ever get such an idea?," violates the guidelines for effective communication. When we judge someone, the person is very likely to stop talking because we have offended him and have made a degrading comment. The same holds for sexist comments, which also demonstrate disrespect.

**EXAMPLE**   A preschool teacher allows only boys to use woodworking tools and allows only girls to bathe dolls: "Girls don't work with woodworking tools. They take care of babies."

Showing contempt for any family or cultural group is outrageous and inhumane, and conveys disrespect about a child's family or culture to a child. If self-esteem develops in a social context, then doing any of these things has the potential for harming children, and this is a violation of the Code of Ethical Conduct for early childhood educators (National Association of the Education of Young Children, 2011).

---

**WORKING** *with* **FAMILIES**    **THE ROAD TO SELF-ESTEEM STARTS IN INFANCY**

Infancy is an important time for developing sense of self. An infant begins to construct ideas about his self as he interacts with responsive parents. Here are practical things that parents can do to help infants build the self.

- **Early infancy.** Make the environment predictable, secure, and gentle. Be flexible, not rigid, about feeding schedules. Make routines predictable and regular. Talk to the baby about what you are doing during diapering and feeding. Pay attention to the baby's cues and respond appropriately—for example, respond to cries quickly.

- **4 to 9 months.** Play games. Traditional games such as "Where are baby's toes?" or peek-a-boo help infants distinguish themselves from others. Use routine times to play word games.

   Encourage play with appropriate toys. Offer safe and clean toys. Do not overwhelm the baby with too many toys at one time. Try offering a toy just within and outside the baby's grasp to encourage an infant to reach. Talk with pleasure about individual toys: "Oh! Look at this pretty blue cube." Encourage babies to grasp toys and offer toys that make a sound and then focus on that sound. Remember that adult interaction with a baby is more important than any toy.

- **9 to 15 months.** Create an environment that infants can manage—small groups with a moderate, not overwhelming, amount of stimulation. Provide simple props for pretend-play: dress-up clothes, pots,

pans, and dolls. Play games that help young children develop self-awareness, such as "Simon says touch *your* nose. Simon says hold *Daddy's* hand.").

- **15 to 24 months.** An adult's response to a toddler's struggle for autonomy influences a child's view of herself. Structure the environment and activities to give children as much control as is safe and possible. Short songs, finger plays, or walks around the block are all appropriate. Toys (for example, blocks, play dough, telephones, books with short stories) should encourage active manipulation, problem solving, and talking.

   Decide how to look at the child's struggle for autonomy. You are most likely to foster all dimensions of self-esteem if you approach this period as a healthy and normal time rather than as a contest of wills and a power struggle. For example, do state limits but state them as positively as possible: "Walk in the house" rather than "Don't run!" Be prepared for a child's testing of the new limits.

- **24 to 36 months.** Continue to provide safe and appropriate toys and to encourage children to play. Communicate genuine respect through words and actions. Give fair and honest feedback about a toddler's feelings and actions: "It really is hard to wait for the basket of crackers" or "I can see that you are upset about Mike taking your block. Let's think of some words to use to tell him that you're angry."

# ANALYZE A VIGNETTE

Refer to the chapter-opening vignettes and to information in the chapter to respond to the following questions.

1. **Infant-toddler vignette:** The teacher focused on self-_____ with the "point to" game. Explain your choice.
2. **Preschool vignette:** Explain how a discussion about the *kindness rules* can help children learn about the concept of the right thing to do. How is the teacher helping the children develop their *moral identity*?
3. **Primary-grade vignette:**
   a. Explain why the "All about Us" chart is an activity deserving of children's time.
   b. Explain how working cooperatively on projects such as the chart can lead to an increased sense of competence and control, two major elements in self-esteem.

# SUMMARY

Children need to develop a stable sense of self in order to live a fulfilling life. A child learns about four different parts of his or her self:

- Self-awareness
- Self-concept
- Self-control
- Self-esteem

There are three components of self-esteem:

- **Competence:** a child learns that she can achieve important goals with effort and work.
- **Control:** children need to learn that they have some control over how things turn out for them and how much effort that they expend on any activity.
- **Worth:** children need to feel that other people like them and that they are worthy of other people's time.

Self-esteem develops as children interact and have relationships with others.

- Children are active in their own development, but adults have a much greater share of the responsibility in relationships with children.

- Adults influence children's self-esteem by reflecting their attitudes about the child to him or her.
- Garbage in, garbage out: This phrase describes the effect of constantly conveying negative attitudes about children to them. Reflected negative attitudes have a negative effect on how children evaluate their self.

Children need to develop a moral self or strong moral identity in addition to positive self-esteem. Moral identity deals with understanding the right things to do and why we do them.

Teachers can help children construct positive self-esteem in many ways. Such techniques include using positive guidance strategies; planning appropriate curriculum and learning activities; using appropriate feedback; and showing respect for all children, families, and cultures.

# APPLY YOUR KNOWLEDGE

1. **Observation.** Observe an adult (parent or teacher) and a young child interacting with each other. Focus on the practices that the adult uses that will likely help the child develop healthy and balanced self-esteem. State specific examples of the appropriate practices and be prepared to present your analysis to your classmates.

2. **Conversation with an expert.** Invite a professional who works with children who are abused to speak to your class. Ask the professional questions that will help you understand why these children are likely to be highly anxious, compulsive, withdrawn, or overly hostile. Explain how abuse helps create negative (unhealthy and unbalanced) self-esteem in children,

that is, how abuse affects a child's evaluation of her competence, control, and worth.

3. **Problem for you to solve: Identify a more appropriate practice.** For each situation, state specifically how someone has been demeaned. Describe how the adult could just as easily have used a more appropriate practice to enhance, rather than bruise, the child's self-esteem.

### Situation

The baseball coach stared out at his team of 7- and 8-year-old boys and said, "You guys swing the bat like girls! Let me show you one more time how it's done."

How has the coach demeaned the boys?

How has the coach also degraded girls?

What more helpful statement could the coach have directed to the boys when he noticed that they used improper batting technique?

### Situation

Five-year-old Matt, pointing to a tree, excitedly said to his grandfather, "Grandpa! Look! An oak tree! I'm learning the names of trees by looking at their leaves." Grandpa pointed to a willow tree and said, "What's the name of that tree?" Matt did not know. Grandpa continued, "Well, you have a lot of learning to do, don't you, young man?"

How has Matt been demeaned?

In your view, what would have been a more appropriate response from Matt's grandfather?

### Situation

Sam, the class's pet gerbil, died during the night, and the aide found Peter crying after he heard the news. "Come on, Peter. Stop crying. You know that big boys don't cry."

How has Peter been demeaned?

In what way has this adult been sexist?

How has the adult demeaned girls as well as boys?

What would have been a better thing to say to Peter?

### Situation

A teacher asked a first-grade child if she would prefer to go to the math or writing center. The child selected the writing center, and the teacher said, "I think that you should start at the math center."

How has this child been demeaned?

What do you think would have been a more appropriate response from the teacher?

# WEBSITES

*National Association for the Education of Young Children (NAEYC)*

http://www.naeyc.org

Home page for the organization. Search for the Early Years are Learning Years (ecly) section of the NAEYC website. You will find short articles designed for teachers or parents.

*National Latino Children's Institute (NLCI)*

http://www.nlci.org

Home page. This website focuses on the full and healthy development of Latino/Latina children.

# CHAPTER 8
# Feelings and Friends

*Emotional and Social Competence*

## Learning Outcomes

- Define terms related to the development of children's emotional and social competence
- Explain the importance of both emotional and social competence in a child's development
- Explain the link between emotional and social competence
- Report on developmentally appropriate ways in which teachers can guide children's social emotional learning (SEL)

---

### VIGNETTES

#### INFANT–TODDLER: COMFORTING THOMAS

*Thomas, 8 months old, seemed startled when he heard the loud noise out in the hallway of the center. He cried loudly even after his teacher picked him up. The teacher held him gently and spoke softly and reassuringly to him. Thomas gradually cried more softly, eventually visibly relaxing in the teacher's arms.*

#### PRESCHOOL: LEARNING THAT USING WORDS IS A GOOD THING

*"You can't play here, Jerry. You pushed me when we were in line," said Sarah, who was upset with Jerry. He responded by sweeping her small blocks onto the floor. Mrs. Johnson, his teacher, spoke privately with him, and one part of her message was this: "You can use words to tell Sarah that you are upset. Try saying, 'I wanted to play with you. I'm upset because you said no.'" She had Jerry say those words, for practice. Then she said, "Would you like to tell her now?"*

#### PRIMARY: LEARNING TO CALM DOWN

*Mr. Santini noticed that his primary class was unusually active and even agitated after the fire drill, and the children had difficulty settling back into their routine. Therefore, he gathered them on the carpet, turned on soft music, and led them in deep breathing exercises.*

---

## :: INTRODUCTION

**Emotions**
Feelings or affective states; they are divided into two groups: basic and complex emotions.

Teachers in the opening vignettes have focused on SEL. Children need to learn about feelings, their **emotions**, which they feel and express but which they do not yet understand. Because they do not understand their emotions, they cannot regulate or control emotions such as anger, anxiety, agitation, disappointment, or even joy on their own. They need adults to help them learn to handle their disappointment and anger and to develop the emotions vocabulary necessary for talking about their emotions. Young children need adult support for developing these skills.

Children also need to develop competence in the social part of life—that is, they need to begin to understand other people and to develop the social and friendship skills necessary for making and keeping friends. The same social skills enable children to get along with others who are not their friends, thus helping them function well in school and other settings. Again, children need adult support in learning these social skills.

The emotional and social domains of development are important all on their own, but never more so than now as the expulsion rate for young children's challenging behavior in preschools soars (Gilliam, 2005, 2012; Ramsey, 2009). Effective teachers understand that they need to focus on children's development in all areas, not just in the cognitive and intellectual domain. Learning to read and to understand math and science is vitally important, but children learn academic material most effectively when they are self-controlled, can handle emotions, and have good social skills.

This chapter describes the development of emotional and social competence. We will explore what it means to be emotionally competent. We will also describe social competence, with an emphasis on social skills that children need for satisfying interactions with other children. You will then learn about practical strategies for teaching SEL. Specifically, you will learn how to support children as they learn about emotions, such as learning an emotions vocabulary, how to deal effectively with feelings of disappointment and anger, and how to develop friendships.

## :: EMOTIONAL COMPETENCE

How well, overall, a person copes with his or her own feelings and whether the person has empathy for and gets along with others is **emotional competence** (Goleman, 2007; Nelson, 2012). Emotional competence is important in a child's development, good mental health, and success in life. Emotionally competent children tend to feel more connected to others and to get along with other children, better than children who do not have these abilities. They feel competent and capable, experience a general sense of balance in their emotions, and are better prepared to deal with conflicts constructively (Brackett, Crum, & Salovey, 2009; Denham, 2006).

**Emotional competence**
How well, overall, a person copes with his or her feelings and whether the person has empathy for and gets along with others

## :: FOCUS ON PRACTICE

This Focus on Practice activity is entitled *Observing an Emotionally Competent Child.* Emotionally competent children are connected to others and tend to get along with other children, better than children who are not as emotionally intelligent. As you complete this activity, note how enthusiastic that Emily is in her approach to interactions.

There are three parts to an emotion, and emotional competence involves all three: the feeling, expressing, and regulating of emotions (Figure 8.1). Every human *feels* emotions. Every human *expresses* emotions. All children, then, feel and express emotions, even infants. However, regulating emotions is learned and *not* everybody learns to control emotions very well, as you can tell from reports of violence appearing every

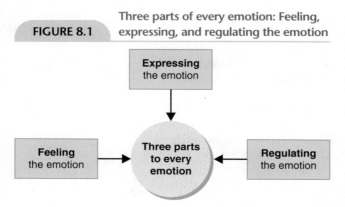

**FIGURE 8.1** Three parts of every emotion: Feeling, expressing, and regulating the emotion

**Perceiving emotions**
Noticing feelings in oneself and others; the least complex emotional competency

**Anger**
A basic emotion present soon after birth; elicited when a person is prevented from attaining a goal

day in the news. Young children are not very good at controlling or regulating emotions, as any parent or teacher of a toddler will tell you. Nevertheless, humans *are capable of learning* to control emotions and that is where teachers come in. Teachers can focus on SEL just as they can about math, science, or reading.

## Perceiving Emotions

**Perceiving emotions** refers to feeling or noticing your own emotions. Feeling or perceiving an emotion is not a very complex thing (Brackett et al., 2009) because we only sense or notice, but noticing does not require doing the work of interpreting, understanding, or managing the emotion. Infants feel the basic emotions of contentment and distress any time from birth to 6 weeks of age. Between 6 and 14 weeks, they feel basic emotions of anger, fear, and joy. By the time they are 2 years old and continuing through early childhood, complex, self-conscious emotions of anxiety, disgust, embarrassment, guilt, hubris (overconfidence or arrogance), jealousy, pride, sadness, and shame appear (Saarni, Mumme, & Campos, 1998; Weir, 2012).

We should not underestimate the power wielded by a child's emotions. Feelings of disappointment, while normal and common, are still distressing for children, especially when they do not know how to deal with the feeling. Some emotions, such as anxiety and anger, are the most difficult feelings with which even adults deal. Anxiety and anger cause great problems for children, making it important for teachers to provide learning opportunities about how to deal with anxiety and anger.

**Anger** is one of the basic emotions and it signals that something is wrong, that something is blocking us from getting something that we need, a goal. Researchers have studied anger in young children for some time and have identified specific, aggravating interactions, such as the following, which tend to arouse young children's anger (Campos & Barrett, 1984; Fabes, Eisenberg, Smith, & Murphy, 1996).

- **Conflict over possessions:** One of the most common interactions in early childhood classrooms provoking anger is a conflict over possessions, which involves someone taking or destroying the target child's property or invading her space. Most conflicts over possessions take place between two children.
- **Physical assault:** This second, most frequently observed cause of anger in early childhood settings involves something done to a child's body, such as biting or hitting. Children do assault other children, but adults also can physically assault children.
- **Assault with words:** This involves taunting, teasing, insults, or making degrading or demeaning statements. It blocks a child's goal of psychological safety. This also includes assault with written words, such as passing nasty notes or cyberbullying in which one child writes insulting, taunting messages about another child.

- **Rejection:** Other children either ignore or refuse to allow a child to play. Rejection by adults is one of the classic forms of emotional child abuse (Garbarino, Guttman, & Seeley, 1986; Centers for Disease Control and Prevention, 2012).
- **Issues of compliance:** This refers to requiring a child to do something that he does not want to do. The child perceives that his teacher's insistence on compliance is blocking his goal for independence. Almost all anger over issues of compliance occurs between an adult and a child.

There are different levels of anger. All children feel angry at times, some more than others. Many young children feel the emotion of low-level anger (irritation), for example, when someone swipes a toy and this is a natural and normal thing. Other children have a much deeper reserve of fear, fury, and rage. Their life experience has started them on a path away from and not toward emotional competence. Someone has aimed anger and aggression directly at these children. Often, an adult has abused them physically, psychologically, emotionally, or sexually, or has ignored their most basic need for safety and security. Whatever the unhealthy experience, they have not developed trust; they feel insecure and unsafe. It is especially difficult for them to confront the normal, everyday, anger-arousing events at school.

Still other children have seen a lot of background anger, anger between others but not directed at the child, especially the high levels of anger-based conflict between their parents (Jenkins, 2000). Anger is the center of their emotional life. Consequently, they do not develop the understanding and skills they need for satisfying relationships. They are very angry and quick to express anger during social interaction, quite often showing aggression in relationships. Like their angry parents, they frequently humiliate and provoke distress in others, mirroring the contempt modeled in their parents' marriages.

**Perceiving Emotions in Other People**  A more complex ability is noticing that other people and animals have feelings. This requires that a child be able to read emotional cues, such as smiling or frowning, in another's face and through another person's body language, such as how a person stands or hold his or her arms (Brackett et al., 2009). Young children differ in their ability to read emotional cues, such as a child not noticing the narrowing of eyes and pinching of lips that indicate another's anger. Young children learn very gradually to notice feelings in other people. For instance, they recognize pleasant emotions such as happiness earlier than they can identify feelings such as anger (Stifter & Fox, 1987). They also create theories after they have several experiences with an emotion, the ideas allowing them to group together things that seem to cause a feeling (Denham, 2006). For example, a child might notice that she and others get upset when somebody makes fun of them.

Some children face additional challenges in reading emotional cues, not paying attention to how others react, thus missing important information, which ultimately has a negative effect on their interactions and relationships. For example, children with an autism spectrum disorder (ASD), have a hard time with other people's emotions, partly because they avoid looking at faces or they look at only part of the face, thus overlooking important facial signals. They tend to look at the lower half of a face, missing information given from the upper half, especially the eyes (Gross, 2004;

**Lela, the child on the left, will develop a theory about why people cry after observing several people who get upset and cry.**

Hopkins, 2005; Hopkins & Biasini, 2006; Hopkins, Ross, & Biasini, 2005). However, they can learn to pay attention to a whole face for clues about emotions by, for example, playing an interactive video game in which they learn to recognize emotions by looking at and following eye movement (Hopkins, Perez, & Biasini, 2007).

As you watch this **video**, you will observe a real-life discussion of feelings. Three young preschool girls have had an unpleasant interaction, with two of the children doing several things to hurt the feelings of the third girl. Notice how the teacher does not shy away from a discussion of the behaviors that brought on the third child's feelings. Notice, too, how the teacher helps the children become more aware of the feelings of other people.

---

### :: *Question for Reflection*

---

## Expressing Emotions

An emotionally competent person expresses emotions so that it helps her interact well in daily encounters and in relationships. She does not try to pretend that the feeling is not there but decides how to deal with it. She might decide not to deal with it until she thinks that she can do so effectively or she might deal with it relatively quickly but in a positive way. This is a difficult skill to acquire and takes years to develop. Any teacher who has uttered the sentence, "Use your words . . ." was teaching children a helpful way to express feelings. All children *feel* emotions: all children *express* feelings. **Expressing emotions** refers to how a person communicates the feelings that they notice. Some classic research with infants, for example, showed

**Expressing emotions**
Communicating a feeling after noticing it

that babies feel happiness or anger, which they then express with their faces and voices (Stenberg, 1982). Some ways of expressing feelings are helpful and some are far less helpful. Let's look at how young children tend to express the feeling of anger.

**How Young Children Express Angry Feelings**   Children tend to express anger in one or more of the following ways (Fabes et al., 1996):

- **Venting** refers to expressing anger through facial expressions, crying, sulking, or complaining, but not doing much to solve a problem. For example, two third-grade girls chattered about how "unfair" it is that the "popular" girls in the class always get picked for things first. Their venting is a way to "blow off steam," but it is an unhealthy approach if the person does nothing to solve the problem that caused the anger.

    Many children can easily detect the difference in power between an adult and themselves, and tend to think that they have much less control when a teacher provokes their anger. With adults, children express anger more indirectly, with strategies such as venting (Fabes & Eisenberg, 1992). Curiously, some children express anger toward a popular child who provokes anger in much the same indirect way as they do toward an adult (Fabes et al., 1996), because children tend to see themselves as having far less control in angry interactions with popular children.

- **Active resistance** involves physically or verbally defending one's position, self-esteem, or possessions in nonaggressive ways, and is a healthy way to express anger. For example, when Luis made a mistake in oral reading, another child called him "dummy." Luis used words to actively resist by saying, "Right! I made a mistake . . . good observation!" Luis's father had taught him this strategy. Teachers encourage active resistance when they tell children to use words to express themselves and then help them learn the words. Children believe that they have some measure of control in interactions with other children, including anger-arousing situations. Therefore, a child who feels angry tends to use direct strategies such as active resistance with other children if they have learned the strategies.

- **Expressing dislike** involves a child telling the offender that he cannot play or that the victim does not like the offender because of an incident. For example, Sarah felt angry after Jerry pushed her. Later, in the chapter-opening vignette for preschool, Sarah refused to let Jerry join a group at a table.

- **Aggressive revenge** means that children retaliate, physically or verbally, against the offender with name calling, pinching, hitting, or threatening. Considered a negative way of expressing anger, teachers most often see revenge-like behavior after a physical assault or rejection. For instance, after snack time the children went to the playground. Jerry, still upset from Sarah's comment at the small blocks table, waited until Sarah walked near him and called to her, "You're a stupid old girl!" An older child might resort to a different way of getting revenge, such as posting hateful things about somebody else on whatever social media the child uses.

- **Avoidance** is a way of communicating anger by trying to escape from or avoid the person with whom the child is angry. For example, Sarah, mildly irritated by the name calling, walked away and played on the other side of the playground.

■ **Adult seeking** involves telling an adult about an incident or looking for comfort from the teacher. In the preschool chapter-opening vignette, after Sarah rejected Jerry and he swept her blocks onto the floor, he turned to his teacher and said loudly, "She said to go away!"

**Learning about Expressing Emotions**    Bronfenbrenner's theory informs us that children develop and learn in a number of systems, such as family and peer group. A family system provides direct lessons based on its *rules* about expressing one's feelings, telling each person how that family expresses anger (Christian, 2006). Peer groups also teach children how each group expresses feelings and children learn about expressing emotions by watching television or movies, playing video games, reading books, and using the Internet. Some systems teach children to express anger by hurting others and then to use aggression when they face normal everyday conflicts at school.

Social learning theory makes clear the value of modeling in children's learning. Constructivist theorists Dewey (1897), Piaget (1970), and Vygotsky (1978) call attention to the value of building some ideas from listening to and talking with more knowledgeable others, teachers and other children. Consequently, children gradually learn how to construct ideas about expressing feelings appropriately. They do this as they interact with others more skilled in expressing emotions—a teacher who responds calmly to another interruption to story time or their friends who "use words" to express irritation assertively but not aggressively.

## Regulating Emotions

**Regulating emotions**
The most complex of the emotional competencies; refers to understanding and managing moods and feelings responsibly

**Regulating emotions** is the most complex and difficult of the trio of feeling, expressing, and regulating our emotions. Regulating an emotion such as anger goes far beyond merely noticing or expressing the feeling. A person who can regulate emotions, control them, *understands* the feeling, can stop and think about it, and interpret it. Regulating emotions refers to understanding and managing moods and feelings responsibly (Brackett et al., 2009). An emotionally intelligent and competent person keeps emotions in check; he or she does not let them run wild and restrains feelings when appropriate. For example, Mr. Santini was astonished and somewhat anxious when a parent shouted and pounded on the table. However, he knew the parent and had figured out that the parent was furious because the school had made a major decision without consulting parents. The teacher could stay calm and regulate his emotions, even though he felt anxious.

Children need to be able to handle disappointment, a mood often rooted in feeling frustrated, for example, over not getting to watch a video, about the rain curtailing a bike ride, or about not getting to sit with a friend at snack. Managing moods is difficult because it requires some higher level understanding and skills, something that humans develop very slowly if they do develop them. A person has to be able to do the following things before he can control any feeling effectively. See Figure 8.2.

■ Monitor feelings: He must be aware that he *has* feelings and that he can keep an eye on them.
■ Delineate feelings: He must be able to tell apart one feeling from another accurately, such as recognizing that feeling anger is different from feeling sad or frustrated.

**FIGURE 8.2**   Children need specific knowledge about feelings and explicit skills in dealing with emotions *before* they can regulate any feeling, such as frustration, disappointment, and anger

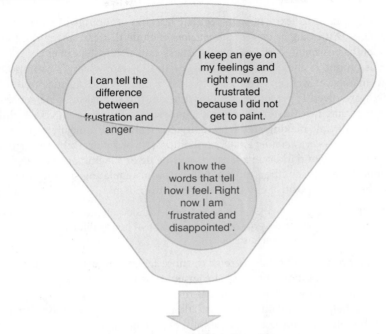

I can tell the difference between frustration and anger

I keep an eye on my feelings and right now am frustrated because I did not get to paint.

I know the words that tell how I feel. Right now I am 'frustrated and disappointed'.

I have learned how to handle *disappointment*.
So, I'll just wait for another chance to paint.
The easel is up every day.

- Experience feelings clearly: He must learn how to figure out what exactly the feeling is—frustration, anger, sadness?
- Label emotions or feelings accurately: This requires knowledge of "the words" that we urge children to use. He must have access to an emotion vocabulary— that is, the particular words to describe feelings. For example, he needs the words *frustrated* and *frustration* in his vocabulary to describe this feeling.
- Must believe in his ability to improve his feelings: This refers to a feeling of optimism in dealing with somewhat scary emotions that wash over all of us. In short, we want children to cultivate an "I can do this!" attitude toward dealing with emotions.
- Must be able to use strategies that will indeed modify the emotions (Brackett et al., 2009; Denham, 2006): He needs to know some options for dealing with a feeling, for example, what he can do about being frustrated at not getting a turn at something that he really wanted to do.

All of this makes regulating emotions extremely demanding, especially for young children who are just starting out with this skill.

## :: *Question for Reflection*

Children have to learn how to regulate specific groupings of emotions (Denham, 2006). *Distressing or unpleasant emotions* include distress, anger, fear, anxiety, disgust, embarrassment, guilt, jealousy, sadness, and shame (Saarni et al., 1998). We will focus on one of these emotions—anger—to illustrate why it is so important to learn to manage it well and responsibly. It is a natural and normal emotion, but chronic, unresolved anger and hostility is a health threat, making a person vulnerable to illness and a weakening of the immune system (Siew et al., 2005). A child will have a difficult time making and keeping friends if she is chronically angry.

*Positive but overwhelming emotions* include joy or pride (but not arrogance). These are pleasant and indicate a sense of well-being or a legitimate feeling of accomplishment. However, children must still learn about regulating such feelings in situations when even a positive emotion can overpower them.

> **EXAMPLE**    Eight-year-old Sheri was overcome with joy after she got three baskets in a row during the recess basketball game and had a very difficult time settling down during the afternoon at school.

*Relevant and helpful emotions* refer to those feelings that help us in interacting with others. The emotion of disgust, for instance, is usually unpleasant but it is certainly relevant when we observe someone mistreating another person or animal, and it would be helpful to retain or preserve this feeling as we reflect on the incident. Guilt, although very unpleasant, is helpful and relevant when we have violated a moral or ethical code. Our guilt helps us focus on what we have done and make decisions about how to repair any damage that we have caused.

*Relevant but unhelpful emotions* are legitimate feelings but might not be very useful in some interactions. Consequently, each culture teaches children how to regulate them. This involves learning complicated rules for expressing emotions. Children must learn, for example, to *mask emotions*, projecting the appearance of one emotion on the outside (pretending to like a gift, for instance) even if they feel something else inside (disliking the gift). The emotion of disappointment on seeing socks as a birthday present is relevant for many children. However, expressing the relevant feeling of disappointment to one's grandmother who gave the gift is not helpful in the relationship. Therefore, a child learns that he is expected to hide the disappointment. Children also learn to regulate how they express an emotion with different people (Denham, 2006), such as the rules for expressing irritation or anger toward a teacher compared to expressing such feelings toward other children.

*Irrelevant emotions* refer to feelings that are not connected to a current discussion or ongoing activity. Children must learn to hold back irrelevant emotions (Denham, 2006), and their failure at doing this is linked to their low-level ability to walk in somebody else's shoes—in other words, take the other person or animal's perspective. For example, a child talks about her father's surgery. Another child horns in with a comment about visiting her grandmother at the hospital and how happy she was to see her grandparent. The second child's legitimate feeling of happiness about her grandmother was actually *irrelevant* to the first child's distress.

# Children's Development Affects How They Understand Feelings

Children do not understand their feelings and need support in learning how to evaluate and deal with emotions (Suveg, Sood, Barmish, Tiwari, Hudson, & Kendall, 2008; Zeman & Shipman, 1996).

**Understanding feelings** refers to reflecting on or evaluating emotions, for example, "I am really sad about my mother's illness. I like having her live near me and I think that I fear losing her." This person has reflected on her sadness and seems to understand it. There are reasonable developmental explanations for why young children can neither evaluate nor interpret how they feel. Three of the major developmental factors contributing to a young child's inability to understand, and therefore to regulate emotions, include:

Memory

Language

Brain development

**Understanding feelings**
The ability to reflect on and evaluate emotions

**Memory**  Children can understand things only if they can remember them. Memory improves substantially during early childhood (Perlmutter, 1986), which makes it possible for young children to retain information about anger-arousing interactions. This is a slow process. Mrs. Johnson, for example, knew that Jerry needed help managing agitation and anger. She helped him remember information about and deal with his feelings, and after a time, he seemed to understand what she meant.

> **EXAMPLE**  Jerry picked out a card with a drawing of an excited and agitated child. "This is how I feel when we stop center time and go to large group, all jumpy." Jerry is remembering the feeling of agitation. She reminded him that he could do some yoga when he feels agitated or excited and use words to say he was upset.

Could Mrs. Johnson expect Jerry to remember her suggestion, or would he regress and use one of his old, unhelpful ways of expressing his anger? Young children such as Jerry remember an unhelpful way to communicate feelings, even after they have learned a more helpful way to remember agitation and to express anger (Freeman, Lacohee, & Coulton, 1995). While a child is learning the new method, his brain can repress an incorrect idea for a short time so that the child can use a new idea. In Jerry's case, it seemed as if he understood Mrs. Johnson because he did remember and he did do yoga or pushups a couple of times to deal with his agitation. However, his previous memories of immediately expressing anger were also very strong, and it is likely that he might at times not remember about how to handle the agitation and go back to immediately expressing anger.

This scenario implies that teachers must be unrelentingly positive and remind certain children, often several times, about a less aggressive way of focusing on agitation and excitement, signals that they need to calm down. Overcoming old, unhelpful memories takes time.

**Language**  How well a child understands emotions depends somewhat on his overall language skills (Denham, Zoller, & Couchoud, 1994). Children have a much easier time learning to talk about emotions if they have good language development in general. Preschooler Ralph, for example, has very good language skills and a large vocabulary, so Mrs. Johnson was confident that he could tell her what had upset him. One of Vygotsky's major ideas centers on discussion between teacher and child. Children glean valuable information from such conversations with an older member of their culture. In terms of managing emotions such as anger, discussions are one of a teacher's most valuable tools. Talking about emotions, as Mrs. Johnson did with Jerry, helps a young child understand his feelings and helps him begin to evaluate them.

**Brain Development**   Early childhood teachers consider the whole child, including the role that a child's brain plays in child development. A brief review of two specific parts of the brain, the amygdala (pronounced ah-MIG-da-la) and the prefrontal cortex, and how they develop, can help us appreciate why young children react as they often do when they feel an emotion and why they express some emotions as they do.

**Amygdala**   The amygdala is an almond-shaped structure located at the top of the brain stem and is almost fully mature at birth, which is important for a caregiver to know. It is a part of the emotional center in the brain and its job is to store a memory of the emotional quality of a child's experience, whether the experience is pleasant or unpleasant. The amygdala also "keeps an eye on" new experience to detect anything posing a danger or anything joyful for the child. It prompts children to recall previously stored memories of emotions, and can seize the brain and keep a child from thinking. For example, a child who has observed parents fighting and who has been hit and yelled at will be "on guard" at school. She might well view everyday mild disagreements at school as threats and as a signal that something bad is about to happen.

This somewhat technical information important to teachers because we deal quite often with children who have "meltdowns" and we can better understand their real distress and inability to control their emotions by knowing a little about their brain development. Getting upset is somewhat normal for very young children whose language and cognitive skills are still developing. However, a child whose life has been filled with distressing interactions will not be able, on her own, to control her reactions because her brain sends such strong signals to her about danger. Her reactions will be much more frequent and much stronger than those of a child with strong and positive relationships with parents.

The conclusion here is that a baby or a toddler's amygdala is up and running at birth, sending warning signs. The baby or toddler or even preschooler, however, does not have any way to deal effectively with things because another part of his brain that he needs for self-control is *not* yet developed.

**Prefrontal Cortex**   The amygdala is almost fully formed at birth. The prefrontal cortex, located at the front of the human brain, has a far different schedule of development. It is not fully formed for years and years, but does show some growth at ages 3 or 4 years; by age 6 the amygdala has developed a little more.

This information is important because the knowledge will help you better understand why toddlers, preschoolers, kindergarteners, and even some primary grade children express emotions as they do, and why they might have difficulty even understanding their anger, for example. A child's prefrontal cortex has an extremely important function: It receives and processes signals from more primitive parts of the brain, such as the amygdala. It helps humans choose how to respond to emotions and helps us make plans. The prefrontal cortex serves as a balance to purely emotional responses of the amygdala. This gives humans an opportunity to step back and think about emotions level-headedly. Children's prefrontal cortex is just starting to develop. Therefore, they do not have the same brain-based ability to deal with emotions as an adult.

Humans need a good pathway or connection between the prefrontal cortex and amygdala so that these two sections of the brain can communicate about what a child feels. The prefrontal cortex has to get information about emotional states from the amygdala in order to make sense of the information. Think of the *prefrontal cortex–amygdala connection* as a cable carrying signals between the two sections of the brain. A weak, underdeveloped, or damaged connection or cable slows or obstructs the passage of signals, placing a child at a disadvantage in managing emotions. His brain is not wired for the prefrontal cortex to communicate with the amygdala. Such a child would very likely misread signals from others and might have a *short fuse,* or be quick to anger. She would rarely use emotion words, would seem unaware of feelings in general, and would get in trouble with other children because of poor social skills.

A strong, well-developed cable or pathway lets those bits of information pass quickly between the amygdala and the prefrontal cortex. This sets the stage for better analysis and management of emotions because the child's brain is wired in a way that allows it to get the information it needs about emotions from one part of the brain to another. This child would have the equipment he needs to read signals from others accurately, would be able to learn about emotion words, and would be aware of feelings. Thus, he would have what he needs in order to learn how to work and play well with other children.

Teachers can help children develop a strong connection between the amygdala and prefrontal cortex so that those signals can get from one to the other. We install the hardware to build this pathway by paying appropriate attention to a child's emotional needs. At times, teachers make a conscious effort to help a child make these connections. At other times, they might not even realize that supportive interactions are helping a child develop the wiring and connections—the hardware—that is essential in managing his feelings. Here are some examples. Let a child know explicitly that her needs are important and worthy of attention. Whoosh, a connection between amygdala and prefrontal cortex! Comfort an anxious or fearful child, another connection. Incorporate calming activities into the day and prevent agitation. Whoosh! Another connection.

## :: SOCIAL COMPETENCE

Children who can regulate their emotions well are better equipped to make and keep friends and to work and play for extended periods with peers. They have what they need to develop skills for positive and ongoing interactions and relationships— including cooperating, searching for help, joining in, listening, and negotiating (Denham, 2006). Therefore, emotional competence goes hand-in-hand with social competence, both then helping children develop essential school success skills.

Socially competent children tune in to their surroundings, relate well to other children, and have effective social skills.

## Socially Competent Children Tune in to Their Surroundings

This refers to how well a child observes others in ongoing activities. Socially competent children are good observers, watch other children at play, and are skillful in assessing their needs or behavior (Mize, 1995). Thus, they have information useful in figuring out what they need to do in different situations, as John demonstrates in the next example.

> **EXAMPLE**    John wanted to join the play at the puppet theater, but observed that all of the puppets were in use. He watched for a little longer, not interrupting, and then volunteered to open and close the curtain to the stage.

Socially competent children deal with disappointment fairly well, not getting too upset when they fail to get what they want. John was successful in his bid to participate in the puppet play, but if the others had rejected his idea, he might have come up with another or might simply have found something else to do.

## Socially Competent Children Relate Well to Other Children

In general, they respond agreeably to others. They are appropriately friendly toward most other people. They are sociable, pleasant, welcoming, and approachable, whether the other child is a good friend or only an acquaintance (Mize, 1995). They relate well to other children at three different levels—interactions, relationships, and with groups of children.

**Interactions**    Generally, they are socially competent in interactions; they have primarily positive *interactions* with other children under a variety of conditions. For example, they may greet others, have positive interactions in large and small groups, in the lunchroom, on the playground, or on the bus.

**Relationships**    Socially competent children are skillful in starting and then maintaining a *relationship*. They have the social skills for starting a relationship and then different social skills for maintaining it. Maintaining a relationship requires getting along with the same person under a variety of circumstances and over time. We see this when children live near one another, go to the same school, are in scouts together, for example. A socially competent child has the social skills and emotional competence to adjust how he relates in these different settings and over extended periods.

**Groups**    Socially competent children also get along well in *groups of children*, indicating that they have the skills needed for getting along with groups of children in school, religious, recreational, and neighborhood settings. Getting along well in groups of children refers to how well liked versus disliked a child is, on average, by members of his or her peer group. Peer acceptance predicts children's academic readiness and classroom involvement (Ladd, Kochenderfer, & Coleman, 1997); peer rejection is linked with negative attitudes toward and avoiding school, as well as not doing very well academically (Ladd, Birch, & Buhs, 1999).

## Socially Competent Children Have Good Social Skills

The emotional competence discussed in the previous section explained that children need to learn how to regulate their thoughts and emotions in order to get along well with others. **Social skills** are observable behaviors that a child uses to control her thoughts and emotions. Key social skills include turn-taking, following directions, coming up with good solutions to conflicts, carrying on a conversation, correctly interpreting another person's actions, and persisting at tasks.

**Social skills**
Observable behaviors through which a child demonstrates the ability to regulate thoughts and emotions

Children can do two things when they have good social skills. First they can initiate appropriate actions, such as carrying on a conversation with a friend who is upset or showing a new member of the class how the lunchroom routine works. Second, and important for behaviors such as dealing with disappointment or angry feelings, they can keep themselves from doing something. For example, children with good social skills can resist the urge to interrupt a conversation. They can, when disappointed, resist the urge to whine. In order to keep yourself from doing something, you have to be able to stop and think. You cannot be ruled by impulses.

Children construct ideas about emotions from models who take the time to give the essential lessons (Corso, 2003; Elias, 2004). It takes many years for children to build knowledge about emotions, acquire a good emotions vocabulary, control themselves, and understand how other people feel, form good friendships, and get along well with others. Let's look at how teachers can guide children's social emotional learning (SEL).

**Cecilia (front, right) gets along well with other children. Today, she invited the other three girls to play a game.**

# :: FOCUS ON PRACTICE

This Focus on Practice activity is entitled *Observing a Socially Competent Child.* Socially competent children share several strengths. As you complete this activity, note Bri'asia's strengths as well as her areas for growth.

## :: SOCIAL EMOTIONAL LEARNING: SETTING THE STAGE

**Social emotional learning (SEL)**
Gaining knowledge about feelings and about getting along with others

**Social emotional learning (SEL)** refers to gaining knowledge about feelings (the emotional domain) and about getting along with others (the social domain). Effective teachers intentionally focus on all areas of development, including emotional and social learning (CSEFEL, 2008; Rimm-Kaufman, 2006). All children benefit from learning about emotions and getting along with others. Children whose families give minimal support or who foster a negative approach to emotions and relationships need SEL even more (Edwards, Shipman, & Brown, 2005).

Learning about feelings and relationships builds brain circuits directly linked to emotions and social development (Goleman, 2007), thus supporting children in learning how to compose themselves, stay calm, and control their impulses. SEL encourages school attendance and higher academic achievement, largely because children gain skills and confidence essential to school success. They display far less challenging behavior because they learn how to deal with emotions and relationships. Teachers who foster SEL successfully use research-based strategies. SEL does not happen by chance. Teachers plan specific learning opportunities for children but first, effective teachers set the stage for SEL. They make sure that the *interpersonal and physical environments* will actually support children's learning.

### Supportive Interpersonal Environments

Children have a better chance of learning social emotional skills in a healthy *interpersonal* environment—that is, when the teacher builds a good relationship with them and when they feel their teacher's respect. Children flourish in positive, trust-building environments (Day & Kunz, 2009; Greenman, 2005; Perry & Szalavitz, 2007; Pianta & Stuhlman, 2004), where teachers communicate genuine respect with a validating and open style of communication; when they are positive, warm, and caring; and when they are highly responsive to what children need, including appropriate limits on behavior (Baumrind, 1996). A healthy interpersonal environment surrounds children with the safety and security (Maslow, 1954/1987) that they need as a base for learning about feelings and for making friends. See Table 8.1 for several realistic strategies that you can use to demonstrate genuine respect for children.

| TABLE 8.1 | Showing respect creates a safe and secure interpersonal environment | | |
| --- | --- | --- | --- |
| **The Strategy** | **What the Teacher Does** | **Example** | **Why This Is Effective** |
| Walk in the child's shoes (take a child's perspective) | Figure out how things look to children. Look at them when speaking. Get down to their level. | The teacher in the chapter-opening infant–toddler vignette seemed to understand how the loud noise might appear to Thomas. | Changes how you see things. Helps children feel worthy of your attention. |
| Observe | Watch carefully. Record observations. Reflect on what you see. Use information to plan for children. | Mrs. Johnson has seen that Jerry gets upset when there is a lot of noise in the classroom. | Helps you recognize children's style and temperament. You discover each child's overload point. You can plan to prevent a child from reaching that point. |
| Communicate caringly | Be unruffled. Speak kindly and avoid loud, stress-inducing speech. Use *appropriate touch* (hand on shoulder or touch a child's hand). Be unrelentingly positive. Acknowledge each child every day. Use active listening. | Thomas, from the infant–toddler chapter-opening vignette, heard his teacher speak kindly and could feel the teacher holding him gently. | Conveys genuine affection for children; helps children pay attention to you; shows them that you are reliable and will help them figure things out about feelings and friends, even when they make mistakes; listening actively tells children that somebody is finally interested in their problem. |
| Focus on calming activities | Allow time for quiet reflection. Teach children how to focus and calm themselves— deep or slow breathing, yoga, for example. | Mr. Santini encouraged his primary grade children in the chapter-opening vignette to calm themselves with deep breathing. | Teaches children to concentrate; gives them time to think and reflect by themselves; trains brain circuits that are responsible for focusing and calming. |

# Supportive Physical Environments

Children also need a pleasant, productive, and peaceful *physical* environment—the arrangement of space and furniture and materials used for their learning. Teachers show respect for how young children learn and develop by arranging space and materials well. Such a physical environment conveys a sense of order, and provides a place for work and play (Greenman, 2005). The teacher arranges the room well and creates an orderly and organized space. This type of physical environment emphasizes active learning and invites children to make choices and to work with other children, which is essential in learning about how to deal with emotions and social skills. Children need an appropriate time schedule, with balance between active and quiet periods and between teacher- and child-initiated activities. An appropriate schedule offers children expanded periods for learning and interacting with others (Hopkins, 2007). For example, work periods of longer than 30 minutes result in higher levels of social and cognitive play (Ostrosky, Jung, Hemmeter, & Thomas, 2003).

Next, we will look at specific elements of a SEL program—that is, specific topics that children need in order to construct understanding about their emotions and social skills.

## :: ESSENTIAL TOPICS IN SOCIAL EMOTIONAL LEARNING

SEL involves gaining knowledge and skills directly related to one's emotions and to social and friendship skills. There are several crucial topics in SEL, and teachers intentionally plan SEL learning opportunities focusing on the essential topics that will help children learn about

- Emotions as normal and having a purpose
- Limits on expressing emotions
- Alternative responses to feelings
- A strong emotions vocabulary
- How to talk about emotions
- Friendship skills

**FIGURE 8.3**   Essential Topics in SEL

Figure 8.3 shows these essential topics in SEL

## Emotions as Normal and Having a Purpose

An emotionally competent person understands that all emotions, even the unpleasant ones such as anger, jealousy, or disgust, are normal. They realize that every emotion has a purpose and an emotion is neither good nor bad, but it is a natural and normal part of existence. Emotions such as anger or disgust should stand out, instead, as bright red flags, trying to get our attention about some issue. Some people attempt to deny an emotion, to pretend that the anger or frustration simply does not exist, but it is not wise and almost impossible to "not have" an emotion. Young children do not automatically develop this idea but, instead, need to learn it. Teachers can help children build the idea that it is normal to have emotions and that emotions have a purpose. This topic is the starting point in successfully handling all emotions well, but is especially so with unpleasant and potentially damaging motions.

**Teacher's Role** Accept the emotions that children have. Avoid denying the existence of any emotion. Communicate your acceptance to children: "It looks like you're frustrated with that pulley." Teach that every emotion sends a message, such as frustration signaling that something is not working out as wished-for: "Yes, the pulley is stuck." This gives information and Vygotsky's theory advises that a more knowledgeable other, the teacher, scaffold a child's understanding of a concept. Accept feelings: "Everybody gets frustrated at times and that's okay." Avoid criticizing children for having any feeling.

Teaching children to accept all emotions that wash over them is not a trivial thing, nor is it an easy lesson. Some adults will find this an extremely difficult topic because they do not believe that all emotions are normal and natural. Some adults, for example, might have been taught that some emotions, such as anger, are not acceptable. Therefore, before you try to plan any learning opportunities for children on this topic, reflect on what you have been taught and what you believe about emotions merely being a signal about an issue and that emotions are normal.

## Limits on Expressing Emotions

Accepting the existence of a child's feeling of frustration does not mean that teachers also approve of any old way of expressing the frustration. Quite the reverse—children need to know how to control their response to a feeling. They need to learn that hurting others or damaging property is *not* acceptable. They need to know that "blowing off steam" and humiliating somebody in the process is *not* acceptable. They need to know that doing these things is not only wrong but will also close the door to friendships and acceptance. Children also need to learn that their teachers can be trusted to help them learn a more positive way to deal with emotions that wash over them. It is very comforting and soothing to children who are angry or disappointed to know that there is somebody who "can turn on the light" and help them find their way to a better way to express feelings.

**Teacher's Role** Accept any feelings, yes, but set limits about expressing emotions. This refers to setting clear, consistent, yet flexible boundaries about how to manage emotions responsibly (Christian, 2006). Let children know that you will help them with learning about emotions. Convey this message simply, firmly, and kindly to children. For example, to a second grader, "There's nothing unusual about how you seem to be feeling. It's okay to feel *frustrated*, but it is not okay to bang the pulley on the edge of the table because you are frustrated." Then, go beyond this and help the child switch to a more optimistic mode by assuring her that you will help her learn a better way: "I will help you figure out another way to say that you feel frustrated." Or, "Do you want me to help you figure out a different way to say that you are really frustrated now or later?" For a child, this can decrease the tension that goes along with strong emotions. Put yourself in that child's shoes. She feels *frustration* and then some *disappointment*, strong feelings, but has no clue as to a solution. This adds fear to the frustration, which confusing for a child. Feeling supported and knowing that "My teacher will help me!" lessens the force of strong emotions and opens the door to children for dealing with the feelings in a different way.

## Alternative Responses to Emotions

Our goal is a realistic one, to scaffold children's understanding about how to deal with the normal emotions that sweep over every person, including every teacher and every child. An essential SEL concept is that children have a choice about how to deal with their emotions. The message to children: You can *choose* what to do when you feel frustrated. You can *choose* what to do when you feel a little irritated or even when you are very angry. Some children have never learned this.

What does this message do for children? It tells them that they will still have the emotion of *frustration*, for example, but will have options, that they can take charge of the feeling and not be at the mercy of their impulses, that they can control those impulses. This bit of self-knowledge—"I can control how I act"—is important for a child to learn. Knowing and believing that one has a choice about how to act is liberating and powerful. Over time, choosing a positive response to unpleasant emotions lets other more helpful and even soothing emotions wash over children. For example, a child who stops and thinks about frustration and then chooses fixing that pulley will feel contentment and a healthy sense of pride in his choosing a positive path. He might even end up, after several such successful dealings with frustration and disappointment, say to himself, "No big deal! I can handle this."

**Teacher's Role**    Teach the child about a different way to act when a feeling creeps up. Teach that the next step after identifying an emotion (I am *frustrated*) is to reject an unkind or hostile response (reject the urge to curse or to slam the pulley against the table edge). Instead, provide suggestions and supports for the child's learning and retention of a different response. For example, "If you are frustrated, then stop and think. Say to yourself, 'When I feel frustrated, I can take s-l-o-w breaths. Then, I won't feel so worried.'" Or, 'When I feel frustrated, I can do a yoga pose.' Or, 'When I am frustrated, I can try to figure things out or ask for help.'" Emotions, even when pleasant, are accompanied by a burst of energy. Learning to calm oneself and think things through is a key emotional skill, but is a process and does not happen overnight. Learning to choose a positive response to anger, fear, jealousy, frustration, or disappointment is a gradual learning process.

Plan discussions around books and stories to get started on intentionally teaching about how to react to anger or other emotions. Literacy-related activities, such as scripted stories and books, help children develop SEL. All children gain when we focus on SEL, but children with communication disorders or challenging behaviors especially need the explicit instruction in a scripted story (Figueroa-Sanchez, 2008). Write a scripted story by combining pictures and words focused on teaching specific skills, such as joining a group or using words to express feelings. Consider using clip art or photographs to develop hard copies of the stories, or simply develop Power-Point slides and show stories with a computer or tablet. Figure 8.4 shows a how to write a scripted story about skills for joining a group of children for play.

| **FIGURE 8.4** | Scripted story for teaching a social and friendship skill: Asking to join in play |
|---|---|

**Write sentences that explain situations and answer questions, such as who, what, where, why.**

- I like to play with other children at school.
- It is fun to play with others.
- Sometime, I see other children already in a group.
- I have to ask if I can play with my friends if they are already in a group.
- It is okay to ask to play with others.

**Write sentences that describe how those involved might feel.**

- I feel a little scared about asking to play sometimes.
- The other children like it when I ask to play.
- My teacher likes it when I ask if I can play with others.

**Write a sentence or two about what the child might do.**

- I will try to remember to ask if I can play.

*Source:* Based on CSEFEL (n.d.—c). Scripted Stories for Social Situations—Tip Sheet.

---

## :: *Question for Reflection*

---

Use books to help children understand feelings and friends (Birckmayer, Cohen, Jensen, & Variano, 2005; Sullivan & Strang, 2002). When you read books about emotions, for example, children get information about the topic, and they make connections between what they hear about feelings in and out of school. They are more likely to view their own emotions as natural and normal when a teacher plans, reads, and follows up on a story about emotions.

As an example, choose books about anger that teach one or more of the major concepts about anger management. For example, a child should express anger without resorting to aggression. (See Figure 8.5). Read and use books thoughtfully, and employ a variety of follow-up activities to the story (Hsieh, Hemmeter, McCollum, & Ostrosky, 2009). CSEFEL (n.d.—d), for example, has developed the "Book Nook," part of its website giving specific suggestions about how to use books—and scripted stories—in SEL. The center gives numerous suggestions for using books such as *Hands Are Not for Hitting*, by Martine Agassi. Suggestions for teaching alternative uses for hands abound in art, music, science, drama, and pretend-play. (Refer to the list of websites near the end of this chapter to find the URL for the CSEFEL website.)

## Strong Emotions Vocabulary

"Use your words . . ." is a wonderful message that supports children in dealing with emotions. What teachers must do is to make sure that a child has the "words" he needs to put a name to those feelings. We do this by helping children develop an emotions vocabulary, the set of emotion words or labels for our feelings, such as

**Emotions vocabulary**
The set of emotion words or labels for feelings, such as angry, jealous, anxious

---

**FIGURE 8.5**   Checklist: Guidelines for choosing books on anger

Follow selection guidelines from Reading Is Fundamental (RIF) (Reading Is Fundamental, 2004) for choosing any picture book, and then check to be sure that the book meets additional, specific selection criteria for stories about anger. Use this checklist to evaluate a book on anger.

1. **How does this book deal with words/vocabulary for angry feelings?**
   - ❑ Uses one word (*mad* or *angry*) exclusively.
   - ❑ Uses two different words (such as *mad* and *angry*) or some other combination.
   - ❑ Uses several different words, thus demonstrating how to describe anger with different words.

2. **Does this book identify the specific event that seemed to elicit the anger?**
   - ❑ Not at all. Anger trigger never mentioned.
   - ❑ Identified a trigger for the anger, but was inaccurate.
   - ❑ Identified the anger trigger, but in a blaming, accusatory way.
   - ❑ Correctly identified the specific thing that brought on the anger, without blaming.

3. **How well does this book convey the idea that feeling angry is a natural and normal experience?**
   - ❑ Not at all. It actually blames the child in the story for feeling angry.
   - ❑ Not very well. It acknowledges that the child is angry but in a guilt-inducing way.
   - ❑ Adequately. It acknowledges anger, but says nothing about it being okay.
   - ❑ Very well. It clearly conveys the idea that anger is a normal emotion.

4. **How does this story urge children to manage their anger (goal: present nonaggressive, optimistic strategies)?**
   - ❑ With aggressive strategies exclusively (such as hitting others—an inappropriate strategy).
   - ❑ Sometimes aggressively (also an inappropriate strategy).
   - ❑ With positive strategies (such as using words—an appropriate strategy).

5. **My decision, based on my checklist analysis:**
   - ❑ Reject the book because it advocates aggression or it blames the child.
   - ❑ Read the book, but make adjustments to fix minor issues.*
   - ❑ Use the book with confidence that it meets most of the selection guidelines.

*It is possible to use a book even if it is less than perfect (assuming it does not advocate aggressive strategies or blame children). Suppose that a book does not identify the event that angered a child. How might you use the book anyway? What might you do to help the children come up with their own ideas about the anger trigger?

---

angry, jealous, distressed, frustrated, or anxious. It takes a long time for children to use words or labels for emotions confidently. Younger children tend to use very few emotion words on their own, such as using *mad* as the only word for angry or annoyed feelings. Older early childhood children, if they have learned the words, are capable of using additional labels, such as *irritated, annoyed,* or *bothered* as synonyms for *angry* or *mad.* Some children are blocked from making progress, however, because they never learn the right words to describe feelings.

| FIGURE 8.6 | Keep the child's age in mind when teaching emotion words |
| --- | --- |

**Glad**

**Cheerful**

**Happy**

Glad
—Delighted
—Pleased

Cheerful
—Jolly
—Jovial

Happy
—Contented
—Blissful
—Elated

**Younger Children**

**Expanding the Range of Happy**

**Older Children**

An emotionally competent person possesses a strong and large enough emotions vocabulary, the set of words or expressions, to describe their feelings, for example: "I was *mad*!" or "I feel *sad* about the puppy" or "I am *disappointed* about not getting to see the movie" or "That odor is *disgusting*!" or (to oneself) "I do feel *jealous*" or "I am so *happy* to be done with that!" or "I'm *afraid* of him" or "When he called me a loser, I was really, really *angry*, almost *enraged*" or "I did feel *guilty* about humiliating her" or "That was *distressing* news to me" or "I felt *embarrassed* when the bus driver called me a slowpoke." Therefore, the first step in dealing with any emotion is to be able to name it. Naming an emotional state, such as *anger*, gives children a foundation for understanding the feeling. Figure 8.6 shows how younger and older children can all learn emotion words, although older children can learn a larger number of words meaning almost the same thing—synonyms. A young child, for example, uses *happy* to indicate lighthearted feelings, but can learn a few other similar words such as *glad* or *cheerful*. Older children can acquire a much bigger set of words representing different states of *happiness*.

Emotionally competent individuals also realize that emotions are complex and have many levels of emotional energy. Children need to learn gradually that every feeling exists on a continuum—that is, each feeling has a range of emotional energy from low to high intensity, from a very mild feeling to something truly substantial, that you can be "a little or teeny-tiny bit angry" or "really, really angry." Children need to learn good labels for the "teeny-tiny bit" of feelings or for more energy-consuming or even threatening "really big feelings." For example, we can feel *happy*, but also *pleased*, *thrilled*, or even swept away with *joy*, *ecstatic* or *overjoyed*, depending on a situation. Another example, a child might feel *frustrated* about the pulley, only *mildly annoyed* with loud noise from outside the classroom during a lesson, and downright *exasperated* with a classmate who dawdles and plods along in any line.

Therefore, adopt a one-word-does-*not*-fit-all approach, especially important when dealing with anger. Dealing with anger effectively, for example, calls for different words about different levels of intensities for this very unpleasant but normal

| FIGURE 8.7 | Different intensities of the same emotion. We need to have a strong enough emotions vocabulary, the words to describe levels of anger, from low to higher intensity |
|---|---|

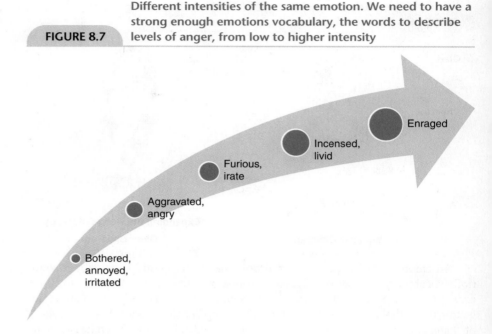

emotion (see Figure 8.7). This knowledge puts the child in charge of correctly labeling the level of feeling that he has and he will be in a much better position to deal more effectively with whatever feeling he has. He might decide, for example, that being just "a little bothered" by something is not a big deal and can simply let the incident pass without a lot of comment.

**Teacher's Role**   Gunning's (2013) explanation of how to teach vocabulary in general is helpful to teachers who are helping children learn a strong emotions vocabulary. Two major ways of helping children build their emotions vocabulary are through a planned and an incidental approach. In the planned approach, a teacher deliberately plans instruction on and methodically teaches emotion words. In the incidental approach, a teacher helps children learn emotion words as the need arises. A blending of planned and incidental vocabulary learning is an excellent approach. However, the emphasis here is on the planned approach with these guidelines for intentionally teaching emotions vocabulary.

- **Provide experiences that are as concrete as possible.**  For example, discussing the class mood when the scheduled visit from the fire truck had to be cancelled provides an experience and the teacher needs to teach the label, the word *disappointed*, to describe the mood.
- **Relate new words to a child's own experiences.**  For example, each child relates a time when he felt similarly *disappointed* about something.
- **Build relationships.**  Show, gradually and not all at one time, how a new emotions word is related to its synonym, such as *disappointed* being similar to

*frustrated* or *saddened,* for example: "The class seemed *saddened* about the fire truck cancellation" or "I noticed that some of you were a little *frustrated* when you heard about the fire truck."

- **Present the new word in different contexts.** For example, a child will better understand the word *disappointed* if she hears it in different settings, such as *disappointed* about the burned pizza, the class was *disappointed* when the principle announced the playground closing, *disappointed* boys and girls left the swimming pool.

- **Present the word several times, not just once or twice.** Real understanding demands several exposures to new words. For example, introduce the emotion word *disappointed* during a large group discussion using a photo of a child whose block tower toppled. Deliberately use the word again at the end of day class meeting when reviewing the day's learning: "When we saw that picture of the child whose tower fell, the word to describe how he felt was *disappointed.*" Read or write a story featuring the word. Show a drawing of a face depicting *disappointment* and ask, "What is the feeling on this face—a *happy* or a *disappointed* look? Showing drawings or photographs of facial expressions of emotions is a good idea because children tend to be more accurate in decoding drawings (MacDonald, Kirkpatrick, & Sullivan, 1996). Another example: "Look at this drawing. Make your face look like this. The word we use when we feel like this is *disappointment.*" Have a child look in a mirror and make a *disappointed* look. Space such learning opportunities out over a reasonable period.

## How to Talk about Emotions: How to Use Your Words

Teachers can deliberately help children learn how to control feelings and to express their emotions accurately and in a positive way, even when they are upset (Weare, 2004). The preschool teacher in the chapter-opening vignettes said, "You can *use words* to tell Sarah that you are upset." It is a supportive strategy because so many young children do not know this concept, this idea of not reacting to every emotion but choosing how to express the feeling and then choosing whether and how to act on the feeling.

Here are three practical steps to helping a child learn to "use your words" to tell how he feels—pay attention to your feeling, slow down and think, and use words to talk about your feelings.

- **Pay attention to your feeling.** Observe children's body and facial language as well as their actions and words. Be prepared to step in before they react to an unpleasant feeling in an aggressive way, if that is possible. For example, two girls, Pearl and Ginger, were working with small plastic blocks when Pearl reached over and took Ginger's remaining blocks. Ginger screeched. (The teacher did work with Pearl but we are focused on Ginger). The teacher said to Ginger, "You seemed to be upset. Is that right?" Ginger: "She always takes things!" Teacher: "Pay attention to how you feel. When somebody takes your things, how do you feel?" Ginger replied, "Mad!"

- **Slow down and talk to yourself.** CSEFEL (2007) calls this the turtle technique—that we teach children to be as slow as a turtle after identifying a feeling. Teach children to calm themselves and then to talk to themselves about how to go forward, how to react to the feeling. We want to help them have an internal dialogue. Teacher to Ginger: "Take a s-l-o-w breath. Look at our turtle drawing. Be as slow as this turtle." Then, firmly but reassuringly, "I heard you make a screechy loud sound. That's not allowed. I want you to use words to tell how you feel. It's okay to be upset but I want you to use words, not to screech. . . . Say, I can use words not screeching." The child repeats, "I can use words, not screeching."
- **Use words to handle the feeling.** Teacher to Ginger: "Listen . . . tell me how to finish this sentence. 'I feel _____.' Okay, mad. Now, you say, 'I am mad.' Good, you have used words to tell yourself how you feel." The teacher then goes on to deal with Pearl and to help Ginger assert her right to get her blocks back. Children need to learn how to use words and benefit from practicing with the teacher before using words with other children. Learning to actually use words is not that difficult, but going forward and saying the words to the person you are angry with is difficult for many people, including children.

After learning about using words, children benefit from being reminded and from practicing. Like any other daunting task, dealing with one's feelings gets less difficult as a person gradually and successfully handles a variety of emotions. Go beyond the initial teaching and build in opportunities for learning and practicing using words to express feelings.

## Friendship Skills

**Friendship skills**
Behaviors through which a child demonstrates the ability to develop relationships with other children

Children need specific **friendship skills**, which enable them to make friends and then to continue to have friendly interactions. Having friends is central to a child's social and emotional development, which makes acquiring the abilities an important task for young children. Friendship skills include getting a friend's attention, giving ideas for and organizing play, greeting others, sharing, being helpful, taking turns, and saying something pleasant to others (CSEFEL, n.d.,—b, c).

**Teacher's Role**   Children do not automatically possess friendship skills, but instead have to learn them. Teachers need to deliberately plan learning opportunities focused on each of the skills. CSEFEL recommends spending about 10 to 15 minutes per day for two weeks teaching these essential friendship skills. For example, a teacher used the morning meeting to teach the children how to greet other children. She showed a photos of two children, Chloe and Donald, and said that Chloe wanted to talk to Donald. So, Chloe watched to see that Donald was not talking to anybody else and said, "Hi, Donald!" Then, the teacher did a role-play with the parent volunteer who had practiced the role-play with the teacher. Teacher: "Good morning, Mr. Colonna." The parent responded, "Good morning, Mrs. Johnson." Notice that the greeting skills run both ways, that the children in the teacher's presentation with drawings and the two adults all participated in the greeting. Responding appropriately to being greeted is also a friendship skill. Teachers can also use large-group time for teaching about the other friendship skills.

## :: SOCIAL EMOTIONAL LEARNING OPPORTUNITIES: DURING LARGE GROUP AND FOCUSED ON THROUGHOUT THE DAY

Teachers plan for social emotional learning by developing lesson plans focusing on the essential SEL topics that you studied in the last section. They teach about the topics directly and in two major ways, in the large-group meeting and then throughout the day (CSEFEL, n.d.—a, c). The first strategy is to use large-group time for direct instruction about any of the SEL topics, such as teaching the friendship skill of greeting other children. Two excellent ways to teach each skill are with modeling and role-playing the skill. The second strategy is to focus on SEL skills throughout the day at school. Group time, small-group learning, centers, routines, and transitions provide numerous opportunities for teachers to acknowledge children's efforts in using new skills, to remind them about a skill, and to practice skills. Weaving SEL learning into children's days transforms SEL into a strong thread running through and making the fabric of children's lives even more beautiful.

This section will illustrate this process. We will use the three issues mentioned in this chapter that every child faces and that can be particularly difficult for them—handling disappointment, managing angry feelings, and developing friendship skills. We have touched on these issues, but will now see how a teacher directly teaches about them in large-group time and then throughout the day.

### Helping Children Handle Disappointment

To recap, every child feels and expresses emotions even though they do not understand the emotions. A teacher's role is to help children build that understanding so that they can then handle or manage an emotion. Every child, therefore, will feel disappointed now and again and will express the frustration. It is important for teachers to help children learn to handle everyday disappointments well so that disappointment does not morph into anger and aggression. Children need to learn, ever so gently, that people simply do not get everything that they want and that things do not always turn out as we hope. They need to know that they can control how they deal with feeling disappointed.

Figure 8.8 shows how Mrs. Johnson, the preschool teacher, intentionally focused on teaching about handling disappointment. She did this first at the morning large-group meeting and then logically wove the information throughout the day. Notice that she targeted only one of the essential SEL topics, that disappointment is a normal feeling and has a purpose. She will focus on this emotion over a number of days and will then revisit the ideas when it seems appropriate to do so.

### Helping Children Deal with Anger

There is quite a bit to teach about dealing with anger, and Mrs. Johnson has proceeded in a step-by-step fashion so that the children had direct instruction about every SEL topic on anger. Today, she decided to focus on the remaining essential SEL topics, how

| FIGURE 8.8 | Teaching children how to handle disappointment |
|---|---|
| **Learning Opportunity Occurs Here** | **SEL Topic: Disappointment Is a Normal Feeling and Has a Purpose*** |
| Large group, morning | Modeling: Teacher shows simple drawings on a flip chart. Child orders chocolate ice cream; clerk says there is no more chocolate; child's face shows disappointment. Parent says, "Uh-oh, no chocolate. You look a little *disappointed*." Child nods. Teacher says to class, "He was *disappointed* because he could not get what he wanted. That happens, doesn't it? |
| | Modeling: Teacher then models the same sort of event with an assistant teacher: Teacher: "It's recess!" Assistant: "Look, it's raining and we can't go out." Teacher: "I wanted to go out." Assistant teacher: "Sounds like you're a little disappointed because you can't play outside." |
| Throughout the day: Centers or project time | Discovery center: Teacher places drawing of a face showing disappointment on table. Places two mirrors on table. Stops by the center as children looking into mirrors mimic the "disappointed" look in the drawing. "The name of the feeling that you are showing in your face is _____?" |
| Throughout the day: Small-group instruction | Teacher and five children at small table, teacher with iPad or laptop. Shows the emotions faces the children have learned about: happy, angry, and disappointed. Asks question: Which face shows how we feel when somebody swiped our play dough when we were using it? Which face tells us how we feel when we get to go swimming? Which face tells us how we feel when we cannot paint at the easel? Which face tells how we feel when we find something else equally interesting to do when we can't paint at the easel? |
| Throughout the day: Routines and transitions | End-of-day routine, review of learning in group: "What is the feeling word that we learned about today?" (Disappointment.) What does your face look like if you are disappointed?" (Children make the face.) "Is it okay to feel *disappointed*?" "What kinds of things tend to make us feel disappointed?" |

*This is only one of the essential SEL topics. You can focus on other essential SEL topics in much the same way.

to talk about emotions—anger in this case. She wanted the children to be able to "use words" in reacting to or dealing with anger. She has used a simple checklist to keep track of teaching the other SEL topics about anger. She has checked off the SEL anger topics that she has already intentionally taught about. She has already taught that anger is a normal feeling and about several good words to express anger. The children were therefore ready, she thought, to "use those words" when they were angry.

**EXAMPLE**   Checklist that the teacher used to decide which SEL topic about anger she should focus on next with her class; the ❏ indicates that the children have already learned about this topic and anger:

❏ Emotions as normal and having a purpose
❏ Limits on expressing emotions
❏ Alternative responses to feelings
❏ A strong emotions vocabulary

How to talk about emotions (how to "use your words" words to talk about anger): all other topics have been checked off and the teacher is focusing on how to

| FIGURE 8.9 | Teaching children how to handle anger |
|---|---|
| **Learning Opportunity Occurs Here** | **SEL Topic: How to Talk about Anger: Use Your Words*** |
| Large group, morning | Modeling with puppets, turtle and child: Child, on playground and just finished racing another child: "Oh!" Turtle: "Your face is all scrunched up. Are you upset?"(Helps child pay attention to a feeling.) Child: "Yes, Sam runs faster than I do." Turtle: "Okay, walk with me. I'm slow, you know! Let's take a s-l-o-w breath. . . . Are you just a little upset or really, really angry?" Child: "Just a little." Turtle: "Okay, so you are *bothered*?" Child: "Yeah, bothered. Just a little upset." (Helps child slow down and talk to himself.) Turtle: "Okay. Now, say, 'I can use words to say how I feel.'" Child repeats the sentence. Turtle: "Now, say 'I am *bothered* because Sam runs faster than I do.'" Child repeats the sentence. Turtle: "Sam didn't do anything mean, did he? So, consider just telling yourself that you are bothered that he runs faster." Child, shrugs in a no-big-deal way: "Sam did not do anything mean; he just ran faster." |
| Throughout the day: Centers or project time | Teacher gave on-the-spot guidance at the sand table. One child was upset when another pushed her over from her place. Teacher: "Sonia, remember . . . use your words to talk to Rita. Use your words to tell her how you feel." |
| Throughout the day: Small-group instruction | *Thinking puppets.* Puppets help children think about many things and solve problems (Keogh, Naylor, Simon, Downing, & Maloney, 2006). Teacher used puppets again to demonstrate using words to tell somebody that you are angry. She demonstrated a mild conflict in which one puppet pinched the other. "Harvey [puppet] is *angry* because this other puppet pinched him. Help Harvey think about what he could do. He's not allowed to yell at or hurt the puppet that pinched him." |
| Throughout the day: Routines and transitions | Transition from outdoors to inside and group time. Teacher starts group time with "turtle time breathing." "Let's take some s-l-o-w breaths." Teacher finds that this is very calming for children and helps them switch gears to a quieter activity. She has found that focusing *before* proceeding with a story prevents agitation. She then says, "Let's practice using our words. I feel calm." |

*This is only one of the essential SEL topics. You can focus on other essential SEL topics in much the same way.

talk about emotions in today's lesson.Figure 8.9 shows how Mrs. Johnson focused on teaching about how "to use your words" to express angry feelings. She used the three practical steps to helping children learn to use their words, the steps including

- Pay attention to your feeling
- Slow down and talk to yourself
- Use words to say how your feel

## Helping Children Learn Friendship Skills

One of the major SEL topics that teachers must focus on are the skills children need to form and maintain friendships. Figure 8.10 shows several examples of how the preschool teacher intentionally planned learning opportunities for teaching friendship skills. She again used large group in the morning to model different friendship skills—direct instruction. She also continued to weave friendship skill learning opportunities throughout the day, in small group instruction, during self-selected center time, and during routines and transitions.

| FIGURE 8.10 | Teaching friendship skills to children |
| --- | --- |
| **Learning Opportunity Occurs Here** | **SEL Topic: Friendship Skills** |
| Large group, morning | (Friendship skills include getting a friend's attention, giving ideas for and organizing play, greeting others, sharing, being helpful, taking turns, and saying something pleasant to others) |
| | Modeling: Teacher and assistant teacher, teacher at computer while assistant teacher stands behind her looking at the computer. Teacher: "Hi, Janet. Do you want a turn with the computer?" Assistant teacher: "Uh-huh." Teacher: "Well, do you want to sit with me and play the game?" Assistant teacher pulls up a chair and sits with teacher. Teacher: "Good, we can both play." (Focused on friendship skills of greeting others, sharing, and taking turns.) |
| Throughout the day: Centers or project time | Teacher notices and acknowledges a child's helpfulness at the writing table (focuses on friendship skill of helpfulness). |
| | Teacher reminds a child about taking turns with the one flashlight in the discovery center (focus on friendship skill of turn-taking) . |
| Throughout the day: Small- group instruction | Friendly vs. unfriendly responses: Teacher made up scenarios and then encouraged the six children to generate a friendly response: "Somebody sits next to you at snack. What would be a friendly thing to say? An unfriendly thing to do or to say?" "Another child wants to play with you. What is an *un*friendly thing to do? What is a friendly thing to do?" "You see that a child is looking at the play dough table while you are working there. What is the friendly thing to do?" (Focused on friendship skills of greeting others and saying something pleasant.) |
| Throughout the day: Routines and transitions | Transition from small-group instruction: Teacher rolls a soft ball to a child and says, "It has been nice working with you!" That child then rolls the ball to another child and says, "It has been nice working with you!" (then leaves the group) . . . and so on. Last child rolls ball to teacher (focuses on friendship skill of saying something pleasant to others). |

## ANALYZE A VIGNETTE

Now that you have read the chapter, analyze the chapter-opening vignette about preschool by answering the following questions.

1. Jerry noticed that he was angry. Which of the types of interactions from the How Children Perceive Emotions section of the chapter would you say fits Jerry's anger?

2. From the section on Expressing Anger, identify the method that Jerry used to express his feeling. Explain your answer.

3. From information in the chapter, explain how Jerry has probably learned to express angry feelings so aggressively.

## SUMMARY

Teachers focus on the whole child, including social and emotional competence. Emotionally intelligent individuals cope well with feelings, have empathy for others, and get along well with others. Children who are intelligent about their feelings are competent and capable, feel connected to others, and have a good sense of balance in their emotions.

The abilities that make up emotional intelligence and competence are:

- Perceiving emotions
- Expressing emotions
- Regulating emotions

Children who are emotionally competent and intelligent are equipped well for making and keeping friends—for developing social competence. Emotional and social competences are linked because good emotional regulation gives children a good chance at developing satisfactory social skills, too. Socially competent children:

- Relate well to other children
- Respond agreeably to others
- Possess developed social and friendship skills

Teachers can guide children's learning about emotions and social development—SEL. They can:

- Create supportive SEL environments. Children need a trust-building interpersonal environment in which they interact with warm and supportive teachers. They need supportive physical environments—that is, classrooms conducive to active, collaborative learning, and they need schedules allowing large blocks of time for their learning.
- Teacher can plan learning opportunities for SEL. Two practical ways to do this include the following: Teach about SEL during the daily large-group meeting. Modeling and role-playing are good strategies for directly teaching about topics such as handling disappointment and anger. Modeling is also useful for teaching friendship skills. Teachers then weave learning opportunities throughout the day—for example, during center time, during small-group instruction, and during routines and transitions.

## APPLY YOUR KNOWLEDGE

1. Analyze one or two books on anger from the list below to decide whether it meets the guidelines for choosing books about emotions/anger. Use the checklist in Figure 8.5 as a guide. Consider adding the completed checklist to your portfolio.

> Bang, M. (2008). *When Sophie gets angry—Really, really angry* (reprint edition). New York, NY: Scholastic Paperbacks.
>
> Kroll, S., & Davenier, C. (2002). *That makes me mad!* San Francisco: CA: Chronicle Books.
>
> Shannon, D. (2000). *The rain came down.* New York, NY: Blue Sky Press.

2. Read a story to children. Access http://www.vanderbilt.edu/csefel. Click on the "practical strategies" link and look over the book nook and scripted stories. Click on the link for a children's book, *Hands Are Not for Hitting*, by Margaret Agazzi. (If you are currently at a practicum site, request permission to read the book to the children.) Request permission to carry out one of the activities described on this web page. The activities will help children understand the major concepts in the book. If you cannot read to a whole group, then consider reading to and doing one of the activities with a single child.

## WEBSITES

*Center on the Social and Emotional Foundations for Early Learning (CSEFEL)*
http://csefel.vanderbilt.edu/index.html

A federally funded, national resources center. Excellent resources on social emotional learning (SEL) for teachers, trainers, and parents. See the excellent examples of scripted stories for SEL, complete with pictures or drawings, in the Resources/Practical Strategies section of the website. These scripted stories are PowerPoint slides that you can use in your teaching.

*Edutopia*
http://www.edutopia.org

A website devoted to what works in public education. Go to the social emotional learning section, which deals directly with social emotional learning (SEL).

# CHAPTER 9
# Resilience and Stress in Childhood

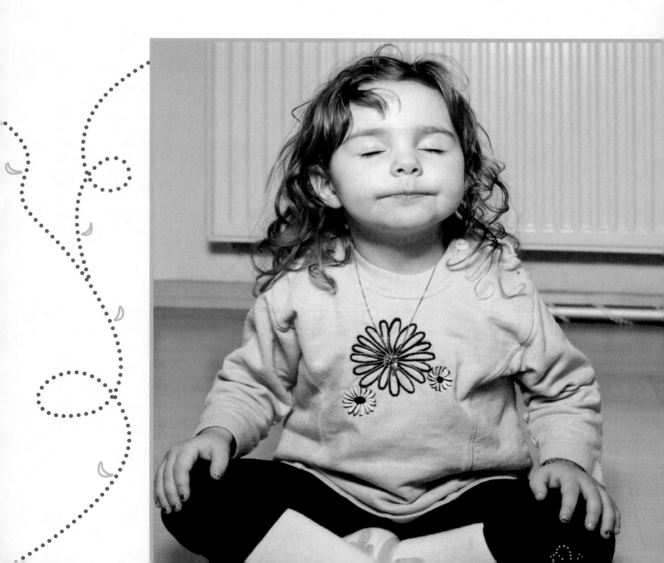

# Learning Outcomes

- Define terms related to resilience and stress in early childhood
- Explain how children become resilient
- Differentiate between acute and chronic stress
- Discuss the major sources of stress
- Describe the likely physical, psychological, and behavioral effects of stress on young children
- Explain the stages that children go through in responding to stress
- Discuss strategies that teachers can use to help children cope effectively with stress

## VIGNETTES

### INFANT–TODDLER: SCHOOL IS A COMFORTING PLACE

*Mr. Bensen realized that 15-month-old Lela's family had moved to a trailer after they lost their house in a flood. Things at home were beginning to settle down, but Lela was still showing signs of stress. The teacher had been working with her and her parents by continuing to make school as predictable as possible. He greeted her warmly every morning, set up interesting and favorite activities and toys, and comforted her as needed. He also invited her parents to spend a little time with Lela in the classroom, and they seem to enjoy this calm and peaceful time together.*

### PRESCHOOL: THE FIRE ALARM RINGS

*Mrs. Johnson and the 4-year-olds had just started their morning meeting when the fire alarm rang out loudly (an unscheduled fire drill). Even though the class had heard the alarm during a practice drill, some of the children were startled. A few showed obvious signs of distress, especially as the sound continued, growing louder and more piercing. The teacher remained calm, called to the children quietly but firmly, and told them to look at her. "That's the fire alarm. We have to leave the building, just as we practiced. Stay with me and watch me." She and the assistant lined up the children and then quickly moved them outside.*

### PRIMARY: ALDEN GOES TO A NEW SCHOOL

*After transferring to his new school, Alden would be in Mr. Santini's mixed-age class. The teacher met Alden and his father after school to orient them to 5-year-old Alden's new classroom. The teacher showed them his cubby, took his picture to add to the class pictures, and showed him where he would nap. They toured the room, and Alden learned where things were and how they worked. Mr. Santini gave a copy of the daily schedule to Alden's father and gave him a choice of children's books about moving to read to Alden. The next day, the teacher assigned a friend to help Alden through routines. He also explained playground rules.*

## :: INTRODUCTION

Children are not immune to stress. They face stress-inducing situations every day, such as those faced by Lela, the preschoolers, and Alden in the chapter-opening vignettes. In this chapter, you will learn about resilience in children and about how stress affects children. We will examine the stages of responding to stress as well as what it takes to cope effectively. You will add to your understanding of why young children have a difficult time coping with stress on their own.

On a practical level, you will learn several general guidelines for helping children with stress. The guidelines can be used to help children who face a variety of stressors. Then we will apply those guidelines to a specific, potentially stressful event—moving to a new neighborhood or school. Finally, you will have an opportunity, in the end-of-chapter activities, to apply this information to other childhood stressors.

## :: RESILIENCE IN YOUNG CHILDREN

**Resilience**
The ability to weather stress and adversity and not be devastated by it

Many children face adversity in their homes and communities. These are the high-risk children about whom we worry so much. What we know, though, is that many, but not all, children who face multiple and severe risks show great *resilience* as they overcome the odds. **Resilience** is the ability to recover relatively quickly from misfortune without being overwhelmed or acting in dysfunctional ways. This implies that a child, for instance, would adapt optimistically under many stressful conditions (Aldwin & Werner, 2007; Werner, 2004). A person who is resilient is calm under pressure, can solve problems, can reflect critically on issues, is autonomous, and has a sense of purpose.

### Resilience Grows in Families, Schools, and Communities

**Stress**
A child's reaction to psychological or physical threats to safety and security

Ecological theory explains that children develop in different systems, each system adding its influence. Many children experience **stress**, a reaction to physical or psychological threats to well-being, and often the stress is traumatic. Some children fare well in spite of very stressful conditions, but others do not. What fosters a good developmental outcome in the face of great stress? Why are some children more resilient than other children?

Children become resilient in the systems in which they grow up—family, peer group, school, neighborhood, and larger society. Those who develop resilience are protected in some way from stress. They still experience stress, but something in the child's systems protects the child from major and potentially negative effects of harmful events. Something or someone buffers or absorbs some of the shock of the stressor, shielding a child and allowing him or her to develop well in the face of adversity (Werner & Smith, 2001).

## :: *Question for Reflection*

# Protective Factors That Foster Resilience

Systems that help children weather trauma provide safety and security in the midst of a whirlwind of stress. In this text, we are interested in what separates families or schools who foster resilience from those who do not. First, adults in these systems have a philosophy or basic core values that put protection of children at the center—the most important thing that they do—over and above their stated role. Your professional code of ethical behavior states that protecting children is the most important thing that teachers do (National Association of the Education of Young Children, 2005a). A resilience-building family or school feels good to children: they like spending time there and understand that the adults really care about them.

Second, resilience-building systems—families or schools—provide a specific type of safeguard called **protective factors**. These protective factors are the key in enabling children to navigate the bumpy road of frustration or adversity and to develop resilience. These three protective factors are (Werner, 2004):

**Protective factors**
Key features of caring systems in which children become resilient

A caring relationship

High expectations

Opportunities for participation.

**Caring Relationships** Adults in resilience-building families or schools tend to be authori*tative*, a style fostering resilience. Children learn to understand and manage potentially stressful events in caring and compassionate adult–child relationships. Resilient children have been able to connect with at least one caring and compassionate person, often a teacher, who serves as a good model of confidence and positive action. An authori*tative* teacher, for example, is high in responsiveness, and one of the most important aspects of high responsiveness is a warm and caring attitude toward children. This teacher tries to develop a good and caring relationship with all children in a class. The teacher acknowledges each child's existence, what that child does and creates, and how that child feels. The teacher knows that a good relationship is especially important for children who do not have a close relationship with parents.

**High Expectations** Authori*tative* caregivers, parents, or teachers have reasonable but high expectations for children. This helps children become resilient, partly because of how the expectations affect a child's self-esteem. Authoritative adults who have high but reasonable expectations help children develop competence, control, and worth, the building blocks of positive self-esteem. Competence, control, and a belief that one is worthy of affection also form the foundation of a resilient spirit.

**Caring relationships help children build resilience.**

As you watch this **video**, notice how the teacher communicates her high expectations to the children, especially to Kaitlin. What does she say to this child to help her wait to talk? What does she do when the child goes ahead and talks when somebody else is talking?

---

## :: *Question for Reflection*

---

**Opportunities for Participation** All humans yearn for validation and group membership. Children have these needs, just as we all do. They require chances to operate as a member of a group, and adults in protective systems make sure that their children get those chances. This can be something as simple as participating in making the limits or rules for a classroom in which caring adults have high expectations. It can also mean participating in family events, activities in one's religious group, Cub Scouts or Brownies, 4-H groups, library reading groups, care and feeding of animals, theater or other arts groups, and athletic teams.

The list of ways for children to participate is long. Children do not need to participate in a large number of activities, only those that give them pleasure and a sense of real belonging. You can do two practical things to help children participate joyfully:

- **Identify interests.** Help a child identify or find those activities that he likes and wants to do. For parents, this might mean spending "registration fees" for activities and letting a child try out the activity. For teachers, this means observing children carefully to discover what they really like to do—not what the teacher thinks a child should like, but what the *child* thinks is interesting and enjoyable. (You will be surprised on occasion!)
- **Encourage participation.** Once a child has found an activity that he likes, make sure that he has opportunities for participating and for feeling like a valued member of the group. For example, Mr. Santini knew that second-grader Sonia liked to play jacks. It was simple for him to set up play for jacks during recess. He also knew that Joseph liked to sing, although the 7-year-old would never admit that in front of the other boys. Therefore, Mr. Santini made sure that the children sang during most of their morning meetings.

## :: TYPES OF STRESSORS

Stressors are forms of excessive stimulation that produce stress. Some of these factors are psychological; others are physical. At times, physical and psychological stressors interact or merge to produce an effect.

## Physical Stressors

**Physical stressor**
Excessive stimulation with potential to damage parts of a child's body

**Physical stressors** refer to forms of excessive stimulation that injure or can potentially injure the tissue of some part of a child's body. There are several such physical stressors: excessively loud noises, extremely harsh lighting, decreased oxygen or lack of oxygen, extreme heat, extreme cold, injuries, infections, and drugs. Children who experience these stressors usually perceive them as painful or unpleasant.

> **EXAMPLE**   Sarah's family was spending a month on vacation at the beach. Sarah's babysitter failed to put sunscreen on 4-year-old Sarah when the child played outside. Sarah was sunburned and her skin blistered. The stressor was unprotected and excessive exposure to sunlight, which affected Sarah's skin.

## Psychological Stressors

**Psychological stressors** are forms of excessive stimulation with the potential to threaten a child's sense of well-being or to keep a child from developing a sense of well-being. Children might perceive several things as psychologically stressful, and children have varying views about what a psychological stressor is. For example, a child might see the death of a beloved grandparent as extremely stressful. Another child might not view a grandparent's death as stressful at all. Psychological stress, then, is a relationship between a child and his environment. Stress is not an *event*, such as the death of a grandparent, but is instead a relationship between a child and her perception of that event.

This relationship involves whether a child understands and can evaluate an event as well as a child's ability to cope with the event. A child is most likely to feel psychological stress when she cannot understand, evaluate, or cope effectively with some internal or external event. She then feels overwhelmed by the inability to cope, thus resulting in stress. Children often feel stress when something keeps them from fulfilling any of several fundamental needs—for security, bonding, acceptance, status, meaning, and mastery.

> **EXAMPLE**   Vincent goes to a school in which close to a third of the children were not born in the United States and who have been here for fewer than 4 years. The school district was not prepared to meet the needs of this influx of children with special requirements and is now struggling to do so. Vincent is having a great deal of trouble adjusting to life in a new country, as are his parents. Six-year-old Vincent does not understand and therefore cannot cope with several aspects of his new school. He is very likely to experience psychological stress because he feels overwhelmed in this new environment.

**Psychological stressor**
Excessive stimulation with potential to thwart or damage a child's sense of security

Some people automatically view specific life events as stressful, such as a move, a new school, a parent's death, or parents divorcing. In reality, these are merely life events, which make them only *potentially* stressful. They create stress only if a child does not understand the event, cannot evaluate the event, or does not have the skills for effectively coping with the event.

For example, many people believe that moving is automatically a stressful life event for young children. It would probably be more accurate to call moving a potentially stressful event; it can possibly create psychological stress, but whether it does depends on a child's understanding of and ability to cope with the move. Vincent, in the example just given, did view moving as stressful.

## Combination of Physical and Psychological Stressors

Often, a child's life includes both physical and psychological stressors that blend. Suppose that somebody hurts a child—a physically stressful event. Then consider what the child might think about this situation: Her thoughts about being assaulted tangle with the trauma itself. Therefore, she experiences psychological stress along with the physical stress. Children physically injured in some way might then fear or display anxiety about similar situations.

> **EXAMPLE**  Daniel is a 2-year-old whose father deliberately burned him with a cigarette as punishment for an accident during toilet learning (often called potty training). The physical stressor was the hot tip of the cigarette. Fear and anxiety in the relationship with a parent who uses sadistic punishment provided the psychological stress.

> **EXAMPLE**  An older child on the way to school has punched Jordan several times. Punching is the physically stressful event. However, this is combined with the anxiety and worry that Jordan feels, making such episodes psychologically stressful as well.

## :: ACUTE AND CHRONIC STRESS

Suppose that a child has perceived a potential stressor as stressful. He does not understand the stressor or might not have the skills for coping with it. The stress that he experiences can be either acute (profound, deep, extreme, intense, short-lived) or chronic (persistent, unceasing, continuous) stress.

## Acute Stress

**Acute stress**
Intense strain that occurs rapidly; usually transitory

**Acute stress** is the most common form of stress. It is intense stress that occurs suddenly. Acute stress can be physical, psychological, or a combination of the two. It occurs quite unexpectedly but tends to subside as abruptly as it arose—for example, a visit to the emergency room to have a broken arm set (physical and psychological stress). How an event affects a child depends, in large part, on how others deal with the event and on how the child appraises it (American Psychological Association, 2004).

> **EXAMPLE**  Six-year-old Jessica stood alone on the front steps of her house, crying. Just minutes before, the fire truck had zoomed into her family's driveway, sirens blaring. The firefighters were at the back of the house in the garage, putting out a fire. Jessica's mother, along with two friends, watched them, looking as though they were at a party, with cigarettes dangling from one hand and drinks in the other. Not one of them explained anything or paid attention to Jessica, other than to tell her to get to and stay in the front of the house. Jessica's apparent upset escalated until she screamed with fear. Her mother strode around the side of the house and angrily regarded her daughter.

## Chronic Stress

**Chronic stress**
Unrelenting, persistent, and ongoing stress

**Chronic stress** refers to persistent stress, which comes into a person's life and remains for a long period or even forever. Chronic stress is like a chronic disease, such as diabetes, because it is a constant part of a person's life. The children in your classes come from a variety of backgrounds and chances are very good that, in any one year, several of the children will be under chronic stress. They will have experienced grinding poverty, homelessness, illness, child abuse, irresponsible or inept parenting, long-term bitterness after parents divorcing, seemingly never-ending daily hassles, and loneliness or lack of friends. The effects of chronic stress seem to accumulate and to cause problems even for children who are well adjusted (American Psychological Association, 2004).

## :: SOURCES OF STRESS

There are two major sources of stress—internal and external (Jackson, 2008; Jewitt & Peterson, 2002). **Internal sources of stress** come from within the child. **External sources of stress** originate outside the child.

### Internal Sources of Stress

Internal sources of stress include hunger pangs in a neglected infant or child, shyness, or headaches. Thoughts about real or imagined dangers can be a source of stress, too. Emotions are also potential internal sources of stress. Anxiety, anger, disappointment, guilt, and even joy are potentially stressful for children if parents and teachers do not help them understand and deal with these emotions. Children do not automatically comprehend and know how to manage emotions.

> **EXAMPLE**   Matthew just transferred to Mr. Santini's kindergarten. In Matthew's former school, his teacher did a morning meeting but it lasted almost one hour, far too long for young children. Matthew experienced a lot of anxiety about going to group and showed signs of the anxiety when he first joined Mr. Santini's class.

### External Sources of Stress

Other potential sources of stress for children are external—that is, they come from the child's environment. Some of these external sources of stress exist within a child's family, whereas others are in a child's caregiving arrangement. Some external sources of stress exist in schools, others come from peers, and still others have their roots in the interaction of several systems. These stressors include the following:

**In a Child's Family**

- Overcrowded living conditions
- Moving
- Daily hassles for parents
- Divorce
- Poverty
- Joint custody arrangements
- Lots of background anger in the family, anger that the child hears and observes but is not directed to the child
- Military deployment of a parent

**Internal sources of stress**
Stress originating within a child

**External sources of stress**
Stress originating outside a child

### In School

- Going to a new school; leaving the old school
- Developmentally *in*appropriate classrooms, such as those dominated by *in*appropriate practices, including too many transitions, inappropriate instructional strategies, no recesses
- Standardized testing

### From Interactions (either at home, in school, or in a child-care facility)

- Experiencing child abuse or neglect directly
- Witnessing child abuse but not experiencing it firsthand
- Anger-arousing social interactions
- Developmentally *in*appropriate guidance, such as harsh discipline or inept guidance
- Loneliness or lack of friends

### From Other Sources

- Observing violence and aggression in newscasts, movies, cartoons, video or DVD games, in real life, or in any other situation
- Death or injury of a friend or even another child who is not a friend but who goes to the same school, such as in the 2013 Sandy Hook school shootings; death of a pet; death of a family member
- Experiencing a disaster, for example the December 26, 2004, tsunami in the Indian Ocean or the Oklahoma City tornados in the spring of 2013
- Illness and hospitalization

---

## :: *Question for Reflection*

---

## :: HOW STRESS AFFECTS CHILDREN

Professionals who work with children can fully expect to experience firsthand a child's reactions to stress. You might wonder why one child suddenly has problems focusing on projects, why another behaves aggressively, or why still another is highly anxious. Stress affects children in a variety of ways, just as it affects adults. Stress takes its toll on children physically, behaviorally, and/or psychologically. If a child used words to express the stress that he feels, he might say, "There's something wrong in my life."

### Physical Effects of Stress

A racing heart rate, dry mouth, a sick feeling in the stomach, a headache—most adults have experienced such physical reactions to some situation that they perceived as stressful, such as giving a speech or seeing the flashing lights of a police car on the interstate. Children can and do experience the same physical effects of stress. Any or a combination of these physical effects usually shows up in cases of acute stress. Given enough stress, as in a chronically stressful situation such as child abuse or a developmentally inappropriate classroom, a child might have even greater physical effects from the stress.

**Stress, White Blood Cells, and Resistance to Infections**  Researchers documented years ago that stress could eventually play a major role in disease (Stein, Keller, & Schleifer, 1981). Recent research has found that chronic stress actually worsens some diseases or suppresses a person's immune system (Meagher, 2007; Miller, Cohen, & Richey, 2002). Stress often disrupts a child's immune system response and makes it difficult for the child's body to deal effectively with infections. Here is an example of how it works.

> **EXAMPLE**  A child gets a splinter in his foot; the splinter breaks the skin and introduces bacteria. The bacteria multiply (the infection) and white blood cells move through the blood to the site of the infection. White blood cells (leukocytes), which contain digestive enzymes, destroy the bacteria in a process called phagocytosis—literally, "cell eating."

The number of white blood cells changes when an abnormal situation arises. A child's white blood cell count tends to rise when a child is overwhelmed by a stressful event. The child's body is trying to protect itself during a time of stress (Nanda, 2005).

**Stress Affects a Child's Brain**  Evidence has steadily mounted attesting to the unfortunate but preventable outcome of continued abuse and neglect on a child's developing brain (Lowenthal, 1999; Child Welfare Information Gateway, 2008). A major stressor such as abuse signals the child's body to prepare for "fight or flight," in which the body prepares to defend itself from danger. Stress hormones, cortisol and adrenalin, are released and prepare the body to respond to stress by increasing blood pressure and heart rate, for example.

A child under constant threat of abuse is nearly always in this state of readiness. The child's body may then produce an excessive amount of stress hormones, which can kill brain cells and reduce the number of connections among brain cells (the synapses). Adults subjected to long-term abuse as children have brains in which the hippocampus has shriveled, for example, and other parts also responsible for tasks such as memory or regulating emotions are smaller. Therefore, chronic stress causes constant activity of the stress response pathways and thus causes alterations in the brain (Child Welfare Information Gateway, 2008; Gallagher, 2004).

# Behavioral and Psychological Effects of Stress

Nail biting, bullying, fatigue, aggression, withdrawal, anxiety, fear—all these and others are behavioral or psychological indicators of childhood stress. The psychological distress that children feel, for example, when abused, when they move, or when they are rejected very often shows up in behavior (see Figure 9.1). Some children react to stress with passive behavior, whereas others display a more active approach. You might find that some children react to stress as they play or work with specific objects.

**FIGURE 9.1**      Behavioral indicators of stress in young children

Children show us that they are experiencing stress in a number of ways:

**Reactions to stress might be passive.**
   Excessive fatigue
   Withdrawing and putting head on table or desk
   Excessive fears

**Reactions to stress might be more active with behaviors that involve only the child.**
   Nail biting
   Manipulating one's hands or mouth
   Repetitive body movements

**Reactions to stress might show up when children interact with others.**
   Stuttering
   Bullying, threatening, or hurting others
   Nervous, inappropriate laughter

**Reactions to stress might show up as children work with objects.**
   Excessive squeezing or tapping of pencils, markers, or crayons
   Clumsy or fumbling behavior

**An Issue to Ponder about Behavioral Indicators of Stress**   Oppositional defiant disorder (ODD) is a psychiatric disorder in childhood. It is quite normal for children to test limits at specific junctures during development, for example, during toddlerhood and early adolescence. The psychiatric community believes, however, that "openly uncooperative and hostile behavior becomes a serious concern when it is so frequent and consistent that it stands out when compared with other children of the same age and developmental level," and when it seriously impairs a child's functioning (American Academy of Child & Adolescent Psychiatry, 2011b). Children diagnosed with ODD have frequent temper tantrums, are touchy, are easily annoyed by others, show a lot of resentment or anger, and argue frequently with adults. AACAP advises that a child labeled as ODD also receive a thorough evaluation to screen for other disorders coexisting with ODD; these other disorders must also be treated.

It is quite possible that some children diagnosed with ODD are also under a great deal of stress. The AACAP even notes that symptoms of ODD tend to increase when a child is "under stress." One of the treatment methods for ODD is training parents. It is possible that parents of some children with ODD have had a major impact on their child's problem with inept or harsh parenting. Inept or harsh parenting is a major psychological stressor for children. Irresponsible parenting is also frequently a physical stressor for children if the parenting includes physical, including sadistically physical, punishment.

The thorough evaluation recommended by the AACAP should not be just an evaluation of the child. It might be more proper and accurate to diagnose a family system as having a problem when a child is given the label *ODD*. We might need a new label for the family system problem. The child would then not be the identified patient; instead, the family system would be the patient.

## :: STAGES IN RESPONDING TO STRESS

A child goes through a series of stages in responding to an event that he does not understand and cannot control. Each of the three stages—alarm, appraisal, and searching for a coping strategy—places different demands on a child's body.

## Alarm

In the **alarm** stage of stress, a child stops what he is doing and orients toward or focuses on the potentially stressful event. A child is aware of the potentially stressful event for the first time. He might become aware of danger in this new situation or remember danger from similar situations in the past. He will be alarmed.

> **EXAMPLE**    Ben, 7 years old, heard his mother's words and closed his eyes (stage of alarm): "We're moving. You have to help me pack your toys and books tomorrow." He and his mother and brother were moving yet again, putting Ben in another new school, his third in 2 years.

> **EXAMPLE**    David, 6 years old, looked up from his game, startled (stage of alarm), when his mom said, "Your father will be here to pick you up soon." David's parents have joint custody of him after their divorce, and David had come to dread visits with his dad, who had married a woman with an 8-year-old child. This older boy bullies David. David's father knows about it but has not done anything to protect David.

**Alarm**
First stage in responding to stress in which a child is first aware of a potential stressor

## Appraisal

The **appraisal** stage is complex and involves reviewing what this event meant in the past. Ben, for example, thought, "I was scared when I went to the last new school, but the teacher helped me find things." Children also try to figure out how to cope as Ben did: "Maybe the new teacher will help me find things." Several things affect a child's appraisal of a potentially stressful event:

**Appraisal**
Second stage in responding to stress; child assesses what such an event meant in the past

- **Developmental level in terms of memory and perception.** Infants and very young children obviously will not be able to perceive and remember or evaluate a stress-inducing event the way that a much older child or an adult would.
- **Child's experience with adults who have modeled how to look at and evaluate events.** A child whose parents model poor anger management skills, for example, will probably appraise an anger-arousing event differently from a child whose parents show responsible anger management.
- **Self-esteem.** Older children with positive self-esteem have a much more positive view of stress-inducing events and their ability to cope with the stressor. Feeling competent is one of the building blocks of positive self-esteem. Children often express competence with statements such as "I can do it."

  > **EXAMPLE**    Ben is a resilient child who has a positive and realistic view of himself. He appraised the situation and said to himself, "The teacher in my last school told me that I know how to make friends and that other children like me."

# Searching for a Coping Strategy

The third stage in responding to stress involves **searching for a coping strategy**. Children, like all of us, do not always cope effectively with stress-inducing events. We know from some older research as well as from current work that children have a better chance of coping successfully when they believe they can control or master an event (American Academy of Child & Adolescent Psychiatry, 2013; Levine, Weinberg, & Ursin, 1978). Controlling or mastering an event depends, first, on whether the child is familiar with and understands an event, and second, on whether he can generate successful coping strategies. Consider the following possibilities.

**First Possibility: A Child Is Familiar with an Event, Has Actively Dealt with It in the Past, and Used a Good Coping Strategy**    This is the best-case scenario because the child has already successfully dealt with a similar stress-inducing event. This enables him to think that he can master the current event.

>    **EXAMPLE**    Tyrell was to get his first barbershop haircut. He had been to the shop on several occasions whenever Dad got haircuts, and Tyrell occasionally sat in the big chair on his own. The barber had demonstrated his haircutting tools, such as a comb, scissors, and towel. Tyrell was thoroughly familiar with the barbershop and, from Dad's observations, seemed not to fear it at all.

**Second Possibility: A Child Is Familiar with an Event, Has Actively Dealt with It in the Past, But Used an Ineffective Coping Strategy**    In this case, the strategy did not work because it was applied incorrectly or was not a good strategy in the first place. This would make a child somewhat wary, or even downright frightened, of the same or a similar stressful event in the future because he has not figured out how to cope.

>    **EXAMPLE**    Luke, 7 years old, had been to the emergency room previously when he put his hand through a garage window. The hospital personnel were not mean to him, but they were efficient; their main goal was to stop the profuse bleeding from his hand and arm. They failed to explain procedures and Luke reacted, understandably, with great fear and upset. Now he was going to the emergency room again, but this time for a skin rash that erupted on a Saturday night. Luke's father also remembered the previous visit to the hospital and tried to reassure his son about the current visit. Despite his dad's calm explanation and reassurances, Luke still viewed the hospital as a frightening place because of his first experience there.

**Third Possibility: A Child Is Familiar with a Stressor But Has Not Dealt with It Firsthand**    The child has only passively dealt with the stressor through secondhand experience; the secondhand source of information made an impact on his level of emotional or physiological arousal.

>    **EXAMPLE**    Jake was Ben's friend in Ben's former neighborhood. Jake's family had never moved, but Jake observed Ben's reactions to having to move to another new school. Jake is somewhat familiar with what happens when somebody moves because his teacher read a story about moving before Ben left. In spite of this, Jake has an incomplete understanding of the process.

**Fourth Possibility: A Child Is Totally Unfamiliar with a Stressor**    In this case, a child who has never dealt with such an event is now thinking about it for the first time and does not yet have a coping strategy. Her degree of anxiety or confusion depends largely on whether adults help her understand the event and whether they help her cope effectively with the stressor.

You can be most helpful to a child who is dealing with a stressful event for the first time in a couple of ways:

- **Change the situation.** You can eliminate the stressful event altogether, as Diana's mother did by taking the new dog from next door back to his own yard after he ambled into Diana's yard.
- **Clarify what the event means.** When the stressor is inevitable and cannot be eliminated, assist a child in comprehending the meaning of an unfamiliar event. Help a child understand as much as he is capable of understanding. If you use this strategy, you will be acting as a buffer to a stressful event. Think of this as *demystifying*, or removing the mystery from, the stressful event for the child.

> **EXAMPLE**  When Tony's family moved (something they had never done before), they did not know anyone in their new neighborhood. Dad took Tony for a get-acquainted walk to meet the new neighbors.

> **EXAMPLE**  Alden's (from the chapter-opening vignette) first trip to the emergency room had all the earmarks of a stressful event when his parents ran to the car with him seconds after he fell off the swing and broke his arm. In the car, Mom kept her composure so that she could help Alden because she realized how frightened he was. "We are going to the hospital, to a special room called the emergency room. A doctor is waiting for you and she will take a special picture so she can see your arm bone. Then she'll fix the bone. Mom and Daddy will stay with you. Then we'll all come home."

## :: COPING EFFECTIVELY WITH STRESS

Suppose that you are working at your computer and your computer freezes; you cannot move the cursor and you cannot type. This has never happened to you before. You sit back and say, "Okay, I have a couple of options. I can get out the manual and try to find out what has happened. I can just turn off the computer and try to reboot it." What you would have done in the process of thinking through your predicament is to have coped. You looked inside yourself and found the knowledge that you needed to get the computer going again and to keep yourself calm.

## What Is Coping?

Coping refers to looking for something inside or outside oneself to come to terms with stressors (Canadian Mental Health Association, 2012). In the computer example, you coped by searching within yourself for the resources (knowledge) that enabled you to deal with the crisis. At other times, a person looks for something outside herself to deal with a stressor.

> **EXAMPLE**  Another person has the same problem with her computer but calls an 800 number for help. She has coped by looking outside herself for the resources (the 800 number) that she needed.

**Coping**
Searching for internal or external resources to contend with stressors

Our goal in working with children is to help them cope as effectively as possible with the stressors that they face. Remember that coping does not necessarily mean a child will have a happy or successful outcome. Some situations, such as child abuse, make it very difficult for a person to achieve a successful solution.

## Different Ways of Coping with Stress

There are many ways of coping with potentially stressful events. There is no one-size-fits-all coping strategy. You will quickly learn to recognize different patterns in different children and in other adults. No single coping method is best for every person, and it is probably wise not to force any specific method on anyone.

**Some People Cope by Getting Information about the Stressor**   Somebody who copes with stress in this way searches his memory for information about how he has dealt with a similar stressor. A person might also look for information outside himself—from other people, self-help groups, a therapist, formal classes, books, pamphlets, movies, television, magazine articles, videos, or the Internet. Bookstores usually stock self-help books that people read for information on almost any stress-inducing event. Early childhood teachers give information on different stressors when they read well-written books to children about specific stressors such as death or moving.

**Others Cope by Taking Direct Action**   Some people take direct action by leaving the scene. Withdrawal can be a healthy way to take direct action and to cope. The withdrawal can be temporary, as when a parent leaves a room to cool off rather than yell at or hurt a crying baby. Such a person chooses either to return to deal with the stressor or to cope by permanently withdrawing. A person who withdraws as a way to cope might either announce his plan to leave or might just leave without notice.

> **EXAMPLE**   Rachel, 5 years old and in Mr. Santini's kindergarten class, was tired of hearing Louie tell her and the other girls that they didn't know how to do certain things because they were girls and that they could not play with certain toys. She dealt with the stress by announcing, "You can just play by yourself, Louie. I'm not going to play with you anymore!" She then left the science table.

Others take direct action by asserting their rights. This implies that the person sees an injustice, which is causing him some stress. For example, asserting one's rights by using words to express the emotion is a good way to deal with the stress of anger.

> **EXAMPLE**   Rachel was clearly upset when Louie sat at her place for lunch. She took direct action this time by asserting her rights and using words, as Mr. Santini had suggested: "Hey, Louie. That's my chair! Your chair is over here."

**Some People Cope by Restraining Movements or Actions**   A person might control her actions because she understands that it would be the most sensible way to deal with a stressor. For example, a teacher instructed a child who did not have friends in class on how to make friends and taught her how to join a group. Specifically, the teacher showed the child how to control her movements and control her tendency to push her way into the group. The next day she practiced and controlled her actions by waiting and observing what the other children were doing before joining them.

It is also possible for children to control their actions out of fear or anxiety. Children who are abused often try to be as quiet as possible around the abuser. They hope that the abuser will not notice them.

**Still Others Cope with Stress by Denying or Avoiding the Problem**  As you remember from your study of psychology, denial is a basic defense mechanism that protects people by allowing them not to face certain situations or to remember unpleasant events.

> **EXAMPLE**  Elena, 8 years old, is the fourth child in a family of seven children, and her parents are seasonal farm workers. Elena's parents love their children; nevertheless, they have to move frequently. All of the school-age children in Elena's family change schools frequently as the family moves from one farm to another. Elena, clearly upset by the turmoil of constant moving, has begun to deny that the family is about to move again as a way of coping with the stress.

Denial is evident in abusive families, with abused children often denying that abuse is even occurring. Denial, in fact, is one of the hallmarks of an abusive family system. Denial does not solve problems, however, and people who are in denial often cope with their problem by engaging in some unhealthy or dangerous activity, such as excessive eating, drinking alcohol, taking illegal drugs, or gambling.

# Can Young Children Cope Effectively with Stressors?

Children's cognitive, physical, social, and emotional development affects whether they can cope with stressors on their own or whether they need adult guidance in order to cope. This section of the chapter focuses first on the requirements for coping successfully. Then the focus shifts to explaining why young children cannot cope effectively with stressors on their own.

**To Cope Well You Have to Be Able to Think about More Than One Thing at a Time**  A person who can sift through several options or solutions has one of the abilities that it takes to cope with stressors. Looking at option A as well as option B requires that the person have the basic cognitive ability to consider at least two things at a time. Essentially, the person must be able to look at a problem from different angles. She might have to take a perspective different from her own.

Can young children think about more than one thing at a time? Usually, they cannot. Young children are not as capable as older people of taking different perspectives (see Chapter 2 for a discussion of perspective taking). They tend to focus on only one thing at a time and cannot seem to pay attention to all helpful and relevant facts. A 4-year-old child who gets upset when he slips away from dad at the grocery store and then cannot find his way back would most likely focus on only one thing—that he is lost.

**To Cope Well You Must Be Able to Invent Alternative Ways of Solving a Problem**  First, a person must believe in the concept that "I can move from this problem to a solution to this problem." Second, he must be able to generate creative solutions for the problem, for example, "I'm locked out of my car. How can I solve this problem?" The person must also be able to look at an array of solutions and categorize or classify groups of options.

Can young children invent different ways to solve problems? Usually, they cannot do this on their own. When children are upset, their emotions often overshadow their ability to solve problems. The preschool child lost in the grocery store would not be likely to think about different ways to handle his problem. He would *not* say, "I can go to the manager and ask her to call my dad on the speaker; I can search each aisle; or I can call out to my dad." He would likely focus primarily on the fact that he is lost.

Young children have difficulty seeing how things can change because they tend to focus on the before and then the after, but not on how they can get from before to after. Consequently, young children have difficulty creating solutions because of their inability to deal with the process of change. Young children also have limited classification skills. They are not able to look at a number of solutions and then classify them into logical groups. For example, they would not say, "I can wait here," or "I can search for dad," or "I can find somebody to help me" (three different groups of things to do).

**To Cope Well You Must Be Able to Manage Unpleasant Emotions**    This implies that a person can pay attention to and that she understands emotions such as anxiety, fear, or anger—emotions often associated with stress. She can evaluate what those emotions mean for her: "I'm anxious about giving this speech because the sale depends on how well I present my ideas today." A person who can manage emotions effectively and appropriately has learned good strategies for managing emotions: "I am well prepared for the speech and I know how to do deep breathing prior to beginning to speak."

Can young children manage unpleasant emotions? Young children, even babies, *have* emotions and they certainly *express* them. However, young children tend not to

**Young children do not understand their feelings and have difficulty regulating how they express emotions.**

understand their emotions or be able to deal with them. Children learn to under-stand or deal with anger when their development allows them to, and then only if they have good models and instruction in managing anger.

**To Cope Well You Must Understand the Effect of Your Reactions**  Again, this implies that an individual can think about at least two things at the same time—his reaction and the stressful event. He could also think about the impact of his actions as well as how another person might feel about them. This requires good perspective taking. It also implies that the person has a broad enough knowledge base and enough life experiences from which to draw the understanding.

Can young children understand how their reactions affect situations? A young child usually is not able to understand how his reactions to a stressor will affect the situation. The child lost in the grocery store does not understand, for example, that his frantic crying (his reaction to stress) affects his ability to listen to or answer questions from the manager.

Young children in general have a limited knowledge base, and some of the children that we teach have an even more restricted knowledge base than do others their age. Young children have less knowledge and experience from which to draw when they face a stressor such as getting lost.

**To Cope Well You Must Be Able to Think Purposefully**  Such a person would be able to think about the obvious in a stressful event but also be able to acknowledge and think about less obvious or hidden factors. Thinking purposefully brings together a person's conscious and preconscious thoughts. Thinking purpose-fully demonstrates that you know that you have thoughts. You also show that you can think about those thoughts—you can "think about thinking."

> **EXAMPLE**  Starting college for the first time is perceived as stressful by many students. The ability to think about this stressor purposefully, however, enables an older person to cope successfully. She would be able to think about the obvious, such as where everything is and how to register for courses. She would also be able to think about what is less obvious, such as her anxiety about meeting new people and making friends, because she understands the concept of anxiety and can think about it.

Can young children think purposefully? Young children are not able to con-sciously reflect—think about thinking—on matters such as how they feel, why oth-ers act as they do, or how others feel. Young children tend to focus on the obvious—their own agitation—and cannot reflect on the less obvious psychological aspects of stressful situations.

## :: GENERAL GUIDELINES FOR HELPING CHILDREN COPE WITH STRESS

Children gradually learn how to manage stress, but only if we actively teach and encour-age them to practice stress management. Many young children live in families that model, teach, and reward poor coping skills. The parents themselves in these families often do not know how to manage stress, so it is nearly impossible for them to teach helpful strategies to their children. These children will come to your classroom having already learned poor coping skills. Other children, fortunately, learn better coping skills.

What follows are general guidelines for encouraging young children to develop good coping skills. After studying the general guidelines, you will have an opportunity to read about a specific experience that is very likely to cause great stress for young children.

## Model Good Stress Management

Modeling is a powerful teaching tool. Children observe many models of stress management—parents; teachers; other adults; and people in videos, movies, videogames, and cartoons. These models influence a child's style of stress management. Children need teachers to model calm, thoughtful approaches to dealing with daily hassles. This is particularly important for children who observe a frenzied, inappropriate approach to stress management in their families or on television.

## Manage Your Classroom to Be a Low-Stress Environment

It is impossible to create a classroom or any other environment that is completely free from stress. However, taking the time and effort to create a developmentally appropriate physical environment will result in a low-stress (not stress-free) classroom. Develop suitable activities and make sure all materials are appropriate. Use positive guidance strategies when dealing with discipline encounters.

# :: FOCUS ON PRACTICE

This **Focus on Practice** activity is entitled *Teachers Can Use Observation to Reflect on Their Practices*. Observation is a very useful strategy in general in early childhood education. Teachers use observation to learn about children but, as you complete this activity, you will see that teachers can also observe themselves and reflect on their teaching practices.

## Acknowledge and Learn about the Variety of Stressors in Children's Lives

This chapter lists several of these stressors and then describes one of them in detail. You will learn the general principles in dealing with stressors, study one or two specific stressors, and then make a commitment to continuing education in this area.

## Act as a Barrier between a Child and a Stressor

You can be helpful to children facing a stressor by acting as a barrier, a buffer, if you stand between them and the stressor as you help them. You will shield them even as you teach them. You cannot always make the stressor disappear, nor would you always want to do so. You can soften (buffer) the effect of the stressor by supporting the child in any of several ways as he deals with the stressor.

> **EXAMPLE**    The manager of the grocery store acted as a buffer between the 4-year-old and the stressor of getting lost. She squatted down so that she was at the child's level, used a calm and even tone, and assured him that they would find his dad. She did not order him to stop crying, but instead continued her soothing talk. He eventually gulped, stopped crying, and stared at her. "I know you're a little scared," she said. "I'll bet that you can tell me your name. Then I can talk on our microphone and tell your dad where we are."

## Teach Children How to Relax and to Calm Themselves

Calming oneself and relaxing are essential skills in managing stress. All children must learn these skills, so it is age appropriate to teach them. Children who live in indifferent, chaotic, abusive, or neglectful families need the lessons even more, making it individually appropriate for an adult to teach them.

Calming down or relaxing helps people get the autonomic nervous system under control. The autonomic nervous system is that part of the nervous system that operates automatically, without our control. The sympathetic nervous system is a part of the autonomic nervous system and puts us in the high-alert stage of alarm when we face a stressor. Learning how to interrupt the action of the sympathetic nervous system is useful in managing stress. You can learn such techniques and you can teach them to children.

Without understanding the biology of the stress response, older preschool, kindergarten, and primary grade children can learn to control how their bodies react under stress by learning how to relax. Children who can actively control their bodies, by deliberately relaxing one or more body parts or by breathing slowly, have strategies that they can use when they are under stress. Adults will undoubtedly have to remind them to use the relaxation strategies because children tend to focus on one thing—their problem—and might well forget about relaxing when they face a stressor. Figure 9.2 gives a few practical suggestions on teaching children how to calm themselves and how to relax.

## Learn and Teach Good Coping Skills

This often involves direct instruction, and specific strategies depend on the particular stressor that a child faces. For example, if a child does not have friends, you might consider teaching him how to approach other children. If a child were under stress because of a lot of anger, you can teach him how to deal with anger and how to do deep breathing. Use books to teach about coping with stress (Thompson, 2009).

## Work with Families

We are much more effective helping children deal with stress when we also work with their families. Family systems theory is a helpful reminder of just how important the

| FIGURE 9.2 | Teach children to stay calm and to relax |
|---|---|

Use these ideas to teach older early childhood children to soothe themselves, to calm down, and to relax. Write lesson plans for teaching these relaxation strategies and teach only one at a time. Consider using one of the calming, relaxing techniques that the whole group can do together at open group times. Encourage children to choose the group-time opening relaxation technique. Make sure that you carefully observe your children and know whether they can perform the physical movements in any of the activities. Plan adaptations for children as necessary.

✓ **Rubber band.** Use a real rubber band to demonstrate stretching it s-l-o-w-l-y. Children then stretch one arm up or to the side just as slowly. Hold the stretch and return slowly to the starting point. Try stretching shoulders down slowly and returning to the starting point.

✓ **Gentle waves.** Create gentle waves in the water table or a sealed jar of water as the children watch. Then listen to the recorded sound of gentle waves. Children move their arms in a slow, wavelike way.

✓ **Swim, fish. Swim!** Children quickly learn that watching the fish swimming in the aquarium is relaxing. Give them permission to pull up a chair and watch. Older children might even enjoy sketching the fish.

✓ **Melting ice cube.** Prepare for this by placing an ice cube in a dish on the science table. Children observe that it melts. At group time, the children become ice cubes, all hard and cold. Then they begin to melt (relax) slowly.

✓ **Yoga stretches.** Teach three or four simple yoga stretches. Place pictures of the poses in the room so children can do the poses whenever they feel the need to relax.

✓ **Paint, sand, and other sensory items.** Remember the power of finger painting (even for primary children) to calm and soothe. The same thing is true for sensory materials such as clean sand, water in a tub, or a sensory table.

✓ **Let's read!** Reading is a powerful way to deal with stress. We can give good information to children by choosing books that help them deal with stress. An example is *A Boy and a Bear:* the children's relaxation book written by Lori Lite and illustrated by M. Hartigan (go to http://www.litebooks.net).

school–family partnership is for children's healthy development and learning. One of the characteristics of a family system that can help you and a family work together to help children deal with stress is equilibrium (Christian, 2006). This refers to a family's sense of balance. Stress is much like a strong wind at times and can throw a family's sense of balance into turmoil. Many military families, for example, have recently been affected by a parent's deployment to a war zone, making it difficult to maintain a sense of balance within the family (U.S. Department of Veteran's Affairs, 2013).

Teachers and schools can work with families to understand how important it is for children to have consistency when stressors appear, including any of the stressors listed earlier in this chapter. They need to know about the concept of stress. Then they need to learn about how stress affects children. Most of all, they need to gain the knowledge and skills for dealing with current stressors that they and their children face. They might also need to learn that children find things such as overscheduling of activities and not getting enough exercise or sleep to be extremely stressful.

Here are three excellent suggestions from Linda Christian (2006) for helping families maintain equilibrium—balance—in the face of potential stressors:

- Invite an expert to talk with parents about important issues that they face. For example, if there is a major flu outbreak, then parents will find good, timely, and accurate information very helpful. They will have concerns, in this case, about whether the school should remain open and, if it does, about the precautions that the school will take to protect their child's health.
- Provide as much consistency as possible in school. This is important all the time but especially so when a family faces stressful events and the off-balance feeling

| FIGURE 9.3 | Schools can help military families during deployment | |
|---|---|---|
| **Phase of Deployment** | **Teacher's Role** | **Why This Is Appropriate** |
| Predeployment | Communicate:<br>• Let parents know that they are welcome to share information about deployment with the school<br>• Figure out good ways for deployed parents to communicate with teachers, such as email, text messages, or Twitter | • Conveys your willingness to listen<br>• Creates a partnership with parents<br>• Fosters continuity in their child's education |
| Deployment | • Observe the child, noting any changes in behavior<br>• Create a section on the school website for military parents who are deployed | • Teachers are with children many hours; can support parents by noticing changes and discussing them with the parent<br>• Deployed parent would have access to information about school |
| Reunion | • Be aware of the date of the reunion<br>• Listen actively to children's questions and concerns<br>• Help children make a welcome-home card or banner<br>• Consult the school psychologist or guidance counselor if a child seems quite anxious; the psychologist can plan special session dealing with reunions | • Listening without judgment encourages children to express feelings without fear<br>• A concrete and gentle thing to do<br>• Gives information to children and helps them to deal with the stress |

*Source:* Based on Military Child Education Coalition (2003). *How to prepare our children and stay involved in their education during deployment.* Harker Heights, Texas: Author.

that goes along with hassles and even trauma. Make your classroom a haven of consistency, where parents and children will be secure in a reliable schedule and with a teacher who is also dependable and trustworthy. Mr. Bensen did this is in the chapter-opening infant–toddler vignette.

■ Help families figure out how to maintain stability and security. For example, help families deal with military deployment of a parent through each of the phases of deployment, as shown in Figure 9.3.

## :: FOCUS ON PRACTICE

This **Focus on Practice** activity is entitled *Key Elements of a Developmentally Appropriate Schedule.* This section has emphasized providing as much consistency as possible in school for young children and their families, and Christian (2006) recommends this as a way to help families maintain balance in the face of stressful events. As you complete this activity, you will see that teachers can support families by explaining how important a consistent and appropriate daily schedule is to children's development and learning.

## ∷ SUGGESTIONS FOR HELPING CHILDREN WHO FACE THE STRESS OF MOVING

There are so many potentially stressful situations faced by families—such as divorce, effects of a recession, job loss, military deployment, death. Recently, foreclosures on mortgages have overwhelmed many families and their ability to cope (ElBoghdady, 2010). Many of these conditions go hand-in-hand with a family's relocation, which is moving the family from one place to another. Moving is indeed stressful for every member of a family, and when it is combined with a divorce, mortgage foreclosure, or job loss, for instance, it is very often even more stressful. In this section, we will focus on the stress of moving on children and families. The reasons for moving are many and varied, but the stress of moving on children in our classrooms is our main concern.

Approximately 1 in 5 children in elementary school change schools every year. Some groups, such as the homeless or migrant, urban, low-income, or abused children move even more frequently than others (Branz-Spall, Rosenthal, & Wright, 2003; Xu, Hannaway, & D'Souza, 2009). In Chicago, in a 3-year period, only about 50% of the children remained in the same school (Kerbow, Azcoitia, & Buell, 2003). The problem of frequent moving also exists in rural areas and contributes to academic achievement gaps (Paik & Phillips, 2002).

Teachers today experience frequently and firsthand the effects of a mobile society, just as they have for the last several decades. Teachers start the school year knowing that some of the children will move to a new school and that they are likely to get new students any time during a year. Teachers witness the stress that moving often produces in children, families, and schools.

## Why Moving Is Stressful for Many Young Children

Moving to a new area is among the most stress-inducing experiences a family faces. Moves are especially difficult for preschool and primary grade children (American Academy of Child & Adolescent Psychiatry, 2011a). For children, moving is a type of loss just as is death or a parent's divorce. A child loses friends, a home, and a school; the losses often result in feelings of sadness and anxiety or even anger. Moving is stressful for many young children for the following reasons (American Academy of Child & Adolescent Psychiatry, 2011a; Steele & Sheppard, 2003).

**Moving Interrupts Friendships and Children Lose Social Support** Children who move to a new area or a new school often think that everybody at school or in the new neighborhood is in a group or has a best friend. Children who lose friendships are likely to go through a mourning process for those friendships. Having somebody dismiss or laugh at the loss intensifies the sadness over the loss. If a child is shy or aggressive or has poor social skills, the move and the need to make friends will be even more difficult and stressful. Many children lose the support of older people, too. Moving away from trusted teachers, a Scout leader, religion teacher, relatives, and neighbors means that a child will not have these adults to turn to for support (Pettit, 2000).

**Moving Elicits Unpleasant Emotions**   Children tend to feel anxious and sad when they move. Young children, however, do not understand their emotions and do not know how to manage them on their own. So added to the already stressful situation of moving is the stress that goes along with emotions that the child cannot manage (American Academy of Child & Adolescent Psychiatry, 2011a).

**Moving Interrupts the Separation Process**   Moving is especially troublesome for children during early childhood because they are in the process of separating from parents and adjusting to adults other than their parents in centers and schools, as well as adjusting to peers. Relocating often pushes young children to return to a more dependent relationship with parents than they might want, thereby interrupting the normal separation process (American Academy of Child & Adolescent Psychiatry, 2011a).

**Moving Requires Children to Adjust to a New Curriculum in School and Different Teacher Expectations**   Children often find that they are behind in some curriculum areas or ahead in others, resulting in boredom or anxiety. Children can withstand the stress if their parents and teachers give them the support that they need (American Academy of Child and Adolescent Psychiatry, 2011a). However, the children who move most frequently are the least likely to get the help that they need for managing the stress of curriculum changes. Their families and schools are often not prepared to give them the support they require.

**Moving Interrupts School and Social Services**   Kerbow (1996) reported that some public school systems, such as those in Chicago, went through reforms centering on promoting greater local school autonomy. Greater local autonomy is based on the assumption that children will attend one specific school consistently enough so that the school can make a difference in the child's achievement. Urban low-income children who frequently change schools lose the benefit of any school or social services that go along with such school reform.

## Act as a Buffer between a Child and the Stress of Moving

Schools, teachers, and policy makers can buffer the stress of moving and changing schools for children. Moving and changing schools does not necessarily have to affect children adversely. With proper support, moving can be a positive experience for children (American Academy of Child & Adolescent Psychiatry, 2011a). Teachers, directors, principals, schools, and policy makers must take the first step and make a conscious effort to help children who are about to move away from or who have just transferred to their center or school.

**When a Child Moves *Away from* Your School or Classroom**   Consider doing some of the following to help a child deal with the stress of moving *away from* your classroom. Our goal is to acknowledge our regret at his leaving, but also to help this child find the strength from within to enable him to deal with his feelings and uncertainties about the move. Another goal is to work with parents so that they can also help their child cope with a move.

- Talk with the child about moving away and help him understand something about his new school. It would help greatly if you took the effort to find out where he is going, the name of his school, and his new teacher. Present this information in a positive way.
- Listen carefully and encourage the child to talk about his feelings about moving away. Avoid being intrusive, however, and do not force a child to talk about feelings.
- Help him say good-bye to his school in a low-key and positive way.
- Give the child a picture of the entire class with him included.
- Make sure that his records are current and accurate and that the records are transferred quickly to the new school.
- Follow your center or school's policy about contacting the new school so that you can give positive information to the new teacher about the child. The goal here is to help the new teacher make the child's transition as smooth as possible.
- Work with the child's parents. Answer their questions and give them information that will enable them to help their child make the move with as little stress as possible (see the Working with Parents feature).

### When a Child Moves *to* Your School or Classroom

Consider the following suggestions as you welcome a child who is moving *to* your classroom. Your goal is to draw your classroom circle to include this new child. Adding a new member to a family or a classroom involves adjusting the boundaries to include that person.

- Obtain the child's file and read it carefully. Follow your school's policy if you need to contact the previous teacher for clarification on any issues.
- Make a home visit if your school encourages teachers to do so. Home visits are a good way to get to know the child.
- Familiarize the child and family with the new school. Invite them to come to school for a tour so that the new school is not so new on the child's first day.
- Make sure that the child and her family know the schedule in your room. Give them a handout of your schedule and encourage parents to talk about their child's new schedule.
- Create a space for a new child by preparing a locker or cubby, cot for napping, and any other individualized areas or materials. Create her space before she arrives.
- Take a new group picture with the new child included. Do this on the first day that the new child enters your room.
- Walk through the routines in your classroom and your center or school (for example, bathroom, snack, or lunch; getting on the bus; waiting for parents). Take your class through the fire safety drill so that everyone, including the new

WORKING
*with*
FAMILIES
## IS YOUR FAMILY MOVING? TIPS FOR HELPING YOUR CHILD COPE WITH THE MOVE

- **Explain and listen.** Explain clearly to your child why the move is necessary. Are you being transferred? Are you starting school in another section of the state? Is the home you've been building finally finished? Is your child's school closing? Your child will understand the reason for the move if you state it simply and clearly. Get comments from your child about what you've explained. Listen closely, clarify anything that your child did not seem to understand, and listen for feelings such as fear or anxiety.
- **Read.** Read a book about moving with your child. This will help children understand the process of moving and deal with some of their feelings.
- **Familiarize and describe.** Acquaint your child with the new area as much as possible. Visit the new area and take your child on a tour of the new house and neighborhood. Consider visiting the public library or parks. Familiarize children with their new

home by using maps (for older children) of the area or photos of a new house or apartment building. Consider obtaining a copy of the local newspaper early to acquaint your child with the comic section if he has a favorite cartoon. Describe something about the new area that your child might like, such as a pool, a pond with ducks, or an amusement park. Give the information in a positive way but do not force your child to be enthusiastic.
- **Get involved.** After the move, get involved with your children in activities in the new community such as synagogue or church, parent's group at school, YMCA, a family education and support program, and volunteer groups such as the humane society.

*Sources:* Based on the American Academy of Child and Adolescent Psychiatry. (2011a). Children and family moves. *AACAP facts for families*, No. 14. Retrieved on May 21, 2013, from http://www.aacap.org/AACAP/Families_and_Youth/Facts_for_Families/Facts_for_Families_Pages/Children_And_Family_Moves_14.aspx

child, knows the procedure. Get the child to tell you about how the new routines are different from or similar to those in her old school.

- Talk with the child and find out what she likes to do in school.
- Include the child in the activities of her new room at her pace.
- Request that other children in the class act as guides for the new class member. Be specific in your requests: "Joe, please walk with Robert to the lunchroom. He will be sitting next to you and I thought that you could show him how lunch is served in our school," or "It's time to put the carpet squares down for group time, Cindy. Please help Jean choose her carpet square and then sit next to her during her first group time with us."
- Be sure that every child wears a name tag so that a new class member can get to know names.
- Read a book about moving with the child or with the class.
- Listen carefully for the feelings that the new class member has about moving. Acknowledge them and avoid commanding her to feel differently.
- Work with parents. See the Working with Parents feature for information that will help parents buffer the effect of moving on their children. Your school might have a formal policy or program in place through which you can help children who are moving. Even if there is no formal program, you can do some things to help parents decrease the stress of moving on their children.

## ANALYZE A VIGNETTE

Refer to the chapter-opening vignettes and information from the chapter. Then answer the following questions.

1. Infant–toddler: Lela is 15 months old. Explain why her teacher's actions are appropriate for a child this age. How do you think that the teacher's actions will help Lela deal with the stress at home? How will the teacher's style help Lela's family maintain equilibrium?

2. Preschool: Explain how Mrs. Johnson has softened the effect of the fire alarm, the stressor, for the children.

3. Primary: Identify the appropriate strategies that Mr. Santini has used to help Alden in moving to a new school. Use information from the chapter as your guide.

## SUMMARY

A resilient child fares well in spite of stressful events. Protective factors such as caring relationships, high expectations, and chances to participate help children become resilient.

Some stressors are physical and damage a child's body. Other stressors are psychological and harm a child's sense of security. Still other stressors combine a physical and a psychological threat. Some stress is acute, which is an intense but brief stressor, while other stress is chronic or persistent and ongoing.

Children can experience stress from internal sources, such as hunger pains or emotions. Another source of stress is external to the child, such as joint custody. Children experience physical effects from some stress, and stress even has the potential to damage a child's brain.

Children go through three stages in responding to stress:

- Alarm
- Appraisal
- Searching for a coping strategy

Coping involves finding some way, with either outside or internal resources, to come to grips with the stress. There are different ways to cope, and young children need adult help in learning how to cope with stress.

## APPLY YOUR KNOWLEDGE

Get a start on developing expertise in one area that can cause stress for children. Do you want to know more about how death, divorce, hospitalization, child abuse, or neglect results in stress? Do you need to know more about how harsh parenting, not having friends, or loneliness causes stress for some children? Choose a specific stressor and then prepare yourself to help children deal effectively with it by completing the following application activities.

1. **Internet and other resources.** Use a search engine to find information on your chosen stressor. Visit or call the extension office in your county and ask the family or child life specialist for written information on your topic. Collect magazine articles about your stressor. Make copies of the information and organize it in a file for later use.

2. **Children's books.** Develop an annotated bibliography of children's books about the stressor you have chosen.

Find and read at least four children's books. Give a brief synopsis of each and then explain how you would use it to help children deal with that specific stressor.

3. **Your portfolio and interview.** Let others know that you have knowledge, skills, and materials for teaching children how to begin to cope with this specific stressor. Decide how to place information in your professional portfolio.

4. **Role-play.** Role-play being interviewed for a teaching position. The director or principal looks over your portfolio, pauses, and says, "I see that you've studied about how children deal with _____ (moving, death, divorce, etc.). How would you see yourself using this information if you're hired to teach in this school?" Be prepared to explain how you would use the material about a specific stress factor to help children and parents.

# WEBSITES

### Center for Effective Parenting
http://www.parenting-ed.org

The Center for Effective Parenting (CEP) is a joint effort of the Department of Pediatrics at the University of Arkansas for Medical Sciences (UAMS) and Arkansas Children's Hospital (ACH). This site has numerous links for parent education information. For information on stress, go to the "search site" box and type in *stress*.

### National Military Family Association
http://www.militaryfamily.org/

An organization "dedicated to serving the families and survivors of the seven uniformed services through education, information, and advocacy." Provides a wealth of information, fact sheets, and other materials about military families. Refer again to Figure 9.3 for information on helping children whose parent is deployed for military service. (Figure 9.3 is based on information from the National Military Family Association.)

# CHAPTER 10

# Aggression and Bullying in Young Children

# Learning Outcomes

- Define terms associated with aggression and bullying
- Explain the nature, different forms, and purposes of aggression, including bullying
- Explain the idea that bullying is aggression in action
- Discuss the process of learning to be aggressive, specifically how children acquire scripts that tell them how to be aggressive, including how to bully others
- Recall and describe strategies which teachers can use to prevent or minimize aggression, including bullying
- Defend the idea that bullying is a form of aggression
- Explain the different forms of bullying
- Summarize strategies children can use to deal with teasing and other face-to-face bullying

## VIGNETTES

### PRESCHOOL: MAYA MOVES IN

*Four-year-old Maya wanted to sit on the yellow carpet square at circle time. When she saw that Nadifa was already sitting on the yellow square, Maya sat down right next to Nadifa and started to nudge her. Nadifa shot a look of annoyance at Maya, who kept prodding Nadifa, finally pushing her off the yellow square.*

### KINDERGARTEN: JESS ATTACKS WITH WORDS

*Jess joined his friend Serena in the dress-up center, but she was finished playing and moved on, leaving Jess by himself. When they went out to the playground, Jess kept an eye out for Serena. When she approached the sandbox, Jess did a little singsong chant, "Serena wears glasses, stupid, stupid glasses! Serena wears glasses . . . ," over and over.*

### PRIMARY: BYSTANDERS CONFRONT THE BULLY

*Third-grader Patrick is a bully who calls himself "Number One," and terrorizes other children. Thomas, in the same grade, is his latest target. As usual, Patrick started with name calling but quickly escalated to physical attacks—tripping, shoving, and punching. At first, the other children, afraid of Patrick, stood by and watched, but today they did something very different. At recess, Thomas ran to retrieve the basketball as it rolled into a remote part of the yard. Patrick ran after Thomas calling out, "I'm coming for you, Science Nerd." Thomas was trapped but then saw the other basketball players coming toward him and heard one of the other boys yell at Patrick, "Leave him alone, Patrick!" Another boy chimed in, "Yeah, leave him alone."*

## :: INTRODUCTION

The chapter-opening vignettes all show some form of aggression. Maya's and Jess's are typical for early childhood, and Patrick's is an example of bullying. Why is it important to understand aggression and bullying? Children often do not feel safe either going to school or while they are at school. This unease or anxiety is often caused by peer abuse, with bullying the most common form (Hazeldon Foundation, 2013). Deadly violence, a complex issue, grows in part out of a progression of traumatizing events such as bullying, constant teasing, isolation, and rejection. Deadly school violence does have warning signs (Block, 2008). It is important to understand aggression and bullying because one of the pathways to violence starts in early childhood.

This chapter focuses on the twin topics of aggression and bullying. We will describe and explain different forms and purposes, or goals, of aggression. Then we will focus on bullying *as a type of aggression*. Third, you will study about the ways in which children gather information on how to be aggressive from different systems. Then you will learn several practical strategies for dealing effectively with bullying and other forms of aggression.

## :: AGGRESSION

**Aggression** is a problem-solving behavior that is learned early in life, is learned well, and is resistant to change. Aggression is any intentional behavior that injures or diminishes a person or animal in some way or damages or destroys property (Gerrig & Zimbardo, 2002).

**Aggression**

Any behavior that a person uses when he or she intends to hurt someone or to destroy or damage property

### Forms of Aggression

Aggression takes several forms, causing damage in many ways. It can cause physical, verbal, psychological, or emotional damage. The attack can be direct or indirect, impulsive or well planned.

> **EXAMPLE** Two adolescents shot and killed 14 classmates and 1 teacher in Columbine High School in Colorado in April 1999. Twenty children and six teachers and other staff members were murdered at Sandy Hook Elementary School in the village of Sandy Hook, in Newton, Connecticut, December 14, 2012 (premeditated, direct, physical aggression).

> **EXAMPLE** Patrick, from the chapter-opening vignette for the primary grades, squeezes another boy's arm as he takes the child's lunch money (intentional and both psychologically and physically harmful aggression).

> **EXAMPLE** Sean called his younger brother a "dummy" (verbal, psychologically harmful aggression). He ripped his brother's list of spelling words to shreds (physical, direct aggression that damages property).

Teachers need a common definition of aggression so that they can recognize and then deal with the different forms of aggressive behavior consistently and effectively. The common thread that ties together all acts of aggression is that the behavior, whatever it looks like, *intentionally* injures a person or animal or damages or destroys property.

Aggression is not the same thing as anger. Anger is an emotion, a feeling. Aggression is a behavior. Angry children might behave aggressively, but not always, and children can be aggressive without being angry. John, for example, was very upset about not getting any chocolate milk but was not aggressive. Mary, on the other hand, pinched another kindergarten child, but was not angry with her. Mary was merely showing her power.

## Gender Differences in Aggression

There are clear differences in aggression between boys and girls, and these differences are evident during early childhood (Baillargeon et al., 2007). The findings tell us that:

- Boys display more aggression than girls do, both physically and verbally.
- Boys display more aggression after watching media violence.
- Older boys are more likely than older girls to counterattack when physically attacked.
- Pairs of boys have more aggressive interactions than a boy/girl or girl/girl dyad (pair).

Researchers document gender differences, but explaining the differences is another thing. One view is that gender differences might result from how we socialize boys and girls (Blakemore, Berenbaum, & Liben, 2009). Our culture has clearly defined attitudes about girls, boys, and aggression, and we can easily observe these attitudes by looking at differing child-rearing tactics used with boys and girls.

Aggression is related to many factors, such as a parent's style of child rearing (Yu, Shi, Huang, & Wang, 2006). Parents' belief systems also affect children's development (Francis & Chorpita, 2009). Some parents expect, permit, and then encourage aggression in boys. Parents tend to use more physical punishment with boys than with girls, and boys might adopt these aggressive methods in interaction with others (Block, 1978). Many parents also manage the environments of boys and girls differently. For example, they choose different toys for girls and boys, and toys often chosen for boys, such as guns or action figures, are aggressive cues, items that seem to elicit aggressive play.

## :: PURPOSES OF AGGRESSION

Aggression, as you see from the definition, is the method that some people use to solve problems. They use aggression for different purposes and it helps them meet different goals. Some people have the goal of hurting a person or animal with violent behavior, but others use aggression only as a means of getting something that they want.

## Instrumental Aggression

A child uses **instrumental aggression** when her goal is to obtain or get back some object, territory, or privilege (Rascle, Coulomb-Cabagno, & Delsarte, 2005). This type of aggression usually springs from simple goal blocking; a child who uses instrumental aggression is usually not even angry with the person blocking his goal.

**Instrumental aggression**
Goal-directed aggression; meant to get or retrieve an object or territory; not anger based

He simply wants to remove whatever is blocking his goal and tends to do something offensive to achieve his end. He uses aggression as an instrument, a tool. In the next example, Maya is not angry with the other child. She merely wants something that the other child is using.

> **EXAMPLE**   Four-year-old Maya whined as she watched Nadifa stirring the cake batter, "It's *my* turn." Then she seized the stirring spoon, setting off a wail of protest from Nadifa.

As we know from many decades of research, instrumental aggression is the most common form of aggression during early childhood. Research from the 1930s (Dawe, 1934), the 1970s (Hartup, 1974), and the 1990s (Fabes & Eisenberg, 1992) demonstrated that young children have most of their conflicts over space and resources, such as toys and other equipment, because they are much more egocentric than older children. There tends to be little hostility involved. They push their way into line, grab things from others, yell, "It's my turn!" and even bite. Children use instrumental aggression because they want something. At the same time, children cannot take another's perspective because of their egocentricity. Frustrated about not getting the desired object, a very young child uses aggression as a tool, a means to get what he wants.

**How to Deal with Instrumental Aggression**   Two of the best things that you can do to help young children who use instrumental aggression include the following, both of which focus on the teaching aspect of guidance:

- Do *not* ignore instrumental aggression. Ignoring it rewards a child for being aggressive. Make sure that a child does *not* get what she wants with aggression. Had the teacher allowed Maya to get her turn by swiping the spoon, she would have actually rewarded Maya's aggression.
- Help the child think of a better solution. Acknowledge her frustration and help her think about the situation. This is what she needs from the teacher now, not punishment. Our long-term goal in guidance is to help children build positive ideas about getting what they want.

> **EXAMPLE**   The teacher took the spoon from Maya, saying, "Maya, Nadifa was stirring. You can stir after she finishes. She has to stir 7 more times, so let's count while you wait."

Notice that the teacher did *not* allow Maya to get her way. Maya handed back the spoon. The teacher also focused on the central issue of fairness to others. "Nadifa was stirring," and suggested a solution that helped Maya deal with waiting: "Let's count as Nadifa stirs." This will teach Maya that she can do something at times like this to help herself wait.

**Hostile aggression**
Anger and revenge-based aggression; it is directed at a specific target

## Hostile Aggression

**Hostile aggression** often strikes an observer as nasty, distasteful, vengeful behavior; some forms of hostile aggression are tinged with evil. It is quite different from instrumental aggression.

**Hostile Aggression Is Anger-Based**   Hostile aggression is bound up with anger aimed directly at a person, animal, or even a country; it is anger-based aggression. The Boston Marathon bombing of 2013, the destruction of the World Trade Center in New York City on September 11, 2001; and the Columbine High School tragedy in 1999 are three of our nation's most glaring examples. Hostile aggression is violence clearly intended to hurt someone or to destroy something.

> **EXAMPLE**   Keith reached into the gerbil house and grabbed one of the gerbils, picking her up by the tail. He dangled her in midair until Mr. Santini intervened. At home, this child intimidates and bullies his dog, laughing as she cowers in fear.

Cruelty toward animals is not a joke; it is outrageous behavior and a warning sign of potential deadly violence. Adults must take it seriously because a young child will not outgrow such cruelty. It is not just a phase (American Academy of Child & Adolescent Psychiatry, 2011c). Ignoring such behavior is akin to participating in the cruel behavior. Ignoring a child's cruelty toward an animal is like giving permission for the behavior. Children who are cruel to animals need help, and teachers must have the courage to observe, document, and then report such behavior to protect the animal and to help the child.

**Perceived Threats to One's Ego Elicit Hostile Aggression**   A person who is angrily aggressive usually is on guard, has his "antennae up" for any behavior that he perceives as a threat to his ego or any sign that someone is showing him disrespect. He either disregards or is incapable of paying attention to relevant social cues, resulting in his belief that the other person has done something mean-spirited when the other person might well have had no such intention. Mistaken beliefs such as this are starting points for physically or psychologically hostile aggression.

> **EXAMPLE**   Patrick and Theng (pronounced "teng") worked on a science project together. Patrick's brothers have been calling him a "dummy," and so now Patrick is on guard at school. When Theng offered to help Patrick solve a problem with Patrick's part of the project, Patrick perceived the offer as a sign that Theng thought him incompetent (perceived threat to self-esteem). Patrick's face got red with embarrassment and anger, and he shouted at Theng, "I can do this, Theng! You think you're so smart," as he slammed his fist into Theng's work (hostile aggression).

**Hostile Aggression Shows Up in Older Children**   Piaget's theory (1970) sheds light on why hostile aggression tends to show up most often in older children, but not young children. A person has to be able to think about what somebody *intended* to do. She must be able to think, for example, that the other person meant to show disrespect. In the previous example, Patrick seemed to think that Theng intended to insult him. Children must be able to take the other person's perspective.

Preschool children, usually in the preoperational or second of Piaget's stages of cognitive development, are somewhat egocentric. They are not yet able to understand or take another person's perspective; this explains why their aggression is most often instrumental.

A very young child who cannot take another person's perspective will also not be able to understand what that other person intended to do. An older child, in a different Piagetian stage, becomes less egocentric and is better able to take another child's perspective. Understanding that other perspective also means that older children, such as Patrick, can begin to guess at another person's intentions.

### Some Older Children Make Mistakes When Interpreting Social Situations

Adlerian theory explains the mistakes that people make in evaluating social interactions (Adler Graduate School, 2012). Some older children have deficits in several aspects of social problem solving. For example, in spite of their greater cognitive ability to detect others' intentions, some older, aggressive children are inattentive to relevant social cues or signals. As a result, they frequently presume that another person had some sort of unfriendly plan in mind, even where no bad feeling was intended (Dodge & Frame, 1982). They repeatedly make mistakes about the intentions of other people, as did Patrick with Theng's friendly offer of help in collaborative learning, but it is a person's perception of reality that matters, even if the perception is a faulty one. Patrick acted on his opinion, faulty as it was, and he reacted with hostile aggression.

---

## ▪▪ *Question for Reflection*

---

## What about Accidental Aggression?

Accidental aggression is *un*intentional injury. All teachers observe a certain amount of this sort of unintended injury or damage. Whether unintentionally hurting others is really aggression is a good question. What does happen, though, is that someone accidentally hurts another person or animal or accidentally damages something.

**The Real Problem with Accidental Aggression**   The child who is accidentally hurt or whose work or possession is damaged often responds aggressively in turn. Recall that young children's development influences their behavior.

> **EXAMPLE**   It was crowded in the coatroom of Mr. Santini's classroom because he used it as a storage area. When Mitchell stowed his backpack and turned to leave, he crashed into Louie (accidental aggression). Louie reacted by pushing back at Mitchell (aggressive reaction to the *unintentional* injury).

Louie retaliated in a hurtful way. Like most young children, who are not able to see things from Mitchell's perspective, he is also not very good at dealing with more than one idea at a time. For example, Louie would likely *not* be able to think on his own about these three things: "It's crowded here. Mitchell is rushing around. He bumped into me by accident." He does not understand yet the difference between an accidental and an intentional act.

Mitchell also had a part in this interaction. He does not pay attention to what he is doing at times. He is somewhat impulsive. The crowded coatroom was perhaps just too much for him to handle.

### How to Respond to Accidental Aggression

- **Teacher's part.** We make guidance mistakes if we always zero in on the behavior first. Practice examining your role and the effect of the environment on behavior. Clearing up issues with how our classroom is set up often clears up accidental aggression.

  **EXAMPLE**  Mr. Santini realized that the cramped coatroom was part of the problem. After removing a table and several boxes, he noticed an immediate change in the children's behavior in this still small but now clutter-free space.

  He worked on one other thing with the children. The teacher and children discussed the issue of *crowding*, which Mr. Santini made into a new vocabulary word. He could simply have limited the number of children who went to the coatroom at any one time, but he decided that the children needed to learn to recognize crowding and to decide whether it was a good idea to enter the coatroom when it was crowded.

- **Children's part.** Avoid problems by teaching skills to children. Mr. Santini realized that the boys lacked some skills that he could easily teach. These skills include paying attention to what you are doing, self-talk to remind oneself to pay attention, practice counting the number of children already in a center and doing self-talk about what to do next, and acknowledge an accident and apologize. These easy steps are appropriate for older preschool, kindergarten, and first-grade children.

## :: BULLYING IS AGGRESSION IN ACTION

"**Bullying** is an aggressive behavior intended to cause harm or distress, occurs repeatedly over time, and occurs in a relationship in which there is an imbalance of power or strength" (American Psychological Association, 2013; emphasis added). Bullying is *not* trivial. It is *not* standard or normative behavior. Parents, teachers, administrators, and children are concerned about the intimidation, terrorizing, and harassment in bullying. Pediatricians are also alarmed about bullying because of all of the physical injuries they are treating that are directly related to bullying. Children's physicians also see the connection of bullying in childhood to violence in adolescence (Sege, Wright, & The Committee on Injury, Violence, and Poison Prevention, 2009). Srabstein (2010) notes survey results showing that 50% of children are bullied at some time during their school years, with 10% of children regularly bullied.

> **Bullying**
> A form of aggression; occurs in a relationship where the power or strength in one party is greater than the other; intention is to cause harm

We usually think of bullying taking place in parks, schools, camps—anywhere we find groups of children. Bullying also takes place in cyberspace, the place where electronic information exists, with middle school children and adolescents putting their tech savvy ways to work to bully others (Lenhart, 2009). Bullying occurs in families as well. In a new study, released ahead of publication, researchers found that siblings attack, threaten, and intimidate a brother or sister, and that this results in the victim's depression and anxiety. This study found that one-third of siblings reported being attacked, threatened, or intimidated and that it was bulling and not normal sibling bantering (Tucker, Finkelhor, Turner, & Shattuck, 2013).

Most information on bullying deals with older children, not those in early childhood. Young children are certainly capable of being aggressive, as this chapter explains, but it is usually a form of aggression not based on anger or hostility. Most young children engage in instrumental aggression and not hostile aggression because they are not able to take the perspective, to figure out what others are thinking or feeling or hoping, and are so focused on what *they, themselves* want. However, this text focuses on helping young children develop the self-knowledge, empathy for others, emotional and social competence, and social and friendship skills that will help them avoid becoming bullies.

## Forms of Bullying

Bullying is aggression and takes many forms—physical bullying, emotional or psychological bullying, verbal bullying, and cyberbullying.

**Physical bullying**
Bodily contact intended to cause harm

**Emotional or psychological bullying**
Aggressive behaviors that are not physical and are intended to cause distress

**Verbal bullying**
Using words to cause distress

- **Physical bullying** refers to any bodily contact intended to hurt another. Examples are pushing, hitting, pinching, and punching. Physical bullying can be mild, moderate, or severe; usually, the victim does nothing to provoke the bully. Whatever the level of the physical bullying, it is still bullying.
- **Emotional or psychological bullying** refers to some nonphysical aggressive behavior. Examples are refusing to let someone play, excluding a child from a work group, spreading rumors, telling other children not to play with them, telling secrets that hurt the person, and withholding information. For example, a work group in third grade might withhold information from one member of the group, leaving that child without the information needed to complete an assignment. Again, the victim usually does nothing to provoke the bully (Prevent Child Abuse Utah, n.d.).
- **Verbal bullying** refers to name calling, making threats, taunting, sarcasm, and teasing (insulting). Victims usually do nothing to bring about the bullying. Teasing, to focus on one form of verbal bullying, is unfortunately very common during childhood and can easily turn into bullying (Vessey, Carlson, Horowitz, & Duffy, 2008; Townsend-Butterworth, 2009). Teasing might seem like playful banter or joking to some people, but it can be aggression when the teaser *intends* to hurt another person. Therefore, teachers need to be acutely aware of this behavior and be willing to intervene and stop or prevent the negative effects of teasing.
- **Teasing** refers to verbal or nonverbal exchanges between children or between a child and an older person—this chapter focuses on child-to-child teasing. There are different views of these interactions. Teasers see their words or actions as funny, but the person or child who is teased most often feels annoyed or humiliated (Vessey, 2006).

It is critical that early childhood teachers understand the real impact of teasing on victims as well as how to help victims protect themselves. The long-term effects of teasing on preadolescent victims include emotional distress, depression, anxiety, and loneliness. Victims of teasing develop negative perceptions about themselves. They also develop negative beliefs about classmates who tease them. For victims, greater negative beliefs about teasers resulted in higher levels of aggression by victims. Teasing can

| FIGURE 10.1 | A Nerf ball and a question: Real help for victims of teasing |

Help victims of teasing develop real coping skills. Teach them effective techniques to use when teased. This will help them feel less helpless and that they can control their reactions—that teasers are not in control. Encourage bystanders to use these same techniques because teasers stop teasing when an onlooker steps in. Here are some suggestions:

- **Nerf Ball.** Teach the child to visualize taunts as a "Nerf ball" that bounces off her. Teach her to say, "Whoa! A Nerf ball! Bounced right off me!"

- **Agree with the Facts.** Agreeing with the fact is one of the most effective ways to stop a teaser in his tracks. A teaser who says, "Hey, Four-Eyes" to a child wearing glasses, hears this from the victim, "Yes, I wear glasses." To the taunt, "You're so short," the victim replies, "You are correct, I am short." This is a disarming strategy. It literally takes away the teaser's ammunition.

- **Ask a Question.** Teaching that one simple word "So?" will also stop the teaser. It conveys indifference and takes the wind out of a teaser's sails.

- **Self-Talk.** Teach children to value their own opinion when the teaser fires away. Give permission to disregard the teaser's opinion. For example, "John is teasing again; I can handle it," or "I like my curly hair; John's opinion stinks."

- **Reframing.** Teach victims to take charge, avoid anger and frustration, and turn the situation around. For example, reframe the taunt, "Hey, freckles. Do those spots peel off?" The victim says, "You like to make observations" or "That's a great put-down." This type of response typically confuses the teaser, who has to then stop and think. It works because the teaser gets no anger, no frustration, no anxiety from the victim—a far different response than she anticipates.

*Source:* Freedman, (2002) and Poussaint (1997).

escalate into harassment and bullying, with violent outcomes well documented in the past several years in American schools (Troop-Gordon & Ladd, 2005). Figure 10.1 gives suggestions for helping victims of teasing.

- **Cyberbullying** refers to bullying with text messaging, tweeting, email messaging, blogs, chat rooms, and any other electronic venue. All bullying is disgraceful, but cyberbullying's speed and scope is alarming. The Olweus Bullying Prevention Program (Hazeldon Foundation, 2013) sees cyberbullying as extraordinarily harmful because it is *anonymous* in many cases, thus making it impossible to avoid the bully as can be done at times in face-to-face bullying. Cyberbullying often leads to *disinhibition*, or losing normal control over being aggressive. Some children, because of the anonymity of cyberbullying, engage in bullying when they would never do the same thing in person. Cyberbullying has an *anywhere and anytime* quality—the bully can get to a victim anywhere and 24-7-365—that is all day and all night, seven days every week, and every day of the year. The number of *bystanders* multiplies greatly in cyberbullying, thereby multiplying the victim's embarrassment and humiliation. Victims of cyberbullying often fear being *punished* by having their electronic media taken away by parents if the victim tells about the bullying. As you can see, cyberbullying eats up a child's time and emotional energy.

**Cyberbullying**
Aggression via electronic media

Figure 10.2 explains the different forms of cyberbullying.

**FIGURE 10.2**   Cyberbullying: Bullying at warp speed

Cyberbullying is common: 42% of children have been cyberbullied; 32% have been threatened online. Common, currently existing, cyberbullying methods include the following:

**Text Messages**   Aggressive messages composed by a bully. Sent to the victim's phone, and then often sent to the bully's contact list. Thus, the information on the bullied child is spread far and wide.

**Email**   Messages from the bully to the victim or from several children led by a bully. Groups of children may blast the victim with countless hurtful messages.

**Website**   Website bullying uses an established site or creates a site specifically designed for bullying. Offensive messages or photos of the victim are posted and the site is shared with many others. Bullies use smart phones to record photographs and videos of victims, for example, at lunch or in gym, and then post the images on the Internet. Website bullying often involves *voting*, for the ugliest, or fattest, or skinniest, or shortest, or whatever the bully decides to vote on. The "winner's" names are posted on the website so that many children can join in on the bullying.

**Chat Room**   *Anonymous*, real-time conversations involving two or more people. For example, a child can pose as someone else and trick a classmate into revealing embarrassing information, which is then used to bully and humiliate the victim.

*Source:* Based on New York Division of Criminal Justice Services (n.d.) and Prevent Child Abuse Utah (n.d.).

## Participants in Bullying

The participants in bullying episodes include the bully, the victim, and bystanders (Olweus, Limber, & Milhalic, 2002). The definitions and explanations in this section are based on the work of Scaglione and Scaglione (2006).

**Bully**
The person bent on causing harm or distress

**Bully**   The **bully** is the perpetrator, the person who intends to cause harm or distress and uses aggression to achieve this goal. It is possible for more than one bully to be directly involved in the aggression. Often, there is a main bully and one or more assistants, such as when a group surrounds a child and the bully beats up the child or when a group of girls excludes one girl from the group. One girl in the group leads the bullying.

**Pure bully**
Someone who bullies; has not been the victim of similar aggression

There are two types of bullies: the pure bully and the bully/victim. They seem to bully for different reasons. The **pure bully** bullies but has never been the victim of bullying. She bullies to establish dominance and power, often has a high view of herself (good self-esteem), and might even be popular. The pure bully likes the power associated with making somebody feel bad. She often is not even angry with the victim; she merely enjoys the power linked to the effect of the intimidation. She chooses victims mainly on how easy it will be to intimidate or harass them.

**Bully/victim**
Someone who has been both a bully and a victim

A **bully/victim** has bullied others but has also suffered bullying. This type of bully tends to feel like a victim but then to behave like a bully. Unlike the pure bully, the bully/victim tends to have a less positive view of himself; he is often very angry about having been bullied. His bullying is seen as more dangerous because of the revenge he needs. This is hostile aggression in action, a child angry about having been intimidated or hurt and turning to bullying others.

**Victim**   The **victim** is the person bullied. The bully seeks out the **pure victim** with the simple goal of tormenting her or showing off her bully power. The pure victim does nothing to provoke the bully; however, the pure victim is simply weaker, smaller, and less powerful—an easy target.

Children with disabilities and special needs might be especially in danger of being victims of a bully, possibly because they are perceived as different. A bully might misinterpret the disability as a weakness. Examples of disabilities and special needs that are sometimes the target of bullying include the following (Health Resources and Services Administration, 2009):

- **Overweight and obesity.** This is a risk factor for bullying. Girls with this problem are very likely to be teased and physically bullied. When the overweight girl *or* boy is in middle school, she or he is very likely to be excluded from activities, a form of relational bullying.
- **Medical conditions affecting appearance.** Conditions such as spina bifida or muscular dystrophy place children at risk for teasing and name calling. Specific names used most often refer to their medical condition.
- **Attention deficit hyperactivity disorder (ADHD).** A child with ADHD is likely to be a victim of bullying and is more likely than many other children to be a perpetrator, a bully.

**Bystander**   A **bystander** observes and witnesses bullying. A bystander can be a child or an adult, such as a teacher. Bystanders observe 85% of bullying episodes (O'Connell, Pepler, & Craig, 1999). The bystander is *not* a passive observer. Instead, he is a dynamic part of the bullying and is closely connected to the bullying. Cyberbullying can involve many more observers, bystanders who receive bullying messages sent to a victim (Hazeldon Foundation, 2013). Teachers have a major role in stopping bullying, but their attitude about it influences what they actually do. If a teacher thinks that bullying is a normal part of childhood or that a child would not be bullied if she were assertive, then that teacher would not likely intervene. Teachers who believe that they should do something do separate the children, and the bullying stops (Kochenderfer-Ladd & Pelletier, 2008).

Many believe that bullying is a relationship mainly between a bully and the victim. However, the bystander has a significant part to play in the whole process of bullying and in stopping the bullying, as explained next.

**Victim**
The person who is bullied

**Pure victim**
Often smaller and weaker or less powerful; does not provoke bullying

**Bystander**
Observes the bullying; can have an important role in stopping bullying

## :: *Question for Reflection*

# Intervening In and Preventing Bullying

Many ways of preventing or intervening in bullying have been proposed and used. The method chosen depends partly on how you look at bullying. Some people view bullying as a two-person issue, something between the bully and the victim, and do not focus on the setting or anyone other than the bully and the victim. This is a

**All of these children and their teacher observed bullying. They are bystanders. The teacher is helping the children understand how to step in to stop bullying.**

dyadic, or two-person, perspective. In this case, prevention usually involves working with individuals, the bully and/or the victim.

Others see bullying in a larger framework, from a systems or ecological perspective (Frey, Hirschstein, Edstrom, & Snell, 2009; Twemlow & Sacco, 2011; Twemlow, Fonagy, & Sacco, 2006). The ecological perspective reflects Bronfenbrenner's perspective on children's development within different systems. This approach sees bullying with a bigger lens, focusing on a triadic or three-person relationship of bully–victim–bystander. Figure 10.3 illustrates the ecological view that bullying has a larger cast of characters than originally thought.

One of the most effective ways to prevent bullying or to stop it is to take this same approach, a systems or ecological perspective. In this perspective, you go beyond looking only at the bully or at the victim and examine the entire system of the school, if that is where the bullying takes place. Researchers Fonagy et al. (2009) found that an ecological approach was successful in decreasing bullying. The entire school was involved, and the researchers focused on creating a more peaceful school environment.

The role of bystanders was of particular interest. Bystanders learned that they had a role in bullying, even if they did not land the punch, start the gossip, or exclude someone from play. Bystanders, including other children, teachers, or even administrators, learned to monitor things and were given permission to step in rather than stand back and watch. Stepping in takes many forms and children need to learn different strategies, such as distracting the bully by saying something like "Mrs. Johnson needs to see you" or telling the

**FIGURE 10.3** Three people are involved in bullying

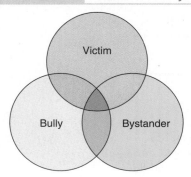

| **FIGURE 10.4** | Help children deal with a face-to-face bully |
|---|---|

We are dealing with a child victim's fear, a basic and normal emotion, in bullying. Child victims need adult and friend support, skills in dealing with a bully, and the courage to use the skills. These tips may lessen some of the child victim's fear a bully thrives on, will help the victim feel supported, and will give him or her specific skills in dealing with a bully.

**Tip 1:** Get the facts. Be available to talk and ask about what has happened. Listen but avoid judging or giving suggestions right away. If a child says that somebody has been *mean*, ask him to say what the other child did that was *mean.* Do not use the word *bully.* Just get the facts. Be positive. Be accepting. Do not belittle the bully.

**Tip 2:** Involve the child. Ask what she has already done. What worked? What did not work?

**Tip 3:** Teach and practice firmness. Teach children about firm statements—that is, assertive things to say to a bully. Practice with the whole class, small groups, or individuals. Some examples: "Get away from me," "Leave me alone," "Looks like you want to fight—I don't," and "This is *my* time at the computer."

**Tip 4:** Teach about walking away. Teach children about why bullies do what they do, that bullies like dominating others and need responses like fighting back or "get backs" from the victim. It fuels the bully fire. Teach children that walking away takes the wind out of the sails of many, but certainly not all, bullies.

**Tip 5:** Avoid a bully and tell a teacher or other adult. Give children permission to tell adults about being bullied.

**Tip 6:** Avoid the bully and be with friends. Bullies are more likely to attack when children are alone. Encourage group play, sitting with others at snack and mealtime, walking from bus stops with friends if possible.

*Source:* Based on American Psychiatric Association (2012); Bullying Statistics (2009).

bully to stop (Davis & Davis, 2007). See the websites at the end of this chapter for specific bullying prevention programs. Figure 10.4 gives suggestions for helping children who are bullied.

## :: HOW CHILDREN LEARN TO BE AGGRESSIVE

The most complete explanation of how children become aggressive is a systems or ecological approach. Professionals taking this approach acknowledge that a child is embedded in a variety of social systems and believe that these systems work together to shape a child's development, including aggression (Huesmann, 1988).

We will emphasize three spheres, or three systems, of influence on children's aggression: family, peer, and media (see Figure 10.5). A child frequently first learns about aggression in his *family* system. Almost equal in

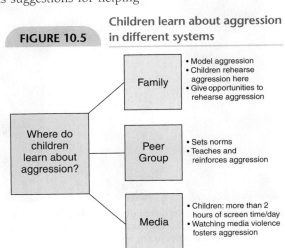

**FIGURE 10.5** Children learn about aggression in different systems

importance to a family's influence is the *media* system, including television, movies in any format, interactive video games, and print, in teaching about aggression. The child's *peer group* is a system that teaches and reinforces aggression. Families and peer groups are themselves embedded in a larger setting, the community and culture, and the teachings about aggression from these settings influence what some families learn and pass on to their children.

## Scripts for Aggression

An actor knows exactly what to say and do onstage because she has a script. Children who behave aggressively, like Patrick in the chapter-opening vignette, also have **scripts for aggression**, files of information that tell them exactly how to hit, punch, kick, grab, insult, extort, threaten, or call names—how to behave aggressively. Other children might not have as many scripts about aggression. They have far less information about how to behave as aggressively as a child who has a large collection of scripts.

> **Scripts for aggression**
> Information stored in memory; focused on how to carry out aggression; gleaned from different systems

Consider the concept of scripts whenever you observe aggressive behavior. Each system *writes* scripts for children. Each system gives children plenty of opportunities to *rehearse* aggressive behavior in the scripts. Children then *store* and *activate* the scripts.

**Children who observe these adults arguing will learn a "script" for aggression. Children can also acquire scripts by watching arguments in the media.**

## Scripts from Aggression-Teaching Families: Writing, Rehearsing with, and Activating the Scripts

**Writing Aggressive Scripts**   Aggression is a learned behavior, and some families teach aggression extremely effectively. An observer would see parents passing on their knowledge about how to hurt others. They teach hurtful or destructive behavior in a variety of ways, and they teach it very effectively. For example, a child might observe verbal aggression or physical attacks, such as using humor as a weapon or making fun of someone else.

Families model aggression, demonstrating behaviors for scripts. Children in such families listen to and observe the family's ways of dealing aggressively with one another, with animals, or with people outside the family. This is the scriptwriting step.

> **EXAMPLE**   A stray cat wandered into Patrick's yard, and Patrick watched his oldest brother yell at the cat, sending the animal running for cover. Patrick's new script is called "Yell at Cats."

As you watch this **video**, notice how the teacher is helping both boys acquire a helpful *script* instead of an aggressive script for getting what they want or need.

Look for a couple of specific statements that the teacher makes or questions that she asks that will help the children deal with frustrating events in a nonaggressive way.

**Rehearsing with Scripts**   In aggression-teaching families, children use newly acquired scripts to rehearse aggressive behavior. Such families give their children many rehearsal sessions with the aggressive scripts.

> **EXAMPLE**   Patrick listened to a talk show in which a man used a racial slur. Patrick learned a new script called "Use Racial Slurs." Patrick rehearsed the new script, calling forth laughter from two of his brothers. There was no adult around to stop them.

Children in aggression-teaching families have many chances to practice using their newly learned aggressive scripts. They practice over and over what they have learned about hurting others (Parke & Slaby, 1983). This is the rehearsal with script step. There is no guarantee, however, that the child will automatically use the script or act it out. Patrick has never used the script that he learned for yelling at cats. In spite of how one of his brothers now treats animals outside the family, Patrick has not rehearsed the lesson very often.

Therefore, learning does not always mean putting the learning to use. In Patrick's case, something in his personality keeps him from acting out almost all scripts for hurting animals. He seems to have also gathered and stored scripts for kind treatment of animals, and these scripts for kindness are more important to him.

**Activating the Scripts**   Children store the scripts for aggression in memory and then activate icons for them, just as we store and activate specific files on our computer screens. A child then retrieves and activates the scripts in settings both inside and outside his family. Suppose that Patrick, the child in the chapter-opening vignette, is in your early childhood class. You observe Patrick's behavior and realize quickly that he has a growing number of scripts for aggressive behavior in his memory. Further observation reveals a pattern. Patrick's scripts for fighting and bullying seem to be stored so that he can retrieve and activate them in a flash. We store frequently used folders on our computers as shortcuts. Unfortunately, Patrick's scripts for quick, aggressive responses are stored as shortcuts. He can simply select the shortcut icon that says "shortcut to name calling."

Three factors induce children to retrieve and activate aggression-packed scripts:

- **Rehearsal.** Children retrieve scripts for aggression if they have rehearsed with scripts. Patrick, our focus child, activates one or more scripts for aggression several times every day; therefore he rehearses the name calling, threatening, and hitting or punching scripts frequently.
- **Cues for aggression, including interactive DVDs.** War toys, guns, or aggressive movies are **cues for aggression**. Playing an aggressive video for a child, for instance, is like showing an actor a cue card. It says, "Here's your cue; time to be aggressive." Children retrieve and activate aggressive scripts after observing specific cues such as war toys or aggressive features on DVDs. Children who play violent video games observe and participate in these interactive games. They learn and then practice new aggression-related scripts. The scripts are then accessible

**Cues for aggression**
Some object, such as a gun, which reminds a person about aggressive acts

for real-life conflict situations. The interactive nature of popular, violent video games puts children right in the middle of the aggression in the video. The child becomes part of the video. Active involvement with violence, even if it is in a video, is still practice. Such practice imprints that script indelibly in the child's memory, giving him a permanent, easily accessed reminder of how to hurt others.

■ **Continued exposure to aggression.** This provides even more scripts. Children who already have a large collection of aggressive scripts will very likely continue to observe aggression, increasing even further the number of aggressive scripts in their collection. The brand-new scripts for aggression, in turn, trigger the recall of existing aggression scripts. It is a nasty cycle.

## Unresponsive Parenting Fosters Aggression

Members of aggression-teaching family systems are not very responsive to each other. Unresponsive parents are often, but not always, insensitive to and do not support their children. This sets the stage for children's increased aggression in a number of ways (Dubow, Heusmann, & Boxer, 2003):

■ **Unmet needs.** Unresponsive adults often ignore and fail to meet a child's basic psychological needs for protection, love, affection, nurturance, play, and self-esteem. Unmet needs result in frustration, and frustrated, angry children frequently act aggressively.

■ **Failure to teach social skills.** Unresponsive adults do not know that they should, or they do not know how to, teach specific social skills to their children. Therefore, the parents omit something that their children need. Their children tend to be low in self-control, and children who are not self-controlled are likely to react with aggression under many circumstances.

■ **Active teaching of ineffective social skills and rewarding aggression.** On the other hand, unresponsive adults actively teach ineffective social skills, either deliberately or unknowingly. These adults also tend to reward aggressive behavior.

■ **Negative or unhelpful discipline strategies.** Using harsh physical discipline, failing to set appropriate limits, disciplining inconsistently, using humor as a weapon, using sarcasm or shame, nattering or nagging, and hurting children with punishment are all unhelpful methods of discipline. Adults in aggression-teaching systems tend to use not just one or two but a whole cluster of negative discipline tactics. Using several negative discipline strategies can increase aggression in children because the strategies demonstrate clearly how to be aggressive.

■ **Providing cues for aggression.** Adults in aggression-teaching systems indirectly influence aggression through their management style. Parents in aggressive systems provide many cues that elicit aggression—media violence in its many forms and toy guns.

> **EXAMPLE** Patrick's parents give him free access to all television shows, including sleazy talk and reality shows and entertainment television.

# Peers: Children Get Scripts from Other Children

One of the conclusions from many different theoretical perspectives and many years of research is this: A child's behavior is remarkably similar to the behavior of her peer group (Prinstein & Dodge, 2008). Peers teach, maintain, and modify a child's aggression (Parke & Slaby, 1983).

**Peers Set Norms for Aggression**   A **norm** is a principle that groups use to guide the behavior of members of the group. Norms tell members of a group what the group considers acceptable behavior. Peer groups influence the aggression of group members by setting norms about a number of things, including the expression of aggression. The norms tell children what the peer group will accept in terms of aggression. Some peer groups, like Patrick's neighborhood friends, have norms permitting and encouraging aggression. Other groups have norms that do not approve of aggression.

**Norm**
A standard used by groups to direct a group member's behavior

**Peers Model Aggression**   Children learn from many different models, including peers. Observe for levels of aggression in a group of children. If the group approves of and models aggression, it will forecast changes in aggression over time for children in that group (Espelage, Holt, & Henkel, 2003).

> **EXAMPLE**   Patrick has observed two friends push their way in line at the bus. The same pair uses aggression to steal lunch money from specific children.

**Peers Reinforce Aggression**   Paul punches Jeff and says, "Give me your lunch money or I'll punch you again." Being punched is a negative and very unpleasant condition. Jeff gives Paul the lunch money, and Paul does not punch. Jeff has stopped the obnoxious negative condition by giving in to Paul. Jeff, however, has actually *reinforced* the aggression, Paul's punching. Paul is very likely to punch again because he has been reinforced for punching. Paul has learned that Jeff will give him money to *stop* the punching.

We reinforce name calling, bullying, pushing, and other forms of aggression when we give in to the bully ourselves or when we watch the aggression and do nothing to stop it.

> **EXAMPLE**   Patrick discovered that children at school readily gave in to his aggression and bullying to stop the attacks. However, they did not realize that the giving in was actually rewarding Patrick and almost guaranteeing that he would attack them again.

# Media: Children Get Scripts from Watching Violence

**Screen time**
Time spent watching action on a monitor of any sort

Children learn from observing different models, including those shown in the media, such as on television and in video games. **Screen time** refers to the time spent watching television programs, movies in a theater, and computer games.

**Children's Screen Time**   Children have a lot of screen time (Page, Cooper, Griew, & Jago, 2010; Rideout, Vandewater, & Wartella, 2003). For instance, 90% of parents report that their children younger than 6 years old have watched television, and watch 1 to 2 hours of televised shows daily. Fourteen percent of children between 6 and 23 months of age watch over 2 hours per day. Thirty percent of infants and toddlers have televisions in their bedrooms, whereas the figure is 59% for children 4 to 6.

The American Academy of Pediatrics (Brown, 2011) has reiterated its older recommendation discouraging media use for children under the age of 2. The group points to both foreground (media very young children watch directly) and background media (television turned on and in the background), and specifically recommends that parents and caregivers avoid exposing infants and young toddlers to both, as much as possible. The group notes that there is little evidence that television watching benefits babies. Young children who watch the most television read less, and they learned to read later than children who do not watch television. Some children, such as those with asthma, have even more screen time (Conn, Hernandez, Puthoor, Fagnano, & Halterman, 2008).

**Effect of Media Violence**   There are a variety of health risks to children who watch too much television or play too many video games (Page et al., 2010). Some of the major health risks are increased aggression from observing so much aggression and obesity connected with inactivity.

**Media violence**
Hostility shown in DVDs, movies, games, and on other screens

**Media violence** refers to brutality, cruelty, and hostility portrayed on screens. There is an overwhelming consensus in the research, public health, and early childhood communities that watching and participating in media violence threatens the development and well-being of young children. Thirty-five years and well over 1,000 studies show that children watch an excessive amount of media violence. The ability to imitate models is present very early in life; thus, children watching a lot of television have many models to imitate. Imitation is the means through which children show that they comprehend screen action (Calvert, 2006).

Children who watch media violence develop aggressive attitudes, values, and behavior. Three major risks go along with watching media violence:

- **Increases aggression.** Media violence can and does increase subsequent aggression in children.
- **Allows acceptance of aggression.** Media violence increases a child's passive acceptance of aggression by others. Not only do children themselves become more aggressive, but they also accept violence by others after watching media violence. Children are most likely to relax their standards if they view violence as effective, justified, reinforced, and commonplace.
- **Increases fear.** Media violence often leads children to think that the world is a violent and scary place in which people hurt and degrade each other. It might create and then increase the fear of becoming a victim of violence. Children who are afraid of becoming a victim of violence develop behaviors through which they hope to protect themselves. It also increases mistrust of others.

# Neutralize Media's Aggressive Message: Help Children Take Charge of What They Watch in the Media

The main goal is to teach children to make conscious decisions about what they watch, and if they will watch at all. Another goal is to decrease the effect of the power and pull of the media—television, DVDs, video games, and computers—on a child. This is a difficult task because of how well and attractively the media packages shows. The shows have a mesmerizing effect on a number of children, and many have developed habits of tuning in to the screen when they have a few minutes of downtime. They are entertained and do not have to think or exert much energy at all.

Experts have long given the same advice for how to help parents and teachers teach children about using media wisely and taking control of what they watch (Levin, 1998; Mayo Clinic Staff, 2010):

- Lead problem-solving discussions with children about the media—for example, about the long-running Power Rangers and all the fighting that they do. Why do they need to fight so much? Is there a way to limit where and when children play Power Rangers on the playground or in the classroom, so that children who do not like the Power Rangers play will not be bothered by it?
- Be clear about limits on imitating certain types of behaviors. Never allow children to imitate hurting animals or other people or damaging property. Talk to them about the reasons, but be firm. This should be a non-negotiable item.
- Teach children how to make good choices and advance planning about their screen viewing. Help them understand that screen time means a combination of television, DVDs, video games, and computers. Give them specific skills for choosing screen time wisely.
- Help children observe themselves and think about the things that they like doing most. Encourage them to schedule time to do these activities in addition to choosing screen time wisely.

# Neutralize Media's Aggressive Message: Watch Television with Children and Comment on Aggressive Content

A realistic approach acknowledges that children will have screen time, some much more than others. Teachers and parents can still be proactive. They can gradually decrease the amount of television watched, monitor what children watch, watch with children, and teach them how to understand what they watch.

> **EXAMPLE**   While John was watching television, his father said, "Why do you think that man kicked his neighbor's car, John?" . . . "Yes, I think he was mad at him for driving his car over the flowers. That still doesn't make it okay to kick his neighbor's car."

Children, who watch media violence with adults and hear a negative evaluation of the violence, as John did, tend to be less aggressive than children who watch the same aggression alone.

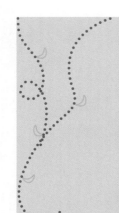

## Cultural Scripts and Guiding Children

### Helping Children Acquire New Cultural Scripts That Prevent Aggression and Bullying

Teachers can help children acquire new and more positive cultural scripts that decrease and prevent aggression. A child will have access to the new knowledge and skills he needs to be less aggressive, less agitated, calmer, and more content. It takes time for children to adopt a new script, but teachers need to teach and then patiently encourage more helpful behavior. Essential elements of the new script include the following.

**Limits Barring Aggression and Bullying**    Base the new cultural script on limits against hurting or disturbing other people and animals, damaging toys or equipment, and bullying. Lead a discussion with children about the need to stop the hitting and hurting and why it is important to treat other people and animals with respect. Firmly but kindly enforce limits. You will begin to help children construct the idea that other people and animals have a right to be safe and secure. You will help them develop values and internal controls about the rights of others.

**Empathy Building**    Infuse the new cultural script with knowledge that aggression and bullying hurt others. Empathic children tend to be more sensitive to another's feelings and to be less aggressive (Feshbach & Feshbach, 1982; Strayer & Roberts, 2004). Give them information by telling the children, for example, "Oh! The gerbils ran and hid and were afraid when you banged on the glass." Avoid simply asking how another child or animal might feel, because young children cannot take the other's perspective.

**Resetting the Norm to Positive Behavior**    Aggressive children, including bullies, possess a limited number of ways to deal with interactional problems. Crowd out aggressive behaviors by teaching children assertiveness, negotiation, cooperation, sharing, and helping. This resets the norm, the expected and valued behavior, from aggression to more positive behavior. Noticing and encouraging positive behavior (Skinner, Neddenriep, Robinson, Ervin, & Jones, 2002) effectively decreases aggression and bullying. Mr. Santini, for instance, taught about helping others when he used a puppet that needed help at the computer and asked someone for help.

**Consequential Thinking**    All children, but bullies in particular, need to understand the undeniable consequence of aggression: somebody gets hurt or something is damaged. Use direct instruction to write this part of the new cultural script. For example, Mr. Santini used clip art to present vignettes, made-up stories not about specific classroom incidents, and asked questions about how the children might have felt about what happened. "When Pam pinched Rita, Rita cried. How do you think that she was feeling? . . . Right. She was hurt and felt bad."

## :: FOCUS ON PRACTICE

This Focus on Practice activity is entitled *Enviornments Can Support Social Emotional Learning.* As you complete this activity, you will observe the teacher as she works through a problem with two children. The strategy that she uses is beneficial for all children, including those who are bullies.

## HELP YOUR CHILD TAKE CHARGE OF MEDIA AND SCREEN TIME

- Slow the pace and focus on your family. Plan a family night every week. Plan fun activities that do not include screen time, activities that everybody looks forward to and enjoys: playing board games, skating, taking a walk, reading, playing charades, playing music, learning about and looking for birds in your area, anything that family members suggest.
- Help your child take an inventory of favorite activities or new things that she or he would like to try:

  Make a list.

  Refer to the list when planning things to do.

  Refer to the list when a child is bored.

  Revise the list when it seems appropriate.

- Model wise, sensible use of your time, including screen time. Let your child see you, not plunking down in front of a screen, but reading books and magazines, exercising, spending time with family, gardening, sailing, or whatever hobby you enjoy.
- Help your child understand the concept of screen time, which includes television, DVDs, computer time, and video games.

- Set a reasonable amount of screen time (less than 2 hours) that your child may have each day.
- Teach your child how to plan reading, play, or screen time.
- Write your family's rules for using television. Let children help write the rules. Then post, use, and evaluate the rules. Change them if necessary.
- Make the television set a less prominent piece of equipment. Turn on the television only for specific, planned shows; avoid letting a television run as background noise.
- Have a motto that works for your family. You may choose examples like "homework first," "chores first," "play with and feed dog first," "think first about what I really want to do," or "what are my choices here?"
- Help your child understand "action figure" characters. Talk with your child about why some of the action figures engage in so much fighting.
- If your child wants to imitate the action figures, consider trying to confine the imitation to specific times and places. Consider how "just saying no" might backfire. However, forbid certain things: hurting animals, hurting other people, and damaging property.

**EXAMPLE** Mr. Santini's school adopted a plan encouraging children to watch out for and report random acts of cooperation and helpfulness. Two children, in one morning, reported that Patrick had helped them with their math.

## ANALYZE A VIGNETTE

Use the information in this chapter to answer the following questions about the chapter-opening vignettes.

1. Preschool: Identify the type of aggression that Maya shows. Explain your choice.
2. Kindergarten: What type of aggression does Jess show? What was the root of his aggressive behavior?

3. Primary: What would lead you to think that Patrick might be a *pure bully*?
4. Primary: What has probably happened at the school to change the behavior of the children who intervened in the bullying incident?

## SUMMARY

There are many types of aggressive behavior, including physical, verbal, psychological, and emotional. All aggression intends to cause harm or damage. Aggressive people have a goal in mind. The two major goals or purposes are:

- Instrumental: The goal is to get or retrieve an object or privilege.
- Hostile: The goal is to do something harmful based on anger. Bullying is aggression. It is repeated over

time, and there is an imbalance between those involved. Bullying can be

- Physical
- Emotional and psychological
- Verbal (for example, teasing)
- Cyberbullying

Participants in bullying are the

- Bully
- Victim
- Bystander(s)

Children learn to be aggressive in different systems by acquiring, rehearsing, and activating scripts for aggression. The systems are

- Family
- Peer group
- Media

Strategies exist for preventing or reducing aggression, such as setting limits on the expression of aggression, teaching, and encouraging more positive and prosocial behavior.

## APPLY YOUR KNOWLEDGE

1. Watch at least 1 hour of television designed specifically for young children. On a sheet of paper, break that hour into 10-minute segments. In each segment, keep a tally of the number of times that you see an act of aggression—any act of aggression—and give a total at the end of the hour. Write a brief description of each act of aggression.
2. Visit a toy store. Find several examples of and describe toys that you think would serve as aggressive

cues that would likely bring out aggression in young children. Were these toys designed for a specific gender? If so, state what led you to this conclusion.
3. Review a prevention program. Choose one of the websites listed at the end of this chapter that is devoted to bullying prevention. Examine one or two of the methods suggested to stop bullying. Say why this method would probably be effective.

## WEBSITES

### Stopbullying
http://www.stopbullying.gov

Home page for a federal government site with accurate and up-to-date information on bullying in it many forms and helpful information on dealing with bullying. Areas of the site targeted to children, parents, and teachers.

### Olweus Bullying Prevention Program (Olweus pronounced ol-VAY-us)
http://www.clemson.edu/olweus/

Main page for this comprehensive, schoolwide program. Used in many different countries. Site contains helpful links that describe and explain the program.

# CHAPTER 11

# Minimizing Challenging Behavior

## Learning Outcomes

- Define terms associated with challenging behavior
- Label observed child behavior as *challenging* or *not challenging* and defend the choice
- Explain why incidents of challenging behavior are the "hot spots" in an early childhood classroom
- List and explain the roots of challenging behavior
- Apply information about roots of challenging behavior to chapter-opening vignettes
- Explain why it is necessary to figure out the function of a child's challenging behavior
- Explain how functional behavioral assessment (FBA) is used in supporting children with specific challenging behavior
- Discuss the major approach to working with infants and toddlers with challenging behaviors

---

### VIGNETTES

---

#### PRESCHOOL: AURELIA SHARES OCCASIONALLY

*Mrs. Johnson is concerned about 4-year-old Aurelia's behavior. Here is a small sampling of her anecdotal records about Aurelia in September. She focused on examples of sharing as well as taking things without asking.*

1. *Aurelia and Justine worked side by side at a table, sorting plastic squares by color. Aurelia leaned over, picked up three of Justine's items, and put them in her own pile.*
2. *Angelo yelled, "Give it back, Aurelia," referring to a boat that Aurelia had taken from him. Aurelia did not give it back.*
3. *Outside: Four tricycles were available. The sign-up list was near the parking area. Moshe waited for his turn. Angelo finished a turn and then returned the tricycle to the parking area. Aurelia scooted in ahead of Moshe, jumped on the tricycle, and rode away.*
4. *Aurelia, Kim, and Pete painted on a long piece of paper taped to the plastic-covered wall. Aurelia shared the three large pots of paint with the others.*

#### KINDERGARTEN: EMILY'S EMOTIONS FLARE UP

*Emily had been in Mr. Santini's class for the last 2 months of kindergarten after moving to the district. Therefore, when school resumed in September, he realized that Emily's angry flare-ups might show up again. The first episode occurred on the third day of school. Emily, now in this teacher's first-grade group, stomped away from the computer center after finding all computers in use. Mr. Santini watched the flood of anger in Emily's face, a clear sign of the emotional storm brewing within this 6-year-old. Later that afternoon, Emily smacked another first grader.*

### PRIMARY: SAMIRA FLITTERS AND FLUTTERS

*Samira speaks two languages fluently, does well in school, and is well liked by other children. Mr. Santini thinks of her as a social butterfly, finishing any work quickly and then flitting off to chat with friends. Samira zips about the room during transitions, too, cheerfully wreaking low-level havoc. During Tuesday's lining-up for lunch, she led the group in a quiet little cheer, "Lunch, lunch, we love lunch!"*

## :: INTRODUCTION

By this time, you have learned about many positive and effective guidance strategies that will certainly work with everyday guidance issues in your classroom. This chapter goes further to address behaviors that do not seem to respond well to normal positive guidance—**challenging behavior**, which tests a teacher's ability to guide a child. Challenging behavior includes but undoubtedly is not limited to biting, disrespectful language, teasing, tattling, hitting, whining, and lying.

There are two major goals in this chapter. The first is to help you learn how to minimize the hot spots of challenging behavior; maximize the calm, cool times in your classroom; and feel competent and confident in the process. You have to give yourself time to learn this process and then to practice it. You will learn how to support children who do not respond to positive guidance strategies and who persist with challenging behaviors. You can indeed support many or most children with challenging behaviors—not all, but many.

The other goal is to support you in developing an optimistic view of challenging behavior, not a Pollyanna-like illogical and unreasonable type of optimism, but a realistic, confident, and hopeful perspective. We can certainly help many children with challenging behaviors by assessing the function of their behavior and deciding on a plan that will best help the child. Some behaviors, in spite of our best efforts in using functional behavioral assessment (FBA), will prove very trying, exasperating, wearisome, and unyielding to even our best practices. Some challenging behaviors may prove to be beyond our training and skills; even then, we can work with other professionals trained in helping children with extremely challenging behaviors. Even at this level, you can be optimistic in that you can still help a child through a proper referral.

**Challenging behavior**
Behavior that tests an adult's ability to support the child; usually in the eye of the beholder

## :: THE NATURE OF CHALLENGING BEHAVIOR

### Challenging Behavior Is "in the Eye of the Beholder"

Suppose that 10 teachers in a workshop watch a video or DVD clip. The film shows a 3-year-old child hiding under a table while the teacher reads a story, lagging behind the group of children as they walk to the library, and crying as he slams his fists on the floor when the teacher reminds him that it is cleanup time. "Do you," asks the workshop leader, "think that you have just seen challenging behavior?" Seven participants state that they have definitely observed challenging behavior. The rest have the opposite opinion: that this child's behavior would not fall into the challenging behavior category. How would you have responded? Why?

**FIGURE 11.1**   Calm and cool times in Jack's morning in kindergarten

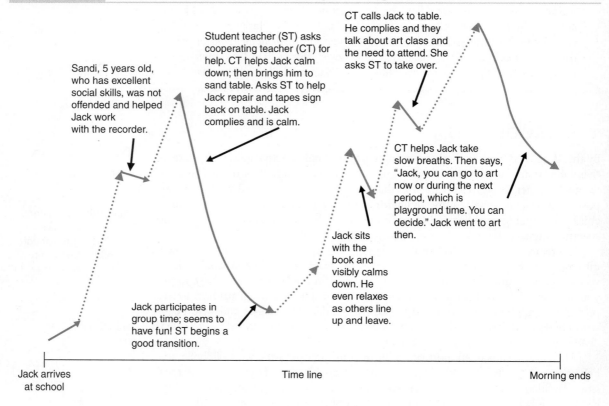

Challenging behavior is in the eye of the beholder because our perspective determines whether we see any behavior as challenging. In the example, some teachers' perspectives led them to see this 3-year-old child as defiant. A different perspective enabled three of the teachers to realize that the child's behavior was predictable for a very young child feeling insecure in a new setting.

Figure 11.1 shows the frame-by-frame sketch of 5-year-old Jack's calm and cool times in his kindergarten class. We will also focus on hot spots of challenging behavior in this child's day as the chapter progresses, and you will have a chance to answer a variety of questions. Jack's behavior presents a challenge to him as he navigates his way through one morning at school.

## Challenging Behaviors Are the Hot Spots in a Classroom

**Hot spots**
Incidents of challenging behavior in a classroom

Figure 11.2 shows several hot spots during only part of one morning. Figure 11.3 explains the nature of each of the hot spots. Examine both figures at the same time. **Hot spots** are the times when a teacher might feel less confident about his

**FIGURE 11.2** Hot spots of challenging behavior in Jack's morning in kindergarten

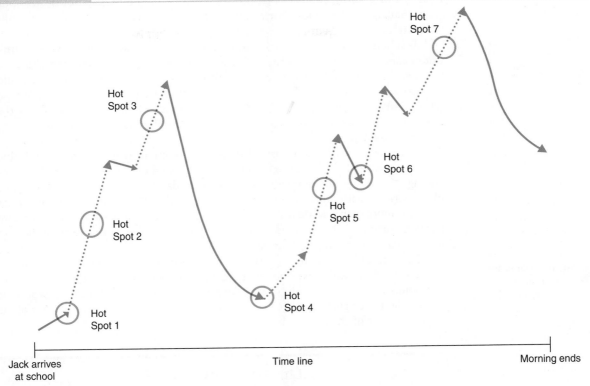

**FIGURE 11.3** Describing Jack's hot spot challenging behavior

**Hot Spot**

1. Jack's father said to the teachers, with Jack listening, "See if you can do anything with him today!" Jack seemed agitated as he started his day and ignored his friend Sandi's cheerful greeting.

2. At the listening center, Jack had a little trouble with the tape recorder. Already agitated, his frustration seemed to increase as he yanked the tape out of the machine.

3. Jack likes Sandi and they had fun together listening to a tape. Then Sandi went to the math center and Jack wandered about the room, not stopping anywhere to work. When the student teacher (ST) asked him to choose his next center, Jack walked away from her without answering. He walked by the sand table, grabbed a corner of the large sign on the table, and ripped the sign in half.

4. When ST started sending children to line up for art class, Jack went to the library, took a book from the shelf, and buried his face in the book.

5. ST called over to Jack in the book corner, "Okay, Jack. Time to line up for art class." "I'm *not* going," he shouted.

6. Jack looked at ST who asked him if he was now ready to go to art class. He ignored her and hung his head. Jack's agitation resurfaced.

7. ST placed her hand on Jack's shoulder as she had seen the cooperating teacher do. Jack shook off her hand with a violent twist. He now showed even more anger and frustration.

guidance—anxious, impatient, or even angry or frustrated. He might question his methods of guiding children because the positive methods may not be working with challenging behavior. For example, good limit setting and restating limits well might not work with some challenging behaviors.

Teachers who have an authoritative caregiving style are kind as well as firm, understand child development, and use this knowledge when guiding children. However, when faced with situations with no resolution in sight, a teacher could feel irritated and edgy. Then many teachers feel guilty for having been impatient with a child. Anger is then likely to get in the way of clear thinking about the challenging behavior. Unpleasant emotions can affect teachers just as they do anybody else.

Hot spots of challenging behavior are also the times when teachers think that their focus has shifted from teaching to crisis intervention. Jack's teacher, the cooperating teacher, spends quite a bit of time every day helping Jack calm down. She likes working with student teachers, but thinks that Jack's challenging behavior might be more than a student teacher can handle. Yet she has found that the student teacher, frustrated and anxious about dealing with Jack, is slowly learning how to help him and is gaining confidence.

Jack's teacher wants to increase the **calm and cool times** in the classroom— time for teaching with fewer hot-spot, challenging behaviors. How does she get to this point? How does she help Jack deal with his anxiety? A good first step would be to consider the origins of his challenging behaviors. We will now examine four of the strongest roots of challenging behavior.

**Calm and cool times**
Periods of relative peace and serenity in a classroom

---

## :: *Question for Reflection*

---

## :: ROOTS OF CHALLENGING BEHAVIOR

Challenging behavior is complex. Even experienced, competent teachers are astounded at how complicated a challenging behavior can be. They realize that a child's demanding or testing behavior grew out of a number of factors. Jack's teacher, for instance, knew that helping Jack would take a lot of time over several months and that she would have to stay focused on his behavior as a complex question with many different answers. The **voice of challenging behavior** speaks through children's actions, their behavior. We begin to help children by listening carefully to what they tell us with their actions.

This section targets the four main roots of challenging behavior:

**Voice of challenging behavior**
What a child's behavior tells a teacher about what the child needs

Developmental characteristics

Unmet needs

Lack of skills

Factors in the classroom (contextual problems)

# :: FOCUS ON PRACTICE

This Focus on Practice activity is entitled *The Voice of Challenging Behavior*. The strategy that you will learn about in this activity focuses on helping teachers clarify the meaning of challenging behavior.

## Developmental Characteristics

**Developmental characteristics** are involved in nearly every challenging behavior. The voice of challenging behavior, in this case, says this: "I am still a child and think like a child. I have trouble taking somebody else's perspective. I can't control my emotions yet and it will be a couple of years before I can really control myself." Some of the developmental characteristics affecting challenging behavior include the following:

- Thinking about one thing at a time: Young children tend to think about one thing at a time. They might focus only on how much they dislike the taste of something, not how the child who brought the treat might feel when she hears, "Yuck!"
- Low-level perspective taking: Young children have difficulty with perspective taking. Perspective taking is a cognitive developmental skill that develops over time, and only if children learn about taking another's perspective and only if they practice this skill.
- Memory of inappropriate response: Children who have learned an unhelpful way to do something retain powerful images of that incorrect method. Even though a teacher tells them, "Use your words," this child will very likely revert to his old and unhelpful method of hitting when angry, stressed, and agitated.
- Unable to understand and control anger: Children feel and express anger but do not understand and cannot manage anger on their own. They cannot contemplate why they feel angry, cannot always generate words for how they feel, and cannot think of how to deal with their irritation.
- Brain development: The development of specific regions of the brain, the amygdala and prefrontal associative cortex, and the link between the two, influence challenging behavior. The part of the brain, the amygdala, sensing danger is fully operational at birth and directs the child's actions for emotional matters. It does not help the child stop and think. It only warns of danger. The prefrontal associative cortex, on the other hand, has a big role in helping us plan, control ourselves, and analyze emotions. However, this part of the brain only has a start in early childhood and is not fully developed until late adolescence or even early adulthood. The circuit or path for shuttling signals between the amygdala and the prefrontal cortex also develops gradually and only if a baby has very responsive and loving parents or caregivers. When

**Developmental characteristics**
Factors in a child's growth that contribute to challenging behavior

**It takes a long time for children to learn to take another person's perspective. When young children grab things from others, they usually do not think about how the others feel.**

children face challenging situations, we want them to begin to stop and think and then act. Their brain development will eventually support this but it is not an automatic process and takes several years.

**EXAMPLE**   In the chapter-opening preschool vignette, recall that Aurelia is 4 years old and grabs things from other children several times each day. Aurelia's inability to take somebody else's perspective is a major developmental root of her challenging behavior.

**EXAMPLE**   In the chapter-opening kindergarten vignette, Emily's overly strong emotional responses also reveal a developmental root to her challenging behavior. Emily's inability to focus on more than one thing at a time is one developmental issue. Emily's inability to manage her emotions is another. A third developmental root is that Emily has remembered and used an ineffective way of dealing with angry feelings.

As you watch this **video**, notice how persistent and firm but kind the teacher is as she works with Tyler on his challenging behavior. How well do you think Tyler, the aggressor, was at taking Dudley's perspective? How did the teacher help the aggressor learn to take someone else's (Dudley's) perspective? What skills did you observe that the teacher also taught to Dudley?

## Unmet Needs

The challenging behavior says, "There is something that I really need. Would you help me get it?" The root of some, but certainly not all, challenging behavior is one or more **unmet needs**. Think about a child's basic needs. What does he need before he can behave well? Here are some of any child's most basic needs (you might have additions to the list):

- Feeling of being loved and appreciated
- Feeling of being safe and secure
- Exercise and physical activity
- Sound sleep and rest
- Adequate nutrition, including enough water
- Basic medical and dental care
- Play
- Classroom structure based on principles of developmentally appropriate practice
- Authoritative, constructive guidance

> **EXAMPLE** In the chapter-opening kindergarten vignette, Emily has several angry outbursts. At home, Emily's parents argue frequently but never argue fairly, instead insulting and degrading each other. Emily hears and sees this background anger, often in the middle of the night, and has observed her father hit her mother on several occasions. One of Emily's most outstanding unmet needs is a feeling of safety and security. Do you think that she has any other unmet needs?

**Unmet need**
One of a child's basic requirements for healthy development and good mental health that have not been satisfied and that contribute to challenging behavior

## Lack of Skills

The challenging behavior says, "There is something that I don't know how to do. Will you teach me?" Many children simply do not have the skills they need for getting along with others and for functioning well in school. They have a **skill deficit**. Observing young children reveals the numerous things that children must learn to be successful in relationships and in school, including the following:

- How to handle joy, disappointment, and anger (or any other emotion)
- How to get attention appropriately
- How to join a group
- How to make and then keep a friend
- How to work with others in small and large groups
- How a group functions
- How to start a project and how to keep it going

**Skill deficit**
Lacking a skill for social emotional development and school success that contributes to challenging behavior

> **EXAMPLE** In the primary-grade vignette, some people might look on Samira's joyful approach to life as challenging behavior. Mr. Santini merely wanted to help Samira learn how to organize herself for moving smoothly through the morning. He did not want to stamp out her joy or the happiness that she brought to the class. After several observations, Mr. Santini decided that Samira needed a day planning chart to help her move to the next center. It worked. Samira is still happy and still socializing, but she now has a destination.

Figure 11.4 is your opportunity to explain how Jack's developmental characteristics, his unmet needs, and his lack of skills all contributed to his challenging behavior.

| **FIGURE 11.4** | The roots of Jack's challenging behavior |
|---|---|

Refer to Figures 11.1, 11.2, and 11.3 when answering the following questions about Jack's challenging behavior.

1. Jack, in kindergarten, came to school in a state of *agitation* and remained upset throughout the morning in spite of his friend Sandi's and his teacher's help. Explain how his current level of brain development played a role in his problem.

2. Explain how at least one other developmental characteristic probably affected Jack's behavior.

3. From the information given, explain what you think Jack's most outstanding unmet need might be and then justify your choice.

4. From your review of the figures and the information, which skill do you think would be most helpful for Jack to learn and what is your reason for your choice?

## Factors in the Classroom (Contextual Issues)

The voice of challenging behavior says, "There's something in our classroom that's making it hard for me to do the right thing. Will you please help me by changing this?" This refers to **contextual factors** that contribute to challenging behavior. Teachers need to examine their own practices when facing ordinary, everyday discipline encounters as well as challenging behaviors. What matters is an unemotional, dispassionate assessment of classroom structure and processes, which requires observation. Early childhood professionals have access to several major observational strategies.

**Contextual factors**
Environmental issues (physical or interpersonal environment or curriculum) contributing to challenging behavior in classrooms

Three ready-made observation instruments are available, one each for infant-toddler, preschool, and K-3 classrooms, which teachers find useful in examining the classroom's environment. They are *rating scales* that yield information but no judgment, and this helps teachers learn about the strengths in their classrooms. The main idea is to use the information to build on these strengths and identify areas for improvement. Improvements involve changing something in the classroom to create an even more developmentally appropriate environment. Here is a brief description of the three environmental rating scales.

- *Infant Toddler Environment Rating Scale—Revised Edition (ITERS–R)* (Harms, Cryer, & Clifford, 2006). ITERS-R is designed for assessing program quality and environments for infants and toddlers, children up to 30 months of age. It assesses health and safety, environment (furniture, equipment, educational materials), educator skill and behavior.

- *Early Childhood Environment Rating Scale—Revised (ECERS–R) (preschool)* (Harms, Clifford, & Cryer, 2005). This scale is designed for assessing program quality in preschool classrooms, for children ages $2\frac{1}{2}$ to 5; it assesses space and furnishings, personal care routines, language and reasoning, activities, interaction, program structure, and parents and staff.

- *Assessment of Practices in Early Elementary Classrooms (APEEC)* (Hemmeter, Maxwell, Ault, & Schuster, 2001). APEEC is designed for assessing how K–3 classrooms use developmentally appropriate practices; it assesses physical environment, instructional context, and social context.

All children in a class benefit when teachers examine the classroom environment, including their own role in events. Those whose challenging behavior is linked to inappropriate transitions, overly long group times, a poorly balanced daily schedule, or inappropriate curriculum or guidance strategies benefit even more. A meeting of the entire class, a morning meeting, for example, is beneficial for children when the meeting is planned and when it is developmentally appropriate. If, however, a kindergarten's morning meeting goes on and on, you can expect some challenging behavior because the group time is much too long. If a first-grade teacher forces children to do one worksheet after another every morning, then he can expect some challenging behavior. Why? The children are sitting and not learning actively, are not collaborating, and are not making choices, a good recipe for challenging behavior.

Effective teachers deliberately walk through the systematic process of choosing guidance strategies. They make sound decisions based on systematically assessing a child's behavior and making decisions about how to support him, the topic we will examine next.

## :: FUNCTIONAL BEHAVIORAL ASSESSMENT AND SUPPORTING POSITIVE BEHAVIOR

Any challenging behavior has a purpose. It serves a function for the child and until we identify that function, we will be puzzled about how to help the child. Once we discover the function of a challenging behavior, we need to figure out how to support a child in adopting a different, more positive behavior and in maintaining the new behavior. This section of the chapter is based on the work of the CSEFEL, the Center on the Social and Emotional Foundations for Early Learning (Fox, n.d.; Fox & Duda, n.d.), and the Outreach Services of Indiana (Indiana Family and Social Services Association, 2010).

### Functional Behavioral Assessment

Functional behavioral assessment (FBA) is a method for figuring out the purpose—the function—that a child's challenging behavior serves. What function, for instance, do frequently interrupting things, teasing, tattling, hitting, lying, whining disrespectful language, and biting serve? We can then go beyond being baffled by the behavior to understanding it. Because all behavior exists in a setting or environment that affects the behavior, FBA considers how the environment has contributed to the child's behavior. Normally, teachers guide children very effectively by using normal positive guidance strategies, but some children do not respond to such strategies. Instead, their challenging behavior makes it difficult for them to participate in normal classroom activities. Teachers begin to help children with challenging behavior by doing a functional behavioral assessment.

**A-B-C Data for Observing Behavior** The "A-B-C" refers to three words, *Antecedent-Behavior-Consequence*. ABC data are gathered to clarify the nature and purpose of a child's behavior and events in the environment linked to the behavior. ABC data collection is usually a part of a functional behavioral assessment and can be collected by an individual teacher or the teacher, parents, and other professionals.

**Antecedent**
An event preceding and possibly predicting an event that follows it

**Behavior**
Refers (when studying children) to a child's actions, conduct, or deeds

**Consequence**
A response that follows a behavior

- **Antecedent** is a word from Latin and means *to go before*. An antecedent is an event preceding and possibly predicting an event that follows it. In observing a child's behavior, therefore, an antecedent is an event occurring before a child's behavior. An antecedent such as hearing a teaser call him "bug-eyes" often activates or triggers the child's behavior of hitting the teaser. Thus, the teasing is the type of event that predicts a specific child's behavior or hitting.

- **Behavior** refers to the child's actions, conduct, or deeds. For our purposes, challenging behavior refers to their own actions that block children's full participation in the life of their classroom. When doing a functional behavioral analysis, teachers need to know some details about the behavior—for example, when does a child hit, who does he hit, where does the hitting take place, how often does the hitting occur?

- **Consequence** refers to a response that follows the behavior. In a functional behavioral assessment, a consequence does *not* refer to what a teacher does. A consequence is something that a child gets or avoids or escapes from because of the challenging behavior. For example, she might "get" the attention of the other children by interrupting group time or might "avoid" having to do something difficult or that frightens her with the challenging behavior. She might "escape from" learning activities in which she feels incompetent by whining so much that the teacher excuses her from the activity.

Understanding how consequences, the result of his behavior, influence a child will help you in dealing with challenging behavior. After we identify the function served by the whining or tattling, for example, we then actually influence or alter the consequence. For example, if tattling about another child gets him attention, then we can refuse to attend to tattling about others and we can react in a different way, thus sending a different message to the child. Instead, we can give attention for a more positive behavior, such as reporting on one's *own* behavior but not on anybody else's, or getting the teacher's attention as he works on a project.

**How to Collect ABC Data**    There are a number of ways to record observations, and what you need in ABC data collection are notes about a child's behavior. Therefore, anecdotal records would work very well for this purpose. There are a variety of ways to record anecdotal records—electronically, or with paper and pen, which would be the first choice. Usually, the recommendation for ABC data collection is a simple table like that in Figure 11.5 used for recording notes about Leo's interrupting. The cooperating teacher recorded these notes about Leo's interrupting a college student (CS) working in his classroom for a semester.

**How to Use the ABC Data**    Analyze the written information. Remember your ABCs.

**Antecedent.** Look for what predicts the challenging behavior (interrupting) in the antecedent column. CS was usually talking to or working with other children when Leo's challenging behavior popped up.

**FIGURE 11.5**    ABC Data Collection Form, Leo interrupts the college student (CS) intern

| Antecedent | Behavior | Consequence |
|---|---|---|
| CS showing new child to class how to wash table | Leo, "Teacher! Come see my blocks." | CS stops. Talks to Leo about his block structure |
| CS reading story to small group of children, including Leo | Leo interrupted another child who was answering CS's question | Group looked at Leo. Child answering question stopped talking. |
| CS giving instruction on fire drill following teacher's instruction to tell children to listen carefully | Leo interrupted with comment about the color of fire trucks | CS said, "Yes, they are red. You are correct!" |
| CS talking to a child who was hanging her coat in her cubby | Leo walked up to CS and child, "Can you read this book to me?" | CS turned to Leo, "Let me see the book, please." |
| CS helping child with coat | Leo walked up to CS, "I can't find my glove." | CS stopped what she was doing and to Leo, "Well, I'm working with Leana but let's look for it." |

**Behavior.** Review how the problem behavior shows up. Leo barges in and makes a request or a demand.

**Consequence.** Then, look and figure out what happens that maintains or keeps the behavior going. You will be determining the function or purpose of Leo's interrupting.

Ask, "Did Leo *avoid or escape* from something by interrupting? Did Leo *gain or get* something by interrupting?" Leo gained the college student's *attention* when he interrupted her and other children. One more question deals with how well the child's problem behavior "worked." How well did Leo's interrupting work? The CS responded by stopping what she was doing in every instance and attended to Leo's interruption: His challenging behavior worked extremely well. Now, you seem to have enough information to make an educated guess or hypothesis about the function served by Leo's interruptions. It is beneficial to actually write the statement, "The function or purpose of Leo's behavior, then, seems to be to gain or get something. He has been very successful at getting attention by interrupting."

# Supporting Positive Behavior

Use the analysis of the ABC data to deal with a challenging behavior. The hypothesis, your statement about the function of the child's behavior, hints at what will help the child to adopt a different approach.

*"The function or purpose of Leo's behavior seems to be to gain or get something. He has been very successful at getting attention by interrupting."*

So, Leo does get something by interrupting—attention. Use this information and ask, "Will it help Leo if I change something in the environment? Will it help Leo if I teach, or *re*-teach, him a different skill? What can I do to help Leo keep a more positive behavior going once he learns it?" Here is what the teacher did to support a positive behavior for Leo.

1. **Confer with college student:** The teacher meets regularly with the CS to evaluate the CS's progress. Today, the teacher talked with the CS about Leo's challenging behavior, which, as it turns out, has been bothering the CS. Teacher showed the ABC table to CS and they discussed the function of Leo's behavior. Teacher noted a need to move forward to supporting a more positive behavior for Leo.

2. **Change the environment:** Teacher and CS decided to give Leo attention at a better time, not when he interrupted. They are changing how the teachers act, are changing the environment so that it supports Leo. They asked Leo to pick something that he would like to do with CS during center time, and he chose a puzzle one day and writing with chalk for another day. His choices were recorded on a clipboard, which was placed on a hook in his cubby. When he came to school, CS or the teacher went over his choice for the day. This strategy gave him the undivided attention from CS that he craved.

3. **Re-teach a skill:** Leo needs to know how to get a teacher's attention but without interrupting. She used the turtle strategy, which Leo had learned already. It involved s-l-o-w-i-n-g down and thinking. If Leo, for instance, saw that CS was helping another child, then he was to be a s-l-o-w turtle and wait for CS to be done. He was to go back to an activity or to find something to do while he waited.

4. **Use a reminder, on-the-spot-guidance, for new or re-learned skill:** Teacher and CS did a role play during morning meeting to teach the "I'm busy right now. Please wait" hand signal. Using a doll that they placed in a chair at the puzzle table, the teacher sat next to the doll, working with the doll on the puzzle. CS approached, "Teacher, can you help me?" Teacher did not look at CS but kept talking to the doll and used the hand signal. CS said, "Oh, I need to be a s-l-o-w turtle and wait." CS bravely used the new reminder, on-the-spot-guidance, the first time Leo tried to interrupt and he stopped. He had remembered to stop.

## Reflect

**Reflection**
An active, intentional, problem-solving process; involves remembering an issue and then analyzing the memories

Willing **reflection** on our teaching practices is a professional disposition. Following up on a plan to support positive instead of challenging behavior gives information on whether the plan was effective. It is fairly simple and easy to follow up with additional ABC data gathering, which involves writing additional observations. You will quickly conclude that the support plan either did or did not help the child to change the challenging behavior. Make adjustments to the support plan if needed.

The whole FBA process is a systematic way to consider the purpose of a challenging behavior. It points to a way to support a child in adopting a positive behavior and dropping the challenging behavior. This might seem cold and clinical at first glance, but guiding children with FBA and supporting positive behavior can help children feel calm and focused as they get their needs met in a positive way.

In the next section, you will apply information on FBA and on supporting positive behavior to some of the more common challenging behaviors facing teachers.

## :: SPECIFIC CHALLENGING BEHAVIORS: APPLY YOUR KNOWLEDGE OF FUNCTIONAL BEHAVIOR ASSESSMENT

This section focuses on several challenging behaviors and follows the FBA process to help a child adopt a positive behavior in place of a challenging behavior. We have already gone through the FBA process with the challenging behavior of constant *interruptions* and are going to go through the entire FBA process with *two* more of the challenging behaviors. We will focus on *biting* and *teasing* by first giving an overview of the topic, then concentrating on determining the function of the behavior, then on supporting a new behavior, and finally on a brief reflection. This in-depth approach will be used for biting and teasing. Then, we will take a briefer approach for other topics—*aggressive behavior*, *whining and pestering*, and *tattling*. For these three challenging behaviors, we will look at topic overviews and ways to support new behaviors for those challenging behaviors.

## Biting

Topic Overview   Biting is an expected but unwelcome behavior in very young children and a major cause for concern among child-care teachers and parents. There are three functions that biting behavior usually serves: attention getting, communicating what they want, and expressing anger.

*Attention Getting.*   Very young babies begin to bite at the same time that they begin teething, usually near their first birthday. An infant might discover biting another person by accident, when she first good-naturedly mouths the skin and then sinks her teeth into the arm, shoulder, or breast of the person holding her, surprising the adult. How the adult reacts to this unintended playful event has a lot to do with whether the infant continues to bite. Some parents think that this first playful biting is cute, they laugh, and essentially tell the baby that it is okay to bite. A baby interprets this as a cool game and a way to get the adult's attention. There is no meanness involved at all on the baby's part.

*Communicating What They Want.*   Between 12 and 24 months, some but not all infants use biting as communication, a way to deal with frustration (babies can feel emotions). Unable to adequately use verbal skills to say and get what they want, usually from other young children, a 15-month-old is likely to bite the child to send the message. They do not intend harm and the biting is a way of saying, "I want that doll," for example.

*Expressing Anger.*   There is a point at which some toddlers adopt biting to express anger, and that occurs between 2 and 3 years of age. Some toddlers who have learned how strong an effect biting has on others now view biting as a weapon and bite intentionally to express angry feelings. They do not have the ability to understand and to regulate this strongest of human emotions.

**FIGURE 11.6**   ABC Data Collection Form, 1-year-old Tom's biting

| Antecedent | Behavior | Consequence |
|---|---|---|
| Morning: Dad brings Tom to child care; nuzzles him | Tom bit on Dad's nose. | Dad, "O-o-h!" and then tickles Tom. |
| Afternoon: Mom picks Tom up | Mom kisses Tom; Tom laughed and bit Mom's chin. | "Ouch! Let's go, silly boy!" Mom hugged Tom. |
| Morning: Mom dropped Tom off, said, "I love you." | Tom wiggled and smiled. Then he bit his mother's hand. | "You should not do that . . . come give Mommy a hug." |
| Teacher holding Tom and reading to him. | Tom leaned against teacher's arm, turned his head, and bit the teacher. | "Ow!" Teacher stopped reading. Tom put arms out (as if to be hugged). |
| Teacher changing Tom's diaper, starts to pick him up. | Tom bit teacher's hand. | "Not again!" (teacher). Tom gurgled and laughed. |

**Determine the Function, FBA**   Use FBA to determine the function that biting serves for a specific infant or toddler. First, look at the child's age. Collect ABC, antecedent, behavior, consequence data. Figure 11.6 shows an ABC data chart for a 1-year-old.

**Analyze the ABC Data**   (A) Antecedent: Parents have normal and pleasant interaction with Tom. (B) Behavior: Tom bit the parent as a part of the interaction. (C) Consequence: Parents smile, coo, tickle, and kiss Tom when he bites. Tom then begins to play the biting game with his teacher, who does *not* like it at all.

Write the statement, your guess or hypothesis, about what the infant is getting or avoiding with the biting, the function of the behavior. *"The function or purpose of Tom's behavior, biting, appears to be to gain adult attention and playful interaction."*

**Support New Behavior**   Even though we are dealing with very young children, our overall message is about the limit on biting, biting is *never* acceptable—for anybody. Children are not allowed to bite. *Adults are not allowed to bite, either. Never bite a child, no matter what you have been told or what you have seen. Never bite a child. Never.*

Dealing with biting depends on the function served by the biting—attention getting, communicating what they want, or expressing anger. For all functions, clearly state, "No biting." For teething and exploring, give children safe items to chew—a clean cloth or teething ring. For attention issues, focus on spending an enjoyable time together and prevent some of the more stressful interactions and offer something else to bite. For expressing anger or frustration, help children acquire a healthy approach to express feelings, such as using words to express anger: "Say, 'I want my doll back.'" You can also help very young children feel a healthy sense of control by giving age-appropriate choices. For example: "Do you want orange or grape juice?" "Would you rather play in the sand or with the paints?"

The function of Tom's behavior was to get adult attention and to play. "Will it help Tom if I change something in the environment? Will it help Tom if I teach, or *re*-teach, him a different skill? What can I do to help Tom keep a more positive behavior going once he learns it?" Here is what the teacher did to support a positive behavior for Tom.

1. Teach a new behavior: The teacher did *not* play with Tom when he bit her, never. She was clear about biting as *not* acceptable. She set a limit, kindly but firmly: "It's not okay to bite me. Here, bite this cloth." She knew that Tom would learn the new behavior but that it would take time.

2. Confer with parents: The teacher met with the parents and discussed biting. The teacher gave them a brief article on biting and emphasized that biting continues and causes problems for children in child care. She told them what she has decided to do. Tom's father said, "You know, I never thought about that."

3. Use a reminder, on-the-spot-guidance, for the new behavior: The teacher stopped Tom just as he was clamping down on her arm: "No biting. Here's your cloth. Bite the cloth." Teacher showed parents how to do the same thing. The main idea was to show affection to Tom and to play with him, but to tell him that biting was not allowed.

**Reflect**   This teacher had dealt with biting before and knew what to do. However, conferring with parents still made her nervous. She knew that helping Tom required her to work with his parents in teaching and maintaining a positive behavior and in stopping the biting. She stayed centered and calm, treating the parents as partners who were obviously in love with their child and who wanted the best for him. The teaching of the new behavior worked, as shown in additional ABC data.

# Teasing

**Topic Overview**   **Teasing** refers to verbal or nonverbal exchanges between children or between a child and an older person. Teasing can be a playful and affectionate thing between friends, with good-natured teasing bringing on good feelings all around. Teasing can also be mocking and spiteful, such as in name calling, ridicule, or insults. This is cruel teasing and damages the victim. Such insensitive teasing can then get even worse and become taunting, in which the teaser torments and harasses the victim (Freedman, 2002). This is aggression and bullying by teasing, a challenging behavior.

> **Teasing**
> Verbal or nonverbal exchanges between children or between a child and an older person; a form of aggression when the teaser intends to hurt the other person

We are interested in teasing as a challenging behavior in this chapter. Teasing is very common in early childhood and it easily turns into bullying (Freedman, 2002; Townsend-Butterworth, 2009). One group frequently taunted is overweight and obese youngsters. These children are teased by both children and adults and in several locations in school (Puhl, Peterson, & Leudicke, 2013). Hostile teasing is not some lighthearted thing but real cruelty that degrades and petrifies victims (Healthy Children.org, 2013). Violent outcomes of years of hostile teasing have been well documented in the past several years in public schools (Cornell & Scheithauer, 2011). A child who is humiliated very often reacts to his angry feelings by striking back at a teaser. Teasing serves many purposes:

**Awkward Way of Establishing a Friendship**   Some children, who would never tease in a hostile way, might use teasing type behavior to try to make a friend.

This is playful and lighthearted teasing, meant to establish a link or a friendship with someone a child likes. The teaser might not know any better way to approach the potential friend. Usually, this type of teasing is clearly not hostile, but the recipient's view of the situation is the important factor here. Some recipients of playful teasing will see it for that but others might be offended.

**Reflects Having Learned Teasing**   Some children have been teased (they were victims of teasing) or have observed teasing either in real life or on screen and are using what they have learned, as misguided as it is. In all likelihood, these teasers are not good at perspective taking, have poor emotional and social skills, and do not fully comprehend the effect of the teasing on a victim.

**Lack of Knowledge of Differences**   Understanding and accepting differences between groups prevents some teasing. Children who do not understand how people can be different might tease the other person. It is not unusual for a young child to note or to ask about differences that she notices. Asking a question out of natural curiosity, however, is different from making fun of a difference—teasing somebody because of a difference.

**Sense of Control**   Teasing somebody gives some children the attention that they crave. The attention is quite negative; however, attention is what they want, negative or positive. Teasing also gives them a sense of control, but this type of control is based on humiliating another person or animal. These children can learn a better and positive way to a feeling of personal control.

**Route to Peer Acceptance**   Humans have a need for relationships and acceptance. Some teasers find that joining with other children to tease a victim, either face-to-face or in cyberbullying, is a sure path to acceptance by peers who practice hostile teasing.

**Determine the Function, FBA**   Use FBA to determine the function that teasing serves for a specific child. Collect ABC, antecedent, behavior, consequence data. Figure 11.7 shows an ABC data chart for a third grade boy who teases a girl.

***Analyze the ABC Data.***   (A) Antecedent: John (the teaser) in situations where he makes contact with Sarah—for example, morning meeting, at their lockers, in the library. (B) Behavior: John asks question about her hair and then uses a nickname. (C) Consequences: Sarah's reactions were not hostile and she did not seem to be offended. Sarah was playful but somewhat assertive. John responded in a good-natured way.

Write the statement, your guess or hypothesis, about what John is getting or avoiding with the teasing, the function of the behavior. *"The function or purpose of John's behavior, teasing, appears to be to establish a friendship with Sarah."*

**Support New Behavior**   Dealing with teasing depends on the function served by the teasing—awkward way of establishing a friendship, having learned teasing, lack of knowledge of differences, sense of control, or route to peer acceptance. For teasers just trying to make a friend, observe the recipient's reaction. If the recipient has good

| FIGURE 11.7 | ABC Data Collection Form, John teases Sarah about her curly hair | |
| --- | --- | --- |
| **Antecedent** | **Behavior** | **Consequence** |
| Sarah and John, third graders, sat at a table in the discovery center. This was the first time they had met. | John looked over at Sarah and asked, "Why is your hair all fluffy? It's curly." | Sarah said, "I don't know. It just is." |
| John greeting Sarah at the lockers. | "Hi Curly Locks!" | Sarah looked at him, smiled, and punched him on the shoulder lightly, saying, "Curly Locks?! That's not my name." Her tone was lively. |
| Large group meeting in morning. John sidled up next to Sarah and sat down, glancing sideways at her, beaming. | John leaned over and whispered, "Hey, Curly." | Sarah sighed, smiled slightly, and said, "It's Sarah, not Curly," sighing again and patting John on the back. |
| Class was in library picking books for the week. | Sarah said to John, "It's okay to call me Curly sometimes." | John, "Sometimes Curly; sometimes Sarah." Sarah rolled her eyes and shook her head. |
| Greeting during morning meeting. Sarah greeting John, "Good morning, John" as they bumped fists. | John then greeted Sarah, "Good morning, Sarah." | Both children greeted each other in a friendly and relaxed way. |

social skills, she might see the teasing as playful and not be offended. If the recipient gets upset, then help the recipient be assertive and teach the playful teaser about other people's view of things.

If the teasing indicates lack of knowledge of differences, then focus on understanding that we are the same but we do have some differences. Set a limit on the teasing. For teasers imitating other teasers, set limits and teach about another person's feelings when they are teased. If the teasing's purpose is for a sense of control or to gain peer acceptance, then establish a clear rule of "no teasing" followed up with helping children be in control in a healthy way. For example, if the teaser has some special skill, such as being good in spelling, then have her help others with spelling practice but forbid teasing during the practice.

The function of John's behavior was a clumsy way of establishing a relationship with a potential friend. Does the teacher need to do anything in this case? Does she need to change something in the environment? Does she need to teach or re-teach John a different skill? Does the teacher need to help John keep a more positive behavior going once he learns it? Here is what the teacher did to support John's positive behavior.

1. The teacher reviewed the consequences on the ABC chart and noticed how well he listened to what Sarah said.
2. She spoke briefly with John, not in front of others, and simply said, "You know, John, I noticed that you and Sarah have become friends. I also noticed that you really listened to her when she said that her name was Sarah and not Curly. I think that she likes being your friend."

**Reflect**   This teacher has seen all kinds of teasing in the school. She wisely observed John and Sarah without interfering because she knew that John was not mean-spirited and she had never seen him tease anybody. She was surprised that Sarah handled things so well, discovering Sarah's skill in interpersonal relationships. Sarah seemed to understand John's motives. The teacher did quietly recognize John's willingness to listen to Sarah. Additional ABC data revealed that John did occasionally call Sarah "Curly" but always in a playful and friendly way, and Sarah accepted this nickname that he had invented for her. After all, he was now her friend.

## Aggressive Behavior (Hitting, Damaging or Destroying Things, Temper Tantrums)

**Aggressive behavior**

Hitting or other forms of fighting, and to damaging or destroying things

**Aggressive behavior** refers to hitting or other forms of fighting and to damaging or destroying things (American Academy of Pediatrics, 2013). Chapter 10 focused on aggression and bullying and Chapter 8 focused on teaching social emotional learning skills (SEL). Here, we will briefly focus on some of the reasons that children use aggressive behavior and then on how to support a more positive behavior. You would use the FBA process to determine the function of a specific child's aggressive behavior.

**Lack of Skills**   Some children use aggressive behavior because they do not have the social emotional skills needed to manage unpleasant feelings well. When they are frustrated or angry, for example, and do not know what to do, they often resort to hitting, fighting, or throwing objects. They might damage or destroy things, have temper tantrums, turn over furniture, or kick chairs or walls. Support positive behavior by setting a clear and unmistakable rule about treating people and things with respect. Then, teach the social emotional learning skills that the child lacks. Teach how to slow down and think about a different way to react to unpleasant feelings. Teach slow breathing to calm themselves and to focus. See Chapter 8 for a full discussion of this approach.

**Experiencing a Lot of Stress**   Some children do know how to control aggressive impulses and do so most of the time. However, these same children may backslide to aggressive behavior when they are under extreme stress, or when many stressors combine and they cannot handle the high level of stress. Support positive behavior by cushioning the effect of the child's stress. Make your classroom a peaceful and productive place. Make sure that you have established a good relationship with each child. Go over the rules for respectful treatment of people and animals. Acknowledge the child's stress and offer help in dealing with fiery feelings, but stress that damaging things or humiliating people or animals is not acceptable.

**Attention Getting**   Aggression is an extremely efficient, although unwise, way to get attention. Teachers and other children usually stop, attend to the uproar (for example, when a child tears through a room by overturning chairs), and even get involved in some way. Some children who resort to aggression are misguided about appropriate ways to get attention. Their thinking is not clear and they do not know how to get the attention which all children deserve and need. If attention getting is the function of the child's behavior, then support positive behavior by first firmly stating the limits about aggressive behavior, that throwing, kicking, or punching things is not allowed. Then, give these children attention for their work, for positive interactions, and for contributions to the life of the classroom.

## Whining and Pestering

Chang and Thompson (2011) defined whining and pestering as a *verbal temper tantrum*, a cousin to a full-blown screaming temper tantrum. Whining and pestering are particularly annoying to many adults. Children who whine and pester soon discover that their annoying and challenging behavior does work because adults will usually do anything to "turn off" the whiney voice and pestering ways. Whining and pestering show up for different reasons and serve different functions. Supporting positive behavior requires that we first of all get across the point that the whining and pestering are not going to work, that you will not meet the demands. Children need to know that they do not get everything that they want and that you will not listen to demands. Then, if you say "no," the child will accept "no." This is the hard part for some adults—saying no, meaning it, and sticking to it.

**Reaction to Being Tired or Under Stress**    Some children whine when they are exhausted or under stress, but usually not at other times. Children gradually acquire self-control and exhibit age-appropriate control over emotions and behavior under normal circumstances. Fatigue, however, diminishes their growing ability to control their emotions and behavior. Supporting positive behavior with a tired, whiney, pestering child focuses on getting the child some rest and helping her wind down. She does need to hear a firm "no" but, in this case, getting the child to rest is also important. She should not get the extra story or extra time at the computer or whatever else she is whining about.

**Child Has Worn People Down with His Whining**    Somebody has given in to whining and pestering with this child. One of the most powerful routes to strong tendencies to whine is to have been rewarded for whining and pestering. Some children in your class have used whining and pestering to wear their parents or grandparents down, and are now simply using what worked for them in the past. They will try their best to wear you down as well. The most potent type of reinforcer is an intermittent or irregularly given reward—that is, the child gets what she wants with whining some of the time but not quite all of the time. Supporting new behavior in this case requires never giving in to whining and pestering. A helpful approach is to state or restate the limit about whining: "No whining and no pestering. I will not listen to you when you whine." Acknowledge their request and give a *brief* reason for your decision: "Yes, you do want more time at the computer, but it's time for math." Then, ignore the child's whining and pestering. Do not argue. Do not keep explaining. Go on about your business. Expect a "bigger and better whine" before the child gets the message, but do not give in to the urge to engage in a battle of wills. It might help you if you remember that a basic principle of child guidance is to combine firmness with kindness and clarity. Kindness and being clear about not whining are not so difficult, but being firm with a previously rewarded whiney and pestering child is very hard.

## Tattling

"Teacher! Joanna spilled the markers and didn't put them all back." "Teacher! I saw John throw his coat on the floor." "Teacher! Jim called Henry an old poopy-pants." These statements are examples of tattling.

"Teacher, the gate is open," or "John's foot is caught in his trike's wheel," or "Teacher, I can't stop the water in the sink. The sink is full of water." These statements are not tattling. Instead, they all refer to issues of safety and we want children to tell us about safety issues. They deal with issues a child cannot handle on her own and we need to hear about these situations from children.

**Tattling**
Unnecessary reporting on the words, actions, and behaviors of others

**Tattling** refers to reporting on the words, actions, and behaviors of others. Tattling usually refers to unnecessary telling and, like whining and pestering, is time-consuming and irritating to teachers. Children are generally aware of the rules and how they are expected to behave. Many children go about the day fully aware of the rules and noticing when activities do not happen as they should, such as not putting all markers back in their containers or throwing a coat on the floor. Some children noticing these things report to the teacher. They tattle. They want to let a teacher know that they know the rules and that someone has broken one. Some children get a teacher's attention by tattling. It is their mistaken belief about how to get the validation, affirmation, and attention that all children need.

**Support Positive Behavior**   Teach a new skill to the whole class. Explain about telling about safety issues, that it is important to tell teachers about broken things, other children in danger, or when somebody might be hurt if they do not tell a teacher. Explain, with puppets, for example, the difference between telling about safety and tattling that would get somebody in trouble. Help a tattler remember the lesson. If a child tattles, say, "Yes, you know about putting things back if you spill them," or "Telling me that Jim belched is not a safety issue. Are you telling me to get Jim in trouble?" Furthermore, if an FBA with ABC data collection reveals that a child's tattling gets adult attention, then help the child learn to get due attention for other, more positive activities, such as her artwork, block building, story writing, physical prowess, ability to concentrate, or kindness to other children and animals.

---

:: *Question for Reflection*

---

## :: SUPPORTING INFANTS AND TODDLERS WITH CHALLENGING BEHAVIOR

When teachers think about challenging behaviors, they do not often think about infants and toddlers. Instead, we tend to concentrate our efforts on 3- through 8-year-old children. However, supporting the very youngest children's social emotional development is important because problems in this domain and in the child's behavior can have a lasting impact on his future development—for example how he views himself, how he gets along with others, how he deals with frustration, or even his level of aggression. Problems in a very young child's social emotional development often indicate future challenging behaviors that a teacher will identify. How can we support infants and toddlers with challenges to healthy social emotional development? How do we support them in preventing future challenging behaviors? The Center on the Social and Emotional Foundations for Early Learning offers excellent strategies (Fox, 2010).

All families need information on children's development, an example of primary- or first-level prevention of challenging behavior. Other families face many challenges, factors placing their infants and toddlers at greater risk for developing challenging behaviors. These families need not only child development information, but also second-level supportive monitoring and referral when that would help them, an example of secondary prevention of challenging behaviors. Some very young children, however, are already showing evidence of delayed social emotional development. This group of children and their parents may benefit from **focused intervention**, a third level of preventing challenging behaviors. Focused intervention is usually done by early intervention professionals trained to work specifically with families and very young children in their homes.

Elements of the focused intervention approach with very young children and their families include these elements:

- First, identifying whether the behavior is developmentally expected or if it is beyond what is expected for a child of this age. Is it so persistent or so intense that it seems to be out of a normal range?
- Familiarizing oneself with the child's developmental and medical status. Understanding the systems in which the child is nested—that is family, community, and culture—because these have an impact on an interventionist's understanding of a child's behavior.
- Concentrating on parent–child interaction when doing focused intervention with infants or toddlers. Parents need to know how to interact with very young children to help the child in coping with difficult situations and in dealing with routines; parents also need to know how to help facilitate a young child's social, emotional, and language development.
- Identifying what a parent of a very young child with delayed social emotional development might need help with and focusing on that. Helping the parent learn strategies that will allow the infant or toddler to feel less frustrated is essential. For example, a parent who finds it extremely frustrating dealing with a screaming infant while preparing a meal would welcome ideas on how to organize mealtime differently to prevent the screaming.
- Providing the information in as natural an environment as possible, such as a home or other setting in the community that would be comfortable. A formal office setting can be very threatening to parents.
- Concentrating on family-centered interventions that help parents gain skill and confidence in focusing on, for example, their baby or toddler's cues and facial expressions. Then, parents needs to know how to interact so that the child learns to solve problems, to begin to regulate her behavior, and to take the first steps toward expressing emotions differently. For example, a parent who has never noticed or has long ignored a baby's "wind up" to screaming, that screwing up and reddening of the face, will benefit from being taught about this emotional signal. The interventionist can then teach the parent to step in when he sees the signal or even before.

**Focused intervention**
Third level of preventing challenging behaviors and usually done by early intervention professionals trained to work with families and very young children in their homes

## SUMMARY

This chapter focused on challenging behavior in children. Some of the main ideas are the following:

- Whether a teacher sees a child's behavior as challenging depends on his or her perspective. We tend to label behavior as challenging when we think we cannot deal effectively with it.
- Challenging behaviors are the hot spots in classrooms, causing both child and teacher great concern. During hot spots, children feel anxious, angry, or afraid, and teachers often feel unpleasant emotions. Our goal is to minimize the hot spots and maximize the calm and cool times for children.
- Challenging behavior has different roots, making dealing with it very complex. However teachers can begin to understand challenging behavior by discerning whether it came about because of developmental characteristics, unmet needs, lack of skills, or factors in the classroom (contextual problems).

- All challenging behaviors have a purpose, serve a function. Functional behavioral assessment (FBA) enables teachers to figure out the function that a child's challenging behavior serves. ABC data is gathered and analyzed, yielding information on the function of the challenging behavior. Support for positive behavior can then be given.
- Specific challenging behaviors, such as interrupting, biting, teasing, aggressive behavior, whining and pestering, and tattling (as well as many other challenging behaviors), can be addressed by using FBA and supporting positive behaviors.
- When working with infants and toddlers with challenging behaviors, a focused intervention approach with very young children and their families is used.

## APPLY YOUR KNOWLEDGE

1. Jack's story occurred on the 35th day of the school year. The calm and cool times were slowly increasing. After reading this chapter, name three factors that you think most likely account for more calm and cool times in Jack's day.
2. Be prepared. Choose two or three challenging behaviors that you are likely to face in your classroom.

Search for reader-friendly, brief articles that you can use for your own reference and that you can hand out to parents. The articles should give accurate information about the roots of the challenging behavior and should give developmentally appropriate information for dealing with the behavior.

## WEBSITES

**Frank Porter Graham Child Development Institute, University of North Carolina at Chapel Hill**
http://www.fpg.unc.edu/

Find information on this site about the environmental rating scales described in this chapter by typing *environment rating scales* in the search box. This chapter described three of the four rating scales available from this site. The fourth rating scale is for family child-care centers.

**PBS Parents**
http://www.pbs.org/parents/

Main page for the site and an excellent site in general. You can access information about challenging behavior by typing *challenging behavior* in the search box.

# Apply Your Knowledge of Child Guidance

**Chapter 12** Apply Your Knowledge: Guiding Children during Routines and Transitions

This chapter gives you a chance to see that guiding children is an applied process. We use guidance throughout the day, such as in routines and transitions, as the example for practicing this applied process. In Chapter 12, we accentuate a teacher's role in supporting children during selected routines and transitions, including arrival and departure, large-group and small-group routines, as well as transitions. In previous chapters, you read about direct and indirect guidance. In this chapter, you will learn how to use both direct and indirect guidance during routines and transitions, a big part of every day at school. You will also learn how visual supports can help you guide children during routines and transitions.

**Chapter 13** Apply Your Knowledge: Use the Decision-Making Model of Child Guidance

In this last chapter, you come full circle: you will now *use* the decision-making model. This model advocates viewing discipline encounters merely as problems to be solved and argues for making active, conscious decisions about how to solve those problems. There are no quick fixes, no easy answers to some discipline encounters. By this point in the book, you should not be surprised to discover that there is no single right way to deal with any discipline encounter; there are many effective and positive approaches. You will get a chance to consider the eclectic approach, which draws from many theories and strategies. This chapter will also help you understand when to refer a child and family for outside help.

# CHAPTER 12

# Apply Your Knowledge

*Guiding Children during Routines and Transitions*

# Learning Outcomes

- Explain how visual supports can assist children in understanding transitions and routines
- Define terms associated with routines and transitions in an early childhood classroom
- List the major routines in a typical early childhood classroom
- Explain why it is important to plan for guidance in everyday routines such as arrival, departure, large group, small group, and during transitions
- State how specific planned transitions can benefit children's development and learning
- Explain how to use direct and indirect guidance to support children during routines
- Explain how to use direct and indirect guidance to support children during transitions

## VIGNETTES

### TODDLER: JOSEPH GOES HOME

*Joseph, 2½ years old, spied his father at the classroom door and squealed with delight. His father said, "Hey, Joey. Let's get your things. Mom is waiting for us." Joseph retrieved a painting from his locker and showed it to his father, "Look, blue!" After putting on his coat, father and son waved good-bye to the teacher and headed out the door, Joseph holding his father's hand and Dad asking about the painting.*

### PRESCHOOL: PRESCHOOLERS LEARN ABOUT SMALL GROUP

*Early in the school year, Mrs. Johnson sat with six children at a table. She was holding a magnet and passed it over a paper clip, picking up the metal item. "Hmm, what happened here?" (Discussion followed.) Then she said as she stood up to retrieve six small baskets, "I have a basket here for each of you. I will hand it to you. Look inside and then you can work with the magnet. You should use things in your own basket but not from anybody else's." (The children worked and discussed magnets for about 5 minutes.) Near the end of the activity, the teacher said, "It's time for outside, so put everything back into your basket." Then she gathered the baskets, sending each child to his or her cubby as he or she handed over the basket.*

### PRIMARY: TEACHERS GREET CHILDREN

*The principal, the assistant principal, and an assistant teacher stood outside the arrival door at school as the buses pulled up. Different teachers took turns greeting children; the principal always greeted the children, unless she was ill or out of town. The drivers opened the doors of the buses, and the children scurried down the steps and toward the entry. The principal and teachers waved and spoke quietly to children, "Remember to walk." "Hi Dave. How is the new puppy doing?" "Good to see you, Theresa." Jake gave a high five to the principal, who said, "Glad you're here, Jake. Have fun today." The children proceeded to their rooms, having been welcomed to a new day at school by adults who genuinely like and care about them. (Based on Freeman-Loftis, 2009)*

## :: INTRODUCTION

Teachers show respect for young children by using direct and indirect guidance throughout the day at school, for example, during routines and transitions. Indirect guidance, that is, well-designed classrooms, curriculum, activities, and materials, supports children's behavior. Direct guidance includes all the positive guidance strategies available to teachers, such as setting and maintaining limits, teaching appropriate behavior, and using redirection well. With the two types of guidance, we give children the information and support that they need for cooperative, kind, and compassionate behavior.

**Routine**

Part of a school day or a day in a school or center; the element occurs regularly, every day

**Transition**

The process of shifting from one part of a school day to another, or from one activity to another

This chapter targets **routines** and **transitions,** two of the regularly scheduled elements in a school day (Malefant, 2006). A **routine** is a regularly occurring, everyday part of the school day, such as arrival, group time, or departure. A **transition** refers to moving from one part of an activity to another or from one activity or part of the room to a different activity or location (Downs, Blagojevic, & Labas, 2006). Because routines such as large group, arrival, and departure are a part of the structure of every school day and because some transitions are essential and unavoidable, our goal should be to minimize time spent in transitions and to structure any routine activity so that we guide children effectively.

We will emphasize a teacher's role in supporting all children during selected routines and transitions. *All* means *all,* each and every child, including, for example, a child with an autism spectrum disorder or a child with hearing loss. Therefore, we will start by looking briefly at the usefulness of visual supports in routines and transitions. Then, we turn to the routines of arrival, departure, large group, and small group to learn about how to guide children effectively during these sections of the day. Finally, we will examine classroom transitions and how effective teachers teach all children about this part of their day.

## :: VISUAL SUPPORTS

The basis of any and all guidance decisions and in the materials that teachers provide for children should always be rooted in how young children develop and what they need to develop well.

**Child Development and Teacher Support**   Young children's development in self-control, social skill development, understanding themselves and other people, and managing stress on their own takes several years, occupying most of early childhood. In addition, the front part of a young child's brain is responsible for planning and self-control, and it takes all of childhood and into young adulthood for this section of the brain to be fully formed. Therefore, we can expect that all young children will need help with things such as learning to control impulses, switching from one activity to another, and planning or thinking through what they want to do. All young children need adult help with dealing with stress, and in a classroom this often means that an effective teacher minimizes children's exposure to unnecessary stress. Transitions are potentially stressful for all young children and become a real source of stress when there are too many transitions during the school day or when they are poorly done. Many children, including but not limited to those with autism spectrum disorders or hearing loss, will have additional challenges on top of their typical developmental needs and will need their teacher's support even more.

**Visual Supports Have a Part in Guiding Children**   There are many direct guidance strategies that teachers use in guiding children, including good limit setting and teaching children positive behaviors and social skills. Teachers have access to a large number of indirect guidance strategies and tools as well, including good room design. Environmental cues are also useful in supporting children, especially so during routines and transitions during a school day. An environment cue is a reminder to children about something needing to be done or remembered in the classroom, much like sticky notes that we adults use.

A **visual support** is such a cue and can be a drawing, photo, gesture, or something in print, such as a sign. Typical examples from early childhood settings include:

**Visual support**
Pictures, photographs, and drawings intended to help children remember the messages implied in the image

- Child's photo in her cubby
- Child's name printed on a card under her photo
- Illustrated hand-washing instructions above a sink
- Drawing of a classroom object, such as a chair, with the word for chair printed in the languages spoken by children in the class
- Emotions chart
- Drawing of blocks placed on the section of a shelf where children are expected to place the blocks after building with them

**Picture Schedules as a Visual Support**   This chapter centers on how to guide children during routines, such as the hand-washing chart over a sink. Visual supports are also a great way to help young children learn how to navigate essential classroom transitions. A particularly helpful visual support for the entire class is a picture schedule of a set of photos, drawings, or clip art depicting the daily schedule. Teachers use these to give a visual cue to children about the flow of the day, and it is difficult to state the importance of such a visual cue. Children have pictures telling them what comes next, and after that until they go home. This is very comforting and anxiety relieving for most young children.

When using picture schedules with young children, Blagojevic, Logue, Bennet-Armistead, Taylor, and Neal (2011) suggest that teachers make this visual cue sturdy by using card stock, laminating each item in the schedule, and attaching Velcro to the back. Children will then be able to work with the schedule easily. It is also important to use the exact words for an activity used by that class. Circle time, if called that in a class, should be labeled "circle time," for example. Teachers can also make the picture schedule most useful by actually using it, placing it where the children can readily interact with it and teaching children what the pictures mean. Examples would be: "This picture shows us all eating at the table. It is for snack time"; "This photo shows our playground and tells us that it is time to go outside to play."

**Use the Picture Schedule During Transitions**   Use the picture schedule to support all children during transitions, from one section of the schedule to another. In this case, you would concentrate, not on the whole set of pictures, but on two. For instance, if the children are moving from circle time to centers, take the photos of these two activities from the board. Focus the group on the circle time photo and then on the center photo. Indicate that they are going to move *from* circle time *to* centers. This is an effective strategy with young children because they do not tend to focus on changes from one state to another, but they gradually understand such change if teachers follow Vygotsky's (1978) theory and have very brief conversations with them about such changes.

In addition to teaching the entire class about transitions by using pictures from the picture schedule, consider making the picture schedule available to everyone throughout the day. Some children will enjoy using the schedule, either on their own or with their teacher's help, to spend more time "reading" the pictures and gaining understanding of how the day flows. A teacher might deliberately plan on working with small groups or individuals needing additional time understanding the schedule as a whole or with moving from one section of the day to another. Children gradually internalize the flow of the day and the concept of transitions from one activity to another when teachers directly teach them about the schedule and about transitions.

We now turn the focus to several classroom routines and to transitions. We will focus on three factors about each routine or transition:

- What children need during the routine or transition
- How to support children with *indirect* guidance during the routine or transition
- How to support children with *direct* guidance during the routine or transition

You will also have an opportunity to say how visual supports could be used effectively during the routine or transition.

**Arrival**
The start of the day at school when children enter the school grounds and their classroom

**Departure**
The routine dealing with leave taking; children exit their classrooms and the school grounds

## :: ARRIVAL AND DEPARTURE

**Arrival** is the beginning of a child's day at school. **Departure** is the time when a child finishes the day at school and goes home. Children go through these routines every day, and it is important that they understand how arrival and departure work. This understanding helps them to feel secure and sets the tone for the day or the tone for the afternoon and evening. A child first arrives at *school* and then arrives in his or her classroom. Arrival and departure are both very good times for building relationships with children. We can send warm and caring messages to children and their families by how we structure both routines.

How you structure arrival and departure depends on how children come to school. Some children, especially infants and toddlers and many preschool and kindergarten children, arrive or depart with one of their parents. Many children ride on buses. In some schools, children go directly to their classroom but in others, they go to a gym, cafeteria, or playground first. Then they go to classrooms with their whole class. Several different factors, therefore, affect decisions about structuring arrival. The same holds for departure.

## What Children Need during Arrival and Departure

Recalling Maslow and Erikson's theories, we can help children meet their needs for security and help them develop trust, autonomy, or initiative during arrival and departure or any other routine. We can build a trusting relationship through these everyday occurrences (Zero to Three, 2009). We support children by taking their perspective and thinking about what they need during arrival and departure.

- **Steps in the routine.** Children need to know the arrival and departure routines, the order of events, and where thing are located. Here is an example of an arrival routine: hang up coat and backpack, go into room, sign in, greet my teacher, say hello to my friends, pick a center, and start to play and work. Knowing what to expect during arrival or departure directly contributes to a feeling of security.
- **Expectations.** Children need to know the teacher's expectations for behavior during the routines that begin and end the day. For example, the child needs the answers to the following questions: Can I go to another center after I am done in one area? Do I have to let everybody play who wants to play in a center where I am working? Can I ask for something that I need? Do I have to take everything that I have in my cubby home with me? When do I line up for the bus?
- **Acknowledgment.** For arrival, all children need to know that the teacher recognizes that they have arrived, that they exist. They need their teacher to greet them warmly, in a low-key way. They also need the opportunity at arrival to greet others. They need a soft introduction to the day, even if arrival is used for instruction. Each child needs to hear the teacher say good-bye to them at departure.

## Indirect Guidance

**Arrival: Soft Landings**   The 10 kindergarten teachers in a very large elementary school had observed the negative effects of the school's mandated arrival process on their 5-year-olds. The children got off the buses and waited in the kindergarten gym, lined up in straight rows, sitting on the floor with their coats and backpacks. They waited until the principal made announcements over the loudspeaker. Then all the kindergarten children filed out of the gym and to their classrooms. By this time, there were usually many children crying, angry, or just plainly frustrated with the waiting.

The kindergarten teachers met with the principal and voiced their concerns. They proposed a new arrival strategy and called it *soft landings*, a good descriptor for their approach. The principal agreed to try the new approach for this age group, an approach in which children arrived by bus, not quite all at once, but within a

15-minute span. Therefore, the teachers needed a good way to get the children started on their day without having to wait for everyone. They also wanted arrival to benefit children and not waste their time.

In the new plan, children placed belongings in cubbies in the hall and came into the room. There, they found the learning centers set up for the day's activities. The teacher greeted children warmly, speaking quietly with each child, asking how he or she was. Then the children were free to go to a center of their choice. The teacher asked most children where they would like to start their day, thus giving support for decision making.

The teachers used indirect guidance by how they had set up the rooms for arrival. They also used indirect guidance by structuring the schedule to allow children to start their center time immediately after saying hello and checking in with the teacher. Children started on their learning activities and did not waste their time by having to wait for the other children.

This method was quite effective. The children seemed far less agitated. They also seemed to know and like the new routine, felt safe in making choices, and did not have to wait. They worked and played with others actively and enthusiastically. Even when children came to school upset about something, teachers reported that this arrival procedure gave them time with the adult so that they could deal with feelings as they started on their day. The atmosphere in all 10 classrooms was quiet and productive. By changing the arrival routine, the teachers had created a "respectful, supportive, and challenging learning environment," as recommended by the National Association for the Education of Young Children (2008).

**Departure: A Calm Ending**   Mr. Santini planned a brief large group just before the children went home. They reviewed the day and planned for the next day. Each child had prepared for departure before large group—gathering things needed for homework and for showing to parents, packing up backpacks, tidying up the classroom, and saying good-bye to the two classroom pets. Finally, they said a formal good-bye to another child. At morning meeting, each child greeted another child in the greeting section of the meeting. Mr. Santini liked the saying-good-bye ending to their day and the children seemed to like it, too. They were usually calm and reflective as they left for the bus.

## Direct Guidance

The kindergarten teachers and Mr. Santini used several of the guidance strategies explained in this book (see the Appendix for an overview of the strategies). Here are three examples:

- **Limit setting.** Children knew the routines and the limits. The teacher had spent time teaching the arrival and departure routines at the beginning of the year. This included setting and then reminding children about limits until everyone knew them. One of the kindergarten teachers restated limits about placing all of their belongings in their cubbies for a couple of the children.
- **Calming techniques.** At departure, during their brief meeting, Mr. Santini taught and then led the children in a calming and focusing exercise, just before

they said their formal good-bye to a friend. His goal was to help them make a psychological transition from their stimulating and busy day at school to the rest of their day at home.

- **Active listening.** One of the children was upset when she could not find the parent letter that she was supposed to take home. Mr. Santini identified the problem as belonging to the child, a strategy from Rogerian theory. Therefore, he used active listening to help her start the problem-solving process.

## :: FOCUS ON PRACTICE

This **Focus on Practice** activity is entitled *Transitions Affect Children's Development and Behavior*. As you complete this activity, you will see that the teacher has deliberately and intentionally planned the brief transition for the children. This strategy is a very effective way to help children learn self-control.

## :: LARGE GROUP

**Large group** refers to gatherings or meetings of all children, along with the teacher, at one time. They participate in a learning experience, all at the same time. Some teachers or programs, such as HighScope, call this *large-group circle time* (HighScope, 2009) or simply *circle time*. The Responsive Classroom model uses the term a *morning meeting* (Kriete, 2002).

Teachers use large groups for many purposes—for example, reflection on how the day went, reading stories, instruction in content areas such as math or science, talking with a guest speaker, dance, drama, or music. Recent research demonstrated that children could learn social skills when teachers embed the skills in a group time (Macy & Bricker, 2007). Some teachers schedule large group for the same time every day. Other teachers might call a large-group meeting to discuss a current topic or problem in their class.

Children benefit greatly from well-managed large-group experiences. They learn academic content, forge friendships, and learn how to be a member of a group. They also practice listening and speaking in a relaxed and natural setting, two important literacy components. Therefore, it is important that teachers learn to manage the large group so that it supports children's learning and development. Poorly managed large groups frustrate teachers, cause anxiety for children, inhibit learning, and often contribute to discipline and guidance problems.

## What Children Need during Large Group

Put your perspective taking ability to work when thinking about large group. As the teacher, you will have a goal for each group, and you are responsible for the tone and content of group time. Children will join in eagerly when they discover that gathering with everybody in class is an enjoyable experience. Think about your professional

**Large group**
Time when all children and the teacher meet; used for a variety of educational purposes

| FIGURE 12.1 | General structure for large groups |
| --- | --- |

**Three Main Parts of a Large Group**

**Beginning**

The starting point for the group.

Teacher gets group started as children arrive; does *not* wait until everyone is there.

The content varies with age group.

Use an attention-getting device such as a song, finger play, or poem.

Focus children's attention and then move smoothly into the main content.

**Middle**

The main content for the large-group time.

Varies, depending on children's needs, learning goals, and the content areas emphasized.

Children should be actively involved.

Directions to children should be clear.

Props make good additions.

**End**

The conclusion to the group time.

Two main purposes are to close the discussion on the topic and help children make a transition to their next activity.

Summarize content.

Do the transition to the next activity: Send individuals or very small groups to their next activity.

*Source:* Based on *Developmentally Appropriate Curriculum*, 5th edition, by M. Kostelnik, A. Soderman, and A. Whiren, 2010, Upper Saddle River, NJ: Pearson Merrill Prentice Hall.

role in managing the large group. What do you need to do to help children participate well? They most often will not know about your goal for learning in any specific group until you tell them, but they will trust you as the leader. Use Vygotsky's theory as a guide to scaffold their understanding of the large-group experience. To participate fully in the large group, children need specific knowledge about and skills in participating in large group.

- **Structure of large-group time.** Children need to know about the general organization of large group or flow of this routine. For example, what comes first, second, or third? How does large-group time start? Who talks first? Figure 12.1 shows the general structure for most large-group times. As with all routines, effective teachers actually teach children about large group at the beginning of the year.
- **Expectations.** Large group goes more smoothly when teachers help children understand expectations for this routine. Many groups fail because teachers forget to state expectations or do not state them clearly enough. Children feel much more secure about participating in large group once they understand the rules or limits.

  For example, teach about the signal for beginning a group. Teach children what to do when you give the signal. Teach about how to listen and respond, for example, to questions about a story. Teach large-group social skills, such as waiting for someone to finish speaking before asking a question or responding respectfully to another person's comment. Teach about the transition *out* of the large group. To do this effectively, think through any specific large group that you plan. Identify expectations that will support children's behavior during that particular meeting. You will discover that there are some limits common to all large groups. In addition, it is a very good idea to identify limits for new activities in large group, as Mrs. Johnson has done in the next example.

> **EXAMPLE**  Mrs. Johnson planned to teach a new song in large group, and it would require children to march in place and swing their arms. The children already knew about carpet squares signaling where to sit. For this new activity, the teacher decided to involve the children in thinking about a different limit for safety. After they were sitting, she said, "I have a new song for you, but you're going to have to move around. We are sitting close to each other. What can we do to make sure that everybody is safe?" The children decided that they should move their carpet squares farther apart.

- **Feedback.** Children need information on how they participate in large group. Observe carefully and acknowledge their effort and success in participating well. Mrs. Johnson said to the problem-solving 4-year-olds, "Good thinking. You have come up with a solution to the problem."

## Indirect Guidance

Use indirect guidance by setting up well for large group. Be deliberate and intentional in how you set up for the group. Some of the most essential considerations include the following:

- **Content worthy of children's time.** Well-chosen content, presented engagingly, supports children's behavior. Group-time content should be worthy of children's time. Mind-numbing drilling and reciting of information is disrespectful to children and *not* worthy of their time. The Responsive Classroom's Morning Meeting is an excellent example of a large group worthy of children's time (Kriete, 2002). The morning meeting has four parts and teachers can insert math, science, social studies, literacy, and the arts into the meeting.
- **Time.** Think about disastrous large groups that you have observed. One of the most common problems in such meetings is that the teacher has too long a group time. Effective and developmentally appropriate large groups for early childhood should last only about 10 minutes, or even less for the youngest children (High-Scope, 2009). The deciding factor, of course, is the age of the children.
- **Seating.** Decide on the best seating arrangement for each particular activity. Figure 12.2 shows several possible arrangements. Some questions to guide your thinking include the following: Will the children sit on the floor or in chairs? Do you need to be able to show an item to each child during the group time? Will some of the children come up to the front of the group? Are you reading a book that everyone should be able to see? Does a child need to be able to see the face of every other person in the group? Do the children need enough space for a movement activity?

| **FIGURE 12.2** | Different seating arrangements for large group |

**Cluster**

This arrangement works when children are supposed to stay in one spot during the group time. Children can sit farther apart if they will do any movement activities.

**Semicircle**

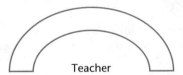

Use semicircle seating with children facing the teacher.

**Circle**

Many teachers prefer using a circle for large group.

The teacher sits in the circle with the children. Morning meetings take place in a circle. Many teachers like to sit on the floor with the children.

- **Arrange seating ahead of time.** This indirect guidance strategy gives a clear signal to children about where to sit. Carpet squares arranged in a semicircle in the large-group area signal children to sit in the semicircle. Children easily figure out the teacher's intention for seating if the teacher arranges the carpet squares in a cluster. Position yourself on the children's level. Sit in a chair if they are sitting on a chair or sit on the floor with them.
- **Materials.** Have *all* materials prepared before large group. Decide where to place the items. This type of preparation allows teachers to concentrate on the activity itself and on assessing children, not gathering materials.

> **EXAMPLE** Mrs. Johnson needed three items for the large-group story—the book, a puppet, and a basket filled with laminated cards with children's names. She placed all items in a box and behind her chair. She brought them out after the children sat down and sang an introductory song. The puppet came out of the box first to introduce the story. Then the teacher put the puppet back into the box and took out the book. She used the laminated name cards in the closing of the large group. She showed a card and the children read the name. The child whose name was shown went to the next activity.

Contrast her approach with that of another teacher, who set all the items on the floor in front of the children. He got upset when one of the children picked up the puppet during the story. Another child sifted through the cards, excitedly calling out names as he went. The teacher's frustration level increased as he kept telling children to put things down.

It is also important to practice ahead of time. Listen to and practice a new song, watch a DVD or video, practice reading a book. Mrs. Johnson, for instance, practiced a puppet play that she presented to the whole class. She discovered that she had difficulty with one of the puppets and decided to substitute another.

## Direct Guidance

Guide directly by using appropriate limits. Reflect on the limits needed for the particular large-group activity. Determine what you need to say to children to support their positive participation.

> **EXAMPLE** Mrs. Johnson reminded the children about a group-time limit. "Stay on your carpet square so that everybody can see the book."

Restate limits as needed, as one teacher did for Timothy when he scooted forward, blocking Serena's view. The teacher reminded Timothy, by saying, "Stay on your carpet square, Tim."

## :: SMALL GROUP

A **small group** refers to a gathering or meeting of only part of the total class, usually up to about six children plus the teacher. All participants in a small group participate in the same learning experience. Small groups take about 10 to 15 minutes to complete. Teachers use small groups with preschoolers, kindergarten, or primary grade

**Small group**
Time when a fraction of the entire class, about four to six children, meets with the teacher for a variety of educational experiences

children. Effective teachers use small groups to introduce children to concepts from any of the content areas (math, science, social studies, literacy, and the arts). Children tend to enjoy small groups because they work with other children in a relaxed learning environment and have a chance to socialize with others as they learn (Graves, 2007).

## What Children Need during Small Group

Children need the same things during small group that they needed in large group. They should understand the general structure of small groups. They need to know what their teacher expects of them in terms of behavior, and they need feedback.

- **Structure of small-group time.** Children need to know that their small-group meeting has a beginning, a middle, and an end. Effective teachers teach children how to navigate small groups at the beginning of the school year. Children need their teacher to be a guide and a facilitator for the small group. For example, children need to know that small groups occur in different places, depending on the learning goals. The teacher supports this understanding by telling children about different possible locations for small groups, such as specific tables, the block area, or the science area.
- **Expectations.** Tell children clearly what you expect when they are in small group. One of the functions of this type of group meeting is to provide social interaction for a small number of children. Children need to know about and how to practice social skills for interacting with only a few other children along with the teacher, which is different from the level of large-group participation. Communicate expectations for respectful and polite communication.
- **Acknowledgment and feedback.** Observe children carefully as they participate in small group. Acknowledge and encourage their positive participation. For example, "You held down the paper for Jerry, Sarah, so that he could write his name. That was a helpful thing to do." If the group met in a new location, acknowledge the children's flexibility.

## Indirect Guidance

Support children by arranging the small-group activity well. Pay attention to time, seating, location of the group, and materials.

- **Time.** As with large groups, small groups are much more effective if they are brief and engaging. Plan on about 10 to 15 minutes for small groups.
- **Seating.** Consider the specific small-group activity and decide whether children need chairs or whether the activity can be done while standing or sitting. In the chapter-opening preschool vignette, the children found six chairs at one table, indicating that they would be sitting. However, some of the children stood up, not using the chairs. Many of the examples of small group on the HighScope

website show teachers and children at tables, the children using chairs in some of the small groups and standing for others.

■ **Location.** Consider where the best location in the classroom might be for specific small groups. Many teachers designate a table for group. For other groups, the floor might be better. Some small groups take place outside the classroom, for example, when children explore the school and yard.

> EXAMPLE   Mr. Santini decided that the small-group math activity—sending small cars down a ramp, marking, and then graphing how far each went— would work best on the tile part of the floor.

> EXAMPLE   The assistant teacher in the kindergarten classroom took a small group to the yard, where they sketched and took photographs of the flowers blooming next to the entryway.

■ **Materials.** A major key to successful small groups is planning and preparing for the experience. One element of planning involves gathering *all* needed items. This helps teachers feel calmer about working with the small group. They are not running around gathering materials at the last moment.

> EXAMPLE   Mr. Santini planned the math activity with racing cars for Tuesday and Wednesday. On Monday afternoon, he gathered everything that he needed: cars, ramp, sheets of paper for graphing, markers, and tape for hanging the graphs. He also placed his digital camera with the materials because he planned to document the activity with photos.

## Direct Guidance

Use direct guidance to state expectations for behavior, such as limits on using only materials in one's own basket. After Mrs. Johnson noticed some of the children standing up as they worked with magnets, she said, "If it's easier for you to work standing up, you can just push you chair back a little." She wanted to give children the room that they needed, and she wanted to prevent tipping over chairs. The children readily complied with this simple suggestion. In the next example, the teacher sets and then gives sound reasons for limits.

> EXAMPLE   For the small group about racing cars and math, Mr. Santini said, "It's very important for our experiment that only one car at a time goes down the ramp. In addition, it is important to start every car at the exact same point on the ramp." Then he touched that starting point.

Choose specific direct guidance or discipline strategies based on the specific small group and the children's needs. For example, when two children squabbled over who was next at the ramp, Mr. Santini used the conflict resolution strategy.

---

:: *Question for Reflection*

---

## :: TRANSITIONS

Transitions are a necessary part of any early childhood program. Some examples of transitions include the following:

Changing from large group to the next activity.

Moving into large group.

Moving from small group back to center time.

Moving from one center to another.

Arriving at or departing from school.

Going from the classroom to work with a specialist.

Moving from the classroom to the gym, lunchroom, or playground.

It is good pedagogical, that is teaching, practice to plan transitions. Well-planned and wisely used transitions are comforting to children, helping them understand how to end one activity and start another, not something that children automatically know how to do. Unplanned transitions create great stress for children.

## :: FOCUS ON PRACTICE

This Focus on Practice activity is entitled *Teachers Plan Routines and Schedules*. Completing this activity will help you understand that well-planned transitions are clearly beneficial for young children.

## What Children Need during Transitions

Transitions are not an end in themselves, but they are part of the day. Children need as few transitions as possible, they need teachers to plan the necessary transitions, and they need to have transitions contribute to their development and learning.

- **As few transitions as possible.** A clear sign of a developmentally *inappropri-ate* classroom is an excessive number of transitions (Burts et al., 1992). While some transitions are necessary, others are *not*. Children need the teacher to reflect on the schedule, making sure that any transition is necessary. Teachers need to eliminate unnecessary transitions.

  **EXAMPLE OF *UNNECESSARY* TRANSITIONS**   A kindergarten teacher rotated children in centers, ringing a bell after 10 minutes. The bell told children that it was time to move to a different center, whether they wanted to or not. During the 1-hour center time, children experienced at least five transitions. Of course, there were numerous other transitions during the day at school. The teacher was puzzled about the amount of *disruptive behavior* (his term) during centers.

> **EXAMPLE** A different kindergarten teacher had the same amount of time scheduled for centers. However, the children chose the centers in which they wanted to work and plan. They went to a different center when they wanted to (a transition). The teacher found that most children worked in about two centers each day.

The second classroom has a more developmentally appropriate approach to centers and certainly to transitions. Children have some choice and control over their activities as they learn. Having a healthy sense of control is a part of positive self-esteem. Children in this room also have enough time to work and play long enough to try ideas, work productively with others, and redo activities if necessary. They do *not* have to stop one activity, move to another, gear up for something completely different, and try to act interested. The only time that they have a transition during centers is when they choose another center.

- **Transitions that have been *planned*.** Thoughtful, reflective, and effective teachers think through every aspect of their teaching, including transitions. Children need teachers not only to identify necessary transitions, but then to plan them. Mr. Santini, for example, planned the general procedure for each major transition one time and then used that plan every time he used the transition. However, he often used a different song, chant, or game. The basic structure of the transition was the same, which the children found reassuring.
- **Transitions that contribute to development and learning.** Consider the amount of time given to transitions. Here is an example. A teacher uses 1 minute to move children from morning meeting (large group) to the next activity. This happens two times each day, for a total of over 6 $\frac{1}{2}$ hours per school year moving from group to another activity. And this is only one transition. If you combine all the transitions in a school day, it quickly becomes apparent that they consume much time.

Transitions are not trivial. A teacher who manages time well and is committed to activities worthy of children's time strives to use children's transition time effectively. Children need transitions that contribute to their development and learning. Teachers can use transition time to help children meet state learning standards in the different content areas.

## Examples of Transitions

Figure 12.3 shows several examples of transitions and the Internet will give many others. You can use transitions not just to move children from one part of the day to the next, but also to foster development and learning. Transitions take time from instruction; therefore, it is a good idea to make a transition a part of your instructional plan. In Figure 12.3, read each transition idea. Then, reflect on how that transition might help a child learn something such as math or might foster his language development. Would the transition help the child develop a social skill, that is, a skill in interacting with others? Would the transition teach the child how to manage her emotions or to calm herself?

**FIGURE 12.3**    Examples of transition strategies

| Transition Idea | Has the teacher used a visual support in this transition? If yes, explain what it is. If not, then say how a visual support might have been used. | For each transition idea in the left column, state how this transition idea would benefit children's development or learning. (The first one is answered as an example). |
|---|---|---|
| Show cards, each with a different child's name. Children read the names and the child whose name is read can move to the next activity. Can also show two cards at one time. | | Benefits language arts, specifically reading. |
| Everyone in the group marches in place. Chant, "March in place . . . 1, 2, 3, 4, 5. Stop. John and Sharon, please go to your cubbies." "March in place. . . ." Continue until every child has left. Change the movement at another group time for variety. | | |
| Show a list of children's names. Say, "If you have a(n) ___ in your name, you can (go to snack or whatever the next activity is). | | |
| Take slow breaths: Move a whole group or a small group by helping them focus on the next activity. "We are all going to walk down to the cafeteria. Let's focus. Take in some air through your nose. Breathe in s-l-o-w-l-y. Hold the breath. Now, let it out through your mouth." | | |
| Roll a beach ball or other soft ball to a child in the group. That child goes to the next activity. | | |
| Say, "If your birthday is in the month of _____ (name the month), you may _____ (get your coat or whatever comes next). | | |
| Show a square of colored paper. Say, "If you are wearing _____ (blue, red, etc.), then you can go to snack." | | |
| Sing a song (tune: "This Is What I Can Do"). "If you're wearing red today, you can leave right now." | | |
| Show a circle (chalkboard, computer screen, or other method). Say, "Everybody draw a circle in the air." When the children are finished, say, " John, Duvall, Jenny, and Sam can get ready for____." Repeat with other shapes until everyone leaves. | | |

# :: FOCUS ON PRACTICE

This Focus on Practice activity is entitled *Schedules Affect Children's Behavior*. Planning schedules and routines has benefits for young children. As you complete this activity, you will learn how such planning helps children learn to cooperate and negotiate.

## Indirect Guidance

In the case of transitions, teachers use indirect guidance by using the least number of transitions possible, planning the necessary shifts in activity well, as you just read. Indirect guidance also includes having all materials for a transition ready before the teacher and the children need it.

> **EXAMPLE** Mrs. Johnson kept a wand that she used occasionally for transitions (for tapping the shoulder of the child who was supposed to move next with the wand) in the large-group area. She also keeps other transition items there—a basket of laminated name cards, a basket of colored squares of paper, and small alphabet cards.

Indirect guidance can also include giving children choices on occasion about which transition song or game to use.

## :: *Question for Reflection*

## Direct Guidance

There are several ways to use direct guidance during transitions. Think about direct guidance as teaching about the transitions and supporting children in participating cooperatively. Here are a few examples.

- **Set clear limits.** Be clear about the limits involved in transitions. For instance, if you use name cards as the transition aid, tell children that they can leave the group when they see their name. Remind those who forget.
- **Teach expected behavior.** For transitions, it is effective to teach about the general process of transitions during the first few days of school. Children like learning about how things work, including transitions, and they will feel more confident after learning the transition process. John Dewey (1938) advocated helping children learn that their individual actions affect others.

> **EXAMPLE** Mr. Santini taught the process for transition from playground back to the classroom, including placing soccer balls in the large basket. He led a brief discussion about why they should store the balls out of the way. One of the girls thought that others could have trouble finding the soccer balls if they were left to roll around the playground.

## ANALYZE A VIGNETTE

Refer to the chapter-opening vignettes to answer the following questions.

1. **Toddler:** How has the teacher supported Joseph and his parents with *indirect* guidance during the departure routine?

2. **Preschool:** Explain how the teacher has supported the children with both indirect and direct guidance.

3. **Primary:** Explain how this arrival routine supports children with *indirect* guidance.

## SUMMARY

Routines and transitions are a necessary part of a school day. They are not an end in themselves, but they are part of the fabric of a child's day. They should have a real reason for existing. For all routines and transitions, even for the necessary and unavoidable ones, we should:

- Use children's time wisely.
- Reflect on how routines and transitions are done, changing them when we discover that they really do not benefit children.
- Keep in mind that routines and transitions are meant to support children's learning and development, not to waste children's time and *not* to be used as filler time.

We support children during routines and transitions by:

- Using children's needs as the foundation for developing each routine or transition.
- Having as few transitions as possible.
- Making sure that each necessary transition benefits children's development and learning.
- Planning routines and transitions.
- Supporting children during routines and transitions with direct and indirect guidance.

## APPLY YOUR KNOWLEDGE

1. Visit the Visual Supports Learning Links and Visuals Templates web page, located at www.ccids.umaine.edu/resources/ec/visual-supports. Develop a visual support for one of the routines described in the chapter.

2. Hand washing is an essential routine and is part of other routines. Explain how you would use *indirect* guidance to support children's learning about hand washing.

3. Explain how you would use *direct* guidance during the hand-washing routine. Use the Appendix as a reference. To get you started, how would you use the direct guidance strategy of setting limits to support children? How could you use direct instruction to teach about hand-washing?

## WEBSITES

***Zero to Three***
http://www.zerotothree.org

A nonprofit organization based at Harvard, Zero to Three focuses on the well-being of infants and toddlers. Reliable and accurate information and excellent resources.

***New Horizon Montessori School***
http://home.earthlink.net/~aletaledendecker/newhorizonmontessorischool/index.html

Home page for this school based on the theory of Maria Montessori. Click on the link *typical day* to see the schedule for the school day. Each segment of the schedule details how teachers support children in the routines and transitions inherent in the program.

***Center for Community Inclusion and Disability Studies***
www.ccids.umaine.edu/resources/ec/visual-supports

Source from the University of Maine for different types of help in developing visual supports.

# CHAPTER 13

# Apply Your Knowledge

*Use the Decision-Making Model
of Child Guidance*

## Learning Outcomes

- Review the decision-making model of child guidance
- Explain each of the four major steps in the decision-making model of child guidance
- Use the decision-making model in everyday discipline encounters
- Use the decision-making model with challenge behavior
- Use the decision-making model to make contextual changes
- Use the decision-making model to change an adult's practices
- Use the decision-making model to change the context and change the teacher's own practices
- Use the decision-making model to write a guidance plan intended to support a child
- Summarize positive outcomes for children when teachers with an authoritative caregiving style use the decision-making model of guidance
- Summarize guidelines for knowing when to refer a child or family to outside resources

---

| VIGNETTE |
|---|

### WHAT SHOULD WE DO ABOUT THE CURSING?

*Mr. Santini is Jake's first-grade teacher as well as the cooperating teacher for student teachers Anne and Sean. The teachers are discussing the day's events.*

*Mr. Santini said, "Okay, you've both noticed that Jake curses."*

*"I suggest time-out," responded Anne.*

*"His father curses, too. I've heard it. Like father, like son!" added Sean.*

*"Could be, but let's avoid blaming," said Mr. Santini. "This is only a problem, so let's do some decision making. Jake is 6 years old and to him, !*!#! is just another word that he has heard. All I want is for Jake to know that there are different words that he can use in school to express his feelings. So I want you to think about who really has a problem here—Jake or us?"*

*"Jake, of course!" sputtered Anne.*

*"Think about that, Anne. What would the P.E.T. [parent effectiveness training] people say?" asked the teacher.*

*"Let me think," said Anne. "Oh, yeah. Figure out who owns the problem. They would probably say that I'm the one with the problem because I get upset when he curses."*

*Mr. Santini. "Probably. So let's help Jake find a different way to say what he feels." He gave each student teacher a list of guidance strategies. "Let's review some guidance strategies," he said. "Do you think we've made it clear that cursing is not permitted here?"*

*"We've never really talked about it at all," responded Sean, "and we probably need to state a limit about cursing."*

*"You might be right. Does that sound okay to you, Anne?"* responded Mr. Santini. She nods. *"Okay, limit setting is our first item. Now, what do you think Jake gets from us when he curses?"*

*"Our attention!"* said Anne. *"We all laugh."*

Mr. Santini said, *"Attention for inappropriate behavior. What can we do instead?"*

Anne looks over the list. *"Use substitution; let's give him a different word to use as a substitute and then encourage him for using the new word."*

*"Good. Substitution and encouragement is item number two in the plan. What if he forgets or even tests our limit and substitution?"* asked Mr. Santini.

*"Sounds like you don't want to use time-out,"* said Sean.

*"Right,"* said Mr. Santini. *"I just don't like using punishment, and anyway, limit setting and noticing the more acceptable word will work in the long run."*

Anne said, *"I think that we should all just stick to the limit and the substitution and not get all upset if he forgets or tests."*

Mr. Santini responded, *"I agree. We should change ourselves a bit. Item number three in our guidance plan is to be calm and restate substitution. Let's stop with three ideas and review the plan that we've made."*

Set limits.

Use substitution.

Calmly restate the limits and substitution, if needed.

*"We'll evaluate it in two days at the next staff meeting. I like how we made this decision."*

## :: INTRODUCTION

Sean, Anne, and Mr. Santini faced a typical guidance or discipline encounter and solved it by making deliberate and intentional decisions, by using the decision-making model of child guidance. Notice that they thought things through carefully. You will apply your knowledge in this chapter by systematically using the four steps of the model.

This chapter will give you an opportunity to practice making decisions just as Sean and Anne have done with support from Mr. Santini, who has scaffolded their learning about child guidance decisions. We will review the decision-making process briefly. Then, we will focus on *using* decision making for four different categories of guidance problems. Finally, we will explore the issue of referring children for outside resources and study a set of guidelines for referral.

## :: DECISION-MAKING MODEL OF CHILD GUIDANCE

The **decision-making model of child guidance** is a process. We use it to construct decisions about how to handle a variety of guidance issues with children. This model focuses exclusively on arriving at a developmentally appropriate solution in a logical and clearheaded way. You will avoid being caught up in emotion when faced with a discipline encounter.

**Decision-making model of child guidance**
Four-step process for making choices about dealing with many different types of guidance issues

# Knowledge, Skills, and Respect:
# The Basis of the Decision-Making Model

Making good decisions about discipline or guidance is more than just common sense. Making good decisions about guidance is not something that people do automatically. Early childhood professionals realize that they have to learn how to make good decisions about guidance, to learn and practice the strategies. Those who use the decision-making model successfully:

Possess a specific knowledge base about guidance.

Have specific child guidance skills.

Respect all children and all families.

**Knowledge Base about Guidance**   A good knowledge base about guidance helps adults use the decision-making model effectively. The most essential knowledge needed is information about how children develop. Understanding what children are like at different ages helps teachers clarify their expectations of children. Adults also need information about how a child's family and culture affect her development and behavior.

### EXAMPLES

Is it reasonable to expect a 6-month-old infant to stop crying just because someone tells him to stop?

How empathic can you expect an abused toddler to be?

How difficult is it for 3-year-old children to wait in line for the next activity?

How likely is it that a 4-year-old whose dad curses will say the same words?

What effect might witnessing a drive-by shooting have on a 6-year-old?

Are kindergarten children able to understand emotions well enough to manage them responsibly on their own?

Are third-grade children able to understand emotions well enough to manage them responsibly on their own?

Will an aggressive preschool child outgrow her aggression by the time he is 6 or 7 years old?

How likely is it that an 8-year-old child whose parents are permissive will willingly follow classroom rules and limits?

A person who can answer these and other similar developmental questions possesses one of the key elements in using the decision-making model, a knowledge base about guidance.

**Skills**   A professional who uses the decision-making model effectively also possesses specific child guidance skills. He can use any one of a variety of developmentally appropriate child guidance strategies. He has the skills to manage the layout of the classroom well and to manage the schedule, curriculum, activities, and materials. He understands current special topics in child guidance, such as self-esteem, bullying, or stress, and has the skills to help children deal with these issues.

**Respect for Children and Families**   Professionals who have a deep-rooted respect for children and families are most likely to use the decision-making model well. A person who does not respect children and families and is not culturally competent will have a great deal of difficulty with child guidance.

Professionals using the decision-making model competently understand that they, the adults, have greater responsibility in any interaction between them and children of any age to recognize signals that children of different ages send. For instance, a child who loudly interrupts would undoubtedly annoy many adults, but it is up to the adult to figure out whether this child needs social skills training, limit setting, and/or a different way of getting adult attention. The adult has to understand that it is her responsibility to ponder the problem and think it through. Here is an example from Mr. Santini's first-grade class.

> **EXAMPLE**   Mr. Santini understands that Jake's cursing is an example of imitation, but is also probably an attempt to be recognized. Irritating? Yes. However, the teacher understands that it is up to him to recognize Jake's attention seeking. He also knows that only he, the adult, can control how he responds to this discipline encounter. He knows that Jake plays a big part in this interaction, but he also knows that he, the adult, has the greatest share of responsibility for deciding how to handle the situation.

Decision making requires a great deal of active involvement. For example, Mr. Santini made an active, conscious, responsible choice about how best to help Jake. He did not just use the first strategy that popped into his head. He did not have an automatic reaction; he had to work at finding a solution. He deliberately walked the student teachers through the systematic process of choosing a strategy. He has encouraged them to recognize their responsibility for choosing the adult behavior most likely to help Jake at this time—that is, to choose individually appropriate strategies. Choosing adult behavior also means consciously rejecting certain strategies that do not fit one's personal philosophy of guidance, as Mr. Santini rejected the time-out strategy.

---

**:: *Question for Reflection***

---

# Eclectic—One Strategy Does Not Fit All

Teachers using an **eclectic approach** select what appears to be the best from several different methods and theories. Mr. Santini, Sean, and Anne reviewed many strategies before making their final decision. They chose the strategies that would be best for Jake at this time. They also changed their own practices. Tailoring a guidance plan to a specific child's needs is the hallmark of the eclectic approach to decision making. They avoided the one-strategy-fits-all model; they did not automatically put Jake in time-out when he cursed. Instead, they thought about what might be best for Jake. They actively rejected a punishment because there is a great potential for harm when using such an approach (see Figure 13.1).

**Eclectic approach**
Guiding children with the best ideas from different theories and strategies

| **FIGURE 13.1** | An *eclectic* approach: What does it mean? |
|---|---|

An eclectic approach does *not* mean "go with the flow" or "do whatever works."

**An eclectic approach requires:**
- Understanding different theoretical approaches, not just one.
- Adults to justify choices in a logical fashion and not defensively.
- Skill with many different guidance strategies.
- A willingness to change the setting or context.

**An eclectic approach implies:**
- That no single approach is appropriate for every child.
- A willingness to examine and change one's own practices.
- That children exist in several different systems (peer, family, school, community, culture).

## Different Children, Different Families Call for an Eclectic Approach

This text is about working with real children in the real and complex world. Typical discipline encounters, such as cursing, are relatively easy to handle. We all face such encounters, regardless of where we teach. Examples include children who wiggle around during group time, children who do not clean up after themselves, or those who exclude somebody from a group. They also include children who grab items from others or who impulsively blurt out answers. It would be foolish to think that an adult could possibly prevent all discipline encounters. It is healthier and more

The decision-making model can be used with children of different ages.

productive to acknowledge that you will run up against many everyday discipline encounters and that you must work to deal with them.

Some children, unfortunately, live under conditions that make it difficult for them to learn appropriate behavior. They present teachers with discipline encounters that are tougher to deal with and challenge us as we guide them. They exhibit difficult or challenging behavior. Examples include the following:

Children who are abused or neglected.

Children whose families move frequently.

Children whose families live in poverty—real poverty.

Children who live in drug-infested areas.

Children whose neighborhoods ring with the noise of gunfire.

Children who live in permissive homes.

Children whose parents model anger, aggression, and lack of empathy.

Children whose parents are self-centered and ignore their children, in spite of having enough money and resources to care for them.

Children who have a diagnosable mental illness (only a qualified professional can diagnose this type of problem).

When you have your own classroom, you will be energized (exhausted on occasion!) by the often confusing, sometimes exasperating, wildly wonderful differences that make each child truly unique. You will meet a new group of individuals every year that you teach—children, yes, but individuals first. Children in your room will be living in the United States, most immersed in the U.S. culture and all exposed to it through the media. The children will have different ethnic backgrounds, and their race will have an impact on how they and their families have experienced life and how they view it. Consider just two examples. You might have a child in your class whose family has lived in the United States for three generations but who observes many of the customs of their Chinese heritage. Another child, born in the United States, might have an African father and a mother who is from Korea, but the parents are now both U.S. citizens.

Each child in your class has a unique family system. Every child, whether an infant or a 9-year-old, whatever his heritage, has a basic style or temperament and a rich personal history of interactions that have taught him how to exist in this large world. Children all come from different families, each with its own scripts and rules, its own communication style, its own cultural history, its own view of how children should behave, and its own style of discipline (Christian, 2006).

Some children have parents who feel secure, who understand children and children's needs. These parents know how to communicate legitimate rules and limits and how to help children live within limits. They know how to demonstrate their love and respect to their children.

Other children have parents who perhaps never felt cherished themselves and who cannot, as adults, meet their children's needs for nurturance and security. These parents do not understand how infants and children develop, how they express their anger, or how to take their children's perspective. They lack empathy for their children; they might well be irritable. Often, these parents have very poor and ineffective child guidance skills; for example, they do not know how to set limits effectively or how to help children accept limits. These parents do not know how to demonstrate the love that they feel for their children.

Authoritative teachers realize that the children with whom they work truly are individuals, which is the best reason for adopting as flexible an approach to guiding children as possible. The decision-making model is an individualized, personal model that allows you to determine the course of action most beneficial for a specific child in specific circumstances. The decision-making model is eclectic—flexible—because it draws from many different ideas about children and guidance. The decision-making model provides the means for you to combine your knowledge and personal strengths to deal more effectively with issues facing individual children. You will be using the decision-making model in this chapter to deal with a variety of problems, including:

Everyday discipline encounters.

More difficult behavior and issues.

The need to change the context or setting in some way.

The need for a teacher to examine her own practices.

## :: STEPS IN THE DECISION-MAKING MODEL

There are four major steps in the decision-making model. The process starts with observation and proceeds to making a decision and then to acting. The process concludes with reflection. See Figure 13.2. Use the steps in the decision-making model to analyze the chapter-opening vignette.

## :: USING THE DECISION-MAKING MODEL IN EVERYDAY DISCIPLINE ENCOUNTERS

The purpose of the rest of this chapter is to help you pull together your knowledge from this textbook and use it to practice the decision-making model of child guidance. You will use the model to deal with the following:

- Everyday discipline encounters.
- More difficult behavior.
- Contextual issues, matters related to the setting.
- Situations in which teachers must change their own practices.

### Outdoor Cleanup Time

This is an example of a normal, everyday discipline encounter. It is time for your kindergartners to go inside for story time, and you notice that Adam and Aziz have left the trucks on the path again instead of putting them in the spot designated for

| FIGURE 13.2 | Four steps in the decision-making model of child guidance |
| --- | --- |

**Observe**

- **Observe the child's behavior.**
- **Focus on the encounter as a problem to be solved.**

  Clearly identify the problem. Decide whether the child or the adult "owns the problem." Focus on solving the problem, not on blaming the child.

- **Examine the "context" of the problem.**

  Ask how the child's age might be affecting her behavior. Ask how the child's family; culture; or the classroom physical environment, activities, or materials have contributed to the problem. The purpose is not to place blame, but simply to get a better picture of the context or setting in which the behavior evolved.

**Decide**

Your observation will tell you what to change. For example, you might need to:

- **Choose a guidance strategy.**

  Use only developmentally appropriate strategies, not punishment. Consult the list of guidance strategies in the Appendix. You would choose a strategy and state why the chosen strategy is appropriate for this child at this time.

- **Change the context.**

  You might decide that you have to change the classroom physical environment or the time schedule.

You might decide that you should choose more developmentally appropriate activities or that materials need to be better organized.

- **Change your own practices.**

  You might decide that you should change something that you are doing. For instance, you might decide to talk with children about playground rules after you realize that you have never set the limits. Do you need to restate a limit? Do you need to lower your voice when talking to a child who has done something inappropriate? Do you need to ignore a child's arguing or sulking about a limit instead of getting angry and fighting with the child?

**Take Action**

- Carry out the guidance strategy, or
- make the contextual change, or
- change the practice that you want to change.

**Reflect**

Think about how things went after you made a change. Specify what went well. State why you think events turned out well. Are there some factors that you still need to change? Why? If you want to make another change, go through this four-step process again to refine your approach.

---

trucks. You and the staff have stated the limits clearly and positively. You have also easily accessible parking spots for the trucks. Adam's parents are permissive by choice and do not set limits. Aziz follows Adam's lead.

## Use the Steps in the Decision-Making Model

1. Observe:
   a. What is the problem?
   b. Whose problem is it—Adam's, Aziz's, Adam's and Aziz's, or yours? Justify your response.
   c. Examine the context of the problem. What is it about Adam's background that is probably contributing heavily to this encounter? How does Aziz's personality contribute to the encounter?
2. Decide, and
3. Plan on Taking Action:
   In this case, the teachers do not have to change the context. They have set up the truck parking very well. They also do not have to change their own practices very much. This encounter calls for choosing a guidance strategy that will help

both Adam and Aziz. Several guidance strategies will help you deal with this encounter effectively. Here are some ideas to get you started.

a. You have effectively stated the limit. Explain why restating the limit is individually appropriate, especially for Adam, who has never had to follow limits, and for Aziz, who follows Adam's lead. Write the exact words you would use to restate the limit.

b. Explain how you could use an I-message (Rogerian approach) to help Adam and Aziz understand your position. Write the I-message, including all three elements (see the Appendix).

c. Explain how you can give helpful feedback to encourage the boys when they do cooperate. Write out the exact statements that you would use. Kohn (2001) makes a very good case when he gives five reasons to stop saying "Good job!" Try to avoid mindless praise as much as possible and, instead, express genuine appreciation for their effort.

d. Explain how you would use scaffolding, from Vygotsky's theory (1978), to help Adam and Aziz. Write a brief statement outlining your plan for scaffolding their understanding of the need to put items away.

e. Explain why punishment, such as time or response cost, is not an appropriate choice in this case.

f. Explain why ignoring this problem is also not appropriate in this case.

4. Reflect:
   a. Which strategy do you feel most comfortable using?
   b. From my perspective, the most effective strategy would be _____.
   c. I deliberately chose not to _____ (name the rejected strategy) because _____.

---

∷ *Question for Reflection*

---

This **video** shows a class making the transition from outdoor to indoor play on a very hot day. Notice how the children's teacher helps the children make the transition by using the decision-making model of child guidance. Notice how the teacher uses each of the four steps of this model.

## ∷ USING THE DECISION-MAKING MODEL WITH CHALLENGING BEHAVIOR

### Smashing Pumpkins in a Primary Classroom

This is an example of how to use the decision-making model when you confront what you perceive as challenging behavior. You are a third-grade teacher. Some of the class, including Kobe and Murphy, are working on a project about pumpkins, the interest having arisen after they read a newspaper story about a farmer growing a very large pumpkin.

Both Kobe and Murphy are famous for their temper outbursts, and you keep a close watch on them. They were working together writing a "newspaper story" about their decorated pumpkins when you heard them start to yell at each other. You were on your way to their workstation when Murphy picked up Kobe's pumpkin and slammed it to the floor, jumped on it, and smashed it to bits. Kobe responded by grabbing the pumpkin that Murphy had decorated.

You said firmly but quietly, "Put the pumpkin down, Kobe. Do it now."

Kobe glared at you and, saying nothing, threw the pumpkin at the wall, smashing it into a slimy mess.

This is an anger-management issue. Many people would consider this challenging and/or difficult behavior because of the aggressive throwing of the pumpkin and glaring at the teacher, seemingly defiantly.

## Using the Steps in the Decision-Making Model

1. Observe:
   a. What is the problem?
   b. Whose problem is it: Kobe's, Murphy's, Kobe's and Murphy's, or yours?
   c. Examine the context of the problem. These are 8-year-old children whose families use harsh discipline and whose lives are chaotic. Kobe is a neglected child, and the human services department is working with his parents. You have been focusing on anger management with both boys, but they occasionally forget your lessons, like today.
2. Decide, and
3. Plan on Taking Action:
   In this case, you will need to make decisions about two issues. First, how will you deal with your own anger about this incident? Second, which guidance strategies will enable you to help Kobe and Murphy with their anger?
   a. You will probably be angry, or at least surprised, immediately after this encounter. How will you get your emotions in check before dealing directly with Kobe and Murphy? State exactly what you would do for yourself.
   b. You realize that this a hot time, with anger flaring. It is not the time to preach or admonish. This is the time to talk, firmly of course but also kindly, with the boys. You do need to be firm, but this does not mean that you should be harsh. Your teacher-directed conversation fits in with Vygotsky's theory (1978) by using teacher–child conversation and scaffolding of the children's understanding. Before you start, decide whether you would separate the children before you talk to them. Why or why not?
   c. What will you say to each child? What will you say if one of them tries to deflect the topic by accusing the other boy? How will you get him to focus only on his own behavior and reaction to the situation?
   d. How do you think you might follow up this incident; for example, the next day, when the boys have both cooled down a bit? This might be a good time to carry out another anger-management activity by scaffolding. Describe at least two things that you can do.
   e. Why is it highly inappropriate to force the boys to apologize to each other?

f. Why is it highly inappropriate to use punishment, such as time-out or taking away recess?

g. Why is it also inappropriate to ignore this incident?

4. Reflect:

a. Which strategy do you feel most comfortable using?

b. From my perspective, the most effective strategy would be _____.

c. I deliberately chose not to use _____ (name the rejected strategy) because _____.

## :: USING THE DECISION-MAKING MODEL TO MAKE CONTEXTUAL CHANGES

### A Preschool Classroom: Keep the Sand in the Pan, Please

You are the head teacher of a group of 4-year-olds. They are interested in writing, and you provide many materials for their use. Today, in addition to all the usual writing materials, you have placed two shallow cookie sheets (with half-inch sides) of dry sand on the table in the writing center. The table is in the carpeted area and when any sand falls onto the floor, it sinks into the carpet.

This was an appropriate activity, with almost all the children using the sand trays to print their names or to print other letters. Nevertheless, you are getting frustrated with having to restate the limit so often, reminding the children "Please keep the sand in the tray." The children unintentionally knocked sand out of the trays and onto the table and floor, which you have to vacuum.

#### Using the Steps in the Decision-Making Model

1. Observe:

a. What is the problem?

b. Whose problem is it: the children's or yours?

c. Examine the context, the setting, of the problem. You see sand spilling out of the tray. How might a 4-year-old child's motor development affect how she uses and moves dry sand around in a large tray the size of a cookie sheet? How has your setup of this activity affected the amount of sand flipped out of the trays (trays with very low sides are on the table; the table is on the carpet).

2. Decide, and

3. Plan on Taking Action:

You have used a good guidance strategy already by stating and then restating the limit of "keeping sand in the pan." Therefore, the solution seems to lie elsewhere, meaning that you do not necessarily need to choose another guidance strategy. You could do so, of course, but there is a better solution.

Simply restating the limit, "Keep the sand in the tray, please," does not seem to be enough. Consider the benefits of changing something about the setting (the context) to be effective.

a. You are using dry sand. How can you safely make the sand itself more stable and less prone to flying up and over the edge of the pan?

b. You decide to continue with the dry sand, fully realizing that your 4-year-olds will probably continue flipping it out of the pans. Consider changing the situation by moving the table aside for a moment and placing a large sheet under the table. Then replace the table; gently flick any sand that spills to the center, under the table. At cleanup, gather the edges of the sheet and pick up the spilled sand. How do you think that this simple change in context would affect the situation?

c. What else can you do about the pans themselves?

d. Do you have to use the pans at all? Can you think of a different place or piece of equipment for this writing activity? What limits would you still need?

4. Reflect:

a. Which strategy would you feel most comfortable using?

b. The contextual change that I think would work best is _____.

c. I do not think that _____ would be very effective. My reason is _____.

## :: USING THE DECISION-MAKING MODEL TO CHANGE AN ADULT'S PRACTICES

### Liam and the Math Workbook

In this scenario, a teacher needs to change her own practices. Liam is in kindergarten, and his teacher uses many developmentally inappropriate practices. For instance, she uses workbooks in three curriculum areas every day. She has set up the curriculum so that every child is doing the same workbook pages in a large group in each curriculum area. Today, for example, all the 5-year-olds are doing page 54 in the math workbook.

Liam dreads these workbook sessions. He sat at his rectangular table with six other children, his workbook and pencil in front of him.

"Alright, everybody! Turn to page 54," called out his teacher. She waited only briefly before issuing the next command. "Pick up those pencils and put your fingers on question 1."

Liam blinked but opened his workbook. He cautiously turned pages, all the while looking at the other children, most of whom had found the correct page. He said nothing but dipped his head a little lower.

"Liam," called the teacher. "Pick up that pencil and get to work!"

Liam picked up his pencil and stared at the page. He bit his lip, as he often did when under stress.

"Get to work right now, Liam!" The teacher seemed irritated.

Liam squeezed his pencil and looked desperately at the book belonging to the child next to him.

"Don't look at my book, Liam," whispered the child.

Liam turned his head back to his own, incorrect page. He sat still, gripping his pencil, a tear forming in the corner of his eye.

Use the Steps in the Decision-Making Model

1. Observe:
   a. What is the problem?
   b. Whose problem is it—Liam's, the teacher's, or both?
   c. Examine the context of the problem. How do you think that the teaching strategy causes Liam's confusion and distress? The teaching strategy consists of using workbooks, and the whole group sitting for direct instruction, all working on the same pages, for several hours each day.
2. Decide, and
3. Plan on Taking Action:
   In this case, the root of the problem is in her instructional style, which is utterly inappropriate and which has directly caused the problem. Liam has done nothing wrong. The teacher needs to change her own practices in order to help Liam.
   a. Describe this teacher's instructional style. For example, does she encourage active, hands-on learning or does she discourage it? Does she use large-group direct instruction? Does she use workbook pages for kindergarten children?
   b. State how you think that the teacher's method of talking with the children, especially how she issues commands, might be affecting Liam.
   c. What does this teacher need to change about her method of talking with the children?
4. Reflect:
   a. Earlier in this chapter, you read that adults who use the decision-making model of child guidance effectively have an abiding respect for children. What is your opinion of the teacher's degree of respect for her kindergartners? On what do you base your opinion?
   b. Suppose that this teacher goes to a workshop and learns about a more developmentally appropriate way of teaching children. On a scale of 1 to 10 ("1" means that she will not adopt better practices; "10" means that there is a very good chance she will change her style of instruction), how likely is it that she will adopt more appropriate practices because of attending such a workshop? State your reasons for your choice.

## :: USING THE DECISION-MAKING MODEL TO CHANGE THE CONTEXT *AND* CHANGE THE TEACHER'S OWN PRACTICES

### A Third-Grade Classroom: Joseph and Chloe Will Not "Sit Still" During the Last Large-Group Lesson

This example demonstrates that problems are complex and that we often need to change a couple of factors, not just one. The teacher in the following scenario needs to change both her own practices and the context in which the children work. She has mistakenly focused on punishing Joseph and Chloe instead of looking at other factors contributing to the problem.

A third-grade teacher was upset because she had ordered Joseph and Chloe to go to time-out yet again during her last large-group lesson before lunch. This problem occurs every morning. Here is the morning schedule for this third grade:

Opening group—30 minutes

Reading groups—30 minutes

Seatwork, workbook pages for different curriculum areas each day—30 minutes

Specialist (music, guidance counselor, art, or physical education)—40 minutes (always large group)

Large group—20 minutes (before playground time)—(the trouble spot for Joseph and Chloe)

## Using the Steps in the Decision-Making Model

1. Observe:
   a. What is the problem?
   b. Whose problem is it: Joseph's and Chloe's, or the teacher's?
   c. Examine the context of the problem. How long are these third-graders spending in group work, whether large-group or smaller groups, every morning? Are the teacher's instructional methods (everything done as a total group, use of workbook pages for every curriculum area, strict division of curriculum into areas) developmentally appropriate? How do you think that all of this might affect Joseph and Chloe's ability to sit through yet another group lesson at the end of every morning?
2. Decide, and
3. Plan on Taking Action:
   This teacher needs to change her own practices. Time-out, a form of punishment, is an inappropriate strategy. Help her understand that her schedule and her instructional methods are the root of the problem. What would you say to her to make her aware of this problem? Remember to be forthright but kind when you tell her. Hearing this type of information often arouses anxiety. People get defensive if they feel attacked.
4. Reflect:
   a. If you could make only two changes in the schedule, what would they be?
   b. Time-out—punishing Joseph and Chloe—was not an appropriate guidance strategy. It has backfired and actually had the opposite effect from what the teacher intended; it seems to have made things worse for Joseph, Chloe, and the teacher. How is this so?

## :: DEVELOP GUIDANCE PLANS

You will use the decision-making method to develop a **guidance plan**, a written document. It is your roadmap for supporting children. Appropriate guidance plans based on clear thinking and good decision making empower you to deal effectively with a variety of guidance or discipline encounters—the typical as well as those that are more challenging. It is very helpful if you write your plan and file it in a child's

**Guidance plan**
Written document based on the process that is part of the decision-making model; outlines how a teacher will support a child

personal file. You can then refer to the plan when reflecting on the child's progress and on any changes that you need to make in your classroom, curriculum, teaching strategies, or way of interacting with children.

Guidance plans grow out of the decision-making model's process. The plans are brief, and they distill all of your thinking during the process. You can do some good observation in the decision-making process. You can write your main findings in the guidance plan. If, for example, you found that your schedule was a bit too long, then you would say that. If you found that you were ignoring a child whose behavior irritated you, then you would record that.

After you have observed the context, you can observe the child and figure out the purpose of her behavior. Record your main finding in the designated space. Figure 13.3a is an example of a blank guidance plan form. See Figure 13.3b for what Mr. Santini wrote in Jake's guidance plan—after going through the decision-making process.

## :: DECIDING ABOUT REFERRING A CHILD AND FAMILY FOR OUTSIDE HELP

Effective early childhood teachers reflect on their own practice so that they can promote positive outcomes for each child in their classes. Applying the decision-making model as explained in this chapter will help you give children the support that they need for social emotional health. The use of positive guidance and good decision making supports teachers in preventing major problems or in minimizing existing problems for children in social and emotional development. On occasion, a teacher who reflects on a situation will conclude that she does not have the knowledge or

| **FIGURE 13.3a** | Guidance plan format |
|---|---|

Guidance Plan
**Date:**
**Child:**
**Behavior:**

**Observation:** Observations revealed the following about the physical environment, curriculum, schedule, my teaching strategies, my interactions with the child or children:


**Observation:** Answering the five "W" questions about the child's behavior reveals that the purpose or function of his or her behavior seems to be:


**What I need to do:** Based on observations, the most significant things that I can do to support this child are:


**Continuing to support the child:** What do I need to do to continue to support the child after she or he learns a different way of behaving?

---

**FIGURE 13.3b**    Filled-out guidance plan for Jake

Guidance Plan

**Date:** *September 20*

**Child:** *Jake*

**Behavior:** *Cursing*

**Observation:** Observations revealed the following about the physical environment, curriculum, schedule, my teaching strategies, my interactions with the child or children:
*We laugh nearly every time Jake curses—we have reinforced this behavior.*
*Jake's father models cursing.*

**Observation:** Answering the five "W" questions about the child's behavior reveals that the purpose or function of his or her behavior seems to be:
*Jake's cursing is simply a part of Jake's way of talking and does not seem to be malicious; he seems to be simply imitating a model.*
*He now seeks our reaction.*

**What I need to do:** Based on observations, the most significant things that I can do to support this child are:
*Change our reaction to the cursing; stop laughing.*
*Set a limit about cursing.*
*Use "substitution."*

**Continuing to support the child:** What do I need to do to continue to support the child after she or he learns a different way of behaving?
*Do not laugh or react when/if Jake tries again to get attention with cursing.*
*Calmly restate the limit and substitution if needed.*

Next, you would decide, based on your observations, on supportive actions that you can take to support the child. Record your brief statement. Finally, think about how you will help the child continue using the appropriate behavior, and record your idea.

---

skills needed to help a child. In such a case, a wise and reflective teacher will decide that she needs to refer a family or a child for services outside of the school setting (CSEFEL, 2008). Some of those times include the following. We will emphasize, though, guidelines for referring a child whose behavior calls for outside help, when his teachers do not have the expertise to help without such outside assistance.

**Child Abuse and Neglect**    Each state has a child abuse law that sets forth legal requirements for dealing with child abuse and neglect. Teachers are mandated reporters in these laws, meaning that they are required to make a report when they suspect that a child shows physical and or behavioral signs of abuse or neglect. Reports go to the outside agency, such as a social services department, designated by the law to receive and investigate such reports. It is the outside agency that makes a decision about whether child abuse or neglect has indeed occurred and the types of services needed to keep the child safe and to assist families.

**Special Education Services**    The Individuals with Disabilities Act (IDEA) has clear guidelines for referring children for special education services. School administrators and special education teachers have the knowledge and expertise to assist regular education teachers in identifying children in need of assessment and then in need of special education services. Teachers work with the team charged with testing and planning for a child's special education services. Merino and Gaytan (2012), discuss problems with the overreferring of Latino children to special education for behavioral and emotional difficulties. They attribute this in part to the cultural clash of teachers who are not Latino and who do not understand the culture from which the children come. Referrals to special education must be made with the whole child in mind and that includes understanding the child's culture.

**Problem Behaviors Beyond the Expertise of a Teacher** A teacher who understands child development and child guidance can deal with many different types of behaviors on his own or by collaborating with other teachers. Even normally challenging behaviors, as described in this book, can be dealt with by a teacher who uses the decision-making model. Teachers, however, see many child behaviors that are fundamentally different from, more puzzling than, and much more difficult to deal with than the issues presented in this chapter. This is when a teacher needs to consult with other professionals with specialized knowledge and skills that a child or family needs.

Therefore, we need to have the wisdom to know the difference between behaviors that we can and cannot deal with on our own. Here are some examples of when to seek help from outside and when to refer children for outside resources (CSEFEL, n.d.).

- **Medical issue.** Some children have medical conditions that bring on or trigger challenging behavior. CSEFEL's example was of a child banging his head on things when he had an ear infection. In this case, the child would benefit greatly from a medical examination and diagnosis. Teachers could also do a thorough behavioral assessment by completing a functional assessment available at the CSEFEL website (http://csefel.vanderbilt.edu/modules-archive/module3a/4.pdf).

- **Family system challenges.** Other children's difficult-to-deal-with challenging behavior is triggered in a family system confronted with problems seemingly beyond their ability to cope with on their own. In this case, a child's school, including the teacher, its administrators, guidance counselor or psychologists, or other professionals work together to refer families to appropriate agencies. For example, a homeless family faces multiple challenges and needs help from a variety of outside resources. If we believe in following Maslow's advice, then helping a family get to the right agency can help them solve some of their problems. Such support assists parents in once again in carrying out different aspects of their parenting role. This, in turn, will help a child in this family and who is in our class to feel safe and secure, one of a child's most basic needs.

- **Behavior continues.** It is disheartening to observe a child's extremely challenging behavior continue in spite of a well thought out decision and in spite of using guidance appropriate for this child. Suppose that Kobe and Murphy's anger did not subside despite your plan arrived at through the decision-making model. A teacher might then decide to consult a professional specializing in doing a thorough functional behavior assessment. The outside professional could help the teacher identify the functions that the child's challenging behavior serves. Then, the teacher could work with the outside professional to devise a plan to support the child.

## :: COMING FULL CIRCLE: AUTHORITATIVE CAREGIVING AND THE DECISION-MAKING MODEL BENEFITS CHILDREN'S DEVELOPMENT

If you started reading this text with Chapter 1, you learned about different styles of caregiving. We will come full circle and end this book by stating what is very likely to happen if you do decide to adopt the authoritative style of caregiving. Authoritative parents and teachers believe that they must create a safe and secure emotional climate for children. They realize that they influence, but do not determine, a child's behavior. By using the decision-making model of child guidance, you will set the stage for many positive outcomes. Using the decision-making model helps children:

- Feel safe and secure
- Develop healthy self-esteem and a strong moral compass
- Honor and respect themselves and others
- Develop healthy self-control
- Learn how to deal with a variety of stressors
- Understand and deal effectively with a variety of feelings: anger, sadness, love, jealousy, disappointment etc.
- Walk a mile in another person's shoes—or an animal's tracks—to be empathic
- Be cooperative, helpful, and generous
- Learn when to be assertive
- Become self-responsible
- Become compassionate and caring individuals

## ANALYZE A VIGNETTE

Use Figure 13.2, the steps in the decision-making model, to evaluate how Mr. Santini and the student teachers applied the decision-making model of child guidance.

1. Describe how Mr. Santini, Sean, and Anne carried out each step. What leads you to think that they observed Jake's behavior? Identify evidence that they viewed the issue simply as a problem to be solved. Who did and who did not—at first? How and when did they examine the context of the problem?
2. Explain what the group decided to do to help Jake. They chose specific guidance strategies. Did they

also decide to change the context? If they did, how were they going to do this? Did they decide to change their own practices? If they did, explain. When did they plan to take action and reflect on their decisions?
3. Name one or two things that you might have done differently. From your perspective, how likely is it that the teachers will deal effectively with this typical discipline encounter? State the reasons for your view.

## SUMMARY

We can use the decision-making model of child guidance to get information and to make deliberate decisions aimed at supporting children. This model gives teachers an eclectic approach for supporting children. The building blocks of this process include the following:

- A knowledge base about guidance
- Specific child guidance skills
- Respect for families and children

The four steps in the decision-making model include observe, decide, take action, and reflect. We can use this process for a variety of guidance or discipline encounters, including:

- Everyday discipline encounters
- More difficult behavior
- Contextual issues, matters related to the setting
- Situations in which teachers must change their own practices

After using the decision-making process, a teacher develops a written guidance plan, a guide for supporting the child. This plan is a logical outgrowth of the decision-making process. Some challenging behaviors call for teachers referring children and families to outside resources. These behaviors include those for which a teacher does not have the expertise to handle on his own.

## APPLY YOUR KNOWLEDGE

### Self-Test: Create a Guidance Plan

Use Figure 13.2 to write a guidance plan for at least three of the following discipline encounters. Go through the steps, just as you did for the discipline encounters that you practiced in this chapter.

- An abused toddler bites other children.
- Five-year-olds in a multiple-age group get younger children to do inappropriate things, such as swearing or throwing objects.
- Third graders push and shove each other while waiting in line for the school bus. They have been waiting for 20 minutes.

- Three- to 5-year-olds push other children while changing activities, such as going outdoors.
- A 4-year-old spits at other people.
- A 4-year-old comes from a family that consistently uses physical discipline such as hitting and pinching. This same 4-year-old hits the teacher when the teacher tries to use even a positive strategy such as restating a limit.
- A 7-year-old tattles several times each day.
- Third graders deface library books.

## WEBSITES

**Scientific American**
http://www.scientificamerican.com/

Organization devoted to publishing information about science. This chapter of your textbook explains the decision-making model of child guidance. You can read a brief article on how making tough decisions affects your brain on the *Scientific American* website by typing *making tough decisions* in the search box. Look for an article, "Tough Choices: How Making Decisions Tires Your Brain."

**Center on the Social and Emotional Foundations for Early Learning (CSEFEL)**
http://csefel.vanderbilt.edu/about.html

Organization focused on providing information about supporting children's social and emotional development. CSEFEL uses research to develop evidence-based practices. There are a large number of practical resources at this website that teachers can use in their guidance work with young children and their families.

# Appendix

## Review: Major Positive Discipline Strategies

This Appendix reviews the major positive discipline strategies described in this text. First, you will read a list of the major strategies. Then each strategy is presented in outline form, along with suggestions of points to remember and to avoid when using the strategy. Every strategy outlined here is described in more detail in other chapters.

## LIST OF MAJOR STRATEGIES

1. Help children save face and preserve their dignity.
2. Set limits well.
3. Teach more helpful behavior.
4. Set up practice sessions and give on-the-spot guidance.
5. Give signals or cues for newly constructed behavior.
6. Change something about a context or setting.
7. Identify problem ownership.
8. Give meaningful feedback to children.
9. Identify mistaken goals and use encouragement.
10. Ignore behavior (only when it is appropriate to do so).
11. Redirect very young children: Divert and distract.
12. Redirect older children: Use substitution.
13. Listen actively.
14. Deliver I-messages.
15. Teach conflict resolution (problem solving).
16. Recognize signs of stress, anxiety, or strong emotion; prevent overstimulation; teach calming techniques.
17. Manage strong emotions responsibly.

## 1. Help Children Save Face and Preserve Their Dignity

*Purpose of the strategy:* To treat children respectfully no matter what positive strategy is used. Children are likely to feel embarrassed in spite of well-done positive guidance.

*How can adults do this?*

- Show respect for children by taking their perspective. Think about how you would want somebody to handle matters if they had just told you to calm down or that you had done something wrong.
- Once you are finished with the positive discipline strategy, let the episode fade into the past and allow the child to move on. Avoid the urge to keep explaining.
- Do not flaunt your power. Avoid saying "I told you so."
- End the interaction quickly, simply, and gracefully. Quietly tell the child, especially if you've helped her calm down, "Let's go back and play now."
- Help the child deal with the root of the upset. Some children might be ready to talk about an emotion-arousing incident, but others need to wait before discussing it. Either way, schedule a time for talking about the original problem with the child. Do what is developmentally appropriate for this child at this time.

## 2. Set Limits Well

*Purposes of the strategy:* State expectations for desired behavior. Clarify boundaries or limits.

*Appropriate limits:* Never arbitrary, limits focus on important matters and are developmentally appropriate.

*Points to remember about stating limits:*

- Involve children in developing some limits in a classroom or other setting.
- Tune in, help children focus on the task, and give good cues.
- Speak naturally but slowly enough so that a child hears the limit clearly.
- Use concrete words and short, natural, and normal sentences. For example, "It's time to put the teacups away."
- Tell a child exactly what to do, for example, "Take small bites of your bread."
- Be as positive as possible.
- Give choices when appropriate.
- Give short, clear, fair reasons for limits.
- Issue only one or two suggestions at a time.
- Give children enough time to carry out the limit or to complete something else before they carry out the limit.
- Restate limits appropriately. Restate limits when it is necessary to do so.

*Avoid the following when stating limits:*

- Avoid giving choices when children really do not have a choice. For example, "Do you want to go to the library?" when the whole class goes to the library.
- Avoid giving a chain of limits.
- Avoid using cute reasons. For example, avoid saying "I think that the teacups want to be put away now." This makes a teacher sound silly.
- Avoid telling children only what not to do. For example, "Don't take such big bites of your bread!"

- Avoid vague limits. For example, "I'm not sure you should be doing that."
- Avoid stating arbitrary or trivial limits. Avoid arguing or playing the "why game" about limits.
- Avoid complex or excessive reasoning about limits.

## 3. Teach More Helpful Behavior

*Purposes of the strategy:* Teach helpful behaviors. For example, using words to express anger. Adults must pinpoint the more helpful behavior.

*Method used:* Several methods can be used. With young children, modeling is effective (demonstrating desired behavior, such as hand washing and table manners; social skills, such as introducing oneself; using words instead of hitting to express anger).

*Steps in teaching more helpful behavior:*

- Observe the child to figure out what it is that he needs to know.
- Identify the behavior causing problems for the child, for example, whining.
- Identify a skill that would be more helpful for the child, for example, asking for items in a normal voice.
- Model more appropriate behavior, for example, model a normal voice for the child.

## 4. Set Up Practice Sessions and Give On-the-Spot Guidance

*Purpose of the strategy:* To give the child a chance to practice a newly learned skill with expert guidance (from the adult or from a more skilled child).

*How to do this:*

- Teach the new skill first, for example, using a normal voice instead of whining.
- Practice the skill with the child. Do this privately if he has just learned the skill, for example, let him ask you for something in a normal voice.
- Give appropriate feedback. For example, tell the child that he seems to know how to use a normal voice when asking for something, or give him hints on how to demonstrate the skill if he makes mistakes in practice.
- Observe the child as he works with other children. Be ready to give on-the-spot guidance if it is needed. For example, Jessie starts to whine when he wants to paint and you step in to say, "Remember, Jessie, use your normal voice for asking." These reminders from you, the expert, are essential in helping a child strengthen a newly learned skill.

## 5. Give Signals or Cues for Newly Constructed Behavior

*Purpose of the strategy:* To help children remember to use the appropriate behavior, part of effective on-the-spot guidance.

*Steps in giving signals or cues:*

- Identify the skill for which you will use a signal or cue, for example, asking for something in a normal voice.
- Figure out what would be a logical signal, such as a quiet verbal reminder, for example, "Normal voice, please," or a hand signal.
- Observe the child to discover when the appropriate skill should be used, for example, asking to join other children.
- Whenever possible, give the signal just before the new behavior should occur and not after the child has forgotten, for example, just before the child asks for something.

## 6. Change Something about a Context or Setting

*Purpose of the strategy:* Figure out what you can do about a situation that will help a child be safe or to enable the child to use a more helpful behavior.

*Ways to change something about a situation:*

- Change the physical environment or time schedule.
- Increase options available to a child: prevent predictable problems, introduce new ideas, introduce new materials.
- Decrease options available to a child: limit choices, change activities.

## 7. Identify Problem Ownership

*Purpose of the strategy:* Determine whether an adult or a child has a problem so that appropriate follow-up can be used.

- When an adult owns a problem: Use strategies focusing on self-responsible, non-accusatory skills, such as I-messages, restating reasonable limits.
- When a child owns a problem: The child's needs are the ones thwarted. Use active listening.

## 8. Give Meaningful Feedback to Children

*Purpose of the strategy:* Give the child helpful information. Feedback is critical to constructing skills and competencies. Good feedback can also help children make changes.

*Suggestions for giving meaningful feedback:*

- Avoid empty praise as feedback. Phrases such as "Good job!" are empty praise.
- Give positive feedback and suggestions for change when appropriate.
- Give positive unconditional feedback, positive information independent of anything the child has done. One example, "I like being your coach."
- Express appreciation, meaningful positive feedback directly related to a child's effort or interest. For example: "You remembered to use words to tell Rachel that you wanted a turn" or "Tom, Larry, and Rob designed the cover for the class photo album."
- Give feedback that helps children construct more helpful skills. Use your expert knowledge and skills to give information so that a child can make a better choice

about how to do something. For example: "Lauren got real angry when you hit her. Let's figure out how to use words to tell Lauren that you were upset with what she did to you."

## 9. Identify Mistaken Goals and Use Encouragement

*Purposes of the strategy:* Identify a child's faulty perception of how to fit into a group. Be aware of what a child does to accomplish a mistaken goal (seeks undue attention, power, or revenge, or demonstrates inadequacy). Explain how an adult usually feels and reacts. Outline a better way to deal with a child who has any of the four mistaken goals.

*Steps in changing how you react to demands for undue attention:*

- Ignore the impulse to give in to the attention-seeking behavior.
- Acknowledge the child's request, but let her know that she can complete the task. Leave the area, if necessary, so that she can finish the job.
- Give the child attention at times when her behavior is more appropriate.
- Encourage a child to take the perspective of others by telling her about their perspective and by helping her learn to cooperate.

*Steps in changing how you react to a child who seeks power:*

- Resist the impulse to fight back.
- Decide to respond differently. (You do not have to be drawn into a power struggle. You can choose to respond differently.)
- Decline the child's invitation to argue or fight. This will surprise a child, particularly if you have previously been locked in power struggles with her. A useful technique is to label the interaction as a power struggle.

*Steps in changing how you react to a child who seeks revenge:*

- Resist the impulse to retaliate or give sermons.
- Focus on helping this child change her view of herself from a person who she thinks is not valued to the view that she is a good, worthwhile person. The goal is to encourage development of self-esteem, the missing ingredient.

*Steps in changing how you react to a child who demonstrates inadequacy:*

- Focus on what a normal child of this age should be able to do. For instance, should a 3-year-old be able to put on her own coat?
- Refrain from performing the age-appropriate task for her.
- Encourage a child who mistakenly believes she has to act like she is incompetent, demonstrate how she can do it, encourage her to try.

## 10. Ignore Behavior (Only When It Is Appropriate to Do So)

*Purpose of the strategy:* To change the adult's behavior, that is, to change the way that an adult reacts to a child; to help the adult stop paying attention to a child's unhelpful behavior.

Do not ignore certain behaviors. I usually like to state things in a positive way, but I find that saying "Do not . . ." seems to be appropriate for this issue.

- Do not ignore behavior that endangers anyone, including the child himself.
- Do not ignore behavior that damages or destroys property or that could potentially damage or destroy property.
- Do not ignore rude, embarrassing, intrusive, or unduly disruptive behavior.

*Guidelines for ignoring behavior:*

- Pinpoint the behavior to which you have been giving inappropriate attention.
- Explain briefly to the child that you will stop paying attention to the behavior.
- Be prepared. You have paid attention in the past to the behavior and it will be difficult to stop giving attention. A child will likely try even harder to get you to pay attention to the same behavior, so be prepared for a "bigger and better whine" before it decreases.
- Decide to thoroughly ignore the behavior—don't mutter to yourself under your breath; don't make eye contact; don't communicate with the child verbally or with gestures.
- Teach and encourage a more helpful skill along with the ignore strategy.

## 11. Redirect Very Young Children: Divert and Distract

*Purpose of the strategy:* To distract a very young child from a forbidden or dangerous activity, and then to divert her to a different activity.

*Factors to keep in mind:*

- Responsible caregivers understand that they must perform most of an infant's or a young toddler's ego functions, such as remembering to keep an infant away from outlets because she does not understand the danger.
- Avoid a power struggle when stopping dangerous behavior.
- Be prepared to act quickly when working with infants and toddlers. This requires constant supervision and observation, even in a baby-proofed area.

*Steps in using diversion and distraction:*

- Identify for yourself what you do not want a baby or toddler to do because the activity is dangerous. An example is playing with an electrical outlet, even if it is covered. We do not want children to do this because it is dangerous.
- Immediately do something to distract an infant or toddler from the forbidden activity, for example, roll a ball to Sari the instant you see her near the outlet.
- Decide whether to tell an infant or toddler not to do whatever it is that is dangerous, for example, "No playing with the outlet, Sari."

## 12. Redirect Older Children: Use Substitution

*Purpose of the strategy:* Form of redirection in which an adult shows a somewhat older child (over age 2½ to 3) how to perform the same activity or type of activity but in a more acceptable and safer way.

*Steps in using substitutions:*

- Specify the activity needing a substitution, for example, while outdoors, zigzagging through the sandbox when others are playing there.
- Develop a substitution: a similar activity or the same activity done more safely, for instance, zigzagging through a set of tires laid flat on the ground.
- Present the substitution to the child, for example, "Looks like you want to do an obstacle course, but please do not zigzag in the sandbox. Try zigzagging through these tires."
- Be prepared for the child to test your substitution. Resist getting drawn into a fight or power struggle. Respond to testing with positive discipline; continue to state the substitution calmly and with goodwill. If two children run back through the sandbox, for example, consider saying, "Tom and Jim, the obstacle course is the set of tires, not the sandbox."

## 13. Listen Actively

*Purposes of the strategy:* Careful, accurate listening to child's feelings. Use when a child owns a problem. Conveys adult's recognition and acceptance of the child and his feelings. Communicates the adult's trust in the child's ability to work through the problem.

*What to remember about active listening:*

- Listen carefully.
- Wait until the child finishes speaking; do not interrupt.
- Try to understand what the message means.
- Listen for what the child is feeling.
- Suspend judgment.
- Avoid preaching, giving advice, or trying to persuade the child to feel differently.
- Merely reflect your perception of the child's feelings.

## 14. Deliver I-Messages

*Purposes of the strategy:* Used when the adult owns the problem. Give information; communicate feelings in a respectful way; give the child a chance to change her behavior (a Rogerian concept).

*Steps in constructing a good I-message:*

- Name the exact behavior causing the problem. Give observable data about the child's behavior—what you see, hear, touch, smell, taste, for example, "Adam, I see that the puzzles you used are still on the table."
- Tell the child how his behavior tangibly affects you. Did it cost you time, money, or effort to do the job he should have done? (". . . and that meant I had to put the puzzles away just before snack").
- Tell the child how you felt, but do not accuse the child of causing your feeling, for example, "I feel annoyed if I have to do somebody else's work." Tell the child how to change the situation, for example, "I want you to do your own work and put the puzzles on the shelf."

*What to avoid in constructing I-messages:*

- Avoid accusing and blaming the child.
- Do not induce guilt.
- Avoid telling the child that he caused your feeling.

## 15. Teach Conflict Resolution (Problem Solving)

*Purposes of the strategy:* Achieve a mutually agreeable solution to a problem without resorting to the use of power. Support creative conflict resolution rather than punishing behavior accompanying conflict between children. For example, teach children who are arguing how to resolve the conflict rather than punishing them for fighting.

*Steps in using the no-lose method of conflict resolution:*

- Identify and define the conflict in a nonaccusatory way, for example, "Vinnie and Reese, you have a problem. You both want the green paint."
- Invite children to participate in fixing the problem, for example, "Let's think of how to solve the problem."
- Generate possible solutions with the children. Accept a variety of solutions and avoid evaluating them, for example, "Yes, you could both use the same paint cup. You could take turns."
- Examine each idea for merits and drawbacks. With the children, decide which to try. Thank the children for thinking of solutions, for example, "Both of you want to use the green paint at the same time."
- Put the plan into action, for example, "You might have to take turns dipping your brushes into the paint. Try your idea."
- Follow up. Evaluate how well the solution worked (teacher comes back in a few minutes): "Your idea of how to solve your green paint problem really worked."

## 16. Recognize Signs of Stress, Anxiety, or Strong Emotion; Prevent Overstimulation; Teach Calming Techniques

*Purposes of the strategy:* To look beyond the visible behavior. To detect an underlying cause, such as stress or anxiety, for a behavior. To get the autonomic nervous system under control.

*Suggestions:*

- Observe carefully, noting signs of stress (Figure 9.1) or anxiety.
- Decide whether to use active listening, to decrease stimulation, or to teach/carry out a calming technique (Figure 5.1).
- Decide whether to change something about the classroom to decrease stress, for example, decide to minimize the number of transitions.

# 17. Manage Strong Emotions Responsibly

*Purposes of the strategy:* To support children in recognizing and learning responsible ways to manage strong emotions such as anger. To avoid simply punishing children for behavior resulting from strong emotions.

*Steps in teaching responsible anger management:*

- Model responsible anger management.
- Create a safe emotional climate. Allow and encourage children to acknowledge all feelings while firmly but kindly not permitting them to hurt anybody because of those feelings.
- Help children understand their anger triggers.
- Help children understand the body's reaction to anger.
- Teach children how to deal with the stress of anger.
- State your expectations for responsible anger management.
- Help some children learn to use words to describe angry feelings, and help others to expand their vocabulary about feelings.
- Use appropriate books and stories about anger management.

# Glossary

**Accommodation** Process of changing an existing concept to include new information

**Active listening** An adult listens reflectively and carefully to a child; does not offer solutions and does not criticize; useful when the problem belongs to the child

**Activity areas** Zones designated for supporting children's development and learning

**Acute stress** Intense strain that occurs rapidly; usually transitory

**Aggression** Any behavior that a person uses when he or she intends to hurt someone or to destroy or damage property

**Aggressive behavior** Intentional behavior aimed at hurting a person or animal or damaging or destroying things

**Alarm** First stage in responding to stress in which a child is first aware of a potential stressor

**Anecdotal record** Brief written notes about an incident; like a snapshot; gives less information that the longer running record

**Anger** A basic emotion present soon after birth; elicited when a person is prevented from attaining a goal

**Antecedent** An event preceding and possibly predicting an event that follows it

**Appraisal** Second stage in responding to stress; child assesses what such an event meant in the past

**Appreciation** Encouraging children with appropriate comments based on a child's effort

**Arrival** The start of the day at school when children enter the school grounds and their classroom

**Assessment** Systematic procedure for obtaining information from observations, interviews, portfolios, projects, tests, and other sources that can be used to make judgments about characteristics of children or programs

**Assimilation** Process of incorporating new information into an existing concept

**Authentic assessment** Children apply their skills and knowledge in a real-world setting

**Authoritarian style of caregiving** Combination of high demandingness and low responsiveness; considered a negative approach

**Authoritative style of caregiving** Combination of high demandingness and high responsiveness; considered a positive approach

**Basic processes of influencing children** Direct and indirect methods of persuasion used by any adult in an interaction with a child

**Behavior** Refers (when studying children) to a child's actions, conduct, or deeds

**Bully** The person bent on causing harm or distress

**Bully/victim** Someone who has been both a bully and a victim

**Bullying** A form of aggression; occurs in a relationship where the power or strength in one party is greater than in the other; intention is to cause harm; Intentionally and repeatedly hurting or humiliating someone. Bullying takes different forms and is done in different ways

**Bystander** Observes the bullying; can have an important role in stopping bullying

**Calm and cool times** Periods of relative peace and serenity in a classroom

**Challenging behavior** Behavior that tests an adult's ability to support the child; usually in the eye of the beholder

**Checklist** Non-narrative method for observing; an inventory of characteristics or behaviors that can be checked as observed

**Child development knowledge** Ability to describe and explain different aspects of children's growth

**Chronic stress** Unrelenting, persistent, and ongoing stress

**Communication style** Manner in which an adult delivers messages to children; indicative of the adult's view of children

**Competence** A child's ability to meet the culture's and her family's demands for success

**Consequence** A response that follows a behavior

**Constructivism** Children's building or constructing knowledge

**Contextual factors** Environmental issues (physical or interpersonal environment or curriculum) contributing to challenging behavior in classrooms

**Control** The extent to which a child thinks that he can influence outcomes of events

**Cooperating** Working collaboratively to complete a job or task; one type of prosocial behavior

**Coping** Searching for internal or external resources to contend with stressors

**Cues** Verbal, nonverbal, pictorial, or written reminders about limits

**Cues for aggression** Some object, such as a gun, which reminds a person about aggressive acts

**Culture** Beliefs, values, and traditions of a group of people; transmitted to the next generation through language, interactions, and relationships

**Cyberbullying** Aggression via electronic media

**Decision-making model of child guidance** Four-step process for making choices about dealing with many different types of guidance issues

**Deferred imitation** Observing an action but delaying imitating it until later

**Demandingness** One of the elements of a person's caregiving style: whether and how the person sets limits and monitors, supervises, and faces issues

**Departure** The routine dealing with leave taking; children exit their classrooms and the school grounds

**Developmental characteristics** Factors in a child's growth that contribute to challenging behavior

**Discipline** Teaching or learning

**Diverting and distracting** Useful with toddlers; redirection in which an adult sidetracks a toddler from one activity and steers him to a safer activity

**Eclectic approach** Guiding children with the best ideas from different theories and strategies

**Ecology of human development** Concept that children grow up and develop in different systems, all nested within one another

**Egocentric** Focused on one's own viewpoint

**Emotional competence** How well, overall, a person copes with his or her feelings and whether the person has empathy for and gets along with others

**Emotional or psychological bullying** Aggressive behaviors that are not physical and are intended to cause distress

**Emotions** Feelings or affective states; they are divided into two groups: basic and complex emotions

**Emotions vocabulary** The set of emotion words or labels for feelings, such as angry, jealous, anxious

**Empathy** Vicariously understanding the thoughts or feelings of another

**Event sampling** Formal method for identifying specific categories of behavior

**Expressing emotions** Communicating a feeling after noticing it

**External sources of stress** Stress originating outside a child

**Feedback** Information that an adult gives to a child about how the child did something

**Focused intervention** Third level of preventing challenging behaviors and usually done by early intervention professionals trained to work with families and very young children in their homes

**Friendship skills** Behaviors through which a child demonstrates the ability to develop relationships with other children

**Guidance or discipline encounter** Interaction between a child and an adult in which the adult helps the child to alter his behavior

**Guidance plan** Written document based on the process that is part of the decision-making model; outlines how a teacher will support a child

**Guidance strategies** The actions that we use in managing guidance encounters

**Helping** Assisting, performing acts of kindness, rescuing; one type of prosocial behavior

**Hostile aggression** Anger and revenge-based aggression; it is directed at a specific target

**Hot spots** Incidents of challenging behavior in a classroom

**I-message** Self-responsible adult behavior useful when the problem belongs to the adult

**Ignore behavior (only when appropriate to do so)** Stop paying attention to a specific action

**Imitation** Performing an action modeled by someone else

**Indirect guidance** Influencing children's behavior through environmental design and appropriate curriculum, activities, and materials management

**Individual learning center** Space for one child to work

**Indulgent/permissive style of caregiving** Combination of low demandingness and high responsiveness; person chooses to be permissive

**Instrumental aggression** Goal-directed aggression; meant to get or retrieve an object or territory; not anger based

**Internal sources of stress** Stress originating within a child

**Large group** Time when all children and the teacher meet; used for a variety of educational purposes

**Large-group area** A space in which a whole class can gather for a variety of learning activities

**Limits** Boundaries; in guiding children, refers to boundaries on children's behavior communicated by a teacher or parent

**Long-term memory** Storage site for permanently stored information

**Media violence** Hostility shown in DVDs, movies, games, and other screens

**Memory** Process used to store information and later retrieve it

**Modeling** Performing an activity and having a child observe it

**Moral identity** Describing oneself by using moral principles such as honesty, kindness, fairness

**Narrative method** Observation that tells a story

**Non-narrative method** Observation method that does not tell a story

**Norm** A standard used by groups to direct a group member's behavior

**Objectivity** Impartiality, detachment, and fairness in recording observations

**Observation** Systematic study; in guidance refers to watching, recording, and reflecting on children's behavior

**On-the-spot guidance** Helping children through direct coaching in daily guidance situations

**Perceiving emotions** Noticing feelings in oneself and others; the least complex emotional competency

**Perception** Process that children use for organizing the information that they gain through sight, hearing, touch, smell

**Permissive style of caregiving** Low in demandingness

**Perspective taking** A basic cognitive developmental skill; ability to see things from another's perspective

**Physical boundary for activity areas** Partition separating one activity area from another

**Physical bullying** Bodily contact intended to cause harm

**Physical stressor** Excessive stimulation with potential to damage parts of a child's body

**Portfolio** Collection of a child's work and the teacher's observation reports and selected observations

**Positive guidance strategies** Methods that rely on teaching

**Praise** A form of intangible feedback for children

**Private space** Place of refuge and relaxation, large enough for only one or at most two children; must be easily monitored by the teacher

**Problem ownership** Concept from Rogerian theory referring to deciding who in a relationship has the problem

**Prosocial behavior** Actions, such as sharing, helping, or cooperating, that promote the well-being of others

**Protective factors** Key features of caring systems in which children become resilient

**Psychological stressor** Excessive stimulation with potential to thwart or damage a child's sense of security

**Psychosocial crisis** Challenges presented at different ages and resolved in either a positive or negative way

**Pure bully** Someone who bullies; has not been the victim of similar aggression

**Pure victim** Often smaller and weaker or less powerful; does not provoke bullying

**Rating scale** Non-narrative method for observing, a listing of activities or characteristics, calls for a summary judgment

**Recall memory** Memories for which a child has to call forth information, either with or without a reminder or cue

**Recognition memory** Feeling of familiarity with something that we know about from our past and that we encounter again

**Reflection** An active, intentional, problem-solving process; involves remembering an issue and then analyzing the memories

**Regulating emotions** The most complex of the emotional competencies; refers to understanding and managing moods and feelings responsibly

**Represent experiences** Major cognitive accomplishment of preoperational thinkers; ability to describe an experience using a variety of means

**Resilience** The ability to weather stress and adversity and not be devastated by it

**Responsiveness** One of the elements of a person's caregiving style; whether an adult meets a child's needs and understands child development

**Routine** (in a school or center) Part of a school day or a day in a center; the element occurs regularly, every day

**Running record** A longer narrative method for observing; tells a longer story; gives more detail than an anecdotal record

**Scaffolding** An adult's modifying support as children develop new knowledge or skills

**Screen time** Time spent watching action on a monitor of any sort

**Scripts for aggression** Information stored in memory; focused on how to carry out aggression; gleaned from different systems

**Searching for a coping strategy** Third stage in responding to stress; strategy chosen depends on whether children are familiar with and understand and whether they can generate a helpful way to deal with the event

**Self** A concept that a child produces in his or her mind; ideas are constructed gradually; consists of four components: self-awareness, self-concept, self-control, and self-esteem

**Self-awareness** Child sees himself as separate from others and able to make things happen

**Self-concept** The accumulation of knowledge that a child gathers about herself

**Self-control** A child's ability to put off gratification until later, to put up with some frustration, and to keep impulses under control; regulating behavior internally and voluntarily

**Self-esteem** A child's overall judgment of the self about which he is aware, knows about, and regulates

**Sharing** Giving, donating; one type of prosocial behavior

**Short-term memory** Temporary storage site for information with which a child needs to work. The child retrieves the information from long-term memory. Also called *working memory*

**Skill deficit** Lacking a skill for social emotional development and school success that contributes to challenging behavior

**Small group** Time when a fraction of the entire class, about four to six children, meets with the teacher for a variety of educational experiences

**Small-group learning center** Space large enough for five or six children; center has a specific function, such as art or discovery

**Social cognition** How children think about how other people feel and about their motives, behavior, and feelings

**Social emotional learning (SEL)** Gaining knowledge about feelings and about getting along with others

**Social skills** Observable behaviors through which a child demonstrates the ability to regulate thoughts and emotions

**Socialization** Process through which children learn the values and traditions of their culture

**Socially competent children** Characteristics of socially competent children include relating well to others, responding agreeably to others, and using good social skills

**Stress** A child's reaction to psychological or physical threats to safety and security

**Style of confrontation** Facing something, often irritating or hurtful, and coping with it

**Subjectivity** Bias or preconception in recording observations

**Substitution** Useful with preschoolers and older children; redirection in which a child learns how to do an activity in a safer, more acceptable way

**Tattling** Unnecessary reporting on the words, actions, and behaviors of others

**Teasing** Verbal or nonverbal exchanges between children or between a child and an older person; a form of aggression when the teaser intends to hurt the other person

**Theory** Not a hunch or a guess; an explanation about something in the natural world, substantiated by observations, facts, and research

**Time sampling** Observes for a limited time period; focuses on a precisely defined behavior; records whether that behavior occurred

**Token** An object that can be felt or held; therefore, it is tangible

**Traffic pattern** Flow of movement in an early childhood classroom

**Transition** The process of shifting from one part of a school day to another, or from one activity to another

**Understanding feelings** The ability to reflect on and evaluate emotions

**Uninvolved/permissive style of caregiving** Combination of low demandingness and low responsiveness; also known as unengaged; person would rather not be permissive

**Unmet need** One of a child's basic requirements for healthy development and good mental health that has not been satisfied and that contributes to challenging behavior

**Verbal bullying** Using words to cause distress

**Victim** The person who is bullied

**Visual support** Pictures, photographs, and drawings intended to help children remember the messages implied in the image

**Voice of challenging behavior** What a child's behavior tells a teacher about what the child needs

**"W" questions about behavior** Questions that observers can answer with well-planned observations. They include What? Who? When? Where? and Why?

**Warmth** Emotional expression of fondness

**Worth** A child's view about how significant he is to others

**Zone of proximal development (ZPD)** Space in which learning and development occur

# References

Adler Graduate School. (2012). Alfred Adler: Theory and application. Retrieved on October 21, 2013, from http://www.alfredadler.edu/about/theory

Aldwin, C. (author), & Werner, E. (foreword). (2007). *Stress, coping, and development, second edition: An integrative perspective.* New York, NY: Guilford Press.

American Academy of Child & Adolescent Psychiatry. (2005). Children's threats: When are they serious? *AACAP Facts for Families,* No. 65. Washington, DC: Author.

American Academy of Child & Adolescent Psychiatry. (2008a). Children of parents with mental illness. *AACAP Facts for Families,* No. 39. Washington, DC: Author.

American Academy of Child & Adolescent Psychiatry. (2008b). Children who cannot pay attention. *AACAP Facts for Families,* No. 6. Washington, DC: Author.

American Academy of Child & Adolescent Psychiatry. (2011a). Children and family moves. *AACAP Facts for Families,* No. 14. Washington, DC: Author.

American Academy of Child & Adolescent Psychiatry. (2011b). Children with oppositional defiant disorder. *AACAP Facts for Families,* No. 72. Washington, DC: Author.

American Academy of Child & Adolescent Psychiatry. (2011c). Understanding violent behavior in children and adolescents. *AACAP Facts for Families,* No. 55. Washington, DC: Author.

American Academy of Child & Adolescent Psychiatry. (2013). Natural disasters and violence. Washington, DC: Author.

American Academy of Pediatrics. (2013). Aggressive behavior. Retrieved on June 2, 2013, from http://www.healthychildren.org/English/ages-stages/toddler/Pages/Aggressive-Behavior.aspx

American Psychiatric Association. (2012). Bullying. Retrieved on June 1, 2013, from http://www.psychiatry.org/mental-health/bullying

American Psychological Association. (2004). *The different kinds of stress.* Retrieved May 1, 2013, from http://www.apa.org/helpcenter/stress-kinds.aspx

American Psychological Association. (2013). This is psychology: Bullying. Retrieved on June 12, 2013, from http://www.apa.org/news/press/video/this-is-psychology/bullying.aspx

Anderson, G., Hilton, S., & Wouden-Miller, M. (2003). A gender comparison of the cooperation of 4-year-old children in classroom activity centers. *Early Education and Development, 14*(4), 441–451.

Arizona Department of Education. (2013). Sample daily schedule. Retrieved on May 24, 2013, from http://www.azed.gov/early-childhood/fullday-kindergarten/sample-sch/

Baillargeon, R., Zoccolillo, M., Keenan, K., Cote, S., Perusse, D., Wu, H.-X., et al. (2007). Gender differences in physical aggression: A prospective population-based survey of children before and after 2 years of age. *Developmental Psychology, 43*(1), 13–26.

Baker-Ward, L., Gordon, B. N., Ornstein, P. A., Larus, D. M., & Clubb, P. A. (1993). Young children's long-term retention of a pediatric examination. *Child Development, 64,* 1519–1533.

Ballas, P. (2009). Reviewer for Medical encyclopedia: Attention deficit hyperactivity disorder (ADHD). Retrieved October 3, 2013, from http://www.nlm.nih.gov/medlineplus/ency/article/001551.htm

Bandura, A.; Ross, D.; Ross, S. A. (1961). "Transmission of aggression through the imitation of aggressive models". *Journal of Abnormal and Social Psychology* 63 (3): 575–582.

Barnard, K. E., & Solchany, J. E. (2002). *Mothering.* Mahwah, NJ: Erlbaum.

Baumeister, R. F., Campbell, J. D., Kreuger, J. I., & Vohs, K. D. (2003). Does high self-esteem cause better performance, interpersonal success, happiness or healthier lifestyles? *Psychological Science in the Public Interest, 4*(1), 1–44. Retrieved June 10, 2009, from http://www.csom.umn.edu/Assets/71496.pdf

Baumrind, D. (1967). Child care practices anteceding three patterns of preschool behavior. *Genetic Psychology Monographs, 75,* 43–88.

Baumrind, D. (1971). Current patterns of parental authority. *Developmental Psychology Monograph, 4*(1, Pt. 2).

Baumrind, D. (1977, March). *Socialization determinants of personal agency*. Paper presented at the meeting of the Society for Research in Child Development, New Orleans, LA.

Baumrind, D. (1979). *Sex-related socialization effects*. Paper presented at the meeting of the Society for Research in Child Development, San Francisco, CA.

Baumrind, D. (1993). The average expectable environment is not good enough: A response to Scarr. *Child Development, 64*, 1299–1317.

Baumrind, D. (1996). Parenting: The discipline controversy revisited. *Family Relations, 45*, 405–414.

Baumrind, D., & Black, A. E. (1967). Socialization practices associated with dimensions of competence in pre-school boys and girls. *Child Development, 38, 291*–327.

Becker, W. C. (1954). Consequences of different kinds of parental discipline. In M. L. Hoffman & L. S. Hoffman (Eds.), *Review of child development research* (Vol. 1). New York, NY: Russell Sage Foundation.

Becker-Blease, K., & Freyd, J. (2008). A preliminary study of ADHD symptoms and correlates: Do abused children differ from nonabused children? *Journal of Aggression, Maltreatment & Trauma, 17*(1), 133–140.

Bedrova, E., & Leong, D. (2005). Self-regulation. *Principal,* September/October, 30–33.

Bell, R. Q. (1968). A reinterpretation of the direction of effect in studies of socialization. *Psychological Review, 75,* 81–95.

Bell, R. Q., & Harper, L. V. (Eds.). (1977). *Child effects on adults.* Hillsdale, NJ: Erlbaum.

Belsky, J., Sligo, J., Jaffee, S. R., Woodward, L., & Silva, P. (2005). Intergenerational transmission of warm, sensitive, stimulating parenting: A prospective study of mothers and fathers of 3-year-olds. *Child Development,* 76(2), 384–396.

Bengtsson, H., & Johnson, L. (1992). Perspective taking, empathy, and prosocial behavior in late childhood. *Child Study Journal, 22*(1), 11–22.

Birckmayer, J., Cohen, J., Jensen, I., & Variano, D. (2005). Kyle lives with his grandmother—Where are his mommy and daddy? *Young Children, 60*(3), 100–104.

Blagojevic, B., Logue, M. E., Bennet-Armistead, V. S., Taylor, B., & Neal, E. (2011). Take a look! Visual supports for learning. *Teaching Young Children, 4*(5), 10-13.

Blakemore, J., Berenbaum, S., & Liben, L. (2009). *Gender development.* New York, NY: Psychology Press.

Block, H. (1978). Another look at sex differentiation in the socialization behaviors of mothers and fathers. In J. Sherman & F. L. Denmark (Eds.), *The future of women: Future directions of research* (pp. 29-87). New York, NY: Psychological Dimensions.

Block, J. (2008, May 6). *Psychiatric factors that can lead to school shootings.* Annual meeting American Psychiatric Association, Washington, DC.

Bolger, K., Patterson, C., & Kupersmidt, J. (1998). Peer relationships and self-esteem among children who have been maltreated. *Child Development, 69*(4), 1171–1197.

Bracken, C. C., & Lombard, M. (2004). Social presence and children: praise, intrinsic motivation, and learning with computers. *Journal of Communication, 54*(1), 22–37.

Brackett, M. A., Crum, A., & Salovey, P. (2009). Emotional intelligence. In S. J. Lopez (Ed.), *Encyclopedia of positive psychology* (pp. 310–315). New York, NY: Blackwell.

Branz-Spall, A., Rosenthal, R., & Wright, A. (2003). Children of the road: Migrant students, our nation's most mobile population. *Journal of Negro Education, 72*(1), 55–62.

Brassard, M., & Boehm, A. (2007). *Preschool assessment: Principles and practices.* New York, NY: Guilford Press.

Brems, C., & Sohl, M. A. (1995). The role of empathy in parenting strategy choices. *Family Relations, 44,* 189–194.

Bronfenbrenner, U. (1979). *The ecology of human development.* Cambridge, MA: Harvard University Press.

Brown, A. (2011). American Academy of Pediatrics Policy statement: Media use by children younger than 2 years. Retrieved on June 17, 2013, from http://pediatrics.aappublications.org/content/128/5/1040.full?sid=90c428d6-df4a-4e16-8862-2ef44f314693

Brown, A. L., & Campione, J. C. (1990). Communities of learning and thinking, or a context by any other name. In D. Kuhn (Ed.), *Contributions to human development: Vol 21. Developmental perspectives on teaching learning and thinking skills* (pp.108–126). Basel, Switzerland: Karger.

Brown, G., Mangelsdorf, S., Neff, C., Schoppe-Sullivan, S., & Frosch, C. (2009). Young children's concepts: Associations with child temperament, mothers' and fathers' parenting, and triadic family interaction. Report. *Merrill-Palmer Quarterly, 55*(2), 184–216.

Burts, D., Hart, C., Charlesworth, R., Fleege, P., Mosley, J., & Thomasson, R. (1992). Observed activities and stress behaviors of children in developmentally appropriate and inappropriate kindergarten classrooms. *Early Childhood Research Quarterly, 7,* 297–318.

Calvert, S. (2006). Media and early development. In K. McCartney & D. Phillips (Eds.), *The Blackwell handbook of early childhood development* (pp. 508–531). Malden, MA: Blackwell Publishing.

Cameron, C., Connor, C., & Morrison, F. (2005). The effects of variation in teacher organization on classroom functioning. *Journal of School Psychology, 43*(1), 61–85.

Campos, J., & Barrett, K. (1984). A new understanding of emotions and their development. In C. Izard, J. Kagan, & R. Zajonc (Eds.), *Emotions, cognition, and behavior.* New York, NY: Cambridge University Press.

Canadian Mental Health Association. (2012). Stress. Retrieved on June 15, 2013, from http://www.cmha.ca/mental_health/stress/

Carlsson-Paige, N., & Levin, D. (1998). *Before push comes to shove: Building conflict resolution skills with children.* St. Paul, MN: Redleaf Press.

Centers for Disease Control and Prevention. (2011). Middle childhood (6–8 years of age) developmental milestones. Retrieved on May 1, 2013, from http://www.cdc.gov/ncbddd/childdevelopment/positiveparenting/middle.html

Centers for Disease Control and Prevention. (2012). *Understanding child maltreatment.* Fact Sheet. Retrieved on June 12, 2013, from http://www.cdc.gov/ViolencePrevention/pdf/CM_Factsheet2012-a.pdf

Chalmers, J. B., & Townsend, M. A. (1990). The effects of training in social perspective taking on socially maladjusted girls. *Child Development, 61*, 178–190.

Chang, R. S., & Thompson, N. S. (2011). Whines, cries, and motherese: Their relative power to distract. *Journal of Social, Evolutionary, and Cultural Psychology, 5*(2), 131–141.

Charlesworth, R., Hart, C., Burts, D., & DeWolf, M. (1993). The LSU studies: Building a research base for developmentally appropriate practice. In S. Reifel (Ed.), *Advances in early education and day care: Perspectives on developmentally appropriate practice, 5,* 3–28.

Child Welfare Information Gateway. (2013). *Long-term consequences of child abuse and neglect.* Washington, DC: U.S. Department of Health and Human Services, Children's Bureau.

Christensen, M., Emde, R. N., & Fleming, C. (2004). Cultural perspectives for assessing infants and young children. In R. Delcarmen-Wiggins & A. Carter (Eds.), *Handbook of infant, toddler, and preschool mental health assessment* (pp. 7–23). New York, NY: Oxford University Press.

Christian, L.G. (2006). Applying family systems theory to early childhood practice. *Beyond the Journal: Young Children on the Web*, 8 pages. Retrieved November 6, 2013, from http://journal.naeyc.org/btj/200601/ChristianBTJ.pdf

Church, R. M. (1963). The varied effects of punishment on behavior. *Psychological Review, 70,* 369–402.

Ciairano, S., Kliewer, W., Bonino, S., & Bosma, H. A. (2008). Parenting and adolescent well-being in two European countries. *Adolescence, 43,* 99–117.

Clark, J. I. (1999). *Time-in: When time-out doesn't work.* Seattle, WA: Parenting Press.

Clark, P., & Kragler, S. (2005). The impact of including writing materials in the early childhood classrooms on the early literacy development of children from low-income families. *Early Child Development and Care, 175*(4), 285–301.

Cohn, J. F., Campbell, S. B., Matias, R., & Hopkins, J. (1990). Face-to-face interactions of postpartum depressed and nondepressed mother-infant pairs at 2 months. *Developmental Psychology, 26,* 15–23.

Coles, R. (1986). *The moral life of children.* New York, NY: Atlantic Monthly Press.

Coles, R. (1997). *The moral intelligence of children.* New York, NY: Penguin.

Coles, R. (2001). *The Erik Erikson reader.* New York, NY: W. W. Norton and Company

Conn, K., Hernandez, T., Puthoor, P., Fagnano, M., & Halterman, J. (2008). Screen time use among urban children with asthma. *Academic Pediatrics, 9*(1), 60–63.

Coopersmith, S. (1967). *The antecedents of self-esteem.* San Francisco, CA: W. H. Freeman.

Copple, C., & Bredekamp, S. (2009). *Developmentally appropriate practices in early childhood programs serving children from birth through age 8.* Washington, DC: NAEYC.

Cornell, D. G., & Scheithauer, H. (2011). Issue editors' notes. *New Directions for Youth Development,* 1–6. doi:10.1002/yd.382.

Corso, R. (2003). The center on the social and emotional foundations for education. *Young Children, 58*(4), 46–47.

CSEFEL. (n.d.—a). Book nook: Ideas for using books to support social emotional development. Retrieved May 1, 2009, from http://www.vanderbilt.edu/csefel/booknook/hands/hands.html

CSEFEL. (n.d.—b). Promoting positive peer social interactions. *What Works Brief #8.* Retrieved on June 14, 2013, from http://csefel.vanderbilt.edu/briefs/wwb8.pdf

CSEFEL. (n.d.—c). Scripted stories for social situations: Tip Sheet. Retrieved on October 12, 2013, from http://csefel.vanderbilt.edu/scriptedstories/tips.pdf

CSEFEL. (n.d.—d). Using classroom activities and routines as opportunities to support peer interaction. What Works Brief #5. Retrieved on June 14, 2013, from http://csefel.vanderbilt.edu/briefs/wwb5.pdf

CSEFEL. (2007). *Tucker Tuttle takes time to tuck and think*. Retrieved on June 9, 2013, from http://csefel.vanderbilt.edu/resources/strategies.html

CSEFEL. (2008). Practical strategies. Retrieved May 1, 2009, from http://www.vanderbilt.edu/csefel/

Damon, W. (2004, April 5). *Studies in the nature of character revisited: Moral identity and its development*. Lecture given at Williams College.

Damon, W. (2009). *The path to purpose: How young people find their calling in life*. New York, NY: Free Press.

Dartmouth Early Learning Center. (n.d.). *Philosophy section and primary grades section*. South Dartmouth, MA: Author. Retrieved on May 10, 2013, from http://www.delc.us/primarygrades.html

Davis, S., & Davis, J. (2007). *Empowering bystanders in bullying prevention*. Champaign, IL: Research Press.

Dawe, H. C. (1934). An analysis of two hundred quarrels of preschool children. *Child Development, 5,* 139–157.

Day, R., Hair, E., Moore, K., Kaye, K., & Orthner, D. (2009). Marital quality and outcomes for children and adolescents: A review of the family process literature. Retrieved on October 10, 2013, from http://aspe.hhs.gov/hsp/08/relationshipstrengths/litrev/index.pdf

Day, T., & Kunz, J. T. (2009). *Guidance based on developmental theory*. Unpublished manuscript, Weber State University, Ogden, UT.

Denham, S. (2006). The emotional basis of learning and development in early childhood education. In B. Spodek & O. Saracho (Eds.). *Handbook of research on the education of young children* (2nd ed.). New York, NY: Routledge.

Denham, S. A., Zoller, D., & Couchoud, E. Z. (1994). Socialization of preschoolers' emotion understanding. *Developmental Psychology, 30*(6), 928–937.

DeVries, R., & Zan, B. (1994). *Moral classrooms, moral children: Creating a constructivist atmosphere in early education*. New York, NY: Teacher's College Press.

Dewey, J. (1897). My pedagogic creed. *The School Journal, LIV*(3), 77–80.

Dewey, J. (1938). *Experience and education*. New York, NY: The Macmillan Company.

Dodge, K. A., & Frame, C. L. (1982). Social cognitive biases and deficits in aggressive boys. *Child Development, 53,* 629–635.

Donfrancesco, R., Mugnaini, D., & Dell'Uomo, A. (2005). Cognitive impulsivity in specific learning disabilities. *European Child and Adolescent Psychiatry, 14*(5), 270–275.

Downs, J., Blagojevic, B., & Labas, L. (2006). Daily transitions —Time for a change. The University of Maine Center for Community Inclusion and Disability Studies. Retrieved November 6, 2013, from http://www.thecommunitypartnership.org/uploads/media/Sept-Oct09.pdf

Dreikurs, R. (1958). *The challenge of parenthood*. New York, NY: Hawthorne Books.

Dubow, E., Huesmann, L., & Boxer, P. (2003). Theoretical and methodological considerations in cross-generational research on parenting and child aggressive behavior. *Journal of Abnormal Child Psychology, 31*(2), 185–192.

Dweck, C., & Leggett, E. (1988). A social-cognitive approach to motivation and personality. *Psychological Review, 95*(2), 256–273.

Dweck, C., & Molden, D. (2005). Self theories: Their impact on competence motivation and acquisition. In A. Elliot & C. Dweck (Eds.), *Handbook of competence and motivation*. New York, NY: Guilford Press.

Edwards, A., Shipman, K., & Brown, A. (2005). The socialization of emotional understanding: A comparison of neglectful and nonneglectful mothers and their children. *Child Maltreatment, 10*(3), 293–304.

Eisenberg, N., Wolchik, S., Goldberg, L., & Engel, I. (1992). Parental values, reinforcement, and young children's prosocial behavior: A longitudinal study. *Journal of Genetic Psychology, 153*(1), 19–37.

ElBoghdady, D. (2010, November 22). Foreclosure takes toll on increasing number of children. *The Washington Post*. Retrieved June 15, 2013, from http://www.washingtonpost.com/wp-dyn/content/article/2010/11/21/AR2010112104255.html?sid=ST2010112202887

Elias, M. (2004). The connection between social-emotional learning and learning disabilities: Implications for intervention. *Learning Disability Quarterly, 27*(1), 53.

Elliott, E., & Dweck, C. (1988). Goals: An approach to motivation and achievement. *Journal of Personality and Social Psychology, 54*(1), 5–12.

Erikson, E. (1958). *Young man Luther: A study in psychoanalysis*. New York, NY: Norton.

Erikson, E. H. (1950). *Childhood and society*. New York, NY: Norton.

Espelage, D., Holt, M., & Henkel, R. (2003). Examination of peer group contextual effects on aggression during early adolescence. *Child Development, 74,* 205–220.

Eysenck, M. W. (2004). *Psychology: An international perspective*. East Sussex, UK: Psychology Press.

Fabes, R., & Eisenberg, N. (1992). Young children's coping with interpersonal anger. *Child Development, 63,* 116–128.

Fabes, R., Eisenberg, N., Smith, M., & Murphy, B. (1996). Getting angry at peers: Association with liking of the provocateur. *Child Development, 67*(3), 943–958.

Fagan, J. F. (1984). Infant memory: History, current trends, and relations to cognitive psychology. In M. Moscovitch (Ed.), *Infant memory: Its relation to normal and pathological memory in humans and other animals* (pp. 1–27). New York, NY: Plenum.

Fantz, R. L. (1966). Pattern discrimination and selective attention as determinants of perceptual development from birth. In A. H. Kidd & J. L. Rivoire (Eds.), *Perceptual development in children* (pp. 144–173). New York, NY: International Universities Press.

Fawcett, L. M., & Garton, A. F. (2005). The effect of peer collaboration on children's problem-solving ability. *British Journal of Educational Psychology, 75*(2), 157–169.

Feshbach, N. D., & Feshbach, S. (1982). Empathy training and the regulation of aggression: Potentialities and limitations. *Academic Psychology Bulletin, 4,* 399–413.

Figueroa-Sanchez, M. (2008). Building emotional literacy: Groundwork to early learning. *Childhood Education, 84*(5), 301–304.

Flavell, J. H., Miller, P. H., & Miller, S. A. (1993). *Cognitive development* (3rd ed.). Upper Saddle River, NJ: Prentice Hall.

Fonagy, P., Twemlow, S., Vernberg, E., Mize Nelson, J., Dill, E., Little, T., & Sargent, J. (2009). A cluster randomized controlled trial of child-focused psychiatric consultation and a school systems-focused intervention to reduce aggression. *Journal of Child Psychology and Psychiatry, 50*(5), 607–616.

Fox, L. (n.d.). Positive behavior support: An individualized approach to address challenging behavior. *What Works Brief #10.* University of North Carolina—Chapel Hill, CSEFEL, NC.

Fox, L. (2010). Supporting infants and toddlers with challenging behavior. Module 4, Handout 4.6. Retrieved on May 4, 2013, from http://csefel.vanderbilt.edu/modules/module4/handout6.pdf

Fox, L., & Duda, M. (n.d.). What are children trying to tell us? Assessing the function of their behavior. *What Works Brief #9,* University of North Carolina—Chapel Hill, CSEFEL, NC.

Francis, S., & Chorpita, B. (2009). Parental beliefs about child anxiety as a mediator of parent and child anxiety. *Cognitive Therapy and Research, 9* pages. doi:10.1007/s10608-009-9255-9.

Freedman, J. (2002). *Easing the teasing: Helping your child cope with name-calling, ridicule, and verbal bullying.* Chicago, IL: McGraw-Hill Contemporary.

Freeman, N., Lacohee, H., & Coulton, S. (1995). Cued-recall approach to 3-year-olds' memory for an honest mistake. *Journal of Experimental Child Psychology, 60*(1), 102–116.

Freeman-Loftis, B. (2009). An administrator shares: A welcoming routine for arrival time. *Responsive Classroom Newsletter, 21*(1), 12–13.

Frey, K., Herschstein, M., Edstrom, L., & Snell, J. (2009). Observed reductions in school bullying, nonbullying aggression, and destructive bystander behavior: A longitudinal evaluation. *Journal of School Psychology, 101*(2), 466–481.

Gallagher, E. (2004). *Abuse, attachment, and animal assisted activities.* Unpublished honors paper, Chestnut Hill, MA: Lynch School of Education.

Gallagher, J., & Reid, K. (2002). *The learning theory of Piaget and Inhelder.* Bloomington, IN: IUniverse.

Gandini, L. (1993). Fundamentals of the Reggio Emilia approach to early childhood education. *Young Children, 49*(1), 4–8.

Garbarino, J., Guttman, E., & Seeley, J. (1986). *The psychologically battered child.* San Francisco, CA: Jossey-Bass.

Gerrig, R., & Zimbardo, P. (2002). *Psychology and life* (16th ed.). Boston, MA: Allyn & Bacon/Pearson Education.

Gilliam, W. (2005, May 4). *Prekindergartners left behind: expulsion rates in state prekindergarten systems.* New Haven, CT: Yale University Child Study Center,.

Gilliam, W. (2012, October 10). *Preschool behavior: A key factor and strategy for school success.* Cromwell, CT: W. C. Graustein Memorial Fund.. Retrieved on June 13, 2013, from http://discovery.wcgmf.org/sites/default/files/resources/preschool%20behavior%20PDF.pdf

Gilligan, C. (1993). *In a different voice: Psychological theory and women's development.* Cambridge, MA: Harvard University Press. (Original work published 1982)

Gilligan, C. (2008, November 17). *Always in a different voice.* Lunch plenary address at the PEN annual conference, 25 Years of Local Education Funds. San Francisco, CA.

Goleman, D. (1995). *Emotional intelligence.* New York, NY: Bantam Books.

Goleman, D. (2007, December 10). Selling SEL: An interview with Daniel Goleman. CASEL Forum, New York City. Retrieved on March 18, 2009, from http://www.edutopia.org/daniel-goleman-sel-video

Gomez, C., & Baird, S. (2005). Identifying early indications of autism in self-regulation difficulties. *Focus on Autism and Other Developmental Disabilities, 20*(2), 106–116.

Gordon, T. (1978). *P.E.T. in action.* Toronto, Ontario, Canada: Bantam.

Gordon Training International (2011). Home page for Gordon Training International. Retrieved on January 11, 2014 from http://www.gordontraining.com/

Graves, M. (2007). *Explore and learn quick cards: 80 activities for small groups.* Ypsilanti, MI: HighScope.

Greenberg, A., & Berktold, J. (2006). Holiday stress. Greenberg Quinlan Rosner Research, American Psychological Association. Retrieved November 6, 2013, from http://gqrr.com/articles/1843/2603_HolidayStress.pdf

Greener, S. (1998). The relationship between emotional predispositions, emotional decoding, and regulation skills and children's prosocial behavior. *Dissertation Abstracts International, 59,* No. 08B.

Greenman, J. (2005). *Caring spaces, learning places: Children's environments that work.* Redmond, WA: Exchange Press.

Gross, T. (2004). The perception of four basic emotions in human and nonhuman faces by children with autism and other developmental disabilities. *Journal of Abnormal Child Psychology.* Retrieved April 2, 2009, from http://findarticles.com/p/articles/mi_m0902/is_5_32/ai_n6234461/

Grusec, J. E., & Lytton, H. (1988). *Social development: History, theory, and research.* New York, NY: Springer-Verlag.

Gunning, T. (2013). *Creating literacy instruction for all children in grades pre-K to 4.* Upper Saddle River, NJ: Pearson.

Hackman, D., & Farah, M. (2009). Socioeconomic status and the developing brain. *Trends in Cognitive Science, 13*(2), 65–73.

Hamre, B. K., & Pianta, R. C. (2005). Can instructional and emotional support in the first-grade classroom make a difference for children at risk of school failure? *Child Development, 76*(5), 949–967.

Harms, T., Clifford, R. M., & Cryer, D. (2005). *Early childhood environment rating scale, revised edition.* New York, NY: Teachers College Press.

Harms, T., Cryer, D., & Clifford, R.M. (2006). *Infant/toddler environment rating scale* (rev. ed.). New York, NY: Teachers College Press.

Harper, D. (2013). *Online etymology dictionary.* Retrieved on May 17, 2013, from http://www.etymonline.com/index.php?term=I

Hart, C., Burts, D., Durland, M. A., Charlesworth, R., DeWolf, M., & Fleege, P. (1998). Stress behaviors and activity type participation of preschoolers in more and less developmentally appropriate classrooms: SES and sex differences. *Journal of Research in Childhood Education, 12*(2), 176–196.

Hart, C., DeWolf, M., Wozniak, P., & Burts, D. (1992). Maternal and paternal disciplinary styles: Relations with preschoolers' playground behavioral orientations and peer status. *Child Development, 63,* 879–892.

Harter, S. (2006). The self. In N. Eisenberg (Ed.), *Handbook of child psychology: Vol. 3. Social, emotional, and personality development* (6th ed., pp. 505–570). Hoboken, NJ: Wiley.

Hartup, W. W. (1974). Aggression in childhood: Developmental perspectives. *American Psychologist, 29,* 336–341.

Haswell, K., Hock, E., & Wenar, C. (1981). Oppositional behavior of preschool children: Theory and intervention. *Family Relations, 30,* 440–446.

Haupt, J. J., Larsen, J. M., Robinson, C. C., & Hart, C. H. (1995). The impact of DAP inservice training on the beliefs and practices of kindergarten teachers. *Journal of Early Childhood Teacher Education, 16*(2), 12–18.

Hazeldon Foundation. (2013). What is cyber bullying? Retrieved on June 17, 2013, from http://www.violencepreventionworks.org/public/cyber_bullying.page

Health Resources and Services Administration/HRSA. (2007). Bullying among children and youth with disabilities and special needs. Retrieved November 6, 2013, from http://www.ldonline.org/article/20001

Healthy Children.org. (2011). Developmental milestones 3 to 4 year olds and 4 to 5 year olds. Retrieved on May 2, 2013, from http://www.healthychildren.org/English/ages-stages/

Healthy Children.org. (2013). Teasing and bullying of obese and overweight children. Retrieved on June 3, 2013, from http://www.healthychildren.org. Go to health issues and then to the article.

Healy, J. M. (2004). *Your child's growing mind: Brain development and learning from birth to adolescence* (3rd ed.). New York, NY: Doubleday/Broadway Books.

Healy, J. M. (2005). Helping children learn to pay attention. *Parents League Review.* Retrieved November 8, 2005, from www.parentsleague.org/attention.html

Helm, J. H., & Katz, L. G. (2001). *Young investigators: The project approach in the early years.* Published simultaneously by New York, NY: Teachers College Press; and Washington, DC: NAEYC.

Hemmeter, M. L., Maxwell, K., Ault, M., & Schuster, J. (2001). *Assessment of practices in early elementary classrooms.* New York, NY: Teachers College Press.

Heritage, M. (2013). *Formative assessment in practice.* Cambridge, MA: Harvard Education Press.

Heyman, G., Dweck, C., & Cain, K. (1992). Young children's vulnerability to self-blame and helplessness: Relationship to beliefs about goodness. *Child Development, 63*(2), 401–415.

HighScope. (2009). Introduction to large group time. Retrieved November 6, 2013 from http://www.highscope.org/Content.asp?ContentId=381

Hildebrandt, C., & Zan, B. (2008). Constructivist approaches to moral education in early childhood. In L. Nucci & D. Narvaez (Eds.), *Handbook of character and moral education* (pp. 352–369). London, UK: Routledge.

Hildyard, K. (2005). An investigation of cognitive mechanisms and processes underlying neglectful caregiving. *Dissertation Abstracts International: Part B The Sciences and Engineering, 66*(2-B), 1172.

Hoffman, M. L. (1975). Developmental synthesis of affect and cognition and its interplay for altruistic motivation. *Developmental Psychology, 11,* 607–622.

Honig, A. (n.d.). Infants and toddlers: The power of sensory experiences. *Scholastic Early Childhood Today.* Retrieved May 20, 2013, from http://www.scholastic.com/teachers/article/infants-toddlers-power-sensory-experiences

Hopkins, G. (2007). The school day: It's not a race. *Education World,* interview with Chip Wood. Retrieved December 17, 2009, from http://www.educationworld.com/a_issues/issues058.shtml

Hopkins, M., & Biasini, F. (2006). *Children with fragile x syndrome and children with autism show distinct impairments in emotional understanding.* Presented at the 18th annual convention for the Association for Psychological Science, New York, NY

Hopkins, M., Perez, T., & Biasini F. (2007). *Children with autism spectrum disorders show improvements in emotion and facial recognition abilities following interactive computer games.* Presented at the 19th annual convention for the Association for Psychological Science, Washington, DC.

Hopkins, M., Ross, L., & Biasini, F. (2005). *Understanding facial expressions: A comparative study of typical children and children with autism or fragile x syndrome.* Presented at the 38th Annual Gatlinburg Conference on Research and Theory in Intellectual and Developmental Disabilities, Annapolis, MD.

Howe, M. L., & Courage, M. L. (1993). On resolving the enigma of infantile amnesia. *Psychological Bulletin, 113,* 305–326.

Hsieh, W., Hemmeter, M., McCollum, J., & Ostrosky, M. (2009). Using coaching to increase preschool teachers' use of emergent literacy teaching strategies. *Early Childhood Research Quarterly.* Retrieved November 6, 2013, from http://dx.doi.org/10.1016/j.ecresq.2009.03.007

Huesmann, L. (1988). An information processing model for the development of aggression. *Aggressive Behavior, 14*(1), 13–24.

Huffman, L. R., & Speer, P. W. (2000). Academic performance among at-risk children: The role of developmentally appropriate practices. *Early Childhood Research Quarterly, 15*(2), 167–184.

Hurley, S., & Chater, N. (Eds.). (2005). Introduction: The importance of imitation. In *Perspectives on imitation: From neuroscience to social science. Volume 2: Imitation, human development, and culture* (pp. 1–51). Boston: MIT Press.

Iannelli, V. (2004). Parenting styles. Retrieved September 7, 2009, from http://pediatrics.about.com/od/infantparentingtips/a/04_pntg_styles.htm

Illinois State University. (n.d.). *Visual supports A Fact Sheet.* Retrieved May 16, 2009, from http://autism.pbisillinois.org/iattap_Visual_Supports_Fact_Sheet_1_.pdf

Indiana Family and Social Services Administration. (2010). ABC (Antecedent-Behavior-Consequence) model. Retrieved October 23, 2013, from https://secure.in.gov/fssa/files/ABC.pdf

Institute for Research on Poverty. (2013). Who is poor? Frequently asked questions about poverty. Retrieved May 19, 2013, from http://www.irp.wisc.edu/faqs.htm

Jackson, S. (2008). *Stress management for health course.* An online health course. Retrieved May 15, 2009, from http://stresscourse.tripod.com/index.html

Jenkins, J. (2000). Marital conflict and children's emotions: The development of an anger organization. *Journal of Marriage and the Family, 62*(3), 723–736.

Jewitt J., & Peterson, K. (2002). *Stress and young children.* ERIC Digest. Retrieved March 24, 2006, from www.ericdigests.org/2003-4/stress.html

Johnson, C., Myers, S., & Council on Children with Disabilities. (2007). Identification and evaluation of children with autism spectrum disorders. *Pediatrics, 120,* 1183–1215.

Johnson, G., Poliner, R., & Bonaiuto, S. (2005). Learning throughout the day. *Educational Leadership, 63*(1), 59–63.

Johnson, L., & Duffek, K. (2008). *Creating outdoor classrooms.* Austin, TX: University of Texas Press.

Kantrowitz, E., & Evans, G. (2004). The relation between the ratio of children per activity area and off-task behavior and type of play in child care centers. *Environment and Behavior, 36*(4), 541–557.

Katz, L. (1993). *Self-esteem and narcissism: Implications for practice.* (ERIC Digest ED358973). ERIC Clearinghouse on Elementary and Early Childhood Education, Urbana, IL. Retrieved on November 6, 2013, from http://www.ericdigests.org/1993/esteem.htm

Keogh, B., Naylor, S., Simon, S., Downing, B., & Maloney, J. (2006, February 22). The puppets project: Puppets.

Kerbow, D. (1996). Patterns of urban student mobility and local school reform. *Journal of Education of Students Placed at Risk, 1*(2), 147-169. EJ 531 794.

Kerbow, D., Azcoitia, C., & Buell, B. (2003). Student mobility and local improvement in Chicago. *Journal of Negro Education, 72*(1), 158–164.

Kernis, M., Brown, A., & Brody, G. (2000). Fragile self-esteem in children and its associations with perceived patterns of parent-child communication. *Journal of Personality, 68*(2), 225–252.

Kishiyama, M., Boyce, W., Jiminez, A., & Knight, R. (2009). Socioeconomic disparities affect prefrontal function in children. *Journal of Cognitive Neuroscience, 21*(6), 1106–1115.

Klinzing, H. (2003, April 21–25). *Improving accuracy of decoding emotions from facial expressions by cooperative learning techniques.* Paper presented at the annual meeting of the American Educational Research Association, Chicago.

Kochenderfer-Ladd, B., & Pelletier, M. (2008). Teachers' views and beliefs about bullying: Influences on classroom management strategies and students' coping with peer victimization. *Journal of School Psychology, 36*(4), 431–453.

Kohlberg, L. (1958). *The development of modes of thinking and choices in years 10 to 16.* Unpublished doctoral dissertation, Chicago, IL: University of Chicago.

Kohlberg, L. (1981). *The philosophy of moral development. Moral stages and the idea of justice* (1st ed.). Cambridge, MA: Harper & Row.

Kohn, A. (1996). *Beyond discipline.* Alexandria, VA: Association for Supervision and Curriculum Development.

Kohn, A. (2001). Five reasons to stop saying "Good job." *Young Children, 56*(5), 24–28.

Kopp, C. B. (1981). *The antecedents of self-regulation: A developmental perspective.* Unpublished manuscript, University of California, Los Angeles, CA.

Kostelnik, M., Purcell, S. E., Nelson, S. E., Schroeder, D. Nelson, Krumbach, E., Hanna, J., Bosch, & DeFrain, J. (2005). *Helping children resolve conflict: Aggressive behavior in children* (Paper 1750). University of Nebraska, Lincoln [Online] Historical Materials from University of Nebraska-Lincoln Extension.

Kostelnik, M, Soderman, A., & Whiren, A. (2010). *Developmentally Appropriate Curriculum,* 5th edition, Upper Saddle River, NJ: Pearson Merrill Prentice Hall.

Kriete, R. (2002). *The morning meeting book.* Greenfield, MA: Northeast Foundation for Children.

Kriete, R. (2003). Start the day with community. *Educational Leadership, 61*(1), 68–70.

Ladd, G. W., Birch, S. H., & Buhs, E. S. (1999). Children's social and scholastic lives in kindergarten: Related spheres of influence? *Child Development, 70,* 1373–1400.

Ladd, G. W., Kochenderfer, B. J., & Coleman, C. C. (1997). Classroom peer acceptance, friendship, and victimization: Distinct relational systems that contribute to children's school adjustment? *Child Development, 68,* 1181–1197.

Lapsley, D. (2008). Moral self-identity as the aim of education. In L. Nucci & D. Narvaez (Eds.), *Handbook of moral and character education* (pp. 30–52). London, UK: Routledge.

Lavallee, K. L., Bierman, K. L., & Nix, R. L. (2005, June). The impact of first-grade "friendship group" experiences on child social outcomes in the Fast Track program. *Journal of Abnormal Child Psychology, 33,* 307–324.

Learning NC. (n.d.). *Zone of proximal development.* Retrieved May 14, 2013, from http://www.learnnc.org/lp/pages/5075#note10

Leary, M. R., & MacDonald, G. (2003). Individual differences in self-esteem: A review and theoretical integration. In M. R. Leary & P. Tangney (Eds.), *Handbook of self and identity* (pp. 401–420). New York, NY: Guilford Press.

Lenhart, A. (2009, May 13). *Cyberbullying: What the research is telling us.* . . . Presentation at the National Association of Attorneys General Year of the Child Conference, Philadelphia, PA.

Levin, D. (1998). *Remote control childhood? Combating the hazards of media culture.* Washington, DC: NAEYC.

Lewis, M. L., & Ippen, C. G. (2007). Rainbows of tears, souls full of hope: Cultural issues related to young children and trauma. In Joy Osofsky (Ed.), *Young children and trauma: Intervention and treatment* (pp. 11–46). New York, NY: Guilford Press.

Lickliter, R. (2011). The integrated development of sensory organization. *Clinical Perinatology, 38*(4), 591–603. doi:10.1016/j.clp.2011.08.007

Linan-Thompson, S., & Vaughn, S. (2007). *Research based methods of reading instruction for English language learners grades K-4.* Alexandria, VA: ASCD (formerly the Association for Supervision and Curriculum Development).

Lindner, J., & Rosen, L. (2006). Decoding of emotion through facial expression, prosody and verbal content in children and adolescents with Asperger's syndrome. *Journal of Autism and Developmental Disorders, 36*(6), 769–777.

Lowenthal, B. (1999, Summer). Effects of maltreatment and ways to promote children's resiliency. *Childhood Education,* 204–209.

Maccoby, E., & Martin, J. A. (1983). Socialization in the context of the family: Parent-child interaction. In P. Mussen (Ed.), *Handbook of child psychology* (Vol. 4; pp. 1–101). New York, NY: Wiley.

MacDonald, P., Kirkpatrick, S., & Sullivan, L. (1996). Schematic drawings of facial expressions for emotion recognition and interpretation by preschool-aged children. *Genetic, Social, and General Psychology Monographs, 122*(4), 373–388.

Macy, M., & Bricker, D. (2007). Embedding individualized social goals into routine activities in inclusive early childhood classrooms. *Early Child Development and Care, 177*(2), 107–120.

Malefant, N. (2006). *Routines and transitions: A guide for early childhood professionals.* St. Paul, MN: Redleaf Press.

Mansager, E. (2004). Parents' prism: Three dimensions of effective parenting. *Journal of Individual Psychology, 60*(3), 277–293.

Mar, R., DeYoung, C., Higgins D., & Peterson, J. (2006). Self-liking and self-competence separates self-evaluation from self-deception: Associations with personality, ability, and achievement. *Journal of Personality, 74*(4), 1047-1078.

Marion, M. (2011). *Guidance of young children* (8th ed.). Upper Saddle River, NJ: Pearson Merrill/Prentice Hall.

Marion, M., Swim, T., & Jenner, L. (2000, November). *Preconference session.* National Association for the Education of Young Children, Atlanta.

Maschinot, B. (2008). The changing face of the United States: The influence of culture on early child development. Washington, DC: Zero to Three. Retrieved on May 16, 2013, from http://main.zerotothree.org/site/DocServer/Culture_book.pdf?docID=6921

Maslow, A. (1954). *Motivation and personality.* New York, NY: Harper.

Maslow, A. (1987). *Motivation and personality.* Hong Kong: Longman Asia Limited. (Original work published 1954)

Mayo Clinic Staff. (2010). Children and TV: Limiting your child's screen time. Retrieved June 16, 2013, from http://www.mayoclinic.com/health/children-and-tv/MY00522

McClellen, D. E., & Katz, L. G. (2001). Assessing children's social competence. *ERIC Digest* [Online]. Retrieved September 1, 2009, from http://wps.prenhall.com/wps/media/objects/486/497735/ObservationFiles/OT17.PDF

McComas, J., Johnson, L., & Simons, F. (2005). Teacher and peer responsivity to pro-social behaviour of high aggressors in preschool. *Educational Psychology, 25*(2–3), 223–231.

Meagher, M. (2007, August 17). *Severe or traumatic stress and inflammation in multiple sclerosis.* Presentation at the symposium Traumatic Stress, Cardiovascular Disease, Metabolic Syndrome, and Neurodegenerative Disease, Annual APA Convention, San Francisco, CA.

Merino, G., & Gaytan, F. (2012). Reducing subjectivity in special education referrals by educators working with Latino students: Using functional behavioral assessment as a pre-referral practice in student support teams. *Emotional and Behavioral Difficulties, 18*(1), 88–101.

Michigan Department of Education. (2013). Center-based curriculum. *Implementation Manual for the Great Start Readiness Program.* Retrieved May 21, 2013, from http://michigan.gov/mde/0,4615,7-140-63533_50451-217313--,00.html

Mikulincer, M., Shaver, P., Gillath, O., & Nitzberg, R. (2005). Attachment, caregiving, and altruism: Boosting attachment security increases compassion and helping. *Journal of Personality and Social Psychology, 89*(5), 817–839.

Military Child Education Coalition (2003). *How to prepare our children and stay involved in their education during deployment.* Harker Heights, Texas: Author.

Miller, G., Cohen, S., & Richey, A. (2002). Chronic psychological stress and the regulation of pro-inflammatory cytokines: A glucocorticoid-resistance model. *Health Psychology, 21*(6), 531–541.

Mirenda, P., MacGregor, T., & Kelly-Keough, S. (2002). Teaching communication skills for behavioral support in the context of family life. In J. M. Lucyshyn, G. Dunlap, & R. W. Albin (Eds.), *Families and positive behavior support: Addressing problem behavior in family contexts* (pp. 185–207). Baltimore, MD: Brookes.

Mize, J. (1995). Coaching preschool children in social skills: A cognitive-social learning curriculum, In C. Carledge & J. F. Milburn (Eds.), *Teaching social skills to children and youth: Innovative approaches* (3rd ed., pp. 237–261), Boston, MA: Allyn & Bacon.

Moffitt, T., Arseneault, L., Belsky, D., Dickson, N., Hancox, R., Harrington, H., . . . Caspi, A. (2011). A gradient of childhood self-control predicts health, wealth, and public safety. *PNAS, 108*(7), 2693-2698.

Morrison, G. M., Brown, M., D'Incau, B., O'Farrell, S., & Furlong, M. J. (2005, December). Understanding resilience in educational trajectories: Implications for protective possibilities. *Psychology in the Schools, 43*(1), 19–31.

Mruk, C. (2013). *Self-esteem research, theory, and practice: Toward a positive psychology of self-esteem* (4th ed.). New York, NY: Springer.

Nanda, R. (2005, February 1. Reticulocyte count. Medline Plus Medical Encyclopedia. Retrieved on November 6, 2013, from http://labtestsonline.org/understanding/analytes/reticulocyte/tab/test

Narvaez, D., & Lapsley, D. (2009). Moral identity, moral functioning, and the development of moral character. In D. M. Bartels, C. W. Bauman, L. J. Skitka, & D. L. Medin (Ed.), *The psychology of learning and motivation* (Vol. 50). Burlington, MA: Academic Press.

National Association for the Education of Young Children. (2003a). *Early childhood curriculum, assessment, and program evaluation: Building an effective, accountable system in programs for children birth to age 8* [Position statement]. Washington, DC: Author.

National Association for the Education of Young Children. (2003b). What to do about biters. *Early Years Are Learning Years*. Washington, DC: Author.

National Association for the Education of Young Children. (2005a, Reaffirmed and updated 2011). *Code of ethical conduct and statement of commitment*. Retrieved November 6, 2013, from http://www.naeyc.org/files/naeyc/image/public_policy/Ethics%20Position%20Statement2011_09202013update.pdf

National Association for the Education of Young Children. (2005b). *Screening and assessment of young English language learners. Supplement to the NAEYC position statement on early childhood curriculum, assessment, and program evaluation*. Retrieved May 18, 2009, from http://www.naeyc.org/about/positions/ELL_Supplement.asp

National Association for the Education of Young Children. (2008). *Physical environment: A guide to the NAEYC early childhood program standard and related accreditation criteria. A position statement*. Washington, DC: NAEYC.

National Association for the Education of Young Children. (2009). Where we stand: Curriculum, assessment, and program evaluation, Retrieved on May 9, 2013, from http://www.naeyc.org/files/naeyc/file/positions/StandCurrAss.pdf

National Association for the Education of Young Children. (2011). *Code of ethical conduct and statement of commitment*. Retrieved May 25, 2013, from http://www.naeyc.org/files/naeyc/file/positions/Ethics%20Position%20Statement2011.pdf

National Institute of Mental Health. (2011). *A parent's guide to autism spectrum disorder*. Bethesda, MD: National Institute of Mental Health–Science Writing, Press and Dissemination Branch.

Nell, M., Drew, W., with Bush, D. (2013). *From play to practice: Connecting teachers' play to children's learning*. Washington, DC: NAEYC.

Nelson, J. (2012). Why feelings matter: The importance of emotional competence in early childhood [Lecture]. Dallas, TX: University of Texas—Dallas, Center for Children and Families, February 24. Retrieved June 10, 2013, from http://ccf.utdallas.edu/programs-resources/spring-lecture-series/2012-lectures.

New York State Division of Criminal Justice Services. (n.d.). Cyber bullying. Retrieved June 16, 2013, from http://www.criminaljustice.ny.gov/missing/i_safety/cyberbullying.htm

Nicholson, E. (2005). The school building as a third teacher. In M. Dudek (Ed.), *Children's spaces* (pp. 44–65). Burlington, MA: Architectural Press.

O'Connell, P., Pepler, D., & Craig, W. (1999). Peer involvement in bullying: Issues and challenges for intervention. *Journal of Adolescence, 22,* 437–452.

Ogu, U., & Schmidt, S. R. (2009, March). Investigating rocks and sand: Addressing multiple learning styles through an inquiry-based approach. *Young Children on the Web*, 9 pages. Retrieved on November 6, 2013, from http://journal.naeyc.org/btj/200903/pdf/BTJSchmidt_Ogu_Expanded.pdf

Olweus, D. (1993). *Bullying at school: What we know and what we can do*. Oxford, UK: Blackwell Publishing.

Olweus D., Limber S., & Mihalic, S. F. (2002). *Blueprints for violence prevention, Book Nine: bullying prevention program*. Boulder, CO: Center for the Study and Prevention of Violence, Institute of Behavioral Science, University of Colorado.

O'Moore, M., & Kirkham, C. (2001). Self-esteem and its relationship to bullying behavior. *Aggressive Behavior, 27*(4), 269–339.

Ostrosky, M. M., Jung, E. Y., Hemmeter, M. L., & Thomas, D. (2003). *What Works Brief 3: Helping children understand classroom schedules and routines*. Champaign, IL: University of Illinois at Urbana—Champaign. Retrieved June 11, 2013, from http://csefel.vanderbilt.edu/briefs/wwb3.pdf

Page, A., Cooper, A., Griew, P., & Jago, R. (2010). Children's screen viewing is related to psychological difficulties irrespective of physical activity. *Pediatrics Digest 126*(5), e1011–e1017; published ahead of print October 11, 2010, doi:10.1542/peds.2010-1154.

Paik, P., & Phillips, R. (2002). *Student mobility in rural communities: What are the effects on student achievement?* Naperville, IL: North Central Regional Educational Laboratory .

Parke, R. D., & Slaby, R. G. (1983). The development of aggression. In P. Mussen (Ed.), *Handbook of child psychology*. (Vol. 4; pp. 547–642). New York, NY: Wiley.

Parten, M. (1932). Social participation among preschool children. *Journal of Abnormal and Social Psychology, 27,* 243–269.

Patterson, J., Mockford, C., & Stewart-Brown, S. (2005). Parents' perceptions of the value of the Webster-Stratton Parenting Programme: A qualitative study of a general practice based initiative [Electronic version]. *Child: Care, Health and Development, 31*(1), 53–64.

Pawlak, J., & Klein, H. (1997). Parental conflict and self-esteem: The rest of the story. *Journal of Genetic Psychology, 15*(3), 303–313.

Pearson. (n.d.). Unit 1: Positive relationships for children's learning, care and development. Retrieved May 15, 2013, from http://www.pearsonschoolsandfecolleges.co.uk/FEAndVocational/Childcare/BTEC/BTEC NationalChildrenSCareLearningAnd Development2007/Samples/Samplematerialfor BTECNationalCCLDStudentBook/BTEC%20 CCLD%20Unit%201%20web.pdf

Perlmutter, M. (1986). A life-span view of memory. In P. B. Baltes, D. L. Featherman, & R. M. Lerner (Eds.), *Life-span development and behavior* (Vol. 7). Hillsdale, NJ: Erlbaum.

Perry, B., & Szalavitz, M. (2007). *The boy who was raised as a dog.* New York, NY: Basic Books.

Petrakos, H., & Howe, N. (1996). The influence of the physical design of the dramatic play center on children's play. *Early Childhood Research Quarterly, 11,* 63–77.

Pettit, B. (2000). Moving and children's social connections: The critical importance of context. *Center for Research on Child Wellbeing Working Paper #98-04.* Retrieved June 10, 2009, from http://crcw.princeton.edu/workingpapers/WP98-04-Pettit.pdf

Piaget, J. (1952). *The origins of intelligence in children.* New York, NY: International Universities Press.

Piaget, J. (1970). Piaget's theory. In P. Mussen (Ed.), *Carmichael's manual of child psychology* (pp. 703–732). New York, NY: Wiley.

Pianta, R., & Stuhlman, M. (2004). Teacher-child relationships and children's success in the first years of school. *School Psychology Review, 33,* 444–458.

Piotrowski, J. T., Lapierre, M. A., & Linebarger, D. L. (2013). Investigating correlates of self-regulation in early childhood with a representative sample of English-speaking American families. *Journal of Child Family Studies, 22*(3), 423–436.

Poussaint, A. (1997). Letter to parents. In B. Cosby (Ed.), *The meanest thing to say* (p. 1). New York, NY: Scholastic.

Power, F. C., Higgins, A., & Kohlberg, L. (1989). *Lawrence Kohlberg's approach to moral education.* New York, NY: Columbia University Press.

Prinstein, M., and Dodge, K. (2008). *Understanding Peer Influence in Children and Adolescents.* New York: Guilford Press.

Project Approach. (2013). Retrieved from http://www.projectapproach.org/

Puhl, R. M., Peterson, J. L., & Luedicke, J. (2013). Strategies to address weight-based victimization: Youths' preferred support interventions from classmates, teachers, and parents. *Journal of Youth and Adolescence, 42*(3), 315–327.

Radke-Yarrow, M., & Zahn-Waxler, C. (1984). Roots, motives, and patterning in children's prosocial behavior. In E. Staub, K. D. Bar-Tal, J. Karylowski, & J. Raykowski (Eds.), *The development and maintenance of prosocial behavior: International perspectives on positive morality.* New York, NY: Plenum Press.

Raffaelli, M., Crockett, L. J., & Shen, Y. L. (2005). Developmental stability and change in self-regulation from childhood to adolescence. *Journal of Genetic Psychology, 166*(1), 54–75.

Ramsey, C. (2009). Analysis of preschool expulsion in California. San Francisco, CA: Child Care Law Center. Retrieved March 30, 2009, from http://www.childcarelaw.org

Rascle, O., Coulomb-Cabagno, G., & Delsarte, A. (2005). Perceived motivational climate and observed aggression as a function of competitive level in youth male French handball. *Journal of Sport Behavior, 28,* 51–67.

Reading is Fundamental. (2004). *RIF's guide to choosing good books for children of all ages.* Washington, DC: RIF. Retrieved November 6, 2013, from http://www.rif.org/assets/Documents/parents/choosing_books.pdf

Reggio Children. (2013). Research. Retrieved October 4, 2013, from http://www.reggiochildren.it/?lang=en

Rholes, W. S., Jones, M., & Wade, C. (1988). Children's understanding of personal disposition and its relationship to behavior. *Journal of Experimental Child Psychology, 45,* 1–17.

Rideout, V. J., Vandewater, E. A., & Wartella, E. A. (2003). *Zero to six: Electronic media in the lives of infants, toddlers, and preschoolers.* Menlo Park, CA: The Henry J. Kaiser Family Foundation.

Rimm-Kaufman, S. (2006). Social and academic learning study on the contribution of the *Responsive Classroom* approach. Retrieved May 4, 2009, from http://www.responsiveclassroom.org

Robins, R., & Trzesniewski, K. (2005). Self-esteem development across the lifespan. *Current Directions in Psychological Science, 14*(3), 158–162.

Rogers, C. (1957). The necessary and sufficient conditions of therapeutic personality change. *Journal of Consulting Psychology, 21,* 95–103.

Rollins, B. C., & Thomas, D. L. (1979). Parental support, power, and control techniques in the socialization of children. In W. R. Burr, R. Hill, F. Nye, & I. Reiss (Eds.), *Contemporary theories about the family* (Vol. 1; 317–364). New York, NY: Free Press.

Rosenkoetter, L. (1999). The television situation comedy and children's prosocial behavior. *Journal of Applied Social Psychology, 29*(5), 979–993.

Rushton, S., Eitelgeorge, J., & Zickafoose, R. (2003). Connecting Brian Cambourne's conditions of learning theory to brain/mind principles: Implications for early childhood educators. *Early Childhood Education Journal, 31*(1), 11–21.

Saarni, C., Mumme, D. L., & Campos, J. J. (1998). Emotional development: Action, communication, and understanding. In W. Damon & N. Eisenberg (Eds.), *Handbook of child psychology, 5th Edition, Volume III: Social, Emotional, and personality development* (pp. 237–309). New York, NY: John Wiley.

Sagi, A., & Hoffman, M. L. (1976). Empathic distress in the newborn. *Developmental Psychology, 12,* 175–176.

Scaglione, J., & Scaglione, A. R. (2006). *Bully-proofing children: A practical, hands-on guide to stop bullying.* Lanham, MD: Rowman and Littlefield Education.

Schaffer, H. R., & Crook, C. K. (1980). Child compliance and maternal control techniques. *Developmental Psychology, 16,* 54–61.

Schneider, W., & Pressley, M. (1989). *Memory development between 2 and 20.* New York, NY: Springer-Verlag.

Schutte, A., Fleharty, H., Hund, A., Uttal, D., Sauter, M., Simms, D., & Genter, D. (2011, July). The development of spatial cognition during childhood. Symposium conducted at the 33rd annual meeting of the Cognitive Science Society, Boston, MA.

Scott-Little, C., Kagan, S. L., & Frelow, V. S. (2006). Conceptualization of readiness and the content of early learning standards: The intersection of policy and research? *Early Childhood Research Quarterly, 21*(2), 153–173.

Seefeldt, C. (1993, May 23). *Parenting.* St. Paul, MN: St. Paul Pioneer Press.

Sege, R., & Wright, J. (lead authors) and The Committee on Injury, Violence, and Poison Prevention. (2009). Policy statement on the role of the pediatrician in youth violence prevention. *Pediatrics, 124*(1), 393–402.

Selman, R. L. (1976). Social-cognitive understanding: A guide to educational and clinical practice. In T. Lickona (Ed.), *Moral development and behavior* (pp. 299–316). New York, NY: Holt, Rinehart & Winston.

Selman, R. L. (2003) *The promotion of social awareness: Powerful lessons from the partnership of developmental theory and classroom practice.* New York, NY: Russell Sage.

SERVE Center of UNCG. (2013). Benefits of messy play. Retrieved October 4, 2013, from http://center.serve.org/SS/toddlersmessy2.php

Shalaway, L. (2013). Classroom organization: The physical environment. Retrieved May 20, 2013, from http://www.scholastic.com/teachers/article/classroom-organization-physical-environment

Shek, D. (2007). Perceived parental behavioral control and psychological control in Chinese adolescents in Hong Kong: A replication. *Adolescence, 42*(167), 569.

Skinner, C. H., Neddenriep, C. E., Robinson, S. L., Ervin, R., & Jones, K. (2002). Altering educational environments through positive peer reporting: Prevention and remediation of social problems associated with behavior disorders. *Psychology in the Schools, 39,* 191–202.

Smith, C. A., & Farrington, D. P. (2004). Continuities in antisocial behavior and parenting across three generations. *Journal of Child Psychology and Psychiatry and Allied Disciplines, 45*(2), 230–247.

Snall, M. (2007, September 15). Conversation with Carol Gilligan. Interview at the Women, Power, and Peach Conference. Retrieved May 27, 2009, from http://www.feminist.com/resources/artspeech/interviews/carolgilligan.html

Snow, C. E., & Selman, R. (2012). Video. Retrieved on May 10, 2013, from http://ccdd.serpmedia.org/research-perspective-taking.php

Snow, C. E., & Van Hemel, S. (Eds.). (2008). *Early childhood assessment: Why, what, and how.* Washington, DC: New Academy Press.

Socolar, R. (1995, January 15). Spanking children is in even though it's out. *The New York Times, 144,* Sec. 1, p. 26.

Spinelli, L. (2008). The early childhood schools of Reggio Emilia. New York, NY: The Parents League. Retrieved June 3, 2013, from http://www.parentsleague.org/publications/selected_articles/the_early_childhood_schools_of_reggio_emilia/index.aspx

Srabstein, J. (2010). AACAP testifies before Congress on cyber-bullying. Retrieved May 10, 2013, from http://www.zoominfo.com/p/Jorge-Srabstein/14197576

Stallings, J. (1975). Implementation and child effects of teaching practices in follow-through classrooms. *Monographs of the Society for Research in Child Development, 40*(78).

Stanger, C., Dumenci, L., Kamon, J., & Burstein, M. (2004). Parenting and children's externalizing problems in substance-abusing families. *Journal of Clinical Child & Adolescent Psychology, 33*(3), 590–600.

Stayton, D. J., Hogan, R., & Ainsworth, M. D. S. (1971). Infant obedience and maternal behavior: The origins of socialization reconsidered. *Child Development, 42,* 1057–1069.

Steele, W., & Sheppard, C. (2003). Moving can be traumatic. *Trauma and Loss: Research and Interventions, 3*(1), 1–2.

Stein, M., Keller, S., & Schleifer, S. (1981). The hypothalamus and the immune response. In H. Weiner, M. Hofer, & A. Stunkard (Eds.), *Brain, behavior and bodily disease.* New York, NY: Raven.

Steinhauer, J. (2005, May 22). Only 4 years old and expelled. Maybe preschool is the problem. *The New York Times, 154,* sec. 4, p. 1, col. 1.

Stenberg, C. (1982). *The development of anger facial expressions in infancy.* Unpublished doctoral dissertation, University of Denver, Denver, CO.

Siew, M., Bishop, G., Enkelmann, H., Tong, E., Yong, P., Ang, J., et al. (2005). Anger, stress, coping, social support, and health: Modeling the relationships. *Psychology and Health, 20*(4), 467–495.

Stifter, C. A., & Fox, N. A. (1987). Preschool children's ability to accurately identify emotions. *Journal of Non-Verbal Behavior, 11,* 34–45.

Strayer, J., & Roberts, W. (2004). Empathy and observed anger and aggression in five-year-olds. *Social Development, 13*(1), 1–13.

Sullivan, A., & Strang, H. (2002). Bibliotherapy in the classroom: Using literature to promote the development of emotional intelligence. *Early Childhood Education, 79*(2), 74–80.

Suveg, C., Sood, E., Barmish, A. Tiwari, S., Hudson, J. L., & Kendall, P. C. (2008). I'd rather not talk about it: Emotion parenting in families of children with an anxiety disorder. *Journal of Family Psychology, 22*(6), 875–884.

Tafarodi, R., Wild, N., & Ho, C. (2010). Parental authority, nurturance, and two-dimensional self-esteem. *Scandinavian Journal of Psychology, 51*(4), 294-303.

Tajima, E. A., & Harachi, T. W. (2006, January 14). *Parenting in the context of immigration: Parenting beliefs and discipline practices of Vietnamese and Cambodians in the U.S.* Presented at the meeting of the Society for Social Work and Research. San Antonio, TX.

Tarr, P. (2001). Aesthetic codes in early childhood classrooms: What art educators can learn from Reggio Emilia. Retrieved December 9, 2009, from http://www.designshare.com/

Thompson, C. (2009). Bibliotherapy and anxiety level of 5th graders. ProQuest Dissertations. Retrieved June 14, 2013, from http://udini.proquest.com/view/bibliotherapy-and-anxiety-levels-of-pqid:1921402311/

Torelli, L. (2002, Spring). Enhancing development through classroom design in Early Head Start. *Children and Families, 44*–51.

Torelli, L., & Durrett, C. (n.d.). Spaces for children's resources. Retrieved July 11, 2009, from http://www.spacesforchildren.com/critera.html

Torelli, L., & Durrett, C. (1996). Landscape for learning: The impact of classroom design on infants and toddlers. *Early Childhood News, 8*(2), 12–17.

Townsend-Butterworth, D. (2009). Teasing and bullying: No laughing matter. Retrieved June 19, 2009, from http://www2.scholastic.com/browse/article.jsp?id=1438

Troop-Gordon, W., & Ladd, G. W. (2005). Trajectories of peer victimization and perceptions of the self and schoolmates: Percursors to internalizing and externalizing problems. *Child Development, 76*(5), 1072–1091.

Tsujimoto, S., Yamamoto, T., Kawaguchi, H., Koizumi, H., & Sawaguchi, T. (2005). Working memory in adults and preschool children: An event-related optical topography study. *Oxford Journals: Cerebral Cortex, 14*(7), 703–712.

Tucker C. J., Finkelhor, D., Turner, H., & Shattuck, A. (2013) Association of sibling aggression with child and adolescent mental health. *Pediatrics,* 2012–3801; published ahead of print June 17. doi:10.1542/peds.2012-3801.

Twemlow, S., Fonagy, P., & Sacco, F. (2006, January 12 online). The role of the bystander in the social architecture of bullying and violence in schools and communities. *Annals of the New York Academy of Sciences, 1036, Youth Violence: Scientific Approaches to Prevention,* 215–232. (Original work published 2004). Retrieved June 17, 2013, from http://www3.interscience.wiley.com/journal/118766611/abstract

Twemlow, S., & Sacco, F. (2011). *Preventing bullying and school violence.* Arlington, VA: American Psychiatric Association.

University of Chicago Medicine. (2013). Cognitive development. Retrieved May 14, 2013, from http://www.uchicagokidshospital.org/online-library/content=P01594

U.S. Bureau of the Census. (2011). *Income, poverty, and health insurance coverage in the United States, 2010.* Washington, DC: U.S. Government Printing Office.

U.S. Department of Veteran's Affairs. (2013). How deployment stress affects children and families: Research findings. Retrieved June 10, 2013, from http://www.ptsd.va.gov/professional/pages/pro_deployment_stress_children.asp

Valentine, V. (2008). The best type of play for kids. Interview with Adele Diamond and Deborah Leong. National Public Radio, February 27. Retrieved May 14, 2013, from http://www.npr.org/templates/story/story.php?storyId=73598288

Varela, R. E., Vernberg, E., Sanchez-Sosa, J. J., Riveros, A., Mitchell, M., & Mashunkashey, J. (2004). Parenting style of Mexican, Mexican American, and Caucasian-Non-Hispanic families: Social context and cultural influences. *Journal of Family Psychology, 18*(4), 651–657.

Vessey J. (2006). ". . . of sticks and stones:" Recognizing and helping kids at psychosocial risk from teasing and bullying. *Program and abstracts of The National Association of Pediatric Nurse Practitioners (NAPNAP), 27th Annual Conference; March 30–April 2, 2006,* Washington, DC.

Vessy, J., Carlson, J., Horowitz, K., & Duffy, M. (2008). Psychometric evaluation of the child-adolescent teasing scale. *Journal of School Health, 78*(6), 344–350.

Vygotsky, L. (1978). *Mind in society: The development of higher psychological processes.* M. Cole, V. John-Steiner, S. Scribner, & E. Souberman (Eds. and Trans.). Cambridge, MA: Harvard University Press.

Walker, J. (2008). Looking at teacher practices through the lens of parenting style. *Journal of Experimental Education, 76*(2), 218–240.

Weare, K. (2004). *Developing the emotionally literate school.* London, UK: Paul Chapman Educational Publishing/ Sage Publications.

Weir, K. (2012). Oh, no you don'! *Monitor on Psychology, 43*(10), 62.

Werner, E. (2004). Commentary, journeys from childhood to midlife: Risk, resilience, and recovery. *Pediatrics, 114*(2), 492.

Werner, E., & Smith, R. (2001). *Journeys from childhood to midlife: Risk, resilience, and recovery.* Ithaca, NY: Cornell University Press.

Williams, D. L., Goldstein, G., & Minshew, N. (2006). The profile of memory function in children with autism. *Neuropsychology, 20*(1), 20–29.

Wise, L., & daSilva, L. (2007, April). Differential parenting of children from diverse cultural backgrounds attending child care. *Australian Institute of Family Studies, Paper number 39.*

Xu, Z., Hannaway, J., & D'Souza, S. (2009). Student transience in North Carolina: The effect of student mobility on student outcomes using longitudinal data. *CALDER Working Paper No. 22.* Retrieved November 7, 2013, from http://www.colorincolorado.org/research/states/north_carolina/

Yu, Y., Shi, J., Huang, Y., & Wang, J. (2006). Relationship between family characteristics and aggressive behaviors of children and adolescents. *Journal of Huazhong University Science and Technology, Medical Sciences, 26*(3), 380–383.

Zahn-Waxler, C., Radke-Yarrow, M., Wagner, E., & Chapman, M. (1992). Development of concern for others. *Developmental Psychology, 28*(1), 126–136.

Zeman, J., & Shipman, K. (1996). Children's expression of negative affect: Reasons and methods. *Developmental Psychology, 32*(5), 842–850.

Zero to Three. (2009). *Love, learning, and routines.* Retrieved July 12, 2009, from http://www.zerotothree.org

Zero to Three. (2012). *Development through your child's eyes: Birth to 8 months, 8 months to 18 months, 18 to 36 months.* Retrieved May 7, 2013, from http://www.zerotothree.org

# Name Index

# Subject Index

f indicates figure, t indicates table

## A

Accidental aggression, 272–273
Accidents
  concrete operational thinkers, 72
  preoperational thinkers and, 72
Accommodation, constructivist
    approach to, 38
Active learning, room design and, 97–98
Active listening, 53–54, 54f, 146, 358
  routines and, 321
Active resistance, 213
Activities
  developmentally appropriate, 117
  and project approach, 115–117, 116f
Activity areas, 99–100
  attractive, 108–111
  development of, 105–106, 106f
  logical arrangement, 106–108, 108f
  physical boundaries for, 107–108, 108f
  sensory-rich, 108–111
Acute stress, 244
Adler, Alfred, 49–50, 51t
Adolescents
  identity v. role confusion stage, 48
  perspective-taking ability, 43f
Adult-child dialogues/discourse, 45
Adult-child relationship, quality of, 196
Adults
  and decision-making model, 345–346
  generativity v. stagnation stage, 48
  integrity v. despair stage, 48
  intimacy v. isolation stage, 48
  perspective-taking ability, 43f
Adult seeking, 214
Aggression. See also Bullying
  accidental, 272–273
  cues for, 281
  defined, 268
  forms of, 268–269
  gender differences in, 269
  hostile, 270–272
  instrumental, 269–270
  learned from family, 279f, 280–282
  learned from media, 279f, 283–285, 287

learned from peer group, 279f, 283
  pumpkin throwing, 342–344
  purposes of, 269
  scripts for, 280–282
  unresponsive parenting, 282
  vignette, 267
  vignette analysis, 287
Alarm stage of stress, 249
American Academy of Pediatrics, 284
Amygdala
  in emotional development, 218
Anecdotal record, 168, 168f
Anger, 210–211. See also Emotions
  active resistance, 213
  adult seeking, 214
  biting causing, 303
  compliance, issues of, 211
  conflict over possessions, 210
  expressing, 213–214
  guidelines for choosing books
    on, 228f
  levels of, 211
  physical assault, 210
  rejection causing, 211
  SEL for handling, 233, 234, 235f
  venting, 213
  verbal assault, 210
Antecedent, 300
Antecedent-behavior-consequence
  (A-B-C), 299–301, 301f
Appraisal stage of stress, 249
Appreciation, 199–200
Appropriate activities, planning, 198
Appropriate behavior, teaching,
  138–139
Arrival and departure
  acknowledgment, 319
  defined, 318
  direct guidance for, 320–321
  expectations for, 319
  indirect guidance for, 319–320
  what children need during, 319
Artistic expression
  to calm and relax, 258f
Artistic expression, as primary interest
  of children, 37

Assault
  physical, 210
  with words, 210
Assessment. See also Observation
  authentic, 161–162
  in decision-making model of child
    guidance
  in early childhood, 160–162
  goal of, 161
Assessment of Practices in Early
    Elementary Classrooms
    (APEEC), 298
Assimilation, constructivist
    approach to, 38
Attention, in Adler's mistaken goals,
    50, 51t
Attention deficit hyperactivity disorder
    (ADHD), 66–67
  and bullying, 277
Attention getting behavior, 303, 308–309
Auditory interest, 110
Authentic assessment, 161
Authentic self-esteem, 197–202
  appreciation, 199–200
  appropriate activities, planning, 198
  authoritative caregiving style,
    197–198
  feedback to children, 198–199
  genuine adult interest in children, 198
  respect, showing, 201
  social skills, teaching, 201–202
  unpleasant feelings, acknowledgement
    of, 200
Authoritarian caregiving
  demandingness, 16–17
  encouraging aggression, 18
  influencing self-esteem, 18
  negative discipline, 19
  negative impact of, 18–20
  responsiveness, 17, 18f
  self-control, 18
  and unacceptable behavior, 19
  vignette, 4–5
  vignette: analysis, 28
Authoritarian style, self-esteem
    influenced by, 18